LIQUOR AND LABOR
IN SOUTHERN AFRICA

LIQUOR AND LABOR
IN SOUTHERN AFRICA

• EDITED BY •

Jonathan Crush and Charles Ambler

OHIO UNIVERSITY PRESS • ATHENS
UNIVERSITY OF NATAL PRESS • PIETERMARITZBURG

© Copyright 1992 by Ohio University Press,
Scott Quadrangle, Athens, Ohio 45701
Printed in the United States of America

Ohio University Press books are printed on acid-free paper ∞

Library of Congress Cataloging-in-Publication Data

Liquor and labor in southern Africa / edited by Jonathan Crush and
    Charles Ambler.
        p.   cm.
    Includes bibliographical references and index.
    ISBN 0–8214–1027–X
    1. Drinking of alcoholic beverages—South Africa—History.
    2. Working class—South Africa—History.   I. Crush, J. S.
    II. Ambler, Charles H.
    HV5118.S6L57   1992
    394.1'3'08623—dc20   92–27473
                                                              CIP

Published in the Republic of South Africa
by University of Natal Press,
P.O. Box 375, Pietermaritzburg 3200, South Africa
ISBN 0–86980–874–5 pbk.
                                          •

The illustrations on the cover and title page have been reproduced
from *Brewers, Beerhalls, and Boycotts: A History of Liquor in
South Africa.* (History Workshop Topic Series Number 2) by Paul
la Hausse, with permission from Ravan Press, Johannesburg.

The title page illustration depicts a rural liquor canteen in the
Eastern Cape in the nineteenth century.

Cover photograph: angry women confronting police in Cato
Manor, June 1959.

CONTENTS

FIGURES AND TABLES

TABLES

ACKNOWLEDGEMENTS

The idea for this book dates to a conversation between the editors at the African Studies Association meeting in New Orleans in 1985. During the next several years it became apparent that a number of other scholars had begun to take notice of the importance of alcohol in the social and labor history of southern Africa. This book brings together a selection of their work. Preliminary versions of a number of the chapters were first presented in a series of panels, organized by Jonathan Crush, at the Canadian Association of African Studies meeting at Queen's University in 1988. Our first debt is thus to the authors for their patience and understanding during the lengthy process of preparing the manuscript for publication. We are particularly grateful to Alan Jeeves, Bill Worger, and Nancy Clark for detailed commentary on the introduction and several of the individual chapters. We would like to thank Ross Hough of the Department of Geography, Queen's University, for drawing the maps and diagrams (excepting those in chapters 7 and 12), and Linda Crush, Shirley Brooks, and Mary Bentley for their editorial assistance. Our thanks also to Holly Panich and Gillian Berchowitz at Ohio University Press and Margery Moberly at the University of Natal Press. For financial assistance we are indebted to the Mellon Faculty Fellowships program at Harvard University, the University of Texas at El Paso Research Institute, the Advisory Research Committee of Queen's University, and the Canada Research Fellowship and research grant programs of the Social Sciences and Humanities Research Council of Canada.

LIST OF CONTRIBUTORS

CHARLES AMBLER is Associate Professor and Chair of History at the University of Texas at El Paso. He is the author of *Kenyan Communities in the Age of Imperialism* (New Haven: Yale University Press, 1988) and articles on the history of eastern and central Africa.

JULIE BAKER is an adjunct Assistant Professor of History at Queen's University, Kingston, Ontario. Her chapter is drawn from a wider study entitled "The Silent Crisis: Black Labour, Disease, and the Politics and Economics of Health on the South African Gold Mines, 1902–1930" which she is currently preparing for publication.

PHILIP BONNER is Professor of History at the University of the Witwatersrand, Johannesburg. He is the author of *Kings, Commoners and Concessionaires: The Evolution and Dissolution of the Nineteenth-Century Swazi State* (Cambridge: Cambridge University Press, 1983) and articles on the social and labor history of the East Rand.

HELEN BRADFORD is Senior Lecturer in the Department of History, University of Cape Town. She is the author of *A Taste of Freedom: The ICU in Rural South Africa, 1924–1930* (New Haven: Yale University Press, 1987).

JONATHAN CRUSH is Canada Research Fellow and Associate Professor of Geography at Queen's University, Kingston, Ontario. He is the author of *The Struggle for Swazi Labour, 1890–1920* (Montreal and Kingston: McGill-Queen's Press, 1987), and *South Africa's Labor Empire: A History of Black Migrancy to the Gold Mines* (Boulder and Cape Town: Westview Press and David Philip, 1991) (with Alan Jeeves and David Yudelman).

RUTH EDGECOMBE is Senior Lecturer in Economic History in the Department of Historical Studies at the University of Natal in Pietermaritzburg. She has published several articles on the history of the coal industry in Natal and is currently completing monographs on the history of Hlobane Colliery and the coal industry in Natal.

STEVEN HAGGBLADE is an Economic Consultant with Bodija Associates in Dhaka, Bangladesh. He has published widely on southern Africa and development issues.

PAUL LA HAUSSE is Research Officer at the African Studies Institute, University of Witwatersrand, Johannesburg. His publications include *Brewers, Beerhalls and Boycotts: A History of Liquor in South Africa* (Johannesburg: Ravan Press, 1988).

PATRICK McALLISTER is a social anthropologist and currently Research Professor and Director of the Institute of Social and Economic Research at Rhodes University, Grahamstown. His publications deal primarily with Xhosa beer drinking and ritual, migrant labor, and rural development.

DUNBAR MOODIE is Professor of Sociology at Hobart and William Smith Colleges in Geneva, New York. He is the author of *The Rise of Afrikanerdom* (Berkeley: University of California Press, 1975). His *Going for Gold,* the first volume of a three-volume work on domination and resistance on the South African gold mines, will be published shortly by University of California Press.

RICHARD PARRY completed his Ph.D. in the Department of History, Queen's University, Kingston, Ontario in 1988 with a study entitled "Birds on a Flat Rock: Black Workers and the Limits of Colonial Power in Salisbury, Rhodesia, 1890–1939," which he is currently preparing for publication.

SEAN REDDING is Assistant Professor of History at Amherst College. She wrote her doctoral dissertation on the history of the town of Umtata in the Transkei, and is currently working on the history of African taxation in South Africa.

CHRISTIAN ROGERSON is Professor of Human Geography at the University of the Witwatersrand, Johannesburg. He is author of over 120 papers dealing with aspects of South African human geography and co-editor of *South Africa's Informal Economy* (Cape Town: Oxford University Press, 1991).

PAMELA SCULLY is completing her Ph.D. in History at the University of Michigan with a thesis entitled "Liberating the Family? Gender, Labor and the State in the Post-emancipation Rural Western Cape, South Africa, 1830–1870." Her publications include *The Bouquet of Freedom: Social and Economic Relations in the Stellenbosch District, South Africa, 1870–1900* (Cape Town: University of Cape Town Centre for African Studies, 1990).

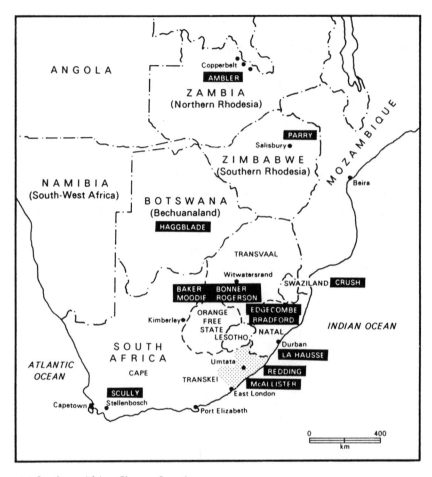

1.1 Southern Africa: Chapter Locations

CHAPTER ONE

ALCOHOL IN SOUTHERN AFRICAN LABOR HISTORY

Charles Ambler and Jonathan Crush

INTRODUCTION

IN JUNE 1976 political demonstrations in the black township of Soweto exploded into an insurrection that would continue sporadically for many months and spread to urban areas across South Africa. In their assault on apartheid the youths who spearheaded the rebellion attacked and often destroyed the state institutions that they linked to their oppression: police stations, government offices, schools, and state-owned liquor outlets. In Soweto alone during the first days of the revolt protesters smashed and burned eighteen beerhalls and a similar number of bottle stores; as the rebellion spread to other South African cities, more stores and halls were destroyed.[1] Those attacks exposed both a moralistic hostility to the institutions that purveyed alcohol in black communities as well as a determination to assault every vestige of state power.[2] But liquor outlets were not simply convenient symbols of oppression. As the essays in this volume show, the anger that launched petrol bombs into beerhalls across South Africa had specific origins in deep and complicated struggles over the control of alcohol production and consumption—indeed over the very meaning of alcohol itself.

Conflict over alcohol has continuously intruded upon the lives of the black residents of southern African towns, cities, and labor compounds and upon the rural communities to which those urban dwellers traced their origins. Popular accounts of urban life repeatedly draw attention to the economic and social importance of alcohol in black communities. Fiction, autobiography, and journalism by writers such as Modikwe Dikobe, Eskia Mphahlele, Nat Nakasa, and Can Themba and volumes of official and semiofficial reports draw the sharp silhouettes of municipal beerhalls and illegal shebeens on bleak urban landscapes, and testify to the obsession of whites—and many blacks—with the prevalence of alcohol in townships and labor compounds.[3] Yet despite the prominence of alcohol production and drinking in descriptions of southern African life, the subject has received little systematic scholarly attention. Moreover, the research that has been done, with a few notable exceptions, has failed to connect the study of alcohol use in southern Africa either to the fundamental issues in the historiography of the region or to the scholarship on alcohol use elsewhere.[4]

This collection explores the complex relationship between alcohol use and the emergence in southern Africa of a modern urban-industrial system, based on mining and the exploitation of migrant labor.[5] The essays collectively focus attention on the ambivalent perspectives of state and capital toward alcohol production and consumption by blacks and on the complex responses of blacks to the regulatory regimes imposed upon them. Those in power saw alcohol as a source of revenue and profit and as an effective tool of social engineering and control, but they often viewed drink also as a dangerous source of disorder, indiscipline, social deterioration, and human degradation. Although many blacks also came to regard alcohol as a source of social decay and a barrier to progress, for most Africans moving into southern Africa's towns and labor camps the preparation and consumption of alcoholic drinks represented a continuity in social and ritual life between the countryside and the town. With the growth of urban black communities, the alcohol trade also became a means to survive economically and to construct a set of cultural and social responses to the harsh experiences of industrial employment, urban residence, impoverishment, and racial segregation.

Throughout southern Africa, colonial governments implemented draconian liquor laws to assert control over black enterprise and leisure. By the 1920s, thousands of black women and men living in the urban areas of South Africa were arrested every year for infractions of the various liquor regulations (Figure 1.2). The graph illustrates both the steady increase thereafter in the number of people convicted of violations of liquor laws and the enormous numbers of people affected. In 1960 alone convictions exceeded 200,000.[6] In short, as this scale of police action suggests and as works like Dikobe's novel *The Marabi Dance* and Mphahlele's memoir *Down Second Avenue* affirm, it was through the application of alcohol regulation that very many of the black residents of urban areas in southern Africa most often and most directly experienced the state. Yet there were few areas of black urban life where the state failed so completely to subordinate the practices of the dominated classes to its own. Ubiquitous daily struggles over alcohol production and consumption, and occasional violent confrontations between brewers and police, were surface manifestations of a deep rejection of state interference and control

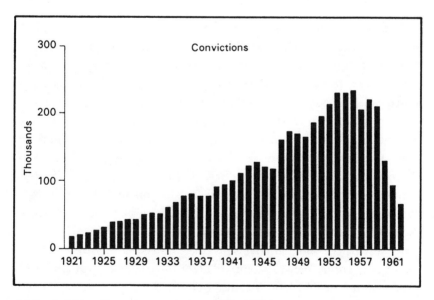

1.2 South African liquor law convictions, 1920–1962

in the arena of drink. Illegal drinking places became sites for the articulation of what James Scott describes as the "hidden transcript" of the dominated: a discourse of opposition that encompassed not only the web of alcohol legislation, but the shared experience of racial oppression and economic exploitation that bound the drinkers together.[7] As the Soweto militants understood only too well, however, the psychological and physiological impact of drinking in such settings was far from unambiguous. Drinking culture fostered compliance as well as resistance, passive acceptance as well as indignant action, hopelessness as well as a sense of empowerment. Thus, the papers in this volume reveal not only the vibrant subcultures nurtured in beerhalls and shebeens, but the worlds of impoverishment and oppression within which these subcultures persisted. Repeatedly, these ambiguities surfaced in the bitter conflicts over alcohol that raged within black communities along the fault lines of age, gender, class, and ethnicity.

THE TEMPTATION OF STRONG DRINK

The basic perspective that has shaped discussions of alcohol in southern Africa emerged out of the late-nineteenth-century confrontation between European and African conceptions of the meaning of alcohol and its role in society. At that time in Europe, and in outposts of European settlement, new thinking about alcohol took root as a result of developments in chemical knowledge and the rise of an aggressive international temperance movement.[8] One of the most important consequences of that particular convergence was the development of the concept of "alcohol" itself. Before the nineteenth century, fermented beers, wines, and distilled spirits—despite recognition of their common psychoactive properties—were each viewed as quite distinct. No one had ascertained the presence in those drinks of a single potentially destructive and addictive substance. Indeed, it was well into the twentieth century before scientists identified the chemical basis and properties of alcohol (specifically, ethanol). As the notion of alcohol took shape, temperance campaigns also steadily eroded the fundamentally positive views of alcoholic drinks that had previously prevailed in Europe and that had led the Puritan preacher Increase Mather to describe drink as "a good creature of God."[9] In England and the English colonies, as well as in the United States, even people who were not committed to temperance came increasingly to see distilled spirits—and to a lesser extent other alcoholic drinks—as unhealthy and potentially dangerous.[10]

The rural black societies of nineteenth-century southern Africa experienced no such change of attitude. In the independent agrarian communities that would shortly fall victim to European imperial expansion, Africans consumed a wide variety of fermented alcoholic drinks produced from various grains and fruits. The offering and consumption of these beers generally held a prominent place at social and ritual gatherings, as tribute to notables, and as reward for the offering of tribute labor.[11] In short, although people recognized and valued the mind-altering properties of grain and fruit beers, they saw them fundamentally as essential substances in both dietary and ritual terms. For the Zulu king Cetshwayo grain beer was "the food of the Zulus; they drink it as the English drink coffee."[12] Such descriptions of beer as an essential food are repeated in numerous European travelers' accounts and in the oral testimonies of Africans.[13] Yet the production of large amounts of alcohol on a regular basis required a command over grain stores and labor that only male notables possessed and thus the consumption and presentation of beer was a mark of both prestige and patriarchal control.[14] For women, youths, and ordinary men, seasonal constraints and the elaborate and time-consuming process of fermentation and brewing—invariably performed by women—sharply limited the quantity of alcohol available. Because grain beer was highly perishable and available to most people only periodically, when people had the chance to drink they often took full advantage of the opportunity. In societies like those in rural southern Africa that condoned a degree of public drunkenness, people found it easy to "get drunk"—even when they had in fact consumed relatively little alcohol.[15]

European observers typically interpreted instances of African drinking they witnessed (or heard about) in terms of their own preconceptions and patterns of alcohol use.[16] They thus tended to see in occasional raucous behavior evidence of excessive drinking and the potential for rampant alcohol abuse. Dudley Kidd, for example, wrote in 1904 of African beer drinking that "the natives can absorb the most prodigious quantities of this stuff; but, after drinking for a day and a half without any needless intervals they are apt to become very quarrelsome. They sometimes drink till they can hold no more, and then lie out in the sun to get rid of the liquid by perspiration, when they set to work once more. This process may be kept up for days together."[17] In a study of colonial Mexican villages in the seventeenth and eighteenth centuries, the historian William Taylor explains how the Spanish misunderstood and misrecorded Indian drinking patterns because they interpreted what they witnessed within a framework of contemporary European notions of moderation and appropriate behavior.[18] A similar process shaped the discourse about alcohol and drinking in Africa. Europeans assumed, for example, that when Africans showed signs of inebriation they had necessarily consumed as much alcohol as Europeans would have done in similar circumstances. African beer parties were often represented as sites of uncontrolled drinking and licentiousness in language not dissimilar to that used by the "respectable classes" of Europe and North America to depict European working-class taverns and public houses.[19]

European notions of racial character and inferiority further distorted descriptions of African drinking. Notwithstanding considerable diversity of opinion among whites as to the susceptibility of Africans to alcohol, in varying degrees Europeans agreed that blacks as a class were more prone than whites to the effects of alcohol. In general, Europeans maintained that only the power of established "tribal systems" contained drinking in rural areas.[20] When traditional authority weakened or when Africans moved into towns and to the mines, it was argued, their resistance to the lure of alcohol dissolved. As a number of the essays in this volume suggest, colonial (and ethnographic) depictions of African alcohol consumption also drew an increasingly sharp divide between "disorderly" urban and "balanced" rural drinking activity. According to a 1942 official investigation, "behind the conflict of interest and theories which have influenced the control of kaffir beer in urban areas can be discerned a desire to respect Native communal customs and to reproduce in the towns . . . something of the social atmosphere of the kraal."[21] In the twentieth century the hysteria among officials about the "orgiastic" character of urban drinking grew out of broader concerns with industrial discipline among black workers, labor migrancy, and the disintegration of rural society.[22] The presence of African women in town also led to "moral panics" among officials concerned with the behavior of women "deprived of 'tribal' restraints."[23] Males, both black and white, commonly portrayed drink and drinking establishments as the "ruin" of black women and the source of unfettered immorality: "When these girls begin drinking," noted an Mfengu headman in 1889, "they go to the bad, and become prostitutes."[24]

In 1893 the Cape Colony Liquor Laws Commission enunciated a perspective on African drinking that until very recently has dominated both scholarly and official representations of the history of alcohol in modern southern African history:

> The difference between the Europeans and natives as regards the use of intoxicants seems to consist mainly in this: That amongst the former a certain proportion is undoubtedly addicted to intemperance, which is found to some extent amongst all classes; but with the tribes on the frontier, the whole population, from the chiefs and headmen down to the lowest amongst the common people, succumb to the temptation of strong drink when it comes within their reach.[25]

In his 1930 examination of alcohol abuse in Africa the missionary and ethnographer Henri Junod summed up that argument with the bold assertion that Africans "are incapable of resisting alcohol."[26] This view that Africans essentially lacked the capacity to refuse alcohol and were thus—unless protected—bound to fall victim individually and collectively to its destructive effects runs through the mass of official and semiofficial investigations and reports, and into the more meager scholarly literature.

Early ethnographic studies in the dominant functionalist tradition subtly sustained that view by portraying drinking in the rural societies of southern Africa as a highly integrated, essentially healthful activity that reinforced the structural order of preindustrial communities. As early as 1932 the anthropologist Eileen Krige, describing alcohol production and use among the Balobedu people of the northern Transvaal, claimed that in the rural setting social controls and practical constraints prevented consumption regarded as excessive.[27] Krige and other functionalist anthropologists argued that alcohol abuse only developed as a consequence of the breakdown of the traditional social order resulting from urbanization and the growth of wage labor.[28] In that tradition Ellen Hellman's examination of a Johannesburg slumyard in the 1930s represented urban settlements as the site of new and destructive forms of brewing and drinking indicative of the disintegration of coherent and cohesive systems of rural values.[29] "The restraints of tribal discipline," she argued, "do not affect the urban native." For Krige, illicit liquor production by urban women was simply "the evil."[30] Similarly, the investigation of the South African Institute of Race Relations into illegal liquor on the Witwatersrand in the 1930s identified a major cause of the "liquor evil" as the divorce of new urban residents from the restraining influence of "tribal custom."[31] The clear implication of those studies was that blacks—individually and collectively—could not control the frequency or intensity with which they consumed alcohol. One of the few historical studies of alcohol use, Bertram Hutchinson's 1961 examination of the eastern Cape Colony in the nineteenth century, described drinking as a "contributing factor in social disorganization," a view that essentially persists in Wallace Mills's otherwise important work on temperance.[32] More recently, Elizabeth Colson and Thayer Scudder's meticulous study of contemporary drinking practices in rural Zambia suggests that a "rising tide of beer" has engulfed an area in which, as recently as the 1950s, the people "never had to learn when to stop drinking, because supplies quickly ran out" and where, consequently, "they drank with moderation."[33] Colson and Scudder link increased drinking to an "African crisis" of social and economic disintegration and decay.[34]

The studies undertaken by the urban anthropologists of the Rhodes-Livingstone Institute in Northern Rhodesia, by contrast, largely eschewed moral commentary, seeing brewing and drinking in Northern Rhodesian towns as crucial elements of relatively stable communities.[35] Similarly, Harry Wolcott's examination of a municipal beer garden in Bulawayo, Southern Rhodesia, in the late 1960s portrayed urban drinking as a stable "integrated" activity that reinforced the structure and norms of urban society.[36] However, if those works dissent from the broad characterization of urban drinking as socially disruptive, they share with other anthropological studies the tendency to romanticize rural African communities as static and coherent and to regard problem drinking—however defined—as an unfortunate, spontaneous byproduct of social change.

As alcohol consumption by Africans came to be defined as an autonomous "social problem," discussion of alcohol use and abuse increasingly occurred within the literature related to health and social welfare.[37] During the late nineteenth century the convergence of new ideas about alcohol and pseudoscientific racial theories inspired a broad imperial assault on the consumption of spirits by Africans.[38] Although temperance purists viewed alcohol as an addictive poison that entrapped drinkers indiscriminately, the wider anti-alcohol movement focused attention on the putative evils of spirits consumption and what was regarded as the particular susceptibility to drink of certain categories of people—notably the European working classes and Africans.[39] In numerous studies and reports, statements regarding the relationship between excessive alcohol consumption and violence, sexual depravity, and genetic disintegration came clothed in scientific language as certain in its tone as it was devoid of fact.[40]

Much of the scientific evidence of the effects of alcohol on blacks and black communities cited in the southern African literature must in fact be read and interpreted as elements of a white discourse about racial difference, making objective investigation of the rates and effects of alcohol consumption extremely problematic. Recent work on the western Cape, for example, draws attention to the health hazards that the long-term consumption of wine rations must have represented for Cape agricultural workers in the late 1800s.[41] But to link the particular regulations or practices of employers or governments to the development of certain kinds of alcohol-related behavior or dependence would be highly speculative given the character and source of evidence on alcohol use by blacks and the present highly contested nature of concepts of inebriation and addiction.[42] Whereas the modern model of alcoholism suggests that certain individuals are innately prone to addiction, the nineteenth-century notion was that alcohol it-self was inherently addictive.[43] By the late nineteenth century, Euro-peans had only recently "discovered" the idea of substance addiction and their definition of it differed markedly from the present popular understanding of alcoholism as a disease.[44]

Whatever specific physiological and genetic relationships scientists may ultimately be able to identify to explain the incidence of alco-holism and the effects of alcohol on behavior, it is clear that cultural as well as chemical factors define the appeal of alcohol and influence the shape of inebriation and the characteristics of dependence.[45] Nu-merous studies document the variations in patterns of drinking and drunkenness across the boundaries of culture, class, and gender.[46] This fact in itself complicates the task of representing the history of alcohol in highly stratified societies like those in southern Africa where the evidence and interpretation of alcohol use by blacks has been expressed largely within a white colonial discourse.

Charles van Onselen's pioneering essay "Randlords and Rotgut" marks a crucial break with earlier perspectives on the history of alco-hol use in southern Africa.[47] Whereas other scholars had portrayed the development of alcohol policy as an ad hoc response to the growth of an autonomous social problem, van Onselen documented in detail the subordination of alcohol regulation to the mining industry's pur-suit of labor mobilization and control. A number of the papers in this collection build very directly on van Onselen's work, applying ele-ments of his argument to other areas of southern Africa and to devel-opments in the twentieth century. Pamela Scully, for example, argues that the voracious demand for black labor in the Cape led to labor shortages in rural areas and to the intensified use of the "tot" (wine-for-work) system on the wine farms of the western Cape in the late nineteenth century. Julie Baker, Dunbar Moodie, and Philip Bonner all explore the struggles inspired by official efforts to enforce prohibi-tion policies in the Transvaal in the face of broad resistance from the black population. The result, argues Baker, was "a fragmented and in-effectual prohibition amid a thriving liquor trade."[48]

These and other essays in this volume also contribute to a broader debate over the character of black and proletarian leisure in the con-text of southern African industrialization and the development of working-class communities.[49] Following van Onselen, many of the contributors emphasize the force of alcohol policy as an instrument of domination. Scully shows how employers used wine rations to control farm workers; Ruth Edgecombe documents the ways that Natal mine owners manipulated supplies of beer to construct a system of debt slavery; and Paul la Hausse, Richard Parry, and Charles Ambler illustrate how the profits of municipal beer monopolies financed the residential segregation and regimentation of urban blacks. However, as English social historians Gareth Stedman Jones and Stephan and Eileen Yeo have argued, the determination of workers to define their own lives beyond work sharply limited the power of the state and capital to structure leisure.[50] The essays in this collection make plain that drinking must be conceived not simply as a weapon of domination but also as a relatively autonomous form of cultural expression— and thus a potent form of resistance. Scully, for example, argues that the daily administration of the tot was at once a ritual of degradation and a site for the production of an alternate laboring culture in which the farmer could not share.[51] In several pieces, including the one published here, la Hausse has unraveled the complex cultures of Durban's legal and illegal drinking establishments and documented the inability of the state to impose its regulatory will.[52] A number of scholars have engaged in a similar exploration of the social history of black culture in the slumyards and townships of Johannesburg and the Rand.[53] For rural southern Africa, the work of Patrick McAllister, in particular, has explored the changing cultural content of forms of alcohol production and consumption.[54] In sum, the essays in this volume represent not only a corrective to the romantic and determinist assumptions that have shaped much of the literature on alcohol use in southern Africa, but also a contribution to the social and cultural histories of black communities in the region.

THE ORIGINS OF ALCOHOL REGULATION

Alcohol has been implicated in the relationships between employers and laborers in southern Africa since the founding of the Dutch colony at the Cape of Good Hope in the seventeenth century. As early as 1658, the Dutch Commandant, Jan van Riebeeck, recorded his recommendation that the young African slaves owned by the Dutch East India Company each be issued daily a glass of brandy and a ration of tobacco "to animate their lessons and to make them really hear the Christian prayers."[55] This is hardly surprising. The Europeans who traded along the southern African coast in the 1600s and who established a settlement at Cape Town in 1652 came from societies where the offering and consumption of alcoholic beverages were deeply entrenched elements of social, economic, and ritual life.[56] By the seventeenth century in Europe alcohol production and consumption had become highly commercialized.[57] Production had moved from the household into breweries and distilleries; inns and taverns had become commonplace features of life not only in cities but in rural communities as well. Distillation technology, which was unknown at the time in sub-Saharan Africa, permitted the production of forms of alcohol that were not only higher in alcohol content but which could be stored for extended periods and transported over long distances.[58] Spirits remained, however, a relatively minor commodity in external trade with Africa until the nineteenth century.[59]

The Europeans who settled in the Cape Colony rapidly established an active commerce in alcohol. The taverns and liquor shops that proliferated in Cape Town and, as the colony expanded, in country hamlets first sold a simple locally produced sugar beer, but by the early 1700s a small brewing industry and extensive vineyards worked by slave labor supplied taverns with beer and wine.[60] With very limited opportunities for export, wine producers relied heavily on the local market—making wine easily available and relatively inexpensive. From a very early stage, estate owners provided tots, or rations, of cheap wine to slaves and free laborers.[61] The provision of rations of wine, beer, or spirits to agricultural workers—free and slave—was common practice at that time in Europe and in America, although both employers and slave owners were clearly ambivalent about permitting their laborers to drink. In seventeenth-century Brazil, for example, amid worries about drunkenness among the slave population, slaves were often provided with tots of rum after completing work.[62] Although detailed research on the development of the practice of providing wine rations in South Africa remains to be done, Pamela

Scully's essay in this volume shows that by the late nineteenth century the system had evolved into a notably debilitating and repressive method of labor control.[63] The political and economic power of the wine industry would ensure its persistence into the twentieth century despite a broad assault on almost every form of drinking by blacks.[64]

The white rulers of the Cape quickly developed concerns about the relationship between the consumption of alcohol and the maintenance of order and control. By the early 1700s the Dutch East India Company had forbidden slaves to purchase wine and spirits, but this regulation—never strictly enforced—was apparently intended to facilitate the control of slaves rather than to limit their consumption of alcohol.[65] Like their contemporaries in Europe and America, the leaders of Cape society condemned the establishments that dispensed alcohol on the open market even as they provided alcoholic beverages to their own slaves and employees. They regarded taverns as centers of vice and criminal activity among both blacks and whites and, in a broader sense, saw them as dangerous refuges from authority.[66] In short, if "respectable people" condemned public drunkenness and the behavior of tavern denizens, they did not extend that condemnation into a general theory of the dangers of alcohol consumption or the susceptibility of certain classes of people to alcohol. Moreover, white officialdom at the Cape made no systematic effort to regulate access to alcoholic beverages.

During the nineteenth century, however, a framework of alcohol regulation was constructed piecemeal that by the early years of the twentieth century had sharply circumscribed the legal rights of black people throughout southern Africa to prepare or obtain alcoholic drinks.[67] The abolition of slavery in the Cape Colony after 1834 and the steady expansion of European political and commercial power beyond the colony's boundary forced colonial rulers and employers to reshape the apparatus of domination.[68] The migration of growing numbers of Africans to the urban areas and agricultural estates of the Cape Colony during the second half of the nineteenth century made whites much more sensitive to signs of disorder among blacks—notably instances of drinking and drunkenness.[69] Public officials began looking with renewed concern at the taverns and grog shops that did legal and illegal trade with blacks.[70] In these new circumstances, the raucous conviviality and communality of taverns appeared to threaten public order and—from the perspective of employers—encourage labor indiscipline.

Many white employers, like their counterparts in England and North America, responded by taking up the temperance cause. Temperance societies had existed at the Cape since the 1830s but encountered "much criticism and ridicule, and little support."[71] By the 1880s, however, temperance ideals enjoyed substantial support, and in the Cape Colony both blacks and whites were active in the numerous temperance societies committed to the prohibition of alcohol to all groups in society.[72] In addition, much larger numbers of whites came to accept temperance ideas insofar as drinking by blacks was concerned.[73] Yet other white South Africans (notably those linked to the wine industry), fearing a reduction in the market for wine as well as disruption of established forms of labor control, opposed regulations that would severely restrict or prohibit the consumption of alcohol by blacks.[74] By the end of the century temperance advocates and their allies had persuaded colonial governments in the Cape Colony and Natal to limit the sale and consumption of alcoholic beverages to Africans, but the political power of the wine industry and its allies prevented any broad attempt at prohibition.[75] The contradictory impulses of alcohol restriction and license would recur repeatedly in the development of industrial capitalism in southern Africa in the late nineteenth and twentieth centuries.

As the legal and illegal alcohol commerce spread at the Cape, traders carried cheap Cape brandy into the independent chiefdoms beyond the frontiers of white settlement.[76] A number of African rulers tenaciously resisted the introduction of distilled spirits into their territories.[77] As early as 1854 the Basotho king Moshoeshoe banned such drinks from his kingdom, declaring that in contrast to locally produced grain beers, "the spiritous liquors of the whites are nothing else than fire."[78] In subsequent decades the Tswana leader Khama would become the hero of temperance advocates for his determined fight against imported spirits and ultimately against all alcoholic beverages, as would Lewanika, the leader of Barotseland.[79] Those men, like many of their European contemporaries, saw brandy and other stronger drinks as substances quite distinct from the fermented alcoholic beverages that were locally consumed. It was not only because those drinks had a higher alcoholic content (and may also have included dangerous impurities), but because they were alien commodities—possession of which required hard cash and not the command over labor power that notables possessed.[80] When cash was available, some African leaders became more concerned with control over the new commerce in alcohol than they were with the effects of consuming those drinks. The royal Swazi villages, for example, were awash with cheap Portuguese wine and spirits during the late 1800s, when concession revenues permitted ostentatious displays of consumption.[81] As Jonathan Crush indicates in his essay in this volume, the Swazi aristocracy continued to regard control over the distribution of alcohol as a crucial element of its power and prestige.

Few whites had any intention of interfering with the household production and consumption of grain beers in rural areas, but they viewed with concern the commercialization of alcohol production in the countryside and especially in towns. That concern turned to alarm when the alcohol produced was spirits. Proponents of strict regulation of African drinking included both those moved by the paternalistic idea that alcohol—chiefly spirits—promoted racial and social disintegration and those with blatant white supremacist fears of alcohol-induced violence and sexual depravity.[82] In the 1890 Brussels Convention and in subsequent agreements culminating in the 1919 Treaty of St. Germain-en-Laye, the major powers agreed to ban the production of spirits in tropical Africa and to forbid the introduction of imported spirits into the areas—beyond the west coast of Africa—where the liquor trade had not yet been established.[83] Although those agreements did not apply to South Africa, governments there ultimately imposed similar and often stricter regulations on the black population. Outside the Cape Province and Mozambique, Africans were forbidden to consume not only spirits but European beer and wine as well. Such measures appear to reflect a determination on the part of whites to preserve the putative noncommercial, "traditional" character of African drinking and to avoid even the suggestion of racial mixing in the consumption of alcohol.[84] The Portuguese, however, permitted the development of distilleries to produce rum from local sugar and, after international pressure forced their closure, encouraged a farflung network of private taverns that purveyed cheap Portuguese-made wines to Africans.[85]

WORK, DISORDER, AND PROHIBITION

The rapid industrialization of South Africa that began with the exploitation of diamonds and gold in the 1870s and 1880s and the concomitant construction of a subcontinental system of labor migrancy decisively recast the patterns of alcohol production and consumption by blacks. During the last decades of the nineteenth century, in the mining areas of Kimberley and the Witwatersrand and in cities such as Durban in Natal (and again decades later in areas like the Copperbelt of Northern Rhodesia) employers saw the easy availability of alcohol as a magnet to draw and hold workers from rural areas—especially those from Mozambique, where a close association already existed between wage employment and drinking.[86] From the inception of organized labor migrancy in southern Africa, alcohol lubricated the mechanisms of movement and control. Gifts of imported spirits helped to secure the cooperation of local notables in labor recruitment, and the provision of drinks became part of the means through which workers were bound into labor contracts and conveyed to and from places of employment.[87] Jeanne Penvenne's work on the labor history of Mozambique describes the incorporation of alcohol sales into the organization of camps where workers were incarcerated before transfer to the mining regions; the routes to the Witwatersrand sprouted with private wine shops that served as way stations for migrants.[88] As the chapters in this volume by Sean Redding and Helen Bradford show, the homesteads of illicit beer sellers in the towns of rural South Africa played a parallel role in the movement of migrant workers there.

Preoccupied with securing and disciplining an industrial workforce, employers made several attempts to control the alcohol consumption of the first black migrants in Kimberley. The mine owners began with an unsuccessful legislative assault on the importation and consumption of "Cape Smoke" in Kimberley's watering holes.[89] Later, they tried to control the black liquor trade through the licensing board and the closed compound. As William Worger and Robert Turrell have shown, the closed compound emerged as a particularly effective system of labor coercion and control in the 1880s.[90] Less remarked upon is the way in which the closed compounds allowed surveillance and supervision of the drinking habits of the workforce. One compound manager later recalled that before the introduction of the closed compound his mine had to "lose Monday" since "labour was disorganised through boys being in gaol and intoxicated." Afterward, the mine issued workers with a tot of Cape brandy a day; then they were allowed no liquor at all. Incarcerated within the compound and denied access to alcohol, workers were supposedly "weaned from the canteen" and became "regular contented workers."[91]

The rapid growth of the Witwatersrand mining region around Johannesburg effectively swept away the ban on sales of alcohol to blacks that the Kruger Republic had promulgated. As thousands of Africans poured into the Witwatersrand goldfields, taverns, liquor stores, and shebeens proliferated. Distilleries in Mozambique and in the Transvaal itself supplied those outlets with a flood of cheap spirits.[92] As in Kimberley, mining interests came to view easy access to drink as a threat to industrial discipline and corporate control of the labor force and devised a successful campaign to close the distilleries and destroy the liquor trade.[93] During the 1890s the major mining companies manipulated white fears of disorderly behavior by blacks and successfully battled and bought off competing industrial and commercial interests to convince the Transvaal government to impose a total prohibition on sales of alcohol to Africans—a prohibition confirmed and extended by the British imperial administration in the aftermath of the South African War. At the same time the British successfully pressured the Portuguese to close down the Mozambique rum distilleries that had operated in violation of international agreements and that had continued to provide a steady flow of liquor to the Rand even after prohibition had been imposed.[94] By early in the century the rulers of South Africa and the British southern African colonies had established a web of alcohol regulations that limited domestic production and consumption of traditional beers to rural areas and permitted urban Africans to obtain those drinks solely from state-owned or licensed outlets or from employers. Africans were generally forbidden to consume all other kinds of alcohol and in the towns of the Transvaal were not even permitted to buy grain beer.[95]

Until the 1930s the Transvaal authorities maintained a prohibition on alcohol consumption by Africans in urban areas, but the chapters by Baker and Moodie show how and why this policy failed to stop Africans from drinking.[96] Even the liquor laws themselves permitted companies to provide their workers rations of "native beer." Indeed, among many employers the view that Africans had to have access to alcohol and that "native beer" was a critical element in the African diet was as strong as the notion that African drinking had to be strictly regulated. Just as the farm owners relied on the tot and extolled the health benefits of wine consumption, urban employers recognized the utility of grain beer in attracting workers and providing a measure of protection against scurvy.[97] Across most of the region, white rulers resisted complete prohibition in favor of various forms of state licensing and monopoly. Employers and local authorities in towns and cities combined not to destroy the liquor trade but to seize control of it, shape it to their needs, and profit from it.[98] As Ruth Edgecombe's grim reconstruction of the use of drink-on-credit on the coal miners in Natal demonstrates, alcohol could be an extremely effective instrument of control.[99]

In the port of Durban, as la Hausse shows in his essay, hundreds of drinking establishments sprang up serving grain beer imported from the surrounding countryside—either unadulterated, distilled, or in some mixture with spirits. Like their counterparts in Johannesburg, the city fathers of Durban were determined to bring drinking under control; but in the face of considerable sentiment for prohibition they sought to construct a system of municipal monopoly. Influenced in part by Scandinavian experiments with alcohol regulation, Durban established in 1909 the first of a network of municipal beerhalls that would give the local state the capacity to shape and intrude upon urban working-class leisure while generating the revenue to provide segregated housing for black workers.[100]

The responses of local governments in the Transvaal and Durban to what they saw as the problem of African drinking represent the two closely related but sometimes contradictory impulses in the design of alcohol regulation: the desire to suppress African consumption of alcohol altogether and the effort to restrict African drinking so that it conformed to and even reinforced the larger objectives of social and economic domination.[101] Both impulses drew on the preoccupation of white officials and employers with the maintenance of order—a concern that had long manifested itself in fears about public drunkenness and tavern life.[102] In addition, as Redding argues in this volume, state concerns about migrant drinking and the presence of female brewers in the urban areas underscored the fears of officials that the migrant labor system itself was disintegrating under the combined pressures of urbanization and rural poverty.

Van Onselen has shown how mine owners played on white anxieties to pursue their campaign for prohibition; but those same anxieties also contributed to the creation of systems of municipal beerhalls.[103] The authorities in South Africa and in Northern and Southern Rhodesia saw public beerhalls as a means to bring the leisure activities of the black population under state scrutiny and control.[104] The chapters by la Hausse and Bradford document a record of persistent and often violent struggle to resist such close regulation and surveillance of drinking. But municipal monopoly—however bitterly contested—also offered the advantage of providing substantial revenues to municipal coffers. The "Durban System" became a model for urban control throughout British East, central, and southern Africa, and by the 1930s throughout the Union of South Africa—including the Transvaal.[105] The beerhalls became one in a nexus of institutions including labor compounds, townships, and rural reserves within which Africans were in some sense incarcerated.[106] In setting the alcohol content of beer and the hours during which it could be consumed, local officials sought to reduce labor indiscipline associated in their minds with unregulated drinking. Furthermore, in determining the location of beerhalls and limiting drinking hours, those officials also hoped to remove African alcohol consumption from white view, and thus create at least the illusion of order.[107]

Ultimately, as the chapters by Baker and Moodie both demonstrate, the most powerful argument against prohibition would be that it created disorder rather than order.[108] With the exception of some diehard temperance advocates, white authorities had come by the

1930s to agree that some provision had to be made for drinking by urban Africans. However, those whites for whom the specter of African drinking inspired violent racist sentiments continued to resist state entry into the liquor trade, as did temperance advocates—including men like Sol Plaatje.[109] Many of the educated and politically active Africans in the Cape Colony in the late 1800s were strong supporters of temperance; and during the twentieth century a sizable proportion of the urban black population—notably devout Muslims and evangelical Christians—rejected drinking and in many instances actively campaigned for its prohibition.[110]

A combative process of conflict and negotiation shaped and reshaped the contours of alcohol control. The essays in this volume make clear that no consensus within the dominant class guided the creation and application of legislation that would govern alcohol. On the Witwatersrand even the mine owners differed in the degree of their commitment to the imposition of sobriety; and those business interests that profited from liquor production and trade bitterly opposed strict restriction.[111] If the Randlords dominated the Transvaal, their sway did not extend to the remainder of southern Africa, where capitalist interests, including the wine industry, succeeded in blocking attempts to impose prohibition.

Not infrequently, the design and enforcement of alcohol regulation put employers in conflict with government. The state at its various levels in Southern Rhodesia and in South Africa had to account to groups within the white community whose views on alcohol did not necessarily conform to those of industrial employers.[112] The case of postwar Johannesburg, discussed by Christian Rogerson in his contribution to this volume, reveals how a combination of pressures from the National Party government and local segments of the white population frightened by the presence of thousands of Africans forced the municipality to close those beerhalls near the city center—a policy that was in many ways inconvenient for employers and cut substantially into municipal revenue. Ruth Edgecombe's essay on the Natal coal mines demonstrates the persistent unwillingness of many Natal officials to support the system of payment in the form of tokens redeemable at company stores and beerhalls that the mines saw as essential to protect their labor supply.[113]

Divisions also emerged between the central and local states over alcohol policy. At the beginning of the century the Durban local authorities successfully avoided the imposition of prohibition by the provincial government of Natal; smaller towns, such as Umtata in the Transkei, were unable to convince the Union government to permit the establishment of beerhalls there.[114] On the East Rand, as Philip Bonner shows, the local authorities and the central government's Barrett-Young Committee opposed each other on the question of municipal monopoly over beer brewing. In Northern Rhodesia, mining interests not only had to contend with local governments dominated by white settlers, but faced as well an imperial state whose broader concern for the maintenance of order sometimes overrode its promotion of industrial profit taking.[115] Not surprisingly, those officials—notably the police—charged with the task of enforcing alcohol regulations in the face of massive defiance of the law were often among the most determined critics of prohibition policies. In fact, Richard Parry suggests that in Salisbury prohibition was sabotaged from within—by an independent judiciary and corrupt law enforcers. The apparent incapacity or unwillingness of governments to enforce alcohol regulations underscores Parry's point that colonialism was often characterized "not by its coercive power but by its inadequacies."[116]

The campaign of employers and governments to control African drinking figured largely in broader attempts by state and capital to shape temporal and spatial orders corresponding to the requirements of capitalist industrial development. As Keletso Atkins has recently argued in a study of nineteenth-century Natal Colony, the expansion of commercial economies directly threatened concepts of time rooted in small-scale rural societies.[117] The introduction of large-scale wage employment imposed a strict categorical distinction between work and leisure time that semisubsistence farming did not require. Estate owners used alcohol rations to segment the day and to mark out free time from work, but industrial employers—in their determination to impose an entirely unprecedented degree of labor discipline—attempted to banish alcohol from the workplace altogether.[118] Julie Baker's essay in this volume documents the close link between efforts of employers to make mines more efficient and their attempts to regulate drinking, often in the guise of the promotion of safety. As both she and Ruth

Edgecombe point out, this drive for efficiency soon pushed industrial employers to extend restrictions on drinking beyond the boundaries of the workplace and the work day and thus establish the absolute primacy of their interests.

The owners of the Natal coal mines, and their counterparts elsewhere in southern Africa, saw the sources of absenteeism and inefficiency in late night and weekend drinking binges and responded with attempts to assert broad control over their workers' lives beyond the mine or factory.[119] Their objectives echoed those of the nineteenth-century English industrialists who sought to eliminate the "St. Monday" extension of the weekend—a phenomenon that was in immediate terms an opportunity to sleep off hangovers and in a deeper sense a refuge for workers from the demands of industrial discipline.[120] As in England, regulations sharply limited legal drinking hours—a plain attempt to prevent extended drinking bouts, the effects of which could invade the work day. In southern Africa, however, such restrictions only encouraged the growth of illegal brewing. For the women who struggled to make a living from preparing and selling beer those developments brought no demarcation to the day and week but, as Helen Bradford shows, a growing burden of work that left such women with little if any leisure at all.[121]

DRINKING AND THE SPATIAL ORDER

Official efforts to impose and enforce liquor regulations aimed not only to subordinate African drinking to the temporal rhythms of industrial employment but to contribute to a definition of urban space appropriate to state control and labor discipline.[122] A number of the essays in this collection illuminate the close connection between prohibition, regulation, and the fundamentally spatial character of alcohol production and consumption. Parry, la Hausse, Bonner, and Rogerson all show the broad relationship between the establishment of alcohol monopolies and the goals of urban segregation. The public beerhalls not only generated the revenue to create and operate separate residential compounds or townships for urban blacks, but they also encouraged Africans to spend their leisure hours in those townships. In some areas, the interaction between drinkers from mine compounds and brewers in neighboring urban communities posed major problems of social control for local municipalities.[123]

Surveillance of African drinking required, in David Harvey's phrase, "command over space."[124] By drawing alcohol consumption into municipal and mine beerhalls, the state and industry sought to circumscribe and police the drinking spaces of the underclasses. Raids against illegal brewers and shebeen owners were as much assaults on the haphazard and covert efforts of Africans to shape their own urban communities and localities as they were attempts to curb African drinking.[125] The authorities aimed to legitimize consumption in certain places and to prohibit it in others. The first step was the legal demarcation of space where Africans were forbidden to produce, consume, or possess alcohol. Drink was forbidden in most public places and many private ones as well. In 1883 the "Robinson clause" of the Cape's Liquor Amendment Act sought to prohibit the sale of liquor to Africans within a radius of five miles of Kimberley.[126] Subsequent colonial regulations in many parts of the region contained such "Robinson clauses" designating the exact spatial limits of the zones within which alcohol production and drinking by Africans were strictly prohibited.

Blanket legislation banning the private manufacture and sale of alcoholic beverages allowed the state to begin to pinpoint those locales where illicit drinking occurred—the boarding houses, private homes, and backyard shebeens. The resulting harassment, prosecution, and imprisonment of illicit brewers and drinkers forced many brewers to move their operations to rural villages beyond the "prohibition zones" and beyond the easy access of the urban population, in the process guaranteeing a market for state-owned beerhalls. The effectiveness of such strategies varied considerably with the surveillance capabilities of the state, the corruptibility of local officials and police, and the tenacity and inventiveness of the brewers and drinkers themselves.[127]

While the state might succeed sporadically in banishing alcohol from the prohibition zones, it rarely tamed the brewers and drinkers. The best that officials could hope to achieve was to drive brewers far enough away from places of employment and mine properties to make their establishments less attractive to customers. As la Hausse shows, the new regime of spatial control in early-twentieth-century Durban was also intended to eliminate the regular movement of non-resident women brewers—and the beer they produced—from the countryside into the city.[128] Crush argues that in Swaziland such spatial strategies of exclusion inadvertently compounded the problem of labor indiscipline since workers were now forced to go longer distances on foot to obtain access to illicit drink.[129] Another spatial strategy adopted by officials on the East Rand in the 1920s and 1930s was to erect fences around locations where women brewed. As Bonner shows, the attempt to keep drinkers (in this case black mine workers) away from producers (Basotho women) through physical restraint failed dismally.[130] Hence, the effective demarcation of prohibition zones required a complementary effort to ensure ease of access to legal drinking space—chiefly the beerhalls.

The authorities in Durban at the beginning of this century saw the beerhall as a tool to establish clear boundaries between the city, dominated by white commercial and industrial interests, and the surrounding rural areas. Decades later, municipal and corporate officials in Southern Rhodesia and on the Copperbelt saw in beerhalls the means to stem the opposite flow of drinkers from the city into the surrounding villages.[131] The women beer protesters in Natal, described in Bradford's essay, clearly understood the personal implications of the strict enforcement of the construction of an artificial urban-rural boundary. The South African, and most colonial, states sought to define cities, towns, and labor compounds as male domains from which women—and especially independent women brewers—were to be excluded as much as possible.[132] As Bradford points out, Natal colonialists believed that female brewers were the ruin of the African male working class and that women drinkers "contaminated the future as well as the current generation of cheap labourers."[133]

Municipalities often tried to locate their public beerhalls to keep African drinking and drinkers as much as possible out of the view of whites, but they deliberately put the halls in prominent and accessible sites in the townships. The halls also reflected white notions of a supposed innate black gregariousness.[134] Beerhalls were constructed in close proximity to other public facilities such as markets, government offices, and especially police stations—which collectively imposed patterns of movement into and within black residential areas.[135] Rogerson notes that beerhalls outside the townships were located close to major industrial areas to capture thirsty patrons as they left work, frequently with pay packets in hand. On the mines, beerhalls were usually sited on private property in or next to the barracklike living accommodations of black miners. Whether inside the townships or not, beerhalls were bleak, functional buildings with little character and no charm, as befitted their purpose. Indeed, patrons often felt they were "drinking in a cage," recognition of the incarceratory impulse that shaped liquor regulation.[136] Some of the less objectionable facilities had adjoining drinking "gardens"—generally a bare, fenced-in area punctuated by small shelters; often the halls were adjacent to the breweries where the insipid beerhall brews were made.[137]

State alcohol monopolies were designed to ensure the absolute racial segregation of drinking. That drinking establishments in southern African cities and towns occasionally attracted mixed clienteles caused considerable concern among the leaders of white society during the early decades of the twentieth century, as did the active involvement of whites in the illegal trade of alcohol to black consumers.[138] The establishment of state control, it was argued, would sharply reduce interracial contact in the alcohol trade. Ultimately, apartheid legislation would make it a crime for liquor to be served at any interracial gathering. Regulations establishing municipal monopolies generally enforced strict bans on whites entering beerhalls, which in any case were usually located in areas removed from the commercial and white residential areas where blacks and whites came into close contact.[139]

Rogerson's chapter on the spatial history of Johannesburg beerhalls describes the gradual elimination of the beerhalls in the industrial and commercial zones of the city as part of the broader apartheid policy of forced population removal. By the 1950s the presence of a beerhall close to the city center that attracted as many as 40,000 patrons in a single day had become intolerable to the whites who lived or worked nearby, and legal drinking was banished to the townships. The redefinition of beerhalls as "noxious facilities" in white discourse accompanied the banishment of legal drinking to the townships. In Rogerson's narrative, the whites-only cocktail party held in the main Johannesburg beerhall following its closure becomes a kind of purification ritual, marking the triumph—albeit temporary—of white values and custom in the cores of South African cities.

Critics—both black and white—regularly denounced the beerhall system in extreme terms, but municipalities tenaciously resisted any moves to dismantle or adjust the state alcohol monopolies. As the essays by Rogerson and Ambler make plain, even hysterical white fears of masses of black drinkers crowded into beerhalls could not persuade town officials to make changes that might shift more of the financial burden of maintaining black residential areas to white taxpayers. In the postwar years, as the cost of providing even meager urban amenities increased, municipalities became more dependent on the income from beer sales to finance urban apartheid and more determined in their defense of beerhalls. Local officials regularly pressed for raids against their competitors—the illicit brewers and shebeen keepers—and lobbied against amendments to alcohol regulations that might reduce revenue.

After 1945, as the publicly owned beerhalls showed increased profits from their sales of mass-produced "traditional" drinks, the highly concentrated industries that controlled the production and distribution of wine, beer, and spirits began to direct increased attention to the African market.[140] The wine industry had long resisted efforts to impose prohibition, especially in the Cape, but after the elimination of the Transvaal distilleries in the 1890s the brewing and spirits industries had focused on the white market. There is no evidence that private capital encouraged the legalization of European beer and wine for African consumption in the 1940s and 1950s in the British colonies, but the South African alcohol industry—plagued by overproduction—pushed hard for the 1962 legalization of African access to European beer, wine, and spirits.[141] The state continued to control production of grain beer in South Africa, but during the 1950s a single private firm gradually took over most of the manufacturing of "traditional" beer for public beerhalls in Northern and Southern Rhodesia and subsequently moved into neighboring countries, including Botswana.[142] There, as Steven Haggblade's essay in this volume shows, the application of corporate economic and political muscle rapidly swept away the cottage brewing industry and left women beer sellers dependent on the male brewery managers and local councillors who regulated the distribution of factory-made grain beer.

The geographical expansion of the alcohol industry was part of a broader commercialization of alcohol production and distribution across southern Africa, urban and rural. During the twentieth century drinking continued to occupy a central position in the social and ritual lives of black people, but brewing was increasingly a source of profit and alcohol itself became a commodity. A growing portion of the alcohol consumed by southern Africans was produced in factories, and even private women brewers used techniques and ingredients unlike those once employed in rural communities.[143]

THE TERRAIN OF RESISTANCE

Beerhalls certainly did not develop into the model institutions that some white officials had envisioned. Although many returned handsome profits to municipalities, the beerhalls failed both to promote orderly drinking and to destroy the private trade. Moreover, the beerhall system inspired enormous resentment and anger in black communities. In 1942 a South African government report noted a pattern—that "raids for detection of illicit liquor have led to struggles ending in bloodshed."[144] Political activists often drew upon opposition to monopoly regulations to build support, and government officials, for their part, eventually came to see the reform of liquor regulations as a means to calm political unrest.[145] Certainly, part of the motivation for the liberalization of South African liquor laws in the early 1960s was a desire to remove a source of discontent at a time when the government was pursuing an intense campaign of political repression and instituting strict controls over residence and movement.[146]

Several of the papers in this volume attest to the anger and outrage that the beerhall could arouse in a wide variety of protesters. Parry, for example, suggests that the quality of beerhall brew was a recurrent source of dissatisfaction for patrons in Salisbury. Rogerson shows that the overcrowded beerhalls in downtown Johannesburg were the site of regular fights between groups of drinkers. Bonner describes how miners from neighboring mines assaulted the police in Payneville location at the instigation of women beer brewers. Both Bradford and la Hausse describe how women themselves launched attacks on the beerhalls, which symbolized their oppression as blacks and as females. Crush recounts how angry strikers demolished a beerhall at the Havelock mine in Swaziland when management attempted to crack down on illicit brewing. Finally, Moodie illustrates how, in the 1980s, mine beerhalls became the focus of intense political struggle between unionized and nonunionized workers.[147]

As these examples attest, Africans tenaciously and often successfully resisted continual efforts by the state and employers to control alcohol production and consumption. Campaigns by patrons and women brewers on beerhalls were generally sporadic and short-lived, partly because of the ready availability of alternative sources of liquor for most blacks.[148] The clearest evidence of the public rejection of the beerhalls was the private and illegal trade in various alcoholic drinks that persisted and even flourished in virtually all urban centers. Indeed, in addition to relying on their own recipes, many women brewers were able to use the beerhall brews as a base for stronger illicit concoctions. Across the region individual brewers and shebeen owners and their patrons defied monopoly regulations and state surveillance. Hence, the rigid definitions of time and space enshrined in the organization of mass beerhalls reflected the determination of the authorities to conceive the black urban population as an undifferentiated laboring class; but that population resisted this classification with equal determination.

The single-sex compound system established on the gold mines of the Witwatersrand allowed management rigorously to exclude women. Mine beerhalls were strictly for employees—by definition male—and this, in part, explains their lack of appeal for generations of miners.[149] Moodie suggests, however, that the "home-boy" networks of migrant miners flourished in such cloistered drinking environments.[150] Moreover, as Moodie, Bonner, and Bradford show, women frequently set themselves up as brewers in competition with the beerhalls; and miners often left the compounds for the illegal drinking establishments that thrived in surrounding areas.

In those parts of the subcontinent—such as the Copperbelt, Swaziland, and the Witwatersrand before 1920—where mine managements experimented with labor stabilization, a different dynamic emerged. Wives and companions (often in the guise of wives) had legal access to mine property, and on many mines the "married quarters" became the center of illicit brewing syndicates and rings—much to the consternation of mine officials, who had assumed that a stable workforce was necessarily more disciplined and "law-abiding."[151] On a more intimate scale, conflict over alcohol revealed the fragility of the moral economies that Moodie and Crush argue governed the conduct of miners and mine managers on the Rand, in Swaziland, and elsewhere.[152]

The promulgation of regulations governing liquor production and consumption was thus only the beginning of the unresolved struggle to control the use of alcohol by the black residents of southern Africa. The texts of statutes served clear practical and ideological objectives, but in societies and communities that recognized no common legal tradition, a great gap existed between those texts and the various experiences of alcohol regulation.[153] While the essays that follow repeatedly document the incapacity and unwillingness of local authorities to enforce the letter of the law, they also dramatically demonstrate the determination of people to resist its enforcement. In Johannesburg the petty liquor dealers, black and white, may have been no match for the powerful mining interests in determining the liquor statutes but, as the essays by Baker, Bonner, Moodie, and Rogerson make clear, they effectively blocked the application of that legislation.[154]

Most important, the ordinary people at whom alcohol legislation was aimed refused to accept its elements or even, in many cases, to recognize its legitimacy. The examples of Durban, Salisbury, the Copperbelt, and Johannesburg covered in this volume show that Africans were determined to shape their own work and leisure lives and build their own community institutions. The most bitter and determined resistance to the enforcement of alcohol regulations came from the ubiquitous small-scale brewers and liquor sellers, mostly women, who depended on the alcohol trade for their livelihood.[155] To those women, police campaigns against illicit alcohol production and consumption meant fines they could not afford to pay and the destruction of brewing or distilling equipment and stocks of beer and liquor that would be expensive to replace. In their view beerhalls represented state-protected competitors. Determined to defend their interests, women brewers and liquor dealers demonstrated and boycotted—in Natal, the western Cape, and the Orange Free State in the 1920s and 1930s, in Northern Rhodesia in the 1950s, and in the dramatic series of protests that rocked the community of Cato Manor near Durban in 1959.[156] In those actions women often joined with temperance advocates and with male opponents of monopoly, but such alliances obscured fundamental differences of interest and objectives among the protesters. While the women sought relief from harassment, their male allies wished to suppress the drink trade or to gain access to it. As Bradford demonstrates in her chapter on women's protests against beerhalls in rural Natal, the experience of oppression and resistance was clearly differentiated by class and gender.

When women migrated to southern African cities, they used the skills they had acquired through the customary tasks of preparing and serving beer to set themselves up as brewers.[157] Aspiring black businessmen objected strenuously to the prohibition of private alcohol production, but men for the most part avoided direct involvement in the illicit alcohol trade. Not only were brewing and beer selling gendered preserves but the very illegality of the activities apparently protected women from competition from men. It was easier for women to elude the police, and women were less likely to be subjected to harsh fines and imprisonment. Not surprisingly, in the 1960s—when Africans were permitted to open bars and bottle stores in Zambia, Malawi, and Rhodesia—men predominated in the trade.[158] Likewise, the recent partial legalization of the shebeen trade in South Africa has resulted in the displacement of women proprietors by male entrepreneurs.[159]

Urban migrants and their descendants gave beerhalls, shebeens, and other drinking establishments in towns and cities a character that differed markedly from the beer parties common to the rural communities from which those women and men originated.[160] As the essays in this volume suggest, the patrons of the drinking establishments that proliferated in labor camps, towns, and cities, constructed or reshaped forms of association that would define new urban communities. In a commentary on the persistence of the shebeen in South Africa in the aftermath of liquor law reform, the journalist Nat Nakasa noted: "It is a mistake to think all these years non-whites have been dreaming about the day they would be allowed to graduate to the status of the white drinker and be welcomed into the lounge. Instead, a different way of drinking has evolved and it cannot suddenly disappear from the face of the Earth."[161] In more intimate terms, the shebeens also represented an escape from the atmosphere of control and surveillance that beerhalls exemplified and from white constructions of African sociability. At the same time, around the beer stores and the brewers' homesteads and in the shebeens and beerhalls themselves, drinkers were engaged in shaping new notions of privacy and communality consistent with the harsh demands of urban industrial life.[162]

By erecting beerhalls and imposing strict alcohol regulations, municipalities and employers attempted to structure the experience of urban blacks. By documenting some of the means that blacks in southern Africa employed to accommodate their incorporation in this system and to insulate themselves from—and even to defy—its harshest and most brutal aspects, the chapters in this volume collectively demonstrate the failure of that attempt. As the essays by la Hausse, Moodie, Bradford, Rogerson, and Ambler show, even the beerhalls nurtured distinctive forms of association and expression quite beyond the control of white rulers and employers.

The women and men who worked in or frequented beerhalls and shebeens pieced together and maintained the social networks that the scholars associated with the Rhodes-Livingstone Institute uncovered in their field studies in the 1940s and 1950s.[163] The patterns of those networks revealed not only the emerging cohesion of communities but the fault lines of differentiation. The women who made and sold beer and those who patronized beerhalls and shebeens were engaged in the redefinition of gender. The same could be said for the husbands and other men whose efforts to control the actions and activism of women Bradford describes in her chapter. Certainly, the violent conflicts that erupted over the beerhall monopolies in Northern Rhodesia in the 1950s and 1960s had as much to do with struggles to delineate the role of women as with concerns over the debilitating effects of alcohol.[164] In the beerhalls and shebeens patrons were mapping out the new boundaries and contours of ethnicity and class.

As urban communities matured, drinking establishments began catering to particular segments of the black population and in the process nurtured the emergence of new expressions of class and consciousness.[165] Many of the accounts of life in urban southern Africa in the 1940s and 1950s describe and even celebrate the "high class" shebeens where well-heeled patrons consumed European drinks and socialized with their peers in relative comfort.[166] In the public beerhalls and beer gardens of the towns of Northern and Southern Rhodesia, better educated and more affluent patrons commandeered separate space for themselves where they imposed patterns of behavior that they regarded as more genteel than those that surrounded them.[167] For these people the existence of regulations that prevented them from consuming spirits and other European alcoholic drinks represented a particularly humiliating symbolic affirmation of a racist order.[168]

When the more affluent patrons of Rhodesian beerhalls attired themselves in imported suits and decorated their tables with cloths and flowers, they were not simply drawing a boundary between themselves and their poorer counterparts. They were acting on an increasingly self-conscious notion of what characterized themselves as a class. The same could be said of the South Africans who frequented elite shebeens, furnished with plush furniture, where brand name spirits and beer were served—and of the ordinary urban workers, who favored much more rakish dress and less-refined behavior.[169] Across southern Africa in beerhalls and shebeens—as at clubs, on football teams, and at the churches and tea parties of nondrinkers— the commonplace behavior of women and men gave some concrete form to human relationships that in new urban circumstances were both in flux and highly contested.[170] Patrons displayed the patterns of speech and dress that were elements of emergent collective identities; they listened to, observed, and performed the vibrant new music and dance that was an integral part of the urban cultures that developed in this century in southern Africa.[171]

Important continuities nevertheless persisted between town and countryside. In towns and cities, residents drew upon diverse rural drinking traditions to shape distinctive patterns of alcohol consumption and drinking institutions. In some areas, rural notables sought to reproduce the "social transactions and cultural meanings" of rural beer drinking within mine compounds.[172] In the towns, the drinking practices of the black workforce could remain closely integrated with those of the countryside as women brought beer to town or men left work to participate in rural beer drinks.

New drinking patterns and tastes also gradually infiltrated the countryside, spreading into farming villages through the drinking establishments where migrants congregated on their way to and from the cities. With the commercial penetration of rural areas and the return of migrants to their homes, new kinds of drinks and new forms of drinking reached deep into the rural areas. Both rural chiefs and critics of colonialism denounced such establishments for siphoning off cash bound for the countryside.[173] But as Bradford and McAllister make clear, brewing enterprises also represented attempts by rural women—impoverished and marginalized by the effects of labor migrancy—to lay claim to the income produced by absent male relatives.

Brewing became an important source of cash for women who needed to buy clothes, feed their children, and pay school fees.[174] Young men returning home with money could demand that beer be brewed, defying the dictates of season and the authority of elders. They could drink as if their time at home were an interval of leisure between periods of work.[175] In the drinking places that sprouted along routes to the cities distinctive social and cultural forms associated with migration took shape. The film *Songs of the Adventurers,* for example, documents vividly how migrants who patronize taverns in Lesotho and the women who work in them comprehend and explain their circumstances through a distinctive form of oral performance.[176]

Drinking and the presentation of gifts of beer also have been central to the rituals of reincorporation of male migrants into rural society. McAllister shows how in the Transkei these rituals were redefined and reinterpreted with changing material circumstances. Xhosa beer-drinking oratory stresses that the migrant's efforts at work have meaning and legitimacy only insofar as they benefit his rural community. Apparently, the emergence in the twentieth century of communal beer drinks in place of the individualized ritual slaughter of livestock was a way of resolving growing conflict between young men and elders; moreover, such slaughter had become "inappropriate as a vehicle for reincorporating returned migrants and making statements about relationships between migrant labor and rural society."[177] The elders summoned the customary power of ritual beer consumption to shore up collective communal identity at a time when migration left rural families increasingly fragmented and vulnerable.[178]

Documentation of the rich heritage of cultural expression that developed around drinking in urban and rural southern Africa does carry the obvious danger that misery is romanticized and suffering minimized. A memoir like Mphahlele's *Down Second Avenue* reveals not only the remarkable vitality, resilience, and autonomy of communities like Alexandra in Johannesburg but also the wreckage of broken families, violence, disease, and alcohol abuse that were as much a part of shebeen and beerhall life as music and dance.[179] We began this introductory essay with the destruction of beerhalls in the 1976 Soweto uprising. In the months that followed, that assault on alcohol spread not only to other cities but to boycotts of the shebeens, which were ubiquitous features of South Africa's black townships. The militants who launched those first attacks and organized the boycotts that followed were not persuaded that beerhalls and shebeens were strongholds of an autonomous black culture and thus elements of resistance to domination. They saw instead repressive institutions that robbed families of wages and sustained crime, violence, and immorality, and drained communities of their strength. The young turks of the National Union of Mineworkers who boycotted mine liquor outlets and attacked older drinkers in the 1980s similarly viewed the outlets as the site of passive acceptance and escapism from the harsh realities of mine life. The "Black Christmas" campaigns that brought boycotts of drinking establishments to South African townships in the mid-1980s may not as yet have effected any deep changes in the patterns and meanings of alcohol consumption. Nevertheless, they sustain a puritanical tradition that has run through the history of black opposition movements since the late nineteenth century, and they are a plain testament that alcohol remains at the center of the complex struggles that will define the future societies of southern Africa.[180]

NOTES

1. B. Hirson, *Year of Fire, Year of Ash: The Soweto Revolt: Roots of a Revolution?* (London: Zed Press, 1979), p. 182; and South African Institute of Race Relations, *Survey of Race Relations, 1976* (Johannesburg, 1977), p. 191.

2. *Rand Daily Mail,* 22 June 1976; 5 July 1976; 14–27 October 1976.

3. M. Dikobe, *The Marabi Dance* (London: Heinemann, 1973); E. Mphahlele, *Down Second Avenue* (London: Faber and Faber, 1959); E. Patel, ed., *The World of Nat Nakasa* (Johannesburg: Ravan Press, 1975); and E. Patel, ed., *The World of Can Themba: Selected Writings of the Late Can Themba* (Johannesburg: Ravan Press, 1985); see also P. Laubscher, "The Magnificent Obsession: The Literature of the Urban Black and the Liquor Question" (B.A. diss., University of Witwatersrand, 1977); and D. Hart, "The Informal Sector in South African Literature," in *South Africa's Informal Economy,* ed. E. Preston-Whyte and C. Rogerson (Cape Town: Oxford University Press, 1991), pp. 68–86.

4. For the comparative literature on alcohol relevant to southern Africa, see the various sources cited in this chapter, as well as L. Pan, *Alcohol in Colonial Africa* (Helsinki: Finnish Foundation for Alcohol Studies, 1975); M. Marshall, ed., *Beliefs, Behaviors, and Alcoholic Beverages: A Cross-Cultural Survey* (Ann Arbor: University of Michigan Press, 1979); D. Heath and A. Cooper, *Alcohol Use and World Cultures* (Toronto: Addiction Research Foundation, 1981); L. Bennett and G. Ames, *The American Experience with Alcohol: Contrasting Cultural Perspectives* (New York: Plenum Press, 1985); J. Curto, "Alcohol in Africa: A Preliminary Compilation of the Post-1875 Literature," *Current Bibliography on African Affairs* 21 (1989): 3–31; J. Verhey, "Sources for the Social History of Alcohol," in *Drinking: Behavior and Belief in Modern History,* ed. S. Barrows and R. Room (Berkeley: University of California Press, 1991), pp. 425–39.

5. This relationship is little commented upon in the large existing literature on industrialization and labor migration in southern Africa. This literature nonetheless provides much of the social and economic context for the essays in this volume; see, for example, F. Johnstone, *Class, Race and Gold*

(London: Routledge and Kegan Paul, 1976); C. van Onselen, *Chibaro: African Mine Labour in Southern Rhodesia, 1900–1933* (London: Pluto Press, 1976); M. Lacey, *Working for Boroko: The Origins of a Coercive Labour System in South Africa* (Johannesburg: Ravan Press, 1981); J. Parpart, *Labor and Capital on the African Copperbelt* (Philadelphia: Temple University Press, 1983); A. Jeeves, *Migrant Labour in South Africa's Mining Economy* (Kingston and Montreal: McGill-Queen's Press, 1985); W. Worger, *South Africa's City of Diamonds: Mine Workers and Monopoly Capitalism in Kimberley* (New Haven: Yale University Press, 1987); and J. Crush, A. Jeeves, and D. Yudelman, *South Africa's Labor Empire: A History of Black Migrancy to the Gold Mines* (Boulder: Westview Press, 1991).

6. The annual *Survey of Race Relations* of the South African Institute of Race Relations (SAIRR) includes published yearly statistics on violations of South African liquor laws; see also South African Temperance Alliance and the SAIRR, "The Illicit Liquor Problem on the Witwatersrand" (Johannesburg, 1935), pp. 58–59; B. Bunting, "Liquor and the Colour Bar," *Africa South* 2 (1958): 36–43; M. Horrell, "The Liquor Laws as They Affect Africans and Coloured and Asian People" (Johannesburg, SAIRR, 1960), pp. 17–19; M. Stein, "State Liquor Policy since 1880" (Paper presented at History Workshop, University of Witwatersrand, Johannesburg, 1981); and W. Schärf, "Liquor, the State and Urban Blacks," in *Crime and Power in South Africa,* ed. D. Davis and M. Slabbert (Cape Town: David Philip, 1985), pp. 48–59.

7. J. Scott, *Domination and the Arts of Resistance* (New Haven: Yale University Press, 1990), pp. 120–35.

8. Jean-Charles Sournia, *A History of Alcoholism,* trans. by N. Hindley and G. Stanton (Oxford: Basil Blackwell, 1990), pp. 43–146; see also W. Crafts, *The Protection of the Native Races Against Intoxicants and Opium* (Washington, D.C.: The Reform Association, 1900).

9. M. Lender and J. Martin, *Drinking in America: A History,* rev. ed. (New York: Free Press, 1987), p. 1.

10. On the historical development of European and American ideas about alcohol, see B. Harrison, *Drink and the Victorians: The Temperance Question in England, 1815–1872* (London: Faber and Faber, 1971); H. Levine, "The Alcohol Problem in America: From Temperance to Alcoholism," *British Journal of Addiction* 79 (1984): 109–19; J. Blocker, *American Temperance Movements: Cycles of Reform* (Boston: Twayne Publishers, 1989); and J. Rumbarger, *Profits, Power, and Prohibition: Alcohol Reform and the Industrializing of America, 1800–1930* (Albany: State University of New York

Press, 1989). The role of women's movements in effecting these changes is explored in B. Epstein, *Politics of Domesticity: Women, Evangelism, and Temperance in Nineteeth Century America* (Middletown: Wesleyan University Press, 1981); J. Dannenbaum, "The Origins of Temperance Activism and Militancy among American Women," *Journal of Social History* 15 (1981): 235–52; and L. Shiman, *Crusade against Drink in Victorian England* (New York: Macmillan, 1988).

11. This depiction of nineteenth-century drinking practices is, of course, highly generalized and is not meant to obscure marked regional differences in brewing methods and drinking practices or the possibility that these changed seasonally, varied from year to year, or evolved over longer periods of time.

12. C. Webb and J. Wright, eds., *Cettiwayo: King of Zululand. A Zulu King Speaks: Statements Made by Cetshwayo on the History and Customs of His People* (Pietermaritzburg: University of Natal Press, 1978), p. 91.

13. For example, H. Callaway, *Religious System of the Amazulu* (London: Folkore Society Publications, 1884), p. 427 fn; and evidence of Johannes Kumalo in *James Stuart Archive,* ed. C. Webb and J. Wright (Pietermaritzburg: University of Natal Press, 1976), 1:252. For repeated assertions of differences in the effects of spirits as opposed to fermented beverages see Cape of Good Hope (G1–'90), "Report of the Liquor Laws Commission, 1889–1890, Minutes of Evidence" (Cape Town, 1890), esp. pp. 498, 652.

14. On the role of alcohol in the exercise and perpetuation of wealth and power in precolonial Africa, see C. Ambler, "Alcohol and Disorder in Precolonial Africa" (African Studies Center, Boston University, Working Paper no. 126, 1987), esp. pp. 11–13. For a more general analysis see M. Aasved, "Alcohol, Drinking, and Intoxication in Preindustrial Society: Theoretical, Nutritional, and Religious Considerations" (Ph.D. diss., University of California, Santa Barbara, 1988).

15. For descriptions of alcohol use and inebriation in rural communities see, for example, Francis Owen, *Diary, 1837–1838,* ed. G. Cory (Cape Town, 1926), pp. 72–74; D. Robinson and D. Smith, *Sources of the African Past* (New York: Holmes and Meier, 1979), pp. 554, 568; D. Fraser, "The Zulu of Nyasaland: Their Manners and Customs," *Proceedings of the Philosophical Society of Glasgow* 31 (1901): 70; D. Mackenzie, *The Spirit-Ridden Konde* (Philadelphia: Lippincott, 1924), p. 35; E. Krige, "The Social Significance of Beer among the Balobedu," *Bantu Studies* 6 (1932): 343–57; and A. Richards, *Land, Labour and Diet in Northern Rhodesia: An Economic Study of the Bemba Tribe* (Oxford: Oxford University Press, 1961 [1939]), pp. 77–81.

16. The social and cultural context of inebriation is exposed in R. Edgerton and C. MacAndrew, *Drunken Comportment: A Social Explanation* (Chicago: Aldine Publishing, 1969); see also N. Lurie, "The World's Oldest On-Going Protest Demonstration: North American Indian Drinking Patterns," *Pacific Historical Review* 40 (1971): 311–32; R. Room and G. Collins, eds., *Alcohol and Disinhibition: Nature and the Meaning of the Link* (Rockville, Md.: National Institute of Alcohol Abuse and Alcoholism, 1981).

17. D. Kidd, *The Essential Kafir* (London, 1904), pp. 326–27.

18. W. Taylor, *Drinking, Homicide, and Rebellion in Colonial Mexican Villages* (Stanford: Stanford University Press, 1969). The cultural content of European comprehension of drinking in Kenya is discussed in C. Ambler, "Drunks, Brewers, and Chiefs: Alcohol Regulation in Kenya, 1900–1939," in Barrows and Room, *Drinking: Behavior and Belief,* pp. 165–83.

19. See J. Roberts, *Drinking, Temperance and the Working Class in Nineteenth-Century Germany* (Boston: Allen and Unwin, 1984); P. Johnson, "Drinking, Temperance, and the Construction of Identity in Nineteenth-Century America," *Social Science Information* 25 (1986): 521–30; and T. Brennan, *Public Drinking and Popular Culture in Eighteenth-Century Paris* (Princeton: Princeton University Press, 1988). In colonial discourse, beer drinking was also connected to an insatiable appetite for meat and therefore inevitably to cattle theft; see T. Beidelman, "Beer Drinking and Cattle Theft in Ukaguru: Intertribal Relations in a Tanganyika Chiefdom," *American Anthropologist* 63 (1961): 534–49.

20. B. Hutchinson, "Alcoholism as a Contributing Factor in Social Disorganization: The South African Bantu in the Nineteenth Century," in Marshall, *Beliefs, Behaviors, and Alcoholic Beverages,* pp. 331–34; G1–'90, "Report of Liquor Laws Commission," pp. 395, 405–6; Mackenzie, *Spirit-Ridden Konde,* pp. 35, 128–30. For discussion of different cultural styles of drinking see J. May, "Drinking in a Rhodesian African Township" (Occasional Paper no. 8, Department of Sociology, University of Rhodesia, 1973), p. 26.

21. Union of South Africa (G.P.–S.42), "Report of the Native Affairs Commission appointed to enquire into the working of the provisions of the Natives (Urban Areas) Act relating to the use and supply of Kaffir Beer" (Cape Town, 30 June 1942), p. 4; see also S. Dubow, "Race, Civilisation and Culture: The Elaboration of Segregationist Discourse in the Inter-War Years," in *The Politics of Race, Class and Nationalism in Twentieth-Century South Africa,* ed. S. Marks and S. Trapido (London: Longman, 1987), pp. 75, 86.

22. J. Crush and S. Redding (in this collection).

23. P. Bonner and P. la Hausse (in this collection).

24. G1–'90, "Report of Liquor Laws Commission," p. 562.

25. Ibid., p. 30.

26. H. Junod, "L'Alcoholisme chez les Africains," *Bibliothèque Universelle et Revue de Genève* 2 (1930), p. 394.

27. Krige, "Social Significance of Beer," pp. 343–57. Functionalist assumptions continued to inform anthropological studies of alcohol use more generally in Africa; see, for example, W. Sangree, "The Social Functions of Beer Drinking in Bantu Tiriki," in *Society, Culture and Drinking Patterns,* ed. D. Pittman and C. Snyder (New York, 1962), pp. 6–21; M. Robbins and B. Pollnac, "Drinking Patterns and Acculturation in Rural Buganda," *American Anthropologist* 71 (1969): 276–84; R. Netting, "Beer as a Locus of Value among the West African Koyfar," in Marshall, *Beliefs, Behaviors, and Alcoholic Beverages,* pp. 328–41; M. Jeffreys, "Palm Wine among the Ibibio," *Nigerian Field* 22 (1957): 40–45; I. Karp, "Beer Drinking and Social Experience in an African Society: An Essay in Formal Sociology," in *Explorations in African Systems of Thought,* ed. I. Karp and C. Bird (Bloomington: Indiana University Press, 1980), pp. 83–119. Largely in the same tradition are the essays in M. Douglas, ed., *Constructive Drinking: Perspectives on Drink from Anthropology* (Cambridge: Cambridge University Press, 1987). For a critique of such assumptions see R. Room, "Alcohol and Ethnography: A Case of Problem Deflation?" *Current Anthropology* 25 (1984): 169–91.

28. For example, M. Hunter, *Reaction to Conquest: Effects of Contact with Europeans on the Pondo of South Africa* (Oxford: Oxford University Press, 1961 [1936]), pp. 253–58, 361–67, 466–67; Richards, *Land, Labour and Diet,* pp. 77–81; and H. Beemer, "Notes on the Diet of the Swazi of the Protectorate," *Bantu Studies* 13 (1939): 199–236. See also C. Davies, "Customs Governing Beer Drinking among the Ama Bomvana," *South African Journal of Science* 24 (1927): 521–24; and F. Brownlee, "Native Beer in South Africa," *Man* 33 (1933): 75–76.

29. E. Hellman, *Rooiyard: A Sociological Survey of an Urban Native Slumyard* (Cape Town: Oxford University Press, 1948).

30. See E. Hellman, "The Importance of Beer-Brewing in an Urban Native Yard," *Bantu Studies* 8 (1934): 60; and E. Krige, "Some Social and Economic Facts Revealed in Native Family Budgets," *Race Relations* 1 (1934).

31. University of Witwatersrand (UW), SAIRR papers, AD 843, B 67.1.1, "Liquor in Native Life" (unpublished report); see also L. Saffery, "The Liquor Problem in Urban Areas," *Race Relations Journal* 7 (1940): 88–94.

32. Hutchinson, "Alcoholism in Social Disorganization," pp. 328–41; W. Mills, "The Roots of African Nationalism in the Cape Colony: Temperance, 1865–1898," *International Journal of African Historical Studies* 13 (1980): 197–213; and "Cape Smoke: Alcohol Issues in the Cape Colony in the Nineteenth Century," *Contemporary Drug Problems* 12 (1985): 221–48.

33. E. Colson and T. Scudder, *For Prayer and Profit: The Ritual, Economic and Social Importance of Beer in Gwembe District, Zambia, 1950–1982* (Stanford: Stanford University Press, 1988), pp. 7, 15; see also L. Molamu, "Alcohol in Botswana: A Historical Overview," *Contemporary Drug Problems* 16 (1989): 3–42.

34. Colson and Scudder, *For Prayer and Profit*, p. 123.

35. G. Wilson, *Essay on the Economics of Detribalisation in Northern Rhodesia* (Cape Town: Oxford University Press, 1941–1942); A. Epstein, *Politics in an Urban African Community* (Manchester: Manchester University Press, 1958), esp. pp. 9–10; and J. C. Mitchell, *The Kalela Dance: Aspects of Social Relationships among Urban Africans in Northern Rhodesia* (Manchester: Manchester University Press, 1971).

36. H. Wolcott, *The African Beer Gardens of Bulawayo* (New Brunswick, N.J.: Rutgers Center for Alcohol Studies, 1974).

37. In South Africa, the persistent strain of blatant racist alarmism in discussions of alcohol use in black communities can be seen in a voluminous series of official and semiofficial reports on the "liquor problem"; see Transvaal (T.K.P. 183), "Report of the Liquor Commission, 1908" (Pretoria, 1910) and Transvaal Archives Depot, C.41, Transvaal Liquor Commission: Minutes of Evidence; Union of South Africa (S.C. 2-'18), "Report of Select Committee on Working of Liquor Laws" (Cape Town, 1918); Union of South Africa (S.C. 7-'18), "Report of the Select Committee on Drunkenness in the Western Districts of the Cape Province" (Cape Town, 1918); Union of South Africa (S.C. 7-'26), "Report of the Select Committee on the Liquor Bill" (Cape Town, 1926); UW, SAIRR papers, AD 843, B67.3.1–2, "Illicit Liquor Commission, 1934"; Union of South Africa (U.G. 50-'37), "Report of the Police Commission of Enquiry. Chapter 8: The Police Administration of the Liquor Law" (Cape Town, 1937); Union of South Africa, "Native Farm Labour Committee. Chapter 6: Kaffir Beer and Other Native Beverages" (Cape Town, 1939); G.P.–S.42, "Commission on Natives (Urban Areas) Act relating to Kaffir Beer"; and Union of South Africa (U.G. 33-'45), "Report of the Cape Coloured Liquor Commission of Inquiry" (Cape Town, 1945).

38. S. Miers, *Britain and the Ending of the Slave Trade* (New York: Holmes and Meier, 1975), pp. 174–81, 273–314; Pan, *Alcohol in Colonial Africa*, pp. 31–38; see also Crafts, *Protection of Native Races*, and the series

of pamphlets, *The Poisoning of Africa,* published by the Aborigines Protection Society in 1895 and 1896.

39. C. Harford, "The Drinking Habits of Uncivilized and Semi-Civilized Races," *British Journal of Inebriety* 2 (1905): 92–103. In the early years of this century there was considerable speculation that excessive drinking had contributed to the poor health of British workers and even to their collective genetic decline; N. Stepan, *The Idea of Race in Science: Great Britain, 1800–1960* (Hamden, Conn.: Archon Books, 1982), pp. 111–39.

40. See, for example, Union of South Africa (U.G. 39–'13), "Report of the Commission Appointed to Enquire into Assaults on Women" (Cape Town, 1913); see also Crafts, *Protection of Native Races,* appendix: "Scientific Testimony on Beer."

41. J. Marincowitz, "Wine and Work in the Western Cape during the Nineteenth Century: The Development of the Tot System" (Paper presented to Symposium on Alcohol in Africa, University of London, 1985); P. Scully (in this collection) and *The Bouquet of Freedom: Social and Economic Relations in the Stellenbosch District, South Africa, 1870–1900* Communications no. 17 (Cape Town, Centre for African Studies, University of Cape Town, 1990), pp. 52–103.

42. Scientific research on the health effects of alcohol consumption is summarized in J. Mendelson and N. Mello, *Alcohol: Use and Abuse in America* (Boston: Little, Brown, 1985) and H. Goedde, *Alcoholism: Biomedical and Genetic Aspects* (New York: Pergamon Press, 1989).

43. H. Levine, "The Discovery of Addiction: Changing Conceptions of Habitual Drunkenness in America," *Journal of Studies on Alcohol* 39 (1978): 143–74; and J. Tropma, "A Contest of Values: A Cultural History of Approaches toward Alcohol," *Journal of Sociology and Social Welfare* 9 (1982): 203–19.

44. H. Fingarette, "Alcoholism: The Mythical Disease," *Public Interest* 91 (1988): 3–22; Sournia, *History of Alcoholism,* pp. 43–146.

45. Scientific knowledge of the effects of alcohol on the brain remains fragmentary. See Mendelson and Mello, *Alcohol,* pp. 163–256. Recent provocative analyses of alcohol abuse and addiction include S. Peele, *The Meaning of Addiction* (Lexington, Mass.: Lexington Books, 1985) and H. Fingarette, *Heavy Drinking: The Myth of Alcoholism as a Disease* (Berkeley: University of California Press, 1988). There has been little systematic study of alcohol abuse and the characteristics of dependency in African societies; see Colson and Scudder, *For Prayer and Profit,* pp. 1–22; and the special number on alcohol in southern Africa of *Contemporary Drug Problems* 16:1 (1989).

46. See, for example, Marshall, *Beliefs, Behaviors and Alcoholic Bever-*

ages; M. Hilton, "Regional Differences in United States Drinking Practices," *British Journal of Addiction* 83 (1988): 519−32; and T. Unwin, *Wine and the Vine: The Historical Geography of Viticulture and the Wine Trade* (London: Routledge, 1991).

47. C. van Onselen, "Randlords and Rotgut, 1886−1903," in *Studies in the Social and Economic History of the Witwatersrand* (London: Longman, 1982), 1:44−102.

48. J. Baker (in this collection), p. 141.

49. D. Coplan, "The Emergence of an African Working Class Culture," in *Industrialisation and Social Change in South Africa: African Class Formation, Culture and Consciousness, 1870−1930,* ed. S. Marks and R. Rathbone (London: Longman, 1982); B. Bozzoli, "History, Experience and Culture," in *Town and Countryside in the Transvaal: Capitalist Penetration and Popular Response,* ed. B. Bozzoli (Johannesburg: Ravan Press, 1983), pp. 16−34.

50. S. Yeo and E. Yeo, *Popular Culture and Class Conflict, 1590−1984: Explorations in the History of Labour and Leisure* (Brighton: Harvester Press, 1981), pp. 128−54; G. Stedman Jones, "Class Expression versus Social Control? A Critique of Recent Trends in the Social History of 'Leisure,'" *History Workshop Journal* 4 (1977): 162−70; and P. Bailey, *Leisure and Class in Victorian England: Rational Recreation and the Contest for Control, 1830−1885,* rev. ed. (London: Methuen, 1987).

51. P. Scully (in this collection), p. 59.

52. P. la Hausse, "Drinking in a Cage: The Durban System and the 1929 Riots," *Africa Perspective* 20 (1982): 63−75; "The Struggle for the City: Alcohol, the Ematsheni and Popular Culture in Durban, 1902−1936" (M.A. diss., University of Cape Town, 1984); and *Brewers, Beerhalls and Boycotts: A History of Liquor in South Africa* (Johannesburg: Ravan Press, 1988); see also I. Edwardes, "Umkhumbane Our Home: African Shantytown Society in Cato Manor Farm, 1946−1960" (Ph.D. diss., University of Natal, 1989); and "Shebeen Queens: Illicit Liquor and the Social Structure of Drinking Dens in Cato Manor," *Agenda* 3 (1988): 75−97.

53. D. Gaitskell, "Laundry, Liquor and 'Playing Ladish': African Women in Johannesburg, 1903−1939" (Paper presented to Workshop on South African Social History, University of London, 1978); E. Koch, "Doornfontein and Its African Working Class, 1914−1935: A Study of Popular Culture in Johannesburg" (M.A. diss., University of Witwatersrand, 1983); C. Rogerson and D. Hart, "The Survival of the 'Informal Sector': The Shebeens of Black Johannesburg," *Geojournal* 12 (1986): 153−66; H. Sapire, "African Urbanisation and Struggles against Municipal Control in Brakpan, 1920−

1958" (Ph.D. diss., University of Witwatersrand, 1989); P. Bonner, " 'Desirable or Undesirable Sotho Women?' Liquor, Prostitution and the Migration of Sotho Women to the Rand, 1920–1945," in *Women and Gender in Southern Africa to 1945,* ed. C. Walker (Cape Town: David Philip, 1990), pp. 221–50; and C. Badenhorst, "Mines, Missionaries and the Johannesburg Municipality: African Sport and Recreation, 1920–1948" (Ph.D. diss., Queen's University, 1992).

54. P. McAllister (in this collection); see also P. McAllister, "Releasing the Widow: Xhosa Beer Drinking Oratory and Status Change," *African Studies* 45 (1986): 171–98; "Xhosa Beer Drinks and Their Oratory" (Ph.D. diss., Rhodes University, 1986); and "Using Ritual to Resist Domination in the Transkei," in *Tradition and Transition in Southern Africa,* ed. P. McAllister and A. Spiegel (Johannesburg: University of Witwatersrand Press, 1991), pp. 129–44.

55. Jan van Riebeeck, *Daghregister,* 2 (17 April 1658): 277 (we are grateful to Robert Shell for providing this reference). See also R. Elphick, *Khoikhoi and the Founding of White South Africa* (Johannesburg: Ravan Press, 1985), pp. 62–63, 96, 157, 166; and N. Worden, *Slavery in Dutch South Africa* (Cambridge: Cambridge University Press, 1985), p. 91.

56. P. Clark, *The English Alehouse: A Social History 1200–1830* (London: Longman, 1983), p. 14; and P. Zumthor, *Daily Life in Rembrandt's Holland* (New York: Macmillan, 1963), pp. 170–75, 182–83, 206.

57. Clark, *English Alehouse,* p. 3; and J. de Vries, *The Dutch Rural Economy in the Golden Age, 1500–1700* (New Haven: Yale University Press, 1974), pp. 67, 126–28, 206.

58. J. Van Houtte, *An Economic History of the Low Countries, 800–1800* (New York: St. Martins, 1977), pp. 147, 171, 255.

59. J. Postma, *The Dutch in the Atlantic Slave Trade, 1600–1865* (Cambridge: Cambridge University Press, 1990), pp. 104–5. During the latter half of the nineteenth century a very substantial trade in cheap, chiefly German, spirits developed with West Africa. See F. Lugard, "The Liquor Trade in Africa," *Nineteenth Century* 42 (1897). On the local impact of the trade, see R. Dummett, "The Social Impact of the European Liquor Trade on the Akan of Ghana (Gold Coast and Asante), 1875–1910," *Journal of Interdisciplinary History* 5 (1974): 69–101; and A. Olurunfemi, "The Liquor Traffic Question in British West Africa: The Southern Nigerian Example," *International Journal of African Historical Studies* 17 (1984): 229–42.

60. E. Rosenthal, *Tankards and Tradition* (Cape Town: Howard Timmins, 1961), pp. 4–32; M. Cairns, "The Land and Its Owners, 1660–1820,"

in *The Josephine Mill and Its Owners,* ed. J. Walton (Cape Town, 1978), pp. 29–46; Worden, *Slavery in Dutch South Africa,* p. 99; and Elphick, *Khoikhoi and White South Africa,* p. 165.

61. Worden, *Slavery in Dutch South Africa,* p. 91; and Elphick, *Khoikhoi and White South Africa,* pp. 165–66, 176.

62. R. Conrad, *Children of God's Fire: A Documentary History of Slavery in Brazil* (Princeton: Princeton University Press, 1983), p. 146; Postma, *Dutch Atlantic Slave Trade,* p. 234. In southern France in the sixteenth century, vineyard workers received an annual ration of more than 900 liters of wine; Emmanuel Le Roy Lauderie, *The Peasants of Languedoc* (Urbana, Ill.: University of Illinois Press, 1974), p. 43. The practice persists to the present, the standard daily ration being two liters; L. Loubere, J. Sagnes, L. Frader, and R. Pech, *The Vine Remembers: French Vignerons Recall Their Past* (Albany, N.Y.: State University of New York Press, 1985), pp. 55, 71.

63. See also Marincowitz, "Wine and Work in the Western Cape"; W. Schärf, "The Tot System in the Western Cape" (mimeo, University of Cape Town, 1987); and J. Bor, "Liquor and Labour at the Cape in the Late Nineteenth Century" (B.A. diss., University of Cape Town, 1978).

64. The Baxter Committee of 1918, investigating drunkenness in the western districts, argued that the tot system "is a fruitful source of drunkenness amongst the Coloured people and against the interests of the farmers whose great need is efficient labour, but to break it down will be no simple matter without the willing co-operation of the farmers." That cooperation was never forthcoming. The Cape Coloured Commission of 1937, the Meaker Commission Report in 1945, and the Erika Theron Commission of the mid-1970s all recommended the abolition of the tot. Such was the power of the farmers, however, that successive governments shied away from implementing the recommendations of their commissions of enquiry. In 1961 the Liquor Amendment Act artfully prohibited the payment of wages in wine but allowed farmers to make "gifts" of wine to their workers; see W. Schärf, "The Impact of Liquor on the Working Class with Particular Focus on the Western Cape" (M.Soc.Sci. diss., University of Cape Town, 1984). Recent studies suggest that the tot system still prevails on many wine farms in the western Cape; see D. Mayson, " 'Hey, You Must Remember We're Living Here on the Farms' " (Paper presented at Conference on "Western Cape: Roots and Realities," University of Cape Town, 1986); and Schärf, "Tot System in the Western Cape."

65. Worden, *Slavery in Dutch South Africa,* p. 99.

66. G. Frederickson, *White Supremacy: A Comparative Study in American and South African History* (New York: Oxford University Press, 1981),

p. 83; Worden, *Slavery in Dutch South Africa,* p. 99; and Rosenthal, *Tankards and Tradition,* p. 41. On the concerns of Brazilian slave owners about taverns, see Conrad, *Children of God's Fire,* pp. 60, 78, 85–86. European taverns were also viewed as centers of vice and criminal behavior; Clark, *English Alehouse,* p. 145; and Brennan, *Public Drinking in Eighteenth-Century Paris.*

67. G1–'90, "Liquor Laws Commission," pp. 25–28, 44, and appendix C, pp. 1004–20; S.C. 2–'18, "Select Committee on Liquor Laws," pp. vi–viii; and Stein, "State Liquor Policy since 1800."

68. M. Rayner, "Wine and Slaves: The Failure of an Export Economy and the Ending of Slavery in the Cape Colony, South Africa, 1800–1834" (Ph.D. diss., Duke University, 1986); J. Marincowitz, "Rural Production and Labour in the Western Cape, 1835–1888, with Special Reference to the Wheat Growing Districts" (Ph.D. diss., University of London, 1985); and J. Mason, "The Slaves and their Protectors: Reforming Resistance in a Slave Society, the Cape Colony, 1826–1834," *Journal of Southern African Studies* 17 (1991): 104–28.

69. Cape of Good Hope (G39–'93), "Labour Commission" (Cape Town, 1893); Cape of Good Hope, (G39–'94), "Report, Labour Commission" (Cape Town, 1894); and Bor, "Liquor and Labour at the Cape."

70. Mills, "Roots of African Nationalism," pp. 210–11; Hutchinson, "Alcohol as a Contributing Factor," pp. 333–45; G1–'90, "Liquor Laws Commission," pp. 405–6, 428, 449, 615; and Rhodes House Library (Oxford), Anti-Slavery Society Papers, Mss. Brit. Emp. S22 G9, "On Drunkenness and Brandy Selling," Cape Colony, 1883.

71. J. Pearce, "The Origins of the Temperance Movement in Cape Town in the 1880s" (B.A. diss., University of Cape Town, 1985), p. 3.

72. Ibid., pp. 11–16.

73. Cape of Good Hope, "Report of the Select Committee on the Working of the Licensing Act, 1884" (Cape Town, 1884), appendix B, A2; J. Stearns, ed. *Temperance in All Nations* (Chicago: World Temperance Congress, 1893) 1:376–78, 385–87, 405–7; Pearce, "Temperance Movement in Cape Town," pp. 58–64. Pearce (p. 45) shows that most of the Cape temperance societies had strong links with their counterparts overseas; see also A. Tiltman, "The Women's Christian Temperance Union of the Cape Colony, 1889–1910" (B.A. diss., University of Cape Town, 1988).

74. M. Ryan, "Anders Ohlsson," in Walton, *Josephine Mill,* pp. 75, 79; and Mills, "Roots of African Nationalism," p. 197. According to the Governor of the Cape, "all subsequent efforts to change the law and to prohibit . . . all sales of liquor . . . to natives have hitherto been frustrated chiefly

by the influence of parties who are supposed to be among the leading correspondents of the Aborigines Protection Society in the Colony"; Public Record Office (London), CO 8339/80, Governor Frere to Secretary of State for Colonies, 6 May 1880.

75. Rosenthal, *Tankards and Tradition,* pp. 85–90; S.C. 7–'18, "Select Committee on Drunkenness in Cape Province," pp. xi, 170–81, 194–201. The Liquor Law Amendment Acts of 1891 and 1898 restricted the sale of liquor to blacks but fell far short of temperance demands for prohibition; Pearce, "Temperance Movement in Cape Town," pp. 14–15.

76. CO 8339/80, Governor Frere to Secretary of State for Colonies, 6 May 1880; Cape of Good Hope, "Select Committee on Licensing Act," pp. 33, 45, 53; and Bor, "Liquor and Labour at the Cape," pp. 6–9.

77. Rhodes House Library, Anti-Slavery Society Papers, Mss. Brit. Emp. S22 69, Summary of Memorial Address to the Governor, Cape Colony, Kingwilliamstown, 1886.

78. "Ordinance against the Introduction and Sale of Spiritous Liquors in the Territory of the Basutos, 8 November 1854" (quoted in Robinson and Smith, *Sources of the African Past,* p. 68); see also L. Thompson, *Survival in Two Worlds: Moshoeshoe of Lesotho, 1786–1870* (Oxford: Clarendon Press, 1975), pp. 199–200.

79. Khama's alcohol policies are described by Rev. J. D. Hepburn, *Twenty Years in Khama's Country* (London, 1895), pp. 140, 151. On Khama as a temperance hero see E. Cherrington, *Standard Encyclopedia of the Alcohol Problem* (Westerville, Ohio: American Issue Publishing Co., 1928), pp. 1460–62. Lewanika's efforts to curb alcohol use are detailed in Zambia Archives, British South Africa Company files, BS 3/168, no. 33.

80. See, for example, the case of Moshoeshoe quoted in Robinson and Smith, *Sources of the African Past,* pp. 54, 68, 70; also Mills, "Roots of African Nationalism," p. 198.

81. J. Crush, *The Struggle for Swazi Labour, 1890–1920* (Kingston and Montreal: McGill-Queen's Press, 1987), pp. 34–36.

82. Pan, *Alcohol in Colonial Africa,* pp. 7–36; P. Winskill, *The Temperance Movement and Its Workers: A Record of Social, Moral, Religious, and Political Progress* (London: Blackie and Sons, 1892) 4:162–63; G1–'90, "Liquor Laws Commission," pp. 498, 626.

83. Miers, *Britain and the Slave Trade,* pp. 171–81, 273–84, 309–10; and Pan, *Alcohol in Colonial Africa,* pp. 37–49.

84. On the purported connection between unregulated drinking and racial intermixing see Union of South Africa, "Commission to Enquire into

Assaults on Women," pp. 1, 16, 20, 23; and S.C. 2–'18, "Select Committee on Transvaal Liquor Laws," p. xiv.

85. J. Penvenne, "A History of African Labor in Lourenco Marques, Mozambique, 1877 to 1950" (Ph.D. diss., Boston University, 1982), pp. 124–46; G. Pirio, "Commerce, Industry and Empire: The Making of Modern Portuguese Colonialism in Angola and Mozambique, 1890–1914" (Ph.D. diss., UCLA, 1982), pp. 178–204, 234–46, 266–94; and W. G. Clarence-Smith, "The Sugar and Rum Industries in the Portuguese Empire, 1850–1914," in *Crisis and Change in the International Sugar Economy, 1860–1914,* ed. B. Albert and A. Graves (Norwich: ISC Press, 1984), pp. 226–35.

86. C. van Onselen, "Randlords and Rotgut," pp. 48–63.

87. P. Harries, "Labour Migration from Mozambique to South Africa" (Ph.D. diss., University of London, 1983), p. 295.

88. C. van Onselen, "Randlords and Rotgut," pp. 51–52; and J. Penvenne, "The Cantina vs The Compound: Labor Control and the Sale of Colonial Wine, Lourenco Marques, 1889 to WWI" (Paper presented at American Historical Society Meeting, San Francisco, 1989).

89. R. Turrell, *Capital and Labour on the Kimberley Diamond Fields, 1871–1890* (Cambridge: Cambridge University Press, 1987), pp. 187–91.

90. Worger, *South Africa's City of Diamonds,* pp. 64–146; and Turrell, *Capital and Labour on the Kimberley Diamond Fields,* pp. 146–73.

91. Transvaal Archives Depot, C41, Transvaal Liquor Commission, Minutes of Evidence, evidence of J. H. Scrutton. When pressed Scrutton admitted that workers devised numerous ingenious ways to smuggle alcohol into the compound and that the mine's attempt to impose prohibition was vociferously opposed by local merchants; see also van Onselen, *Chibaro,* p. 171.

92. C. van Onselen, "Randlords and Rotgut," pp. 57–67; and S.C. 2–'18, "Select Committee on Transvaal Liquor Laws," pp. vi–vii.

93. C. van Onselen, "Randlords and Rotgut," pp. 53–96.

94. Clarence-Smith, "Sugar and Rum in the Portuguese Empire," p. 230. Portuguese wine interests also lobbied for the prohibition of colonial liquor production.

95. P. Jones, *The Liquor Laws of the Colony of the Cape of Good Hope* (Cape Town, 1907); South African Temperance Alliance and SAIRR, "The Illicit Liquor Problem on the Witwatersrand," pp. 8–9, 28–39, 46–57; A. H. Ashton, "Liquor Laws of Central Africa" (Paper delivered to the Conference of Non-European Administrators, Livingstone, Northern Rhodesia, 1960); Stein, "State Liquor Policy since 1880"; and Schärf, "Liquor, the State and Urban Blacks," pp. 97–105.

96. See also C. Dugmore, "Shebeen versus the State: The Conflict over Black Access to Alcohol in Johannesburg, 1902–1939" (B.A. diss., University of Witwatersrand, 1986); and K. Eales, "Race, Class and Liquor: Towards an Understanding of Prohibition for Africans in South Africa, 1902–1928" (Paper presented to Department of History seminar, University of Witwatersrand, 1988).

97. J. Baker, "The Silent Crisis: Black Labour, Disease, and the Politics and Economics of Health on the South African Gold Mines, 1902–1930" (Ph.D. diss., Queens University, 1989).

98. See P. la Hausse, R. Parry, and C. Ambler (in this collection); also Eales, "Race, Class and Liquor."

99. R. Edgecombe (in this collection), pp. 193–96.

100. P. la Hausse, "Struggle for the City."

101. See T.K.P. 183, "Report of the Liquor Commission, 1908"; and S.C. 2–'18, "Select Committee on Liquor Laws."

102. *The Liquor War in South Africa* (Papers prepared for the World's Temperance Congress, London, 1901); T. Schreiner, *Natives and Liquor: Transvaal Commission Recommendations Analysed* (Cape Town, 1911); J. Orpen, *Natives, Drink, Labour. Our Duty* (East London: Crosby and Sons, 1913).

103. See la Hausse, "Struggle for the City," pp. 140–42; and files related to monopoly legislation in Central Archives Depot (Pretoria), NTS 6065 31/322/2 1938.

104. R. Parry and C. Ambler (in this collection).

105. P. la Hausse (in this collection); see also M. Swanson, " 'The Durban System': The Roots of Urban Apartheid in Colonial Natal," *African Studies* 35 (1976): 159–76.

106. C. van Onselen, *Chibaro,* pp. 34–73, 128–94; M. Channock, "The Ecology of Coercion: Criminology and Criminal Law in a New State, South Africa, 1902–1930" (Paper presented at the Social Science History Association Meeting, Minneapolis, 1990); W. Worger, "Industrialization and Incarceration: Punishment and Society in South Africa in the Late Nineteenth and Early Twentieth Centuries" (Paper presented at the American Historical Association Meeting, New York, 1990); and J. Robinson, "'A Perfect System of Control?' State Power and Native Locations in South Africa," *Society and Space* 8 (1990): 135–62.

107. South African Temperance Alliance and SAIRR, "Illicit Liquor Problem on the Witwatersrand," p. 34; see also C. Rogerson and C. Ambler (in this collection); F. Baddeley, "African Beerhalls" (M.A. diss., University of Cape Town, 1966).

108. See also Eales, "Race, Class and Liquor," pp. 32–34, 48–50.

109. A. Cook, "Municipalities and Kaffir-Beer: Why Not the Durban System" (Cape Town: South African Temperance Alliance, 1922); South African Temperance Alliance and SAIRR, "Illicit Liquor Problem on the Witwatersrand," p. 41; B. Willan, *Sol Plaatje: South African Nationalist, 1876–1932* (Berkeley: University of California Press, 1984), pp. 118–19, 135, 141, 379–85.

110. Mills, "Roots of African Nationalism," pp. 197–213; J. Midgely, "Drinking and Attitudes Towards Drinking in a Muslim Community," *Quarterly Journal of Studies on Alcohol* 32 (1971): 148–58; and K. Eales, "Patriarchs, Passes and Privilege," in *Holding Their Ground,* ed. P. Bonner *et al.* (Johannesburg: Ravan Press, 1989), pp. 110–11.

111. C. van Onselen, "Randlords and Rotgut," pp. 84–87.

112. R. Parry, "Birds on a Flat Rock: Black Workers and the Limits of Colonial Power in Salisbury, Rhodesia, 1890–1939" (Ph.D. diss., Queens University, 1988); Eales, "Race, Class and Liquor."

113. R. Edgecombe (in this collection).

114. P. la Hausse and S. Redding (in this collection).

115. C. Ambler (in this collection); and "Alcohol, Racial Segregation and Popular Politics in Northern Rhodesia," *Journal of African History* 30 (1990): 295–313.

116. R. Parry (in this collection), p. 135.

117. K. Atkins, " 'Kafir Time': Preindustrial Temporal Concepts and Labour Discipline in Nineteenth-Century Colonial Natal," *Journal of African History* 29 (1988): 229–44; see also F. Cooper, "Urban Space, Industrial Time, and Wage Labor in Africa," in *The Struggle for the City: Migrant Labor, Capital, and the State in Urban Africa,* ed. F. Cooper (Beverly Hills, Calif.: Sage Publications, 1983), pp. 7–50; and J. Crush, "Tin, Time and Space in the Valley of Heaven," *Transactions of Institute of British Geographers* 13 (1988): 211–21.

118. P. Scully (in this collection); van Onselen, "Randlords and Rotgut," pp. 95–96. The role of drinking in the definition of time is examined by J. Gusfield, "Passage to Play: Rituals of Drinking Time in American Society," in Douglas, *Constructive Drinking,* pp. 73–91.

119. C. Ambler, P. Bonner, J. Crush, and D. Moodie (in this collection).

120. See E. Thompson, "Time, Work Discipline and Industrial Capitalism," *Past and Present* 38 (1967): 56–97; W. Lambert, "Drink and Work-Discipline in Industrial South Wales," *Welsh Historical Review* 7 (1975): 289–306; and D. Reid, "The Decline of St. Monday, 1766–1876," *Past and Present* 71 (1976): 76–101.

121. See also G. Chauncey, "The Locus of Reproduction: Women's Labour in the Zambian Copperbelt, 1927–1953," *Journal of Southern African Studies* 7 (1981): 135–64; D. Gaitskell, "Female Mission Initiatives: Black and White Women in Three Witwatersrand Churches, 1903–1939" (Ph.D. diss., University of London, 1981), chap. 3; Bonner, " 'Desirable or Undesirable Sotho Women?' "; M. Miles, "Missing Women: A Study of Swazi Female Migration to the Witwatersrand, 1920–1970" (M.A. diss., Queen's University, 1991); and B. Bozzoli, "Life Strategies, Household Resilience and the Meaning of Informal Work: Some Women's Stories," in Preston-Whyte and Rogerson, *South Africa's Informal Economy,* pp. 15–33.

122. Cooper, "Urban Space, Industrial Time, and Wage Labor"; and Robinson, "State Power and Native Locations."

123. P. Bonner (in this collection).

124. In "The Restless Analyst: An Interview with David Harvey," *Journal of Geography in Higher Education* 12 (1988): 16.

125. G.P.–S.42, "Commission on Natives (Urban Areas) Act relating to Kaffir Beer," p. 12; and R. Chicken, *A Report on an Inquiry into the Prevalence of Illegal Brewing and Its Causes and Effects on Urban Areas near the Railway Line in Northern Rhodesia* (Lusaka: Government Printer, 1948).

126. Turrell, *Capital and Labour on the Kimberley Diamond Fields,* p. 189.

127. Chicken, *Prevalence of Illegal Brewing;* H. Sapire, "The Stayaway of the Brakpan Location, 1944," in *Class, Community and Conflict,* ed. B. Bozzoli (Johannesburg: Ravan Press, 1987), pp. 369–71; and P. Bonner, H. Bradford, P. la Hausse, and R. Parry (in this collection).

128. P. la Hausse (in this collection), pp. 85–86, 101.

129. Crush, "Tin, Time and Space."

130. P. Bonner (in this collection), pp. 290–292.

131. "Report of the Committee Appointed to Enquire into the Working of the Kaffir Beer Act, 1936" (Salisbury, Government Printer, 1937).

132. Baddeley, "African Beerhalls"; H. Bradford, R. Edgecombe, and C. Rogerson (in this collection).

133. H. Bradford (in this collection), p. 210.

134. S. Hope Redford, "Report of the Durban System of Control of Native Beer" (Durban, 1921).

135. Union of South Africa, "Commission on Natives (Urban Areas) Act relating to Kaffir Beer," p. 4; *Rand Daily Mail* 3 March 1938; and H. Sachs, "The Role of Beerhalls in the Municipal Townships of Johannesburg," 2 vols. (mimeo, Johannesburg, 1962).

136. P. la Hausse, "Drinking in a Cage."

137. Wolcott, *African Beer Gardens of Bulawayo.*

138. U.G. 39–'13, "Commission to Enquire into Assaults on Women," pp. 1, 16, 20, 23, 26; South African Temperance Alliance and SAIRR, "Illicit Liquor Problem on the Witwatersrand," pp. 9–12; Eales, "Race, Class and Liquor," pp. 10–13, 15–20; and J. Baker (in this collection).

139. G.P.–S.42, "Commission on Natives (Urban Areas) Act relating to Kaffir Beer," pp. 5, 12.

140. C. Rogerson, "A Strange Case of Beer: The State and Sorghum Beer Manufacture in South Africa," *Area* 18 (1986): 15–24; N. Rothman, "The Liquor Authority and Welfare Administration in Lusaka," *African Urban Studies* 1 (1978): 27–38; and M. Fridjhon and A. Murray, *Conspiracy of Giants: The South African Liquor Industry* (Johannesburg: Divaris Stein, 1986), pp. 280–81.

141. Fridjhon and Murray, *Conspiracy of Giants,* pp. 280–81.

142. C. Rogerson and B. Tucker, "Commercialization and Corporate Capital in the Sorghum Beer Industry of Central Africa," *Geoforum* 16 (1985): 357–68; B. Tucker, "Interaction Behaviour and Locational Change in the South African Brewing Industry," *South African Geographical Journal* 67 (1985): 62–85; and Rogerson, "Strange Case of Beer."

143. P. la Hausse, *Beerhalls, Brewers and Boycotts.*

144. G.P.–S.42, "Commission on Natives (Urban Areas) Act relating to Kaffir Beer," p. 4.

145. Ambler, "Alcohol and Popular Politics."

146. Rogerson and Hart, "Shebeens of Black Johannesburg," pp. 161–64; Horrell, "Liquor Laws," pp. 14, 30–32; and *Rand Daily Mail,* 28 January 1960, 20 June 1961.

147. R. Parry, J. Crush, H. Bradford, P. la Hausse, C. Rogerson, and P. Bonner (in this collection).

148. See H. Bradford and J. Crush (in this collection).

149. D. Moodie, "Migrancy and Male Sexuality on the South African Gold Mines," *Journal of Southern African Studies* 14 (1988): 228–56.

150. D. Moodie (in this collection); and J. K. McNamara, "Brothers and Work Mates," in *Black Villagers in an Industrial Society,* ed. P. Mayer (Cape Town: Oxford University Press, 1980), pp. 310–20.

151. N. Kagan, "African Settlements in the Johannesburg Area, 1903–1923" (M.A. diss., University of Witwatersrand, 1978); S. Moroney, "Mine Married Quarters: The Differential Stabilization of the Witwatersrand Workforce, 1900–1920," in Marks and Rathbone, *Industrialisation and Social*

Change, pp. 259–69; Chauncey, "Women's Labour in the Zambian Copperbelt," pp. 135–64; and K. Eales, "Jezebels, Good Girls and Mine Married Quarters" (African Studies Institute seminar paper, University of Witwatersrand, 1989).

152. See also D. Moodie, "The Moral Economy of the Miners' Strike of 1946," *Journal of Southern African Studies* 13 (1986): 1–35.

153. See the editorial introduction to J. Brewer and J. Styles, eds., *An Ungovernable People: The English and Their Laws in the Seventeenth and Eighteenth Centuries* (New Brunswick, N.J.: Rutgers University Press, 1980), pp. 1–20.

154. See also Eales, "Race, Class and Liquor"; S.C. 2–'18, "Select Committee on Liquor Laws"; and J. Nauright, "Black Island in a White Sea: Black and White in the Making of Alexandra Township, South Africa, 1912–1948" (Ph.D. diss., Queen's University, 1992), pp. 53–72.

155. H. Bradford (in this collection); Eales, "Jezebels, Good Girls and Mine Married Quarters"; and Bonner, "'Desirable or Undesirable Sotho Women?'."

156. P. la Hausse, *Brewers, Beerhalls and Boycotts,* pp. 29–38, 60–63; L. Ladlau, "The Cato Manor Riots, 1959–60" (M.A. diss., University of Natal, 1975); and Edwardes, "Shebeen Queens."

157. Chauncey, "Women's Labour in the Zambian Copperbelt," pp. 135–64; E. Koch, " 'Without Visible Means of Subsistence': Slumyard Culture in Johannesburg 1918–1940," in *Town and Countryside in the Transvaal,* ed. B. Bozzoli (Johannesburg: Ravan Press, 1983), pp. 151–175. Sapire, "Stayaway of the Brakpan Location;" pp. 370, 373–75; Hellman, *Rooiyard*; S. Redding (in this collection). For a description of the work of a woman brewer see "Nomvula: Beer Brewer," in *Working in South Africa,* ed. K. Dovey, L. Laughton, and J. Durandt (Johannesburg: Ravan Press, 1985), pp. 41–42.

158. Colson and Scudder, *For Prayer and Profit,* pp. 94–95; V. X. Smith, "Excessive Drinking and Alcoholism in the Republic of Zambia (M.A. diss., Howard University, 1973), pp. 88–154; A. Haworth, M. Mwanalushi, and D. M. Todd, *Community Response to Alcohol Related Problems in Zambia, vol. 1: Historical and Background Information* (Lusaka, Institute for African Studies, 1981); also S. Haggblade (in this collection). Women remained active in the illicit trade, which continued to thrive.

159. Rogerson and Hart, "Shebeens of Black Johannesburg," pp. 162–63; Fridjhon and Murray, *Conspiracy of Giants,* pp. 267–72, 281, 291–98.

160. See M. de Haas, "Of Joints and Jollers: Culture and Class in Natal Shebeens," in Preston-Whyte and Rogerson, *South Africa's Informal Econ-*

omy, pp. 101–14; W. Schärf, "Shebeens in the Cape Peninsula," in Davis and Slabbert, *Crime and Power in South Africa,* pp. 97–105; Edwardes, "Shebeen Queens"; and G. Malahlela, "Liquor Brewing: A Cottage Industry in Lesotho's Shebeens," *Journal of Eastern African Research and Development* 15 (1985): 45–55.

161. Nat Nakasa, "And So the Shebeen Lives On," in Patel, *World of Nat Nakasa,* p. 15.

162. See, for example, Hellman, "Beer Brewing in an Urban Native Yard," pp. 38–60; G.P.–S.42, "Commission on Natives (Urban Areas) Act Relating to Kaffir Beer," pp. 7–9; Sapire, "Stayaway of the Brakpan Location," pp. 369–81; and D. Pinnock, "Stone's Boys and the Making of a Cape Flats Mafia," in Bozzoli, *Class, Community, and Conflict,* pp. 422, 429–431.

163. See J. C. Mitchell, ed., *Social Networks in Urban Situations: Analysis of Personal Relationships in Central African Towns* (Manchester: Manchester University Press, 1969).

164. Ambler, "Alcohol and Popular Politics," pp. 306–12.

165. Sachs, "Role of Beerhalls," 1: i–ii; Rogerson and Hart, "Shebeens of Black Johannesburg," pp. 166–67; and C. Rogerson, "Consumerism, the State and the Informal Sector: Shebeens in South Africa's Black Townships," in *Economic Growth and Urbanization in Developing Areas,* ed. D. Drakakis-Smith (London: Routledge, Kegan Paul, 1990), pp. 287–303.

166. *Rand Daily Mail,* 1 February 1960.

167. B. Gussman, "African Life in an Urban Area: A Study of the African Population of Bulawayo" (mimeo, Bulawayo, 1953), pp. 241–46; Wolcott, *African Beer Gardens of Bulawayo;* May, "Drinking in a Rhodesian African Township."

168. Ambler, "Alcohol and Popular Politics," pp. 298–302; Horrell, "Liquor Laws," p. 30; and M. West, " 'Equal Rights for All Civilised Men': Elite Africans and the Quest for 'European Liquor' in Colonial Zimbabwe" (unpublished paper, 1991).

169. Can Themba, "Let the People Drink," in Patel, *World of Can Themba,* pp. 158–65; la Hausse, *Brewers, Beerhalls and Boycotts,* pp. 54–59; Rogerson, "Consumerism, the State and the Informal Sector"; and de Haas, "Joints and Jollers."

170. Badenhorst, "Mines, Missionaries and the Johannesburg Municipality"; J. Lotter, "The Structure and Function of Shebeens in Black and Coloured Communities," in *Report of the Conference on Alcohol in Perspective* (Pretoria, 1991), pp. 223–36; and Rogerson and Hart, "Shebeens of Black Johannesburg."

171. D. Coplan, *In Township Tonight! South Africa's Black City Music and Theatre* (London: Longman, 1985); M. Rorich, "Shebeens, Slumyards and Sophiatown: Women, Music and Cultural Change in Urban South Africa, c1920–1960," *The World of Music* 31 (1989): 78–104; and C. Ballantine, "Music and Emancipation: The Social Role of Black Jazz and Vaudeville in South Africa between the 1920s and the Early 1940s," *Journal of Southern African Studies* 17 (1991): 129–52.

172. J. Crush (in this collection), p. 372.

173. Dr. John Mackenzie noted in 1889 that "I have travelled largely in Bechuanaland, and I know there are chiefs there who have done all they could to prevent their people coming here, because they were unmanned by learning the curse of strong drink"; G1–'90, "Liquor Laws Commission: Minutes of Evidence," p. 417.

174. Crush, *Struggle for Swazi Labour,* pp. 126–27; M. Hedlund and M. Lundahl, "The Economic Role of Beer in Rural Zambia," *Human Organization* 43 (1984): 61–65; Molamu, "Alcohol in Botswana."

175. Richards, *Land, Labour and Diet,* p. 77; Colson and Scudder, *For Prayer and Profit,* p. 42. Other useful studies of changing roles and conceptions of rural drinking include B. O'Laughlin, "Mbum Beer Parties: Structures of Production and Exchange in an African Social Formation" (Ph.D. diss., Yale University, 1973); T. Herlehy, "Ties that Bind: Palm Wine and Blood Brotherhood at the Kenya Coast during the Nineteenth Century," *International Journal of African Historical Studies* 17 (1984): 283–308; J. Pottier, "Reciprocity and the Beer Pot: The Changing Pattern of Mambwe Food Production," in *Food Systems in Central and Southern Africa* (London: School of Oriental and African Studies, 1985), pp. 101–37; S. Heald, "Mafias in Africa: The Rise of Drinking Companies and Vigilante Groups in Bugisu District, Uganda," *Africa* 56 (1986): 446–66; and Molamu, "Alcohol in Botswana."

176. See also D. Coplan, "Performance, Self-Definition, and Social Experience in the Oral Poetry of Sotho Migrant Mineworkers," *African Studies Review* 29 (1986): 29–40; "Eloquent Knowledge: Lesotho Migrants' Songs and the Anthropology of Experience," *American Ethnologist* 14 (1987): 413–33; and "The Power of Oral Poetry: Narrative Songs of the Basotho Migrants," *Research in African Literatures* 18 (1987): 1–35.

177. P. McAllister, "Beasts to Beer Pots: Migrant Labour and Ritual Change in Willowvale District, Transkei," *African Studies* 44 (1985), pp. 132–33.

178. P. McAllister (in this collection).

179. Mphahlele, *Down Second Avenue.*

180. For evidence of the character of this hostility to alcohol, see *Rand Daily Mail,* 12, 14, 25, 27 October 1976; Miriam Tlali, *Amandla* (Johannesburg: Ravan Press, 1980), pp. 178–79, 238–39; and Mewa Ramgobin, *Waiting* (New York: Random House, 1986), pp. 154–56, 191.

CHAPTER TWO

LIQUOR AND LABOR IN THE WESTERN CAPE, 1870–1900

Pamela Scully

INTRODUCTION

THE PRACTICE OF giving out wine in return for labor in the western Cape dates back to the early years of white settlement in the mid-seventeenth century, but the tot system was only fully elaborated during the slaveholding period and became firmly entrenched in the eighteenth century.[1] In the 1680s Khoi pastoralists and dispossessed *strandlopers* (indigenous coastal people living on fishing and foraging) were induced to enter service on white farms and in the towns with payment of tobacco, bread, and wine.[2] The Dutch East India Company initially limited trade in alcohol, reserving it mainly for gifts to Khoikhoi leaders. The spread of colonial settlement and the colonists' growing need for agricultural labor transformed the politics of reciprocity into a politics of domination in which alcohol was to play a particularly important role.[3] The giving out of wine as part of the "wage" emerged as one way of accelerating a process of proletarianization.[4] The use of liquor in the creation and reproduction of a rural working class extended into the nineteenth century, when both unfree and nominally free workers received wine at regular intervals throughout the day. The system continued for similar reasons in the postemancipation period, particularly among marginalized farmers who were short of cash and who struggled to find sufficient laborers at cheap wages.[5] By the 1870s farmers in the western Cape had long secured their dominant position in the world of the farm by making the drinking of alcohol one of the reference points of the laborer's experience.

THE TOT SYSTEM

The operation of the tot system in Stellenbosch district (see Figure 2.1) in the period 1870 to 1910 raises questions about how power was exercised and contested, camouflaged and reproduced. The oral testimony of Olga Starke, a farmer's daughter from Muldersvlei near Stellenbosch village, helps illuminate the extent to which the dynamics of exploitation became intrinsic to the daily experience of male farm laborers:

> Now the men didn't come home for lunch. So Arend, we had the wine here they used to get their dop [tot]. More or less, say a pint a day. Now this old Arend had a long pole. This side he had a basket that he carried the food in and another basket at the back with the wine. If the women arrived late with their husbands' food, he didn't wait. He walked down the road screaming back but he didn't stop. They had to catch up to him.[6]

That reminiscence has multilayered meaning for the historian of rural life in the late-nineteenth-century western Cape. The quote provides an entry to understanding the pivotal role played by alcohol in social and economic relations on the farms. The tot system cut down the outlay of cash wages while farmers also sought to secure an inwardly focused workforce linked to the farm by ties of alcohol dependence. As an insidious means of attempting to dominate and control a rural underclass, the tot system had few equals.

The repressive atmosphere of the farm world and the arduous and repetitive nature of the work made alcoholic stupor an understandable means of coping for laborers, while the giving of a bottle and a half of doctored wine per day from the age of twelve also did much to

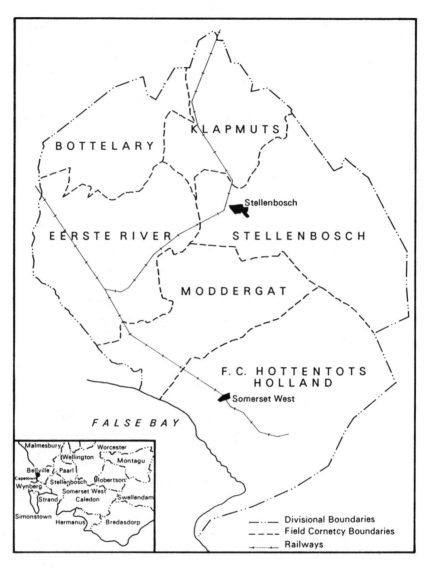

2.1 Stellenbosch District, Cape Colony, c. 1890

produce a rural class of alcoholics. For most of the nineteenth century workers were given up to two quarts of wine a day during the week, and a bottle per day on the weekends. Tot wine was reject wine— made of grape husks, the residue of the second pressing, water, and sometimes brandy.[7] The tot was given at mealtimes and also at about

11 o'clock in the morning and again at four in the afternoon. The farmer's coffee break was thus duplicated but inverted elsewhere on the farm into a ritual of degradation.[8]

Laborers were thus both the instruments and the victims of their own oppression, and relations of power were reproduced and constantly refashioned in practice at the very site of the labor process. Work time came to be marked by the intervals between the pouring of the tot. Paradoxically, a kind of time discipline that slipped easily into work discipline was based on alcohol, a substance that undermined both those concepts. Domination was thus knitted into the labor process of wine farming so that the very rhythms of daily life facilitated and affirmed the farmer's control. Alcoholism accounts for the eagerness with which the laborers in the Muldersvlei vineyard awaited the lunchtime tot, and the worker Arend's haste, while described in comical terms, underscores workers' alcohol dependence. Olga Starke's humorous account also suggests the manner in which the tot system allowed farmers to put domination into practice, into behavior. Drunkenness became comical, domination ritualized, power hidden.

Laborers came to see the daily ritual of the tot as an immutable feature of their experience on the farm. Pieter Cupido, a laborer from Genadendal said that on one farm he had had a good master: "I could drink as much as I liked."[9] Farmers inculcated domination in practice, but practice resonated with other meanings too. Every day of the working year, three times a day, laborers met at a corner of the vineyard to drink their tot. The ritual of daily drinking may have constituted a site for the production of a laboring culture. In the very act of meeting and drinking the tot, workers created a social moment in which farmers could not share. Farmers might supply the wine but they could not fully determine the interaction that took place at the site of drinking the tot; they could not participate in the jokes, the conversation, nor fully restrict the meaning of the tot system to that with which they wanted to invest it. Farmers could only laugh at their workforce from the outside.

The recollections of Olga Starke tell us something of the notions of identity that helped frame the farmers' world. In the postemancipation period the terrain of domination shifted from one that had been rooted in visible violence and authority vested in possession of people to increasingly bureaucratized and diffuse institutions of power.[10] This shift undermined farmers' sense of identity as ultimate holders of power on the farm. The continued use of the tot system in the post-emancipation period might partly have served a symbolic function by reactivating older forms of domination. In giving out wine, farmers could perceive themselves as generous; in response they expected obedience. Notions of *herrschaft*, of domination and reciprocity, underlie the farmers' outrage in the period from 1870 to 1900, when their monopoly of the labor force of the western Cape was weakened as the locus of the colonial economy shifted away from the Cape.

DAILY LIFE AND SOCIAL PRACTICE

Domination and social control were as much components of the rural world in Stellenbosch district in the late nineteenth century as the visual symbols of wine farming in that region: the vineyards and the gabled houses. Although farms in the district differed very much in terms of size, they shared an organization of space. The manor house of H-plan Dutch design dominated the landscape. The vines were planted in rows on ground close to the house. On a "progressive" farm the bushes would be placed in regular rows, with the ground neatly cleared in between. On most farms the bushes ambled across the veld in irregular lines, with overgrowth and even trees visible between the vines. Farther away from the house might lie wheat or oat fields. Bordering the house was the all-important wine cellar. The workers' dwellings sheltered behind a clump of trees or in a depression, out of sight of the farmhouse but close enough for the workers themselves to be conscious of the farmer's presence. The spatial organization of the farm thus gave the presence of the farmer—and his family as representatives of his authority—a significant role in defining the boundaries within which the laborers constructed their social world.

A period of intense work during the summer picking and pressing season was followed by a relative lull from April to October. A permanent body of laborers was required to work in the vineyards all year round. On a farm with a large number of vines (say 300,000) a regular workforce of twelve to fifteen workers was necessary. In winter laborers "skoffeled" the soil between the vines in order to aerate it and to clear the worst of the undergrowth (the horse-pulled hoe was only introduced in the 1880s). In July the soil would be trenched and manured and new cuttings were planted about four feet apart. These cuttings would not be pruned for two years. In older vineyards, pruning took place in May and again in August. Farmers tended to rely for pruning on the services of pruning teams, working under contractors, who toured the wine districts. In February began the backbreaking work of picking the grapes from the low bushes and throwing them into baskets on one's back, all in the intense heat of the Cape summer. In defending the tot system some farmers and their supporters argued that "if workers are in a hot climate and sweat for the whole day in the open air . . . and drink 2 bottles of white wine a day, we don't think this is too much."[11] The grapes were collected in bushel baskets, which contained about fifty pounds of grapes. The baskets were then carried on the wagon that waited in the road between the vineyards. After pressing, the must would be put in the barrels to aid fermentation and the wine would lie for a few months before being sent to firms such as Collisons in Cape Town or the Van Rijn Wine and Spirit Company in Stellenbosch for blending and marketing.

The complexity of labor relations in an era of transition makes any easy categorization of laborers difficult. Permanent laborers included Africans from Mozambique and Delagoa Bay working on contracts of up to five years (who were employed increasingly in the district from the 1870s) as well as local laborers, paid by the month, week or day who worked for a farmer for a continuous period of over a year. Laborers paid by the month most often had access to a house and plot provided by the farmer. Day laborers tended to live in the villages, traveling to the farm each day for work. Traditionally, workers who worked on the farm only at peak seasons did not have access to houses provided by the farmer, but that was to change in the period under review. Seasonal and permanent laborers received wages in cash and kind, and the tot was increased during peak periods in order to lure seasonal workers to the farm.

At peak periods, during picking and pressing, the farmer employed up to double the number of regular workers, recruiting temporary, seasonal labor from the mission stations of Genadendaal, Raithby, and Pniel, although by the 1880s farmers complained that the stations could not fulfill all their labor needs. They partly offset their dependence on the mission stations by employing the family members of permanent workers during peak periods. Indeed, the authority of a farmer to lay claim to the labor of a permanent worker's family whenever extra labor was needed on the farm was an unwritten code of rural labor relations.[12] The peak seasonal labor force thus contained more women and children than the labor force for the rest of the year.

The day began with the ringing of the old slave bell.[13] Work in the vineyard lasted from sunrise to sunset. In summer, when the sun in the western Cape sets as late as 9 o'clock, that could mean a fifteen-hour working day.[14] The crucial punctuations of the farm day were breaks for meals and for the ration of wine. Typically, half an hour was given for breakfast and an hour for lunch. Breakfast rations were eaten outside with the first tot of the day.[15] Working conditions varied for different categories of laborers. The elite among the farm laborers seem to have been the shepherds. As skilled laborers, they were paid more than vineyard workers. They also enjoyed greater freedom during the working day. Unlike the vineyard workers, who were under the supervision of the farmer or an overseer, the shepherds fashioned their own timetable. Klaus, a shepherd, described his day: "I went with my sheep towards Eerste River Railway Station. I left my sheep in the veldt and went for a bottle of beer at the canteen. After partaking of the beer I went back to the sheep."[16] That testimony reveals the way workers fashioned spaces of independence and of how the day was punctuated by drinking.

Of course, the tot system had other ramifications. It reached into the social experience and practice of the farm workers' world, helping to make alcohol consumption a feature of rural underclass culture. Men "club together, buy an anker of wine [a small barrel of 8 and a half gallons] . . . each pays his share and then they divide up the wine on the farm."[17] Canteens also provided an important venue for social interaction between members of the rural underclass. Farm and other laborers met in canteens on Mondays (an unofficial weekly holiday) and in the evenings.[18] Canteens provided an environment potentially subversive of the farmer's authority.[19] The anti-tot lobby in Stellenbosch saw the presence of the canteens as part of the problem in that they encouraged "anti-social unchristian behaviour."[20] The canteens also provided another avenue of dispensing poor quality wine and brandy, however, as well as further binding laborers to farm employment by encouraging addiction. Farmers, particularly those without capital to invest in the sophisticated vats and machinery to make quality wine, were content to exploit this market. After 1846, the law regarding the number of canteens permitted in any area was revised to permit more such licensed houses to operate.[21] In 1865 there were eight canteens in the whole of Stellenbosch district. By the 1890s Stellenbosch village had ten canteens alone, while there were five in the village of Somerset West.[22] Laborers often fell into debt with canteen owners, sometimes with farmers themselves. This tied the workers even tighter to their employer in order to earn money to pay off the debt. Some farmers saw a very real link between access to labor and the presence of canteens. J. Molteno observed that "many farmers hold that canteens do good; they make laborers work for drink, they absorb their wages rapidly, and compel them to work for more to supply the craving. One farmer actually told me that he preferred to have a canteen near his farm, as it ensured him a good supply of labour."[23]

THE EXPANSION OF THE LABOR MARKET, 1870–1900

The mineral and transport revolutions of the late nineteenth century brought about the first major reformulation of social and economic relations in the western Cape since emancipation. The region entered the nineteenth century with an economy resting almost solely on agricultural production and ended it with a new and substantial income from diamond mining operations in the northern Cape, a development that spawned the expansion of transport networks and urban centers like Cape Town and Port Elizabeth. This expansion created new demands for proletarian labor and helped realign the margins within which class relations were negotiated on the farms of the western Cape. Farmers turned to a range of strategies in order to secure both permanent and seasonal labor. Since emancipation, competition for cheap labor had existed among farmers in the western Cape. J. H. Hofmeyr, editor of the *Zuid Afrikaan,* observed in 1875 that the perception of a labor shortage stretched from "the beginning of the years until now."[24] For the first six decades of the century farmers had a stranglehold on the rural labor market, although competition existed between the producers of different crops. Farmers were not forced to confront the practical implication of a postemancipation, "proletarian" labor force for many decades. However, the late nineteenth century brought a level of competition for which farmers were unprepared.

The economic climate of the 1880s and 1890s helped forge deeper cleavages between those farmers who successfully capitalized their farming operations and those who were either unwilling or financially unable to do so. Recession and phylloxera (an insect that destroys vines) brought about many bankruptcies in the district which resulted in the sale or subdivision of many farms. Bankrupt farmers either left the district or sold their farms to kin members. Other farmers maintained their farming operations against all odds owing to the generous mortgage arrangements of the Stellenbosch District Bank, which was financed with local capital. In the last decade of the century entrepreneurs such as Cecil B. Rhodes, John X. Merriman, and James Sivewright bought land in the district. The marriage of those mining entrepreneurs with the progressive Dutch-speaking elite was seen in the Afrikaner Bond of J. H. Hofmeyr.[25] The last three decades of the nineteenth century thus witnessed the consolidation of a capitalizing farming elite, as well as a growing divide between those farmers and the more marginal farmers in the western Cape. The divide was most clearly articulated in the differing attitudes of those groups to the changing tenor of labor relations.

The discovery of diamonds in 1867 in Griqualand West, and of gold in the Transvaal almost twenty years later, created a new economic context in the Cape. From the early 1870s, the major source of competition over labor came from the mines and the railways that began to fan out from Cape Town in the late 1860s. For the first time, farmers in Stellenbosch and other western Cape districts faced competition for labor from the state. In 1890 a select committee report on the labor question stated that:

> In the western Districts, the employment of "Cape Boys" on the Railways, Harbours and other Public Works, the conditions of pay and other privileges offered to labourers by those in charge of such works, does materially and seriously affect the labour market to the detriment of corn and wine farmers, especially during pruning, ploughing, reaping and wine making seasons.[26]

The problem facing farmers in Stellenbosch and other western Cape districts was not so much a shortage of labor as a lack of cheap labor on traditional terms of employment (where farmers had immense power over laborers since members of the rural underclass had little choice but to work on the farms). As the labor market expanded so did the opportunities for laborers. At the same time the farmers' monopoly over rural labor in the western Cape declined, as did their perceived immunity to market forces regarding wage rates.

Farmers reluctantly witnessed the crumbling of the bridge linking their status as a class in the present to the authority and control they had enjoyed in the past. They resented the fact that the rural balance of power was no longer unequivocally theirs and that the texture of class relations had begun to shift. The farmers' world was being shaken, although they tended to exaggerate the degree of instability. A farmer complained that "it is obvious that the servant is striving not to be under his master, but over him, in fact to be in the place of the master."[27] Farmers thus made strenuous attempts to bolster existing mechanisms of control.

The slight gain in economic independence by rural workers led to farmer demands for a stringent amendment to the Masters and Servants Act of 1856, which had helped provide farmers with legal power over their postemancipation labor force. The first amendment occurred only one year after the granting of responsible government in 1872. The legislation now drew a distinction between farm and other servants, and introduced harsher penalties for farm workers. Servants were bound to a five-year contract, criminally punishable if broken. The Act also made "offending behaviour by the servant" a criminal offense; there were twenty-eight such clauses, ranging from insolence to leaving the farm without permission. For a first offense a farm worker was fined £2; an ordinary worker was fined only half that amount.[28] Farmers who had difficulty paying competitive wages were accommodated by the coercive mechanisms of the Act which provided for the imprisonment of farm workers. This was in line with legislative precedents in Britain and the Caribbean which aided marginal farmers.[29] However, farmers' attitudes towards the Masters and Servants Act were ambivalent. Many resented the penetration of state power into farm relationships, preferring the immediate and intimate power that could be exercised on the body of the laborer through physical violence and the tot system.[30] Poorer farmers complained too about the clauses in the Act which allowed for the imprisonment of laborers since this resulted in a shortage of labor on the farm. Wealthier farmers were not as troubled by this aspect as they tended to employ a larger number of laborers and were satisfied to bring laborers to court merely to demonstrate and bolster their authority through law.

With the expansion of the Cape economy in the late nineteenth century these contradictions came to the fore. The farmers of Stellenbosch district liked the fact that "free" wage laborers could be dismissed at times in the agricultural calendar when a large labor force was burdensome, but farmers welcomed wage labor as long as conditions suited the farmer rather than the laborer. Their desire was, at base, contradictory. Farmers wanted an economy that was at once "capitalist and stable, traditionalist and hierarchical."[31] It is noticeable that in the very period that Stellenbosch and other rural societies were shifting into a higher capitalist gear, labor relations were dominated by the use of strategies that subverted the concept of free labor. As Brass has noted about nineteenth-century Puerto Rico, "in the absence of trade unions, the bargaining power of a rural worker consists of an ability to move from farm to farm (or other employment sectors) in search of better paid work."[32] It is precisely because farm laborers in the western Cape began to use this power that farmers relied even more heavily on an armory of hidden weapons such as tied rent, the advance system, and the tot, ensnaring the rural underclass in debt, alcoholism, and dependence.

In the tied-rent system, a farmer offered a laborer a house on the farm or in a nearby village at a nominal rent. In return the worker agreed to provide labor during the crucial seasons of picking and pressing.[33] A leading farmer in Stellenbosch district, J. P. du Toit, made a laborer work one day a week in return for a house.[34] This system of labor tenancy became increasingly important in the period under review, though some workers complained that it gave them little time to cultivate their own plots. Augus Viane, a laborer, observed before the 1893 Labour Commission that "even if farmers give a laborer a free house and a piece of ground as big as the Braak [the Stellenbosch village square] it does not help him a bit. It should be a condition that he be allowed to work his own plot on Saturdays."[35]

The advance system also grew in importance during the late nineteenth century. The system ensnared a laborer in debt and ensured his presence on the farm when his labor was required most. Wine and wheat farmers competing with each other for labor both used the advance system. Wheat farmers in neighboring districts such as Malmesbury and Caledon (fig. 2.1) offered wage advances to laborers at the end of the harvest to try and guarantee a labor supply the following October. That tended to deprive wine farmers of labor at a crucial time since workers tended to live off their advances right through the grape-picking season. Wheat farmers also actively touted for labor in the wine districts, to the dismay of the wine farmers.[36] While the advance system tied workers in a web of debt, it could also be exploited to their own advantage since the system arose out of the farmers' weak position. In Stellenbosch district, the majority of cases tried under the Masters and Servants Act in the period under review related to desertion by a servant either after an advance had been given or in response to an advance promised by a competing farmer. The laborer Barend Philimon was particularly adept at manipulating the system; he was "in the habit of going about getting advances from masters and promising to work but [did] not do so."[37]

Tied rent and the advance system were used mainly by wealthier farmers who had the cash to offer advances or owned additional properties. Practically all farmers, however, used the tot to secure seasonal labor and to aid in controlling laborers. For farmers unable to pay competitive wages, the tot remained virtually the only way of attracting and keeping labor. In the 1870s the size of the tot seems to have increased. As complaints about labor shortage grew and competition for labor heightened between wheat and wine farmers, wheat farmers too began to offer the tot as part of the wage. For many of these farmers the tot was not a means of disposing of surplus wine—in fact, they had to buy tot wine in order to be able to dispense the tot.[38] The effectiveness of the tot system in recruiting labor was acknowledged by the Labour Commission of 1893. The commissioners argued that alcoholism ensured that there would be a number of workers prepared to work under virtually any circumstances.[39]

The tot system also helped farmers dispose of surplus wine in an era when the industry was known more for the volume of production that the quality of the product.[40] The effective closure of the British market after 1861 (owing to the abolition of preferential duties) also contributed to the growth of a colonial market for low-quality wine and brandy.[41] From the 1880s Cape farmers encountered increasing competition for the brandy markets after the establishment of the first distillery in the Transvaal.[42] Brandy was produced mainly for the African trade and production more than doubled between 1865 and 1875.[43] By at least 1880, the demand for brandy outstripped that of wine on the Transkei border.[44]

Legislation passed during the worst years of the depression of the mid-1880s points to the tensions and ambivalence that were to become more explicit in the following decade. As wine and brandy producers turned to the local market, mining interests began to lobby for restrictions on the sale of liquor to Africans on the grounds that alcoholism contributed to low productivity on the diamond mines.[45] The Liquor Licensing Act of 1883 prohibited the sale of liquor in proclaimed "native areas," while in the same year all country canteens in the Orange Free State were closed. The measures threatened the markets of the Cape wine and brandy farmers, but other sections of the Act accommodated the needs of farmers who secured labor through the provision of liquor. Africans were permitted to obtain liquor provided they showed evidence of employment—an obvious recognition of the effectiveness of alcohol in fashioning a proletariat.

The Liquor Licensing Amendment Act of 1885 allowed farmers to sell liquor on the premises in quantities of not less than eight gallons to people in their employ. Africans' relations to liquor, both as consumers and producers, came increasingly to depend on, and be legally linked to, their working for whites. This trend climaxed with the passing of the Innes Liquor Law (Act 28 of 1898), which effectively gave licensing courts the power to prevent Africans from buying or brewing liquor unless they were employed by whites. So important was the sale of poor-quality wine to the livelihood of wine farmers, however, that the state made no moves to limit the sale of wine to the so-called "coloured" population, nor to abolish the tot system. The provision of wine as part of the wage was so central to the labor history of the western Cape that it spread beyond the boundaries of the farm. Reverend Weeber of the Rhenish Mission church stated in 1893 that he had been told by laborers on the railways that contractors on the Somerset West railway gave very large quantities of wine as part of the wage.[46]

THE CONTRADICTIONS OF CONTROL

In the competitive labor market of the late nineteenth century, the reliance on coercive and extra-economic measures to secure sufficient labor became ever more important to both capitalizing and marginal farmers. The contest over access to and control of labor played a key role in the capitalization of agriculture in Stellenbosch district. The exploitation of labor power was one means by which marginalized farmers clung to economic survival, while it formed part of the base from which capitalizing farmers were able to intensify their agricultural production. Those means of securing labor were problematic, however. The advance system set wheat farmers against wine farmers, while the tied-rent system heightened the advantages that wealthier farmers enjoyed over their poorer neighbors. In particular, debate was initiated in the 1890s on the merits of the tot system both as a means of securing labor and as a mode of control. The debate fed into the much larger debate about the prohibition of liquor sales to Africans.[47]

The growing volume of wine and brandy dispensed to rural workers in the late nineteenth century had its own contradictions. While it provided farmers with a short-term means of securing labor, in the long

run it tended to undermine farming operations. Workers could be induced by ties of alcohol dependence to stay on the farm, but inebriation hardly contributed to an efficient labor force. Farmers began to
complain that drunkenness and alcohol abuse was on the increase in
the rural districts.[48] H. Auret, Civil Commissioner in neighboring
Paarl district, argued that "among the labouring classes the love of liquor is formed as children in consequence of the existing custom
among farmers of giving wine three or four times a day to boys for
10–12 years."[49] Reverend Pauw of Wellington said that masters gave
servants too much liquor and that children were given tots six times a
day. "Coloureds are retrograding as a race," he said.[50] J. P. Louw, a
progressive farmer, argued that seasonal laborers were more vulnerable to drink than resident laborers since they were unaccustomed to
drinking regularly.[51]

The tot system was challenged by farmers who sought to reconcile
themselves to the shifts that had occurred in the colonial economy by
the end of the nineteenth century. Some wealthier, capitalizing farmers
indicated a willingness to pay an extra 3d per day instead of providing
wine as part of the wage, while others offered coffee instead of wine.[52]
They did this partly out of recognition that it was the "better class of
labourers" who were leaving the farms and that in order to attract
them it was necessary to offer higher wages.[53] Those farmers were
also mechanizing their operations. Mechanization allowed a smaller
workforce, but it also required a higher level of skill.[54] Perhaps they
were also those farmers whose definition of self more successfully
shifted from being bound with ritualized and intimate domination of
their labor force to one that was comfortable with the more deper-
sonalized and distanced control of the cash nexus.

Most farmers acknowledged the drawbacks of daily wine consumption, but many also felt that the tot system was a necessary component of rural labor relations in the western Cape.[55] Farmers testified
that they could not get labor without the attraction of wine. They
were reluctant to translate wine into equivalent cash wages and that
might have been one of the reasons laborers refused the offer of 3d.
Adolf Abraham, a laborer living at Genadendal, said that if "a farmer
will give 6d per day all his men will give it up," but they would not
accept 3d as that was "not the value."[56] Much wine might have seemed

a better bargain than three pence, which might be spent on wine anyway. A labor force with much of its social discourse based on drinking would not easily respond to some farmers' new incentives. Laborer Pieter Cupido said that he would not take the cash value of the wine since he preferred drinking. He started drinking at sixteen and "got the craving for it."[57]

The report of the Labour Commission of 1893 stated that "the giving of wine or other liquor to farm servants by their employers in some parts of the Colony has been mentioned by many witnesses as either in itself injurious, or inducing an immediate craving, or tending to form a habit which leads them to indulge in excess."[58] The Commission went on to argue that the system was "forced upon farmers" by the demands of their employees. Given the "present scarcity of labour" the farmers felt they were powerless to resist. The Commission's words highlight the changing attitudes of some farmers to the use of liquor as a means of social control and self definition. The report also points to the increasing leverage of temperance advocates and the contradictions faced by farmers as they struggled for control of the rural proletariat. Farmers spoke to the commission with an ear open to public attitudes regarding liquor consumption, and it is hard to ascertain if farmers were as ready as they claimed to kick the habit of pouring out the tot. Jakobus Gabrielse, a former farm laborer, told the Commission, "I formerly got this 3d extra [instead of wine], but I understand that the farmers do not care about giving it now. I do not know whether it is so."[59] The statement also suggests the extent to which farmers had to bow to worker demands in a period of competitive employment opportunities. The extension of the tot system to the railways highlights the leverage enjoyed by laborers at that time.

CONCLUSION

A study of Stellenbosch district in the late nineteenth century illuminates the interrelationship between regional economic transformation and consciousness. In the competitive labor market of that time, the reliance on coercive and more hidden means of social control permeated labor relations in the rural western Cape. The contest over access to and control of labor played a key role in the capitalization of agriculture in Stellenbosch district. The maximum exploitation of labor power was one of the means whereby marginal farmers were able to subsist, while for capitalizing farmers it provided a base from which to intensify production.

The tot system formed a node at which the concerns of two groups met and diverged. Partly because of a recognition of the detrimental effects regular wine consumption had on laborers, and also because they were reconciling themselves to a different definition of rural social relations, progressive farmers were somewhat prepared to halt the tot system. Poorer farmers, on the other hand, remained bound by immediate concerns to hold on to labor at any cost, since they were unable to match the wages offered by wealthier farmers and the public works. The poorer farmers' economic insecurity only buttressed their need to reactivate notions of authority rooted in the region's slaveholding past.

Liquor played a central role in Stellenbosch district as a means of reconstituting and fashioning identity. For some farmers it was a means of linking them to a more secure past. For others the abandonment of liquor as a means of labor control linked them to what they perceived as a more progressive and productive future. For laborers, liquor and the places and times associated with drinking might have represented paradoxical testimony to the incompleteness of farmers' domination—an arena where a rural working class identity could be fashioned, however painfully.

By 1910 farmers no longer complained of labor shortages. On the contrary, they talked of an oversupply of labor, and especially of unskilled labor. The Public Works schemes were coming to an end, closing one area of alternative employment for farm laborers, while the increasing movement of Africans into the western Cape increased the size of the labor force, thus reducing the bargaining power that laborers of the western Cape had enjoyed while the labor market was undersupplied. The 1909 report on the wine districts claimed that "a number of witnesses stated that on several occasions parties of labourers had volunteered to work without wages if only they could be supplied with food."[60] The dilemmas of paying workers in wine receded and the tot system faded from public view, but not from farm practice. In the late twentieth century it is still found on some farms in the district of Stellenbosch.[61]

ACKNOWLEDGEMENTS

I am indebted to Clifton Crais and Ellen Furlough for their comments on this chapter.

NOTES

1. For a discussion of the minimal impact of liquor on Khoi society in the early years of white settlement see R. Elphick, *Khoikhoi and the Founding of White South Africa* (Johannesburg: Ravan Press, 1985), pp. 165–66; see also C. L. Leipoldt, *300 Years of Cape Wine* (Cape Town: Stewart, 1952), pp. 78–80; J. S. Marais, *The Cape Coloured People, 1652 to 1937* (Johannesburg: Witwatersrand University Press, 1957), p. 3: W. Schärf, "The Impact of Liquor on the Working Class with Particular Focus on the Western Cape" (M.Soc.Sci. diss., University of Cape Town, 1984), p. 26.
2. Elphick, *Khoikhoi and White South Africa*, p. 165.
3. For an innovative treatment of trade and reciprocity in the Cape Colony, see C. C. Crais, *White Supremacy and Black Resistance in Pre-Industrial South Africa: The Making of the Colonial Order in the Eastern Cape* (Cambridge: Cambridge University Press, 1991).
4. On the link between alcohol and proletarianization in the late nineteenth century see C. van Onselen, "Randlords and Rotgut, 1886–1903," in *Studies in the Social and Economic History of the Witwatersrand* (London: Longman, 1982), 1:52. Similar provisions were used in the late nineteenth century to lure Xhosa to the farms of the western Cape.
5. J. Marincowitz, "Rural Production and Labour in the Western Cape, 1838–1888" (Ph.D. diss., University of London, 1985); P. Scully, *The Bouquet of Freedom: Social and Economic Relations in Stellenbosch District, South Africa, 1870–1900* Communications no. 17 (Cape Town, Centre for African Studies, University of Cape Town, 1990).
6. Interview with Olga Starke, Muldersvlei Central, 25 November, 1985. She is referring to the first decade of the twentieth century.

7. Schärf, "Impact of Liquor," p. 30.

8. A. Giddens, *Central Problems in Social Theory* (Cambridge: Cambridge University Press, 1981).

9. Cape of Good Hope (G3–'94), "Labour Commission 1893," evidence of Pieter Cupido, p. 385.

10. See M. Foucault, *Discipline and Punish: The Birth of the Prison* (London: Vintage Press, 1982); also Crais, *White Supremacy,* chap. 7.

11. *Zuid Afrikaan* (*ZA*), 17 December 1889; Cape of Good Hope (G1–'90), "Report of the Liquor Laws Commission," evidence of W. A. Krige, p. 216.

12. See E. Boddington, "Domestic Service: Changing Relations of Class Domination, 1841–1948: A Focus on Cape Town" (M.Soc.Sci. diss., University of Cape Town, 1983); also P. Scully, "Liberating the Family? Private and Public Worlds of Emancipation in the Rural Western Cape, South Africa, c. 1830–1842," in *Breaking the Chains: Slavery and Its Legacy in Nineteenth-Century South Africa,* ed. C. Crais and N. Worden (forthcoming).

13. Cape Archives (CA), Magisterial Records of Stellenbosch District (1/STB) 2/45, summary trial, 26 April 1875. This practice continued into the twentieth century; P. van Ryneveld (of the Black Sash), interview with Oom Flip, an ex-farm worker, in *Cape Times,* 2 April 1987.

14. These long working hours contributed to the movement of laborers to the railways, where there was a uniform eight-hour working day; G3–'94, evidence of J. P. Louw of Neethlings Hof, p. 297; CA, 1/STB 2/54, case 1441, n.d. (1885).

15. CA, 1/STB 2/41, case 2654, 24 November 1868; interview with Olga Starke; see also 1/STB 2/68, case 3, 4 January 1895.

16. CA, 1/STB 2/45, summary trial 26 April 1875.

17. G3–'94, evidence of George B. West, constable at Genadendal, p. 386.

18. G3–'94, evidence of Richard Conway, chief constable, Paarl, p. 293; evidence of J. P. Louw, p. 292.

19. This was certainly the case in workers' cafes in France, which were the locus of political activism. I am grateful to Ellen Furlough for pointing this out.

20. *ZA,* 28 January 1880.

21. Schärf, "Impact of Liquor," p. 30.

22. Cape of Good Hope (G20–'66), "Census 1865"; G3–'94, evidence of Petrus Jakobus Bosman, mayor of Stellenbosch, p. 307; Colonial Office 3706, Resident Magistrate to Secretary of the Land Department, 28 February 1892.

23. J. Molteno, *Liquor Problems and Legislation: An Address Delivered at the Annual Meeting of the Church Temperance Society, Cape Town, 1893*

(Cape Town: Church Temperance Society, 1893); also see G3–'94, evidence of J. P. Louw, p. 301.

24. *ZA*, 11 December 1875; Marincowitz, "Rural Production."

25. Scully, *Bouquet of Freedom,* chap. 2; H. Giliomee, "Farmers and Ethnic Politics: The Cape Boers during the Late Nineteenth Century" (Paper delivered to the Tenth Biennial National Conference of the South African Historical Society, 1985); T. R. H. Davenport, *The Afrikaner Bond: The History of a South African Party, 1880–1911* (Cape Town: Oxford University Press, 1966).

26. Cape of Good Hope (A12–'90), "SCR on Labour Question," p. ii.

27. G3–'94, evidence of D. H. Joubert, p. 288.

28. Cape of Good Hope (A5–'72), "Report of the Select Committee appointed to consider and report on the Masters and Servants Acts: Act 18 of 1873." Subsequent amendments to the Cape Masters and Servants Act continued the discrimination against farm laborers. Act 7 of 1875, for example, permitted the arrest of deserting laborers and negated the need for a warrant of arrest in the case of rural laborers.

29. C. Bundy, "The Abolition of the Masters and Servants Act," *South African Labour Bulletin* 2 (May-June 1975): 37–46.

30. See the chapter on slave discipline in N. Worden, *Slavery in Dutch South Africa* (Cambridge: Cambridge University Press, 1985), and the responses of farmers to the 1893 Labour Commission in G3–'94.

31. In this they shared a perception with other agrarian elites in a period of intensifying capitalist relations. The quote is from E. Hobsbawm and G. Rude, *Captain Swing* (New York: Norton, 1975), chap. 2. Also see E. Foner, *Nothing But Freedom: Emancipation and Its Legacy* (Baton Rouge: Louisiana State University, 1983) and I. Berlin, S. Hahn, S. Miller, L. Reidy, and L. Rowland, "The Terrain of Freedom: The Struggle over the Meaning of Free Labour in the U.S. South," *History Workshop Journal* 22 (1986): 108–30.

32. T. Brass, "Free and Unfree Labour in Puerto Rico during the Nineteenth Century," *Journal of Latin American Studies* 18 (1986): 181–94.

33. CA, 1/STB 1/44, case 160, 13 July 1874.

34. G3–'94, evidence of J. P. du Toit, p. 312.

35. G3–'94, evidence of Augus Viane, p. 327.

36. CA, 1/STB 2/44, case 3, 3 August 1874; G3–'94, evidence of J. P. du Toit, p. 312. Wheat farming became increasingly important during the latter half of the nineteenth century. In Stellenbosch district wheat production increased by 45 percent in the decade after 1865, partly in response to the poor outlook for wine.

37. CA, 1/STB 2/59, case 136, 6 May 1890, testimony of A. de Waal. See also 1/STB 2/44, case 101, 27 April 1874; 1/STB 2/48, case 54, 4 March 1880; 1/STB 2/59, case 135, 16 May 1895; 1/STB 2/64, case 272, 12 November 1895.

38. See the valuable thesis by J. Bor, "Liquor and Labour at the Cape in the Late Nineteenth Century" (B.A. diss., Department of History, University of Cape Town, 1978), p. 23.

39. G3–'94, p. 177.

40. M. Rayner, "Wine and Slaves: The Failure of an Export Economy and the Ending of Slavery in the Cape Colony, South Africa, 1806–1834" (Ph.D. diss., Duke University, 1986), chap. 1.

41. Schärf, "Impact of Liquor."

42. See van Onselen, "Randlords and Rutgut," 1:44–102.

43. In 1865 431,000 imperial gallons were produced in the Cape Colony, and in 1875 1 million; CCP, *Blue Book 1879,* part 4, section Q10.

44. See Bor, "Liquor and Labour", p. 5. I have relied heavily on this work for the discussion of the growing link that was made between liquor and labor in the 1890s.

45. Cape of Good Hope (A100–'82), "Petition of Merchants regarding the Housing of Natives at Kimberley."

46. G3–'94, evidence of Rev. J. Weeber, p. 252.

47. Schärf, "Impact of Liquor," p. 152.

48. *ZA,* 30 September 1880; *ZA,* 9 October 1888; *ZA,* 9 September 1890; CA, 1/STB 19/156, residents of Stellenbosch to Resident Magistrate, 12 February 1909. Cases of drunkenness in Paarl District increased from twelve in 1871 to fifty-seven in 1873; Native Affairs, 172, Civil Commissioner to Secretary for Native Affairs, 12 December 1873.

49. CA, Native Affairs, 172, Civil Commissioner to Secretary of Native Affairs, 12 December 1873.

50. G3–'94, evidence of Reverend J. C. Pauw, p. 280.

51. G3–'94, evidence of J. P. Louw, p. 299.

52. G3–'94, statement by Commissioner Neethling, p. 321; evidence of J. P. Louw, p. 309.

53. Cape of Good Hope (G1–'90), "Liquor Laws Commission," p. 26; G3–'94, p. 329.

54. See Scully, *Bouquet of Freedom,* chap. 2, for a discussion of agricultural innovation in the period under review.

55. *ZA,* 16 September 1882; *ZA,* 21 September 1882; *ZA,* 10 October 1882; *ZA,* 31 October 1886; *ZA,* 4 November 1886; G1–'90, p. 26.

56. G3–'94, evidence of Adolf Abraham, p. 385.

57. G3–'94, evidence of Pieter Cupido, p. 385.

58. G3–'94, p. xv.

59. G3–'94, evidence of Jakobus Gabrielse, p. 321.

60. Cape of Good Hope (G47–1909), "Report of a Commission appointed to enquire into the economic condition of the 'Wine Districts' of the Cape Colony," p. 7.

61. Schärf, "Impact of Liquor."

CHAPTER THREE

DRINK AND CULTURAL INNOVATION IN DURBAN: THE ORIGINS OF THE BEERHALL IN SOUTH AFRICA, 1902–1916

Paul la Hausse

INTRODUCTION

IN THE EARLY 1930s Gilbert Coka, an organizer of the Industrial and Commercial Workers' Union, commented that the "liquor question" was a "peculiarity of Natal."[1] Coka was not suggesting that liquor legislation aimed at Africans was confined to Natal. Rather, he was drawing out the particular form that liquor laws had taken in the province and the widespread popular opposition to the controls imposed on African production and consumption of alcohol.

In 1908 the Natal Legislative Assembly passed legislation that made provision for the establishment in the colony of municipal beer monopolies. The Durban Town Council, which had been the prime mover in the passage of the legislation, implemented the provisions of the Native Beer Act in 1909. After this date, the legal consumption of *utshwala* (a nutritious fermented, grain-based drink usually of low alcohol content) by Africans living in Durban was permitted only within the confines of municipal beerhalls.[2] By 1915 the monopoly system had spread to most of Natal's larger towns.[3] In Durban, the institution of a municipal beer monopoly provided the basis for the elaboration of the "Durban system": a particular form of urban Native Administration that became a model for the control and exploitation of Africans living and working in South African towns.[4]

The widespread interest expressed in the Durban system elsewhere in South Africa is best understood in terms of this absence of a coherent state urban policy. While local government in Johannesburg grappled with the problem of financing the accommodation of its African population, in Durban the social costs of black labor were heavily subsidized by the massive revenue generated by the beer monopoly. This revenue provided the platform for a singularly repressive system of urban control. After 1909 beerhall revenue was ploughed into the maintenance and establishment of migrant worker barracks, beerhalls, hostels, and beer breweries, as well as into the costs of police and Native Administration in the town. Until 1929, the year in which a mass boycott of Durban's municipal beerhalls was instituted, Durban was the only town in South Africa with a self-supporting Native Revenue Account.[5]

The following discussion explores the local struggles through which the beerhall (together with the principle of municipal beer monopolies) was established as a lasting feature of the South African urban landscape. Pioneering studies, most notably that of Charles van Onselen, have examined the changing significance of the production, consumption and supply of alcohol within the context of regional political economies and patterns of proletarianization in industrializing South Africa.[6] This chapter attempts to relate the institution of the beerhall system in urban Natal to a critical moment in a broader process of restructuring of social relations in the colony. It seeks to explore the social origins of Durban's beer brewers, the nature of the pre-1909 liquor trade, and the way in which an understanding of those areas illuminates processes of African class formation. Central to this study, too, is the way in which the cultural meaning of alcohol, and beer in particular, was constructed by Durban's dominant classes and contested by subaltern society in the town.

AFRICAN LABOR AND MORAL PANIC
IN POSTWAR DURBAN

In 1904 Durban was still essentially a nonindustrial urban center. The contours of the local economy were significantly shaped by Durban's position as the most important port town in southern Africa. Local merchant capital was held by shopkeepers and traders (who dealt in goods such as tea, coffee, and sugar), as well as numerous stevedoring and shipping companies. By the early 1900s economic activity had become predominantly based on inland commerce. Railway works and engineering shops were established to service coastal sugar estates and the northern Natal coal-mining industry, while the wool-processing industry along with shipping offices and brokers shifted to Durban.[7] The African working population, which numbered 18,929 in 1904, was channeled into four main sectors of the local labor market: togt (day) laborers (largely comprising dockworkers), washermen, ricksha pullers, and monthly-contract workers (many of whom were domestic servants and storehands). The largest group were the dockworkers. Of the 76,700 black males in wage employment in Natal, 5,100 were to be found on the docks in Durban (fig. 3.1).

All workers were obliged to register, either as togt laborers or monthly servants, within five days of entering the town. The togt labor system, although partly rooted in the need to depress wages and to accommodate the fluctuating labor requirements of local merchants (particularly stevedoring companies), was also the outcome of a complex process of cultural and economic negotiation between employers and migrant workers in the nineteenth century.[8] The togt worker was obliged to pay a monthly registration fee, wear a togt badge, and accept any work that paid at a rate above an official minimum. Contravention of those regulations could result in a twenty-shilling fine or imprisonment with hard labor. Ricksha pullers and washermen were obliged to comply with regulations framed along similar lines. Registration as a monthly worker brought an individual under the penal discipline of the Masters and Servants Act.

These continual attempts to regulate the labor market and police migrants' working lives extended into a struggle over forms of cultur-

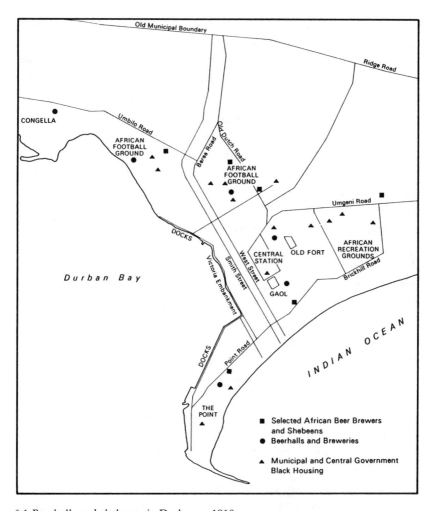

3.1 Beerhalls and shebeens in Durban, c. 1910

al expression and the control of urban space defined along racial and class lines. Bylaws were enacted to control "disorderliness," "provocative language," and "indecent conduct." The Vagrant Law of 1869 provided the basis for the imposition of a 9 P.M. curfew on Africans without a pass, while the Identification of Native Servants Act (1888) was amended in 1901 in an attempt to further control the movement of Africans into and within the town. By the turn of the century, then, an embryonic system of Native Administration in Durban was in place and largely financed by worker registration fees and fines, which were paid into the Togt Fund.

Yet colonial legislative fiat and expressed administrative ideals foundered on the reefs of everyday reality in the colonial town. By 1902 these regulations, and the police coercion that accompanied them, had not achieved their desired ends. Local authority tried, for example, to house all togt workers in municipal barracks paid for out of Togt Fund revenue. Zulu migrants, however, carved out space for themselves in an urban world constituted by backyard sheds, slum dwellings, and rented rooms in Indian and sometimes white working-class houses—"dens of vice" from which administrators were virtually powerless to remove workers. Even after an attempt to tighten up registration bylaws through the Togt Labour Amendment Act of 1902, it still proved impossible to force workers out of informal dwellings into unpopular barrack accommodation, which workers compared to jails. In desperation, an ultimately abortive scheme was drawn up for the erection of closed compounds along the lines of those in existence on the Kimberley diamond fields.[9] While the free five-day pass allowed for the legal entry of Africans into the town for the purpose of visiting friends and relatives, or in order to seek employment, it was used by thousands of African women and children to gain both temporary and permanent access to the town or, at least in the eyes of the Superintendent of the Borough Police, "to lead an idle life or to sponge upon their friends." Pass forgery, pass swapping, and outright evasion led to the system being described officially as "useless" in 1905, a period during which around 8,000 Africans were being arrested annually for violation of various municipal and government laws.[10] As Robert Jameson, prominent manufacturer and Town Councillor, lamented, "I have become more and more convinced that the existing system, or, more correctly, want of system, of rule, control, and provision for the native is, in many respects, deplorable. . . . he is almost out of control."[11]

For Jameson, together with some members of the Town Council and representatives of local capital, the solution to many of those problems was seen to lie in the creation of an urban location where African workers could settle with their families. That idea, although hardly new, was advocated with increasing intensity during the early years of the century and resulted in the passing of the Native Location Act (No. 2) of 1904.[12] Yet opposition to the idea of a location expressed by employers of African labor, especially stevedoring companies, was partially responsible for Durban's failure to establish a location. The debate over the location system hinged partially on the question of the nature of the control to be exercised over Africans and the form in which urban African labor was to be reproduced: in short, whether Africans would be allowed to settle under family conditions in an urban location or be compelled to live as migrants in barracks close to the workplace.[13]

The resolution of the debate threw into stark relief the discrepancy between the abstract necessities of and the concrete possibilities available to Durban's ruling classes. Many local employers were both unwilling and unable to bear the costs of reproducing an urban African proletariat. Their opposition to an urban location was underpinned by a fiercely segregationist discourse which, in its most articulate form, held that Africans "should for many years to come, be regarded as mere visitors to the town; they do not contribute to municipal rates, and therefore have no right to share the same privileges that regular citizens do. . . . Permanent residence in town should, as far the great majority are concerned, be distinctly discouraged."[14] Moreover, in a colony generally starved of finances and in a town where the intensity of African arrests by the borough police was importantly premised on the possibility of fines accruing to an undercapitalized Togt Fund, it is little wonder that the idea of a costly location system was stillborn.[15]

Yet the inability of local authority in Durban to establish an effective system of political domination and labor coercion in relation to Africans was not simply the outcome of an embattled local bourgeoisie and undercapitalized Native Affairs bureaucracy. It was also the outcome of ongoing conflict and negotiation between local authority and employers of labor on one hand and the town's subaltern classes on the other, over the terms of African residence in the town. This struggle, although seldom constituted in forward-looking political terms, was not unpolitical. It was deeply rooted in common sense notions and traditional views of social norms and behavior. Africans had come to determine, in a variety of ways and with a remarkable degree of success, the terms under which they lived and labored in Durban. The first decades of colonial rule in Natal witnessed important concessions to the commonsense notions and resilient precapitalist belief system of Zulu wage workers.[16] The late nineteenth century, however, saw increasingly concerted efforts to redraw the boundaries of this moral economy and remold elements within African "plebeian culture."[17]

As already suggested, this proved to be a difficult and contradictory project. Municipal officials did not have to look far to find confirmation of the subversive autonomy of African workers, particularly during conditions of labor shortage produced by the economic boom of 1902–1903. Togt workers at the Point embarked on a series of "spontaneous strikes" between 1901 and 1903.[18] The claim that Africans "have no right in the Boro' when they refuse to work for a fair wage" was a thinly disguised reference to the bargaining power of workers at particular moments.[19] Migrants, regardless of which sector of the labor market they entered, registered as togt workers in order to avoid coming under the more strict regime of Masters and Servants legislation. Others took out togt badges as a convenient cover for their entry into town or, in the words of the Chief Constable, "to plunder"—a thinly disguised reference to the emergence of *amalaita* gangs within the ranks of Durban's over 4,000 domestic workers.[20] In a town where notions of private space, codes of sexual conduct, racial etiquette, and ideas of a fair wage were continually challenged from below, it was perhaps little wonder that the "Native Convict" came to be regarded "more in the light of A Hero than Criminal" by many Africans themselves.[21]

The massive social dislocation that the South African War (1899–1902) carried in its wake added impetus to attempts to restructure and refine relations of domination and subordination in Durban. White refugees from the Transvaal settled in the port town and rapidly became involved in prostitution and the drink trade. Described variously as "refuse from other colonies," "vagabond whites," and "low class Jews and foreigners," these immigrants created enclaves of nonracial association in the backyards, brothels, shebeens, and eating houses of the town. The profound challenge posed by the "contaminating influence of the cosmopolitan crowd" to the elaboration of a racially defined order of class domination and territorial separation was expressed in a series of moral panics centering on the "lawlessness," "familiarity," and "demoralisation" attendant upon urban African wage labor.

Established in 1904, the Natal Native Reform League formally articulated these deep-seated colonial anxieties about the inability of authority to police racially defined master-servant relationships.[22] White fears of the violence of the casual laborer, the dangerous nocturnal autonomy of Durban's over 1,200 ricksha pullers, incipient worker rebellion fueled by drink, and the turbulent appropriation of streets and sidewalks by stick-wielding domestic workers, found articulation in a well-developed language of social pathology.[23] Yet as economic boom gave way to depression after 1904, the real and imagined threat presented by Africans to a stable urban social order was increasingly apprehended through popular drunkenness and the presence of "idle and suspicious" African women "without any visible means of subsistence" in the town.

RURAL WOMEN, BEER BREWERS, AND THE RISE OF URBAN SHEBEENS

The daily entry of hundreds of African women into Durban on five-day passes had been a feature of the town's landscape even before the turn of the century. The majority brought rural produce—such as fowls, eggs, sticks, *dagga* (marijuana—the smoking of this intoxicating weed was widespread among workers), herbs, and skins—to sell in the town. *Utshwala,* too, had always been sold in this way, but by 1902 became an increasingly prominent aspect of the trade. In 1906, for example, the magistrate of Umlazi Division reported that African women and girls were constantly conveying large quantities of beer, by rail, to Durban:

> It was a Friday practically the first day of what may be termed the weekend. Some sixty to seventy large gourds, calabashes and paraffin tins, full of Kafir beer, surrounded by . . . chattering Native girls, occupied a great deal of the station platform. Their number was considerably augmented as time slipped by. When the train departed for Durban, it carried

away 168 vessels containing beer. These native females—mostly girls—ranged from 12 to 30 years of age. In conversation with them it was elicited that this beer was destined for brothers, sweethearts, and, in a few cases fathers, at work in Durban, who defrayed all the expenses.[24]

At many other railway stations in rural areas around Durban this scene was duplicated every weekend. Between June 1905 and June 1906 an estimated 25,680 pots and vessels of beer—up to 9,000 gallons—seeped into Durban.[25]

While the scale of the post-1905 African drink trade in Durban was unprecedented, the question of alcohol and its sale and consumption by Africans, both in the towns and the countryside of Natal, had been the subject of agitated debate within white colonial society for decades. For the colonial state and undercapitalized white farmers the question of African alcohol production and consumption was inextricably linked to the difficulty in securing an adequate supply of African labor. During the 1870s one magistrate ascribed the apparent increase in the use of intoxicating liquor and drunkenness among Africans to "the growing wealth and change of habit of the Natives" together with their "freedom from adequate taxation"—an explanation that no doubt found support from within the ranks of an embattled civil service.[26] Extensive beer brewing among Africans in Natal suggested the extent to which African grain surpluses were being converted into alcohol.[27] If the production of *utshwala* came to symbolize the relative resilience of African agricultural production and the ability of Africans to resist wage labor on white farms and government works, popular drunkenness provided commercializing white farmers with the clearest index of this independence.

By the 1880s, however, important shifts in the political economy of Natal witnessed a more thoroughgoing attack on African economic independence and traditional social and political institutions. The growing ascendancy of white commercial farmers' interests within the colonial state was accompanied by concerted legislative initiatives aimed at proscribing African liquor production and consumption.[28] Paradoxically, just when the African homestead economy in Natal was beginning to manifest the stresses of early industrialization, the reported increase in the consumption of *utshwala*, together with stronger drink (such as colonial rum or cane spirits, and *isishimeyana*), was ascribed to "light taxation, increasing amabele crops, higher wages, peace and plenty and less difficulty in earning money."[29] Rural beer drinks, in particular, attracted the ire of farmers, not least because of their association with the disruption of labor supplies and the erosion of time-discipline associated with wage labor.[30]

No doubt many of the reports of increased beer drinking were exaggerated. Yet significant transformations had been, and continued to be, wrought in African colonial society. The commercialization of white agriculture after 1880 resulted in increasing pressure on land and the web of kinship ties constituted around the African homestead. The destruction of chiefs' power on white-owned farms, together with the circumscription of the rights of African squatters and the reduction of many Africans to the status of labor tenants, was paralleled by the general weakening of chiefly authority, the collapse of the *amabutho* system, and the undermining of the position of homestead heads. The erosion of chiefs' and homestead heads' control over women and youth perhaps illustrated most vividly those centripetal forces acting on African society.[31] The changing definition of *lobola,* the appropriation of key spheres of chiefly legal jurisdiction by the colonial state, and the creation of alternative sources of authority in the mission stations served to significantly undermine traditional views of social norms and obligations.

The conflict over liquor was but one aspect of a more generalized struggle to transform the way of life of Natal's rural underclasses. The panic over African liquor consumption and the prominence of women in its production revealed the contradictory nature of these processes of transformation. At the heart of the processes, however, was a deep ambiguity: a need to restructure African society to suit the needs of agrarian and industrial capitalism, but at the same time to preserve and indeed to selectively use elements of precapitalist African social and political formations to effect this long transition. Not surprisingly then, the question of "native custom" and its appropriate uses loomed large in this "reformation" of African society, while conflict and negotiation over traditional forms of life such as beer brewing emerged in peculiarly stark form.

There can be little doubt that the "innovation on the Kafir customs" perceived by whites in the late nineteenth-century beer drink had a basis in fact. Attempts to regulate rural beer drinks were not only a response to reports of increasing "faction fights" at rural beer drinks, but also to the emergence of novel cultural institutions based on the sale of drink.[32] At gatherings such as *itimiti* (an ironic reference to the mission-based tea meetings of Christian Africans), upon payment of a prescribed fee, beer would be supplied free from any further charge. Similarly, the *oshisanyama* (a term that would later be used to describe eating houses frequented by African workers) were usually peri-urban gatherings at which meat, drink and, it seems, prostitutes, were available to patrons. Based on their traditional production of beer within rural homesteads, African women retained a significant degree of control over the distillation of agricultural surplus into beer and, by the later decades of the nineteenth century, rapidly turned this situation to their advantage by engaging in the widespread sale of *utshwala*.[33] Indeed the colonial state was forced to recognize this fact. Although Act 36 of 1899 prohibited the sale or supply of any intoxicating or fermented liquor to Africans, Section 4 of the Act allowed "the sale and supply of Native Beer by Native women, according to their usual practice, and not as a permanent business." According to government officials, it was precisely "the abuse of this privilege, particularly in the neighbourhood of the towns" in "sinks of riot and debauchery" that was "contrary to Zulu law and custom," and increasingly threatening to labor supply, discipline, and social order.[34]

A battery of confusing liquor laws, based on a particular understanding of the meaning of beer brewing and consumption in a hazy Zulu past, proved ill equipped to deal with new conditions of life emerging in Durban. In the local context, contradictory liquor laws were subject to relatively flexible interpretation. African consumption of sorghum beer was permitted in the town on the grounds that it was a customary and nutritious low-alcohol drink the consumption of which would be virtually impossible to police.[35] No doubt, too, many whites feared that its prohibition could lead both to the withdrawal of Africans from local wage labor and the consumption of stronger drink.[36] Yet the rapidly changing local social and economic conditions outlined above, which were themselves closely bound up with massive rural hardship brought by rinderpest and war, provided a context for the more energetic proscription and redefinition of the meaning of the production, consumption, and sale of "the natives' traditional beverage."

Thus, in 1902 the first concerted attempt was made to control the local trade in *utshwala* through a system of licenses provided for in the Sale of Native Beer Regulation Bill. In countering critics who saw in the Bill the establishment of the principle of the sale of beer "contrary to Kafir custom," the Secretary for Native Affairs appealed for measures that took account of what the Natal Native Affairs Commission of 1906 was to call the "unobserved disintegration of the tribal system."[37] "Beer in the past," he claimed, "has been used as an article of food, and, as matter of hospitality, beer has been given away. . . . But the conditions have changed altogether when the people go in for this sale of beer, and have it not only as a food, but develop the drinking of it into an orgie [*sic*]."

While some defenders of the Bill saw it as an attempt to "confirm and re-establish customs," others viewed it, more accurately, as an attempt to reform popular cultural practices—an initiative worthy of support. As the local press put it: "We must temper our worship of the 'native custom' fetish with common sense, and if the native custom is harmful, not only to the natives themselves, but to Europeans and to the best interests of the Colony, then the custom must undergo some modification."[38] The Bill was thrown out by the Natal Legislative Council, a development that underlined the unevenness of attempts to redefine aspects of "traditional life" from above, as well as the resilience of popular institutions, such as the urban shebeen, produced by rapid social change.

Shebeens in Durban flourished as the beer trade grew. In 1906 there were over a hundred shebeens in the town, variously described as "frightful dens" which were "hotbeds of immorality" providing a "rendezvous of native women of loose character."[39] Yet what is striking about this booming beer trade was its socially differentiated nature. A significant part of the trade was in the hands of African women. Thousands of females took advantage of their right to temporary entry into the town to supply beer to extended-kin networks living in the backyards, rented rooms, and ricksha sheds of the town. There can be little doubt that widespread worker resistance to the barrack system stemmed from the fact that informal housing facilitated the creation of particular social networks in which women occupied a central position. Such relationships were inconceivable in the closely policed world of the barrack. In a situation where large numbers of workers migrated from neighboring magisterial divisions, many of those women entering Durban with beer were wives or relatives of men working in town.[40] Certainly, workers in town bore the cost of both many of the women's train fares and their brews. Clearly, too, many of these rural women sold beer in the town. Popular memory records the fact that many women sold their beer outside Durban station near a series of large boulders whose Zulu name was *ematsheni*—"the place of the stones"—a name subsequently given to Durban's beerhalls.[41] So extensive was this female beer portage into Durban that official suggestions were made to control the ingress of women and girls, together with their beer, through appropriate railway legislation.[42]

There are no reliable statistics to indicate the size of the African female population of Durban at this time, though the 1911 Government Census put the number at 1,165.[43] Most of these women obtained jobs as domestic servants, nursemaids, and washerwomen, while available evidence suggests that many of them were *amakholwa*—Christian, mission-educated Africans. Given the scant openings for African women in the local labor market, the visibility of a large floating African female population fed into deep white anxieties about the inexorable "demoralisation," "degradation," and "ruination" of African women in the town.[44] Moreover, in a colony where white notions of African respectability were integrally bound up with an imagined view of a hierarchically ordered rural world governed by strict moral codes and social sanctions created in a timeless Zulu past, the apparently autonomous female beer seller became virtually synonymous with the prostitute. These particular constructions of social reality proved ill equipped to grasp the more complex processes of class formation in colonial society. As A. J. Ncama, solicitor's clerk and prominent member of Natal's small *amakholwa* community, was at pains to point out, it was the "*respectable* natives" whose kin brought "beer in for them to consume."[45]

If the temporary supply and sale of beer by rural women in the town revealed the essential continuities between town and countryside, the forces impelling some women to establish beer selling more permanently must have been profound. The imposition of a poll tax on all unmarried adult African males in 1906 precipitated mass rural revolt among Africans in Natal, accelerated the pace of African proletarianization, and added a significant new tax burden to rural households.[46] The erosion of chiefly authority in the face of increasing pressure on social and economic organization around the homestead was reflected in the increasing independence of women. By the turn of the century growing numbers of females began using the missions and divorce actions in the Native High Court to escape the increasingly harsh exactions made on them by embattled homestead heads.[47] As migrancy became an increasing feature of the colonial economy, such strategies were also designed to cope with the loss of husbands to wage labor on the Witwatersrand mines and growing industrial towns. Undoubtedly many of these women moved more or less permanently into Durban and engaged in prostitution or became active in the urban-based shebeen trade.[48] It is possible that the entry into Zulu vocabulary of the word *ihuzu*—"low-town kaffir"—around this time was related to the growing independence of African women. Certainly the complaints of chiefs about their loss of control over women underlined these developments.[49]

By 1907 it was estimated that fully a quarter of black women in Durban were active in the beer trade.[50] The more permanent urban-based shebeen, as opposed to the seasonal entry of rural African female beer suppliers, was rooted in a new set of social relationships. According to official reports, many African men and their wives, most notably from the Inanda and Lower Tugela magistracies, moved to Durban with the "sole purpose" of earning a living from the preparation and sale of *utshwala*. As early as 1906 the Chief Magistrate noted with apprehension the emergence of a "class of people" in the town who depended "almost entirely upon beer traffic for a living."[51] Houses were frequently rented by Africans from Indian landlords and it was in such places that *utshwala* or more potent alcohol, such as *isishimeyana*, was stored and sold.

Contemporary reports suggest that African women were the principal brewers, doing the manual work for a "male retainer." Brewing could be conducted by women while men were engaged at their "ordinary callings" during the day, and if questioned about the presence of women in their rooms, the worker usually responded that the woman was his spouse.[52] As the Secretary for Native Affairs explained, men used "some female, not necessarily a relation . . . as a figure-head to conduct the business, in order to evade the provisions of the law as they exist, and under the shelter of selling under the name of that female they carry on a very large and a very deleterious business."[53]

Detectives who entered the threatening world of the shebeen sometimes reported whole families engaged in the beer trade. In Shepstone Street at the Point, one five-room house served as a flourishing shebeen run by thirteen women and twenty men. In the rooms stood fifty-seven casks, drums, and kerosene tins in which the various brews were stored. The beer, often laced with spirits of some kind, usually sold for 6d a tin.[54] Rooms in such houses could be rented from Indian landlords at 15 to 20 shillings a month. The shebeens also provided meeting places for numerous gangs of African youths who subsisted largely through petty theft and gambling. At least six of these *amalaita* gangs made the shebeens their arena for inter-gang fighting. In addition to these organized bands of youths, nine gangs of housebreakers were involved in the brewing trade. Their role is not altogether clear but it appears that they assisted in the distribution of drink around the town.[55] In the Congella district of Durban (see fig. 3.1), ricksha pullers, dockworkers, and domestic servants occupied various premises. Here "disturbances, dancing and noises" reportedly commenced on Saturday and continued "far into Sunday nights."

The character of shebeens in "Darkest Durban" (a term conjured up by the local press to describe what they saw as a dangerous, drink-sodden town) was captured in one police account:

> The premises are in all cases dwelling houses, some very old, and mostly with boarded floors, and in all respects quite unsuitable for the use to which they are now put. The beer is produced in kitchens, bathrooms, open dusty yards, behind sanitary conveniences, and in fact in any recess, shanty, or space which affords a convenient standing place for the open receptacles.[56]

Alongside large-scale shebeen operations were numerous smaller brewing enterprises—many, no doubt, merging with the institutionalized supply of beer to kin and workers by migrant women. Africans working in the central areas of town had access to a "honeycomb of beer sellers." Large quantities of beer were supplied by women living illegally in ricksha sheds, often centers of dancing, concertina playing, and drinking. It was hardly surprising, then, that during the Bambatha Rebellion in 1906, one official noted that the "greatest enemy" facing Durban's white population was not the rebels but "drink."[57]

The image of the African beer trader living independent of wage labor and free from the discipline of a master was particularly disturbing to Durban's white population. Although the Chief Constable claimed that "the Native is still too much a child to carry on a business," he also noted that most houses that served as shebeens were "the best in the locality, and the rents paid well above what would be paid by an ordinary tenant . . . another indication of the extent and lucrativeness of the business."[58]

One of the most popular (and notorious) shebeens was that run by Matshikiyana Gumede at his house on Warwick Avenue. The case of Gumede provides some insight into the extent to which the brewing trade was internally differentiated and how, in some cases, brewing could provide a crucial means of capital accumulation for an emergent class of African entrepreneurs. In 1906 Gumede was in his late sixties and was prominent in the local community of "progressive" mission-educated Africans (or *kholwa*). As a first generation *kholwa* he had spent much of his early life on the Amahlongwa Mission Station, south of Durban, where he farmed twenty acres of rented land and owned a few cattle. No doubt with a view to accumulate further capital for rural investment, he established himself as a beer brewer in Durban.[59] Gumede, like at least one African brewer in Pietermaritzburg during this period who was reported to have earned over a thousand pounds in the trade, shows every sign of having accumulated substantial wealth through his shebeen, which was open day and night and provided patrons with facilities for sleeping over if in danger of being arrested for drunkenness. In November 1907 Gumede was arrested for being in possession of 200 gallons of beer. J. S. Stuart, First Assistant Magistrate, found Gumede not guilty, whereupon he successfully sued the Durban Corporation, claiming £45 for damages and illegal arrest.[60]

Like Gumede, a number of African men saw significant economic potential in the booming drink trade. In 1904 over a hundred unlicensed African men, all of whom had invested large amounts of capital in the necessary brewing equipment (including hundreds of wooden barrels), were earning £1 a day selling hop beer in Durban. Significantly, over a quarter of these men appear to have been part of a fractured, largely Christian, middle-class group attempting to carve out space for itself in the interstices of a racially oppressive colonial economy.[61] This increasingly popular drink was brewed and sold in Native eating houses or various "kaffir" markets. In the first decade of the twentieth century, the streets of Durban were dense with privately licensed eating houses that provided food for African workers as well as another outlet for beer and recreation. Of approximately 139 eating houses in 1905, over 100 specifically catered for Africans and were mostly run by "non-Britishers," and the "lower class Jew and white man."[62] In all the eating houses, hop beer was freely available. In 1906 the Chief Constable reported an alarming increase in African drunkenness due to the "indiscriminate sale of hop beer." No license was required to manufacture and sell hop beer, provided it did not contain more than 2 percent proof spirit. However, sugar could be added to make it a highly intoxicating beverage.

In an attempt to keep Africans from strong drink, crippling fines of up to £50 were imposed for the sale of hop beer stronger than that allowed by law. When "European liquor," frequently supplied to Africans by Indians, was unavailable, Africans in search of strong drink reportedly drank methylated spirits sold by chemists at sixpence per bottle.[63] Even *utshwala,* frequently referred to by colonial officials as the wholesome "natural beverage" of Africans, began to assume the character of other illegal intoxicating drinks which were high in alcohol content. Alternative definitions of "traditional beer" came to reflect broader social conflicts between whites and African underclasses in Durban. The Chief Constable noted, "native beer which is sold in town is much stronger than that specially provided at the kraals"—or, as one member of the colonial government put it, "there is no definition of Kafir beer . . . they may put in a little whisky and call it Kafir beer."[64]

The historical experience of Europe suggests that the making of the working classes in the early stages of industrial capitalism, insofar as they were made from above, was facilitated by alcohol. The supply of alcohol to a newly proletarianized workforce could ensure increased dependence on wage labor, produce a more stable workforce, and provide workers with cheap recreation.[65] In Natal, where sugar farmers were not averse to supplying plantation workers with *isishimeyana,* perceptions of the possible uses of alcohol were not lost on employers.[66] In Durban, precisely because its production had been appropriated by the subordinate classes themselves, alcohol had become an integral part of a resilient alternative culture that was inimical to the production of a suitably coerced and disciplined African workforce. The assertion that Africans should "spend the time harmlessly between working hours" involved in some "legitimate amusement" was based on an understanding of the potentially subversive meanings and values contained within this alternative culture.[67] At the height of the postwar depression between 1906 and 1908, and in the wake of the outbreak of the Bambatha rebellion, thousands of Africans entered Durban and remained there, many of them unemployed, to implicitly challenge relations of domination and subordination in the town.[68] It was at this crucial moment in the restructuring of social relations in Natal that the local authority embarked on a concerted campaign to redefine the meaning of beer and transform the context in which it was popularly produced and consumed.

ORGANIZED TRADERS, NATIONALISM, AND THE INSTITUTION OF A BEER MONOPOLY

The growth of the hop beer trade and the consumption of stronger liquor was viewed with increasing official concern. In 1907 Natal's Prime Minister, F. R. Moor, asserted that Africans preferred "their own drink" and called for the complete prohibition of "this other taste"—hop beer.[69] One of the first moves to formalize control over the African drink trade and unlicensed eating houses had already been made in 1905 when the municipality formed a committee under Robert Jameson to investigate the establishment of municipal eating houses. This initiative came in the wake of the passing of the Stamps and Licences Act of 1905, which imposed a £5 license fee on all African eating houses.[70] Then the flourishing center of the African hop beer trade in the Queen Street Market became the main target of the committee. Jameson proposed a takeover of the market:

> We could realise £336 by a charge of 6d per day, and this reduction would alone ensure . . . the getting rid of a most objectionable and discreditable as well as insanitary condition of affairs on municipal property. . . . the whole place being under Municipal control would enable us to deal more effectively with the hop beer traffic. . . . the advantages are so obvious as not to require discussion.[71]

White officials were clearly aware that control over the profits from the beer trade would generate considerable income for administrative purposes. African petty traders were quick to respond to this threat to their livelihood. A petition to the Town Council, signed by 940 Africans, argued that the market served the African population as an orderly enterprise separate from residential areas and sold only the produce of Natal.[72]

The municipality did not close the market but in May 1905 opened Durban's first municipal eating house, and granted a contract to a white caterer for £600 a year. The municipal eating house generated significant municipal revenue but did little to halt the drink epidemic. On the contrary, the consumption of beer in the municipal outlet could not be rigorously controlled. At least seventy African traders in the municipal eating house supplied hop beer from fifty-two large barrels. At any time of day between one and three thousand Africans could be found on the eating house premises "sitting with absolute security, drinking as much hop beer" as wages allowed, and talking to "as many girls" as they wished to "court." Moreover, liquor was still freely available in numerous forms and outlets both within the town and on its outskirts.[73] It was clear that it would take more than a single municipal liquor outlet to transform local drinking patterns and associated forms of cultural expression.

In the face of a burgeoning hop beer traffic and a continuing stream of arrests for drunkenness after 1906, the council decided to enforce more stringently its own pragmatic ruling forbidding the consumption of any fermented drink containing more than 2 percent alcohol.[74] The first target of the police raids was, ironically, the municipal eating house itself. In March 1907 two hop beer traders, the first of many, were arrested and charged with supplying intoxicating liquor to African workers. Magoyela and Kuzwayo, the two traders, were found guilty of being in possession of hop beer with an alcohol content slightly over the 2 percent maximum. In sentencing the traders, however, Percy Binns, Durban's Chief Magistrate, expressed "amazement" that "the body charged with prosecuting under the Act receives proceeds of the breach of that law," and went on to remind the court that the Liquor (Amendment) Act (No. 36) of 1899 had deemed *utshwala* a prohibited intoxicating drink.[75] In short, Africans were to be prohibited access not only to hop beer and *utshwala,* but any fermented drink regardless of alcohol content.

Instead of introducing prohibition, as was the case in other urban centers of Natal, the municipality defied the Chief Magistrate and introduced a private bill into the Legislative Assembly.[76] The Durban Hop Beer Bill (No. 17) of 1907 sought to legalize the production and consumption of hop beer *only* in municipal eating houses. The idea of a state liquor monopoly, supported by the historical examples of Russia and Sweden, had already received publicity as a possible strategy of liquor supply in the South African context.[77] Although some members of the Town Council favored licensing private beer sellers, the monopoly scheme won out. The Council proposed that the profits be ploughed into the Togt Fund "for the benefit of Natives in Durban."[78] With few exceptions, the Bill was supported by large employers of labor, missionaries, temperance advocates, and churchmen. They anticipated that it could be used to force Durban's shebeens to close, prevent the importation of *utshwala,* and ensure a sober workforce. The colonial government, however, was not prepared to make an exception of Durban and the Bill was withdrawn in August 1907. In October, Durban was compelled to introduce prohibition, a strategy foisted on the municipality by what the *Natal Mercury* called "the stupid obstinacy of the Government and their supporters"—a reference, no doubt, to commercializing farmers who feared the attraction this form of liquor supply might offer to rural labor.[79]

If the situation was not already sufficiently confused, in January 1908 the Native High Court, in an appeal ruling, held that *utshwala* was *not* an intoxicating liquor in terms of the law.[80] The brief days of prohibition dissolved into an unprecedented boom in the beer trade among Durban's underclasses. By the beginning of 1908, there were 76 known shebeens, although the actual figure was probably closer to 200. In September that year, at least 112 shebeens, employing over 200 brewers, were reportedly producing an estimated 4,000 gallons of beer between Saturday afternoon and Sunday morning.[81] Paradoxically, *utshwala* came to be perceived in the same light as hop beer, which was now officially referred to as a "harmless concoction compared to the vile native beer sold by the gallon to natives in native public houses of the most disreputable type."[82]

Finally, in October the Native Beer Act (No. 23) of 1908 was pushed through the Natal parliament. The government had had time to reflect on its earlier opposition and, with the failure of prohibition and the obviously imprecise liquor laws, the new legislation was virtually a formality.[83] In terms of the act, boroughs and townships could opt either for a licensing system whereby private individuals could produce and sell beer under strict municipal supervision or a monopoly system whereby the municipality itself would brew beer and sell it in beerhalls. Profits accruing from municipal beerhalls were to be paid into a Native Administration Fund and used to build locations, barracks, schools, hospitals, or "any other object in the interests of Natives residing in the town."[84] In January 1909 Durban became the first local authority in Natal to opt for a municipal beer monopoly.

In the same month the Chief Constable held meetings with 320 African traders scattered around the town, including many women, and informed them in detail of the implications of the legislation. They were given a week to destroy their stocks of beer.[85] The authorities also hoped that rural women would be informed of the new law by black policemen and migrants returning home. In response, the hundred or so beer traders at the municipal market organized themselves into the Municipal Eating House Standholders' Organisation (one of the first formally constituted urban-based African associations in the history of Natal) and petitioned the Town Council not to enforce the beer monopoly. While "appreciating the efforts of the Corporation in encouraging them to support themselves by trading," the beer traders appealed to the Council to recognize their position, which they had "worked so hard and spent so much money to attain."

When it seemed clear that the monopoly would be enforced regardless of their protests, the traders requested that the municipality ease the blow by buying their stock-in-trade, in which they had invested so much capital. Their final fruitless appeal was to "acquire the benefit in full of the whole monopoly system." Matshikiyana Gumede, as a prominent independent beer trader, petitioned the authorities on his own. In language that reflected his social origins and the stirrings of African nationalism he made a call for African-run eating houses to be established in Durban. "It is said in the Scriptures," his petition began, "that you must pray and pray again and again and shall not be given stones."[86] In fact, Gumede, together with his fellow traders, were given stones in more ways than one. The new beerhalls became known as the *ematsheni*.[87]

The first three beerhalls were built on Victoria Street, Bell Street, and Ordnance Road. Physically, the beerhalls were stark and uninviting. Access to beer was tightly regulated:

> The building is divided by a high wire fence and one portion is set aside for the sale of native beer, where only male natives . . . may purchase a ticket for three pence and not more than sixpence worth of beer from the overseers at the office; he then passes through a turnstile and presents the ticket to the native barman who cancels the ticket and places it in a tin receptacle. The native on being supplied with beer in a suitable tin adjourns to the sitting accommodation. . . . he leaves the building through an exit turnstile. This method prevents natives from getting more than one drink, and is most effective in preventing indiscriminate drinking and idling.[88]

Municipal beerhalls and eating houses (on the same premises) were located in those areas of town with the highest concentrations of African living quarters. Municipal *utshwala* was available throughout the day (from 8 A.M. to 8 P.M.) and sold to any male over the age of fif-

teen. The beerhalls together with the eating houses were well patronized and began to generate large revenue (table 3.1).

The introduction of the municipal beer monopoly in Durban was
the specific outcome of a period of conflict over what constituted the
most appropriate means of controlling and reproducing African labor
in the town. As Hemson notes, the monopoly system was not the result of a carefully planned strategy on the part of local authority.[89] The
principle of the beer monopoly was first mooted in 1902, and many of
the possible benefits of a monopoly had been registered by officials
for nearly a decade. The ideological justification for this innovative
measure to rework an alternative culture and marginalize the resilient
economic institutions in which it was based was rooted in the manip-
ulation of notions of Zulu tradition. As one Native Affairs official put
it in 1908, the beer monopoly would "teach [the African] moderation
in regard to [his] own beverage to which he has been accustomed
from time immemorial."[90]

The beerhall system also embodied a sophisticated form of urban
control. Workers were not compelled to drink municipal beer and yet
in doing so they subsidized their own control by the municipality. The

Table 3.1: Durban beerhall and eating house revenue, 1909–1922

| Year | Revenue (£) | |
	Beer	Eating Houses
1909	7,937	932
1910	15,849	857
1911	19,690	1,293
1912	23,521	1,596
1913	25,033	1,953
1914	18,656	2,034
1915	21,232	2,054
1916	24,163	2,387
1917	28,079	2,640
1918–21	not available	
1922	42,994	3,302

Source: *Durban Mayor's Minutes,* 1909–1923.

monopoly also undermined the livelihood of a relatively small but growing class of African entrepreneurs who were reaping not insubstantial profits from beer sales. Moreover, the legislation provided grounds for the expulsion of African women from Durban. As Councillor Jameson noted before the passing of Act 23: "When such a scheme had been started in Durban there would not be the necessity for the women coming into the town."[91] In short, the Native Beer Act promised to deprive rural women of the urban social and cultural space they had previously enjoyed and, in the process, support the cheap reproduction of an African male migrant workforce. A piece of liquor legislation, then, was to provide the key support for "a more intensive and comprehensive programme of paternalistic administration than ever before."[92]

At a time when Africans still retained significant rural ties and partial access to the homestead economy, the essentially exploitative and coercive nature of the monopoly was obvious to the colonial bureaucracy and employers. As Dr. W. H. Addison, district surgeon of Umlazi, noted of the beerhall: "It keeps them at work longer. They have not quite so much money to take home, and consequently they work longer in the towns. We have more labor in the towns than we had."[93] Before 1909, local government had been unwilling or unable to adequately finance the costs of reproducing urban African labor. After 1909, substantial beer profits began to bear an important part of those costs. Although togt registration fees continued to draw revenue from the African workforce, they were relegated to a secondary role by the municipal beer monopoly. While the togt system had never affected more than a third of Africans in Durban, the monopoly raised revenue from all sections of the population. What was known as the "Durban system of supply and control of Kaffir beer to Natives" possessed a wider significance than the mere control of alcohol to Africans. The revenue from Durban's beerhalls provided the support for a greatly expanded Native Affairs bureaucracy and was used to pay for "police services connected with the Administration of Act 23."[94]

Revenue was also ploughed into barrack and hostel accommodation for workers. Additional beerhalls were constructed in 1912 and 1914. In 1913 a sophisticated two-storey municipal brewery was built with beer revenue accumulated over the previous four years. By 1916 the brewery was producing 1,023 gallons of *utshwala* a day which meant that each year some 320,000 gallons of beer were distributed to five municipal beerhalls. By 1916 over £122,000 had been spent on beerhalls, breweries, and hostels and compounds for Africans.[95]

Scarred by the struggle to push through monopoly legislation, and extremely sensitive to criticism about the morality of municipalizing the supply of beer to Africans, local authority in Durban was at pains to preach the benefits of Durban's beerhalls. Officially the monopoly was an unqualified success—a fact readily gauged from the remarkable drop in arrests for African drunkenness.[96] Clearly, of course, the Borough Police would have had every reason for tempering the diligence with which they arrested Africans for drunkenness once the municipal beer monopoly was in place and there certainly is evidence to suggest that that was the case.[97] S. E. Kambule, a prominent *kholwa* landowner based at Driefontein, claimed that the Durban authorities "keep drunkenness quiet, and do not bring these cases before court."[98]

In 1910 the colonial government suggested confidentially that in view of both the "considerable profit reaped" from beer sales and the "comparatively speaking very small" wages of Africans, the price of beer should be reduced. Not surprisingly, those views went unheeded. Criticisms of the beer monopoly were to surface in more public form in 1914 when the African section of the Women's Christian Temperance Union under Mrs. Ncamu organized a petition signed by 4,000 black women calling for the abolition of the beer monopoly because of the growing indebtedness of male kin working in Durban, their failure to remit wages to rural households, and the consequent "grievous condition" of rural families."[99] In a statement that turned out to be prophetic, T. L. Schreiner, liberal Cape politician and leading temperance advocate, said that the motive for the monopoly was "laudable" but that "the financial interests and profits accruing will in the long-term outweigh every other consideration, especially if these profits claim to be devoted to the public benefit."[100]

This criticism echoed that of members of Natal's black *kholwa* elite. Indeed, the response of men such as Kambule was seldom unambiguously in favor of prohibition.[101] While frequently expressing their personal support for the principles of teetotalism, they also had political objections to Natal's beerhalls, arguing that it was unjustifiable for whites to appropriate and profit from the "raw native's traditional right to produce and consume his national drink." Perhaps most outspoken in this regard was Stephen Mini, *kholwa* chief at the Edendale Mission Station near Pietermaritzburg:

> The right of beer brewing is only in the hands of Europeans in this Province that is beer which does not belong to their nationality, and beer which the Creator gave to the native. . . . the Europeans make this which they do not know how to make, and they serve it to the natives not knowing how much should be consumed by them, as it does not belong to them. . . . if the making of native beer was left in the hands of the native under certain regulations it would be far better.[102]

Rev. Abner Mthimkulu, Wesleyan minister and future African National Congress spokesman in Natal, was more direct. He explained that Africans "think that the whiteman has come to take the profit from the beer because the black man is making it." This position was elaborated on by middle-class Africans with keener entrepreneurial instincts. By 1916 Skweleti Nyongwana, editor of *Ilanga lase Natal* was calling for Durban's sorghum beer brewery to be "floated into a company in which the natives could take up shares."[103] In the same year the leadership of the Natal Native Congress requested that "respectable and well accredited Native Citizens" be given permission to brew beer, and appealed for statements of the manner in which beer revenue was being expended in Natal's towns.[104]

But what of those thousands of migrant workers who provided the beerhalls with their daily trade and the Native Administration Fund with its substantial revenue? In reshaping the boundaries of a local system of political rule and economic appropriation, the Durban Town Council did not precipitate any overt worker resistance. Workers thronged to the beerhalls, not only to drink but also to purchase food and other necessities from the stalls of African petty traders in the animated proletarian society of the adjoining eating houses. Although the beerhall system was an indirect form of taxation and exploitative in nature, it did represent something of a concession to ordinary migrant workers. Where prohibition was the rule in other industrial centers such as the Witwatersrand at this time, workers in Durban retained access to beer even if it was produced and supplied under importantly novel circumstances. The support of local beerhalls by workers, however, was never unconditional and appears to have rested significantly on a number of assumptions. The beer itself had to be of a popularly acceptable quality. When foul beer was produced by the municipal brewery in 1913, for example, there was an extensive informal boycott of the beerhalls, resulting in a significant loss of revenue.[105] Moreover, a range of beliefs, not least about the dangers of the production of beer with machinery and by whites, formed an integral part of migrants' consciousness. It was precisely these ideas, when melded with a more articulate nationalist ideology of political leadership and associated with starvation wages and increasing rural impoverishment, that produced a violent and lengthy boycott of Durban's and Natal's beerhalls in the late 1920s.[106] Evidence also suggests that illicit brewing of beer continued alongside the production by workers of *mahewu*—a nutritious drink of fermented porridge that was permitted in compounds.

But perhaps the early acceptance of the system by workers was not surprising for other reasons. While illicit brewing continued within the town itself on a smaller scale than previously, shebeens flourished on the outskirts of Durban. There brewers such as Matshikiyana Gumede reestablished their trade in Springfield, Sydenham, Cato Manor, and South Coast Junction. Durban's Chief Magistrate reported that whites and Indians let rooms to "unemployed" Africans "from all parts of the colony" and that rooms let by Indian racketeers attracted the "riff-raff of Durban . . . to sell this beer."[107] Taking advantage of a loophole in the "five-mile ruling" of the Native Beer Act, and the uneven policing of the peri-urban areas, hundreds of workers moved across the borough boundary to drink at these shebeens every weekend.[108] It was in these rapidly growing areas of African settlement that the proposed erection of a beerhall in 1928 resulted in the first in a series of confrontations between Africans and the municipality that led to the fierce popular riots and beer boycott of the following year.

CONCLUSION

The successes of the Durban system in securing a more pliant black workforce and in generating a major source of municipal revenue attracted widespread attention after Union in 1910. In 1913 the system was extended to Bulawayo in Southern Rhodesia with the establishment of a municipal beer monopoly there. Administrators in British colonies as far afield as Kenya, Uganda, and the Sudan expressed considerable interest in the system.[109] In 1921 the Deputy Principal Medical Officer of the Uganda Protectorate visited Durban and wrote a lengthy report recommending the Durban system for Uganda.[110] In South Africa itself the Johannesburg Town Council issued an extensive report on the workings of the monopoly system in relation to the delivery of African housing in 1916.[111] By 1918 numerous other local authorities in South Africa were making enquiries into the workings of the Durban system. Then, in 1923, many of the features of the system were embodied in the Natives (Urban Areas) Act—the first decisive attempt by the South African state to centralize African urban management and control.

NOTES

1. G. Coka, "The Story of Gilbert Coka of the Zulu Tribe of Natal, South Africa," in *Ten Africans,* ed. M. Perham (London: Faber and Faber, 1980), p. 312.

2. A. T. Bryant, *A Description of Native Foodstuffs and Their Preparation* (Pietermaritzburg, 1907).

3. Municipal beer monopolies were instituted in the following towns: Newcastle (1908), Pietermaritzburg (1909), Greytown (1910), Dundee (1912), Ladysmith (1912), Vryheid (1913), Estcourt (1915); see An. 139–1943, "Report of the Native Affairs Commission Appointed to Enquire into the Workings of the Provisions of the Natives (Urban Areas) Act Relating to the Use and Supply of Kaffir Beer." Other Natal towns introduced the system after 1915.

4. See M. Swanson " 'The Durban System': Roots of Urban Apartheid in Colonial Natal," *African Studies* 35 (1976): 159–76.

5. See P. la Hausse, "Drinking in a Cage: The Durban System and the 1929 Riots," *Africa Perspective* 20 (1982): 63–75.

6. C. van Onselen, "Randlords and Rotgut, 1886–1903," in *Studies in the Social and Economic History of the Witwatersrand 1886–1914* (London: Longman, 1982), 1:44–102.

7. See M. Katzen, *Industry in Greater Durban, Part I* (Pietermaritzburg: Town and Regional Planning Commission, Natal, 1961).

8. See D. Hemson, "Class Consciousness and Migrant Workers: Dockworkers of Durban" (Ph.D. diss., University of Warwick, 1979), chap. 2; P. la Hausse, "The Struggle for the City: Alcohol, the Ematsheni and Popular Culture in Durban, 1902–1936" (M.A. diss., University of Cape Town, 1984), chap. 1; and K. E. Atkins, "The Cultural Origins of an African Work Ethic and Practices: Natal, South Africa, 1843–1875" (Ph.D. diss., University of Wisconsin-Madison, 1986).

9. See Natal Archives (NA), Superintendent of Police Report Books (PRB), no. 6, report 4 February 1903; no. 7, report 2 November 1905; and NA, Durban Corporation Letterbooks (DCL), no. 547, Palethorpe and Plum Ricksha Co. to R. Jameson, May 1904. Out of 2,080 registered togt workers, only 290 were living in licensed private accommodation.

10. NA, DCL, no. 555, Chief Constable to Chairman, Police Committee, 2 December 1905. For pass forgery see NA, PRB, no. 6, report 6 October 1902; and NA, DCL, no. 582, Chief Constable to Chairman, Police Committee, May 1909. On the arrests, see *South African Native Affairs Commission* (SANAC), Minutes of Evidence, vol. 3, p. 645, evidence of R. C. Alexander.

11. NA, DCL, no. 548, Proceedings of the First Natal Municipal Conference, Pietermaritzburg, 22 September 1904.

12. The Act enabled local authorities in Natal to establish locations and compel Africans to live in them. R. C. Alexander, Durban's farsighted Chief Constable, had been advocating such a scheme since the 1880s.

13. Hemson, "Dockworkers of Durban," pp. 100–109; and la Hausse, "Struggle for the City," pp. 38–46.

14. NA, *Natal Native Blue Book*, 1904, p. 77. These were the views of James Stuart, Durban's First Assistant Magistrate and pioneering recorder of Zulu custom and folklore.

15. For a discussion of the discrepancy between African contributions to colonial revenue through taxation and the amount spent on Native Affairs, see NA, Government House (GH), vol. 1550, Report of the Secretary for Na-

tive Affairs, 24 December 1907; and for the importance of fines imposed on Africans for local revenues, see GH, vol. 1546, Governor to Prime Minister, 3 November 1903. The cost of a location, given the existing fiscal basis of local government in Durban, would have been prohibitive. Apart from the purchase of land and erection of houses, in terms of the Location Act the owners of all "kafir premises" would have been eligible for compensation in the event of their closure upon the erection of a location.

16. K. Atkins, "African Work Ethic."

17. For discussions of culture and moral economy see R. Williams, *Problems in Materialism and Culture* (London: Verso, 1980); S. Hall, "Notes on Deconstructing 'the Popular,'" in *People's History and Socialist Theory*, ed. R. Samuel (London: Routledge and Kegan Paul, 1981); and E. P. Thompson, "The Moral Economy of the English Crowd in the Eighteenth Century," *Past and Present* 50 (1971): 76–136.

18. NA, PRB, no. 6, report 7 June 1901 and report 4 March 1903.

19. NA, PRB, no. 6, report 4 March 1903.

20. For a more detailed discussion of the *amalaita* in Durban, see P. la Hausse, "The Cows of Nongoloza: Youth, Crime and Amalaita Gangs in Durban, 1900–1930," *Journal of Southern African Studies* 16 (1990): 79–111.

21. NA, PRB, no. 7, report 1 August 1904.

22. See, for example, NA, DCL, no. 547, C. R. King, Hon. Sec., NNRL, to Durban Town Council, 6 February 1905.

23. For togt worker violence see *Natal Advertiser,* 19 September 1902; for white fears of the threat posed by ricksha pulling, see NA, PRB, no. 6, report 6 January 1902 and report 26 May 1902; for violent deaths in ricksha sheds see NA, PRB, no. 7, report 4 April 1906; and NA, GH, vol. 1550, report of RCA Samuelson, 24 December 1907; for fears of drink riots, see SANAC, Minutes of Evidence, vol. 3, p. 752. For domestic workers and the *amalaita* in particular see la Hausse, "Cows of Nongoloza."

24. NA, SNA, vol. 1/1/351, 294/1906, Magistrate, Umlazi to Under SNA, 1 October 1906.

25. NA, SNA, vol. 1/1/418, 3762/1908, General Manager, Railways, to Secretary, Railways and Harbours, 4 January 1909; and J. Stuart to Under SNA, 22 December 1908.

26. See Natal Legislative Council, *Correspondence re Increased Drunkenness among the Native Population,* Separate Publication no. 17 (1877), Acting Resident Magistrate, Umvoti to SNA, 11 September 1876, p. 13.

27. African *amabele* (sorghum) production between 1867 and 1897 was far greater than settler production in Natal; P. Harries, "Labour Migration

from Mozambique to South Africa; with special reference to the Delagoa Bay hinterland, c. 1862–1897" (Ph.D. diss., University of London, 1983), pp. 82–84. This period produced the first attempts to tax African-grown *amabele* and to limit the size of land on which it was grown. These initiatives were abortive because of fears that open rebellion would follow any such moves.

28. Law No. 18 of 1863, which prohibited the sale of intoxicating liquors to Africans, proved unworkable not least due to the numerous rural canteen keepers who willingly sold spirits to Africans. Although Law No. 10 of 1890 prohibited the sale and disposal of intoxicating liquor to Africans, Law No. 18 of 1888 permitted the sale of *utshwala* by license holders. The passing of Act 38 of 1896, and then Act 36 of 1899, were attempts to tighten control over African access to liquor with high alcohol content, yet they failed to explicitly define *utshwala* as an intoxicating liquor.

29. *Isishimeyana* was made from fermented treacle. References to African production and consumption of this brew, not surprisingly, frequently emanated from coastal sugarcane-growing regions of the Colony, where treacle was easily available. It is difficult to pinpoint the first appearance of this brew, although it is possible that it was first produced by Indians working on cane farms. Other recorded names for this brew are *isiqedaviki, isiqatha, izingodo,* and *umfangqokisaka;* see D. N. Bang, "The History and Policy of Kaffir Beer in South Africa" (Paper presented to the Fifth Annual Conference of the Institute of Administrators of Non-European Affairs, 1956). Act No. 27 of 1905 prohibited the production and consumption of *isishimeyana* by Africans. See also "Report of the Select Committee on the Supply of Liquor to Natives," no. 37 (1891), p. 616.

30. See, for example, NA, Colonial Secretary's Office (CSO), vol. 1394, 2074/1895, Extract from the Memoranda of Resolutions, Natal Farmers Conference, 22 March 1894; and *Debates of the Natal Legislative Assembly,* 6 April 1897, p. 135.

31. See J. Lambert, "Africans in Natal, 1880–1899: Continuity, Change and Crisis in a Rural Society" (Ph.D. diss., University of South Africa, 1986).

32. Government Notice No. 32, 1903, Rules for controlling and regulating the gathering of Natives belonging to different kraals or homes for the purpose of feasting or beer drinking.

33. As van Onselen has suggested, the distillation of agricultural surplus into alcohol provides one of the clearest visible links between a declining agriculturally based feudal regime, and a modern industrial capitalist order; see van Onselen, "Randlords and Rotgut," p. 45; and R. E. F. Smith, "Drink

in Old Russia," in *Peasants in History,* ed. E. J. Hobsbawm (London, 1980).

34. NA, GH, vol. 1546, SNA to Governor, 18 May 1902; and Governor to SNA, 2 June 1902.

35. This pragmatic ruling was made on the basis of the Beer Act of 1901, which imposed an excise tax on all liquor containing more than 2 percent alcohol.

36. The use of beer as a means of procuring and retaining an African labor supply was not lost on colonial officials; see for example, the comments of F. R. Moor (SNA, 1899–1903, and Prime Minister of Natal, 1906–1910) on this subject in *Debates of the Natal Legislative Council,* vol. 14 (1890), p. 18.

37. For this debate see *Debates of the Natal Legislative Assembly* vol. 31 (1902), pp. 465ff.

38. *Natal Mercury,* 26 April 1902.

39. *Natal Mercury,* 19 May 1908.

40. In 1904, 67 percent of Durban's African workers came from Natal proper and of these a large percentage hailed from the reserves in Mapumulo, Kranskop, Lower Tugela, Umlazi, and Ndwedwe; see *Natal Census Report* (Pietermaritzburg, 1904).

41. Interview with G. Zungu, Umlazi, Durban, 5 June 1987; interview with S. B. Borquin, Westville, Durban, 23 January 1982.

42. NA, SNA, vol. 1/1/351, 294/1906, Magistrate, Umlazi to Under SNA, 1 October 1906.

43. U.G. 32–'11, *Census, 1911. Preliminary Returns,* p. 8.

44. See, for example, NA, SNA, vol. 1/1/367, 1116/1907, Report of Magistrates, Alexandra and Umlazi divisions, January 1907.

45. Central Archives Depot, (CAD), K 373, evidence before the Commission Appointed to Enquire into Assaults on Women, 1912, Minutes of Evidence, p. 3. Emphasis added.

46. See S. Marks, *Reluctant Rebellion* (Oxford: Oxford University Press, 1970).

47. As early as the 1880s it was being reported that "when young women quarrel on some trivial matter with their husbands and are not granted a divorce . . . they go off to Durban or Pietermaritzburg for the expressed purpose of catching syphilis"; NA, SNA, vol. 1/4/3, C5A/1884, Annual Report of the Administrator of Native Law, Lower Tugela for the year 1883.

48. In discussing the increasing independence of rural women, Rev. Hans Nilson disagreed that the town was demoralizing in itself. Although he agreed that nine-tenths of African women living in Durban were "immoral,"

he claimed that they had come to town after having been "degraded" in the countryside; CAD, K373, Commission appointed to inquire into Assaults on Women, Minutes of Evidence, p. 22.

49. CAD, K373, Assaults Commission, Minutes of Evidence.

50. NA, SNA, vol. 1/1/361, 197/1907, R. H. Arnold to Chief Magistrate, 14 January 1907.

51. NA, SNA, vol. 1/1/335, 407/1906, Chief Magistrate to SNA, 6 February 1906.

52. NA, DCL, no. 574, Chief Constable to Town Clerk, 15 April 1908.

53. *Debates of the Natal Legislative Assembly,* vol. 31 (1902), p. 467.

54. NA, SNA, vol. 1/1/399, 1530/1908, CID report re Preparation and Sale of Native Beer in Durban, 11 May 1908; also NA, PRB, no. 7, 1 October 1908.

55. NA, SNA, vol. 1/1/361, 197/1907, R. H. Arnold to Chief Magistrate, 14 January 1907.

56. NA, DCL, no. 576, Inspector of Nuisances to Town Clerk, 9 April 1908; see also NA, DCL, no. 572, Chief Constable to Town Clerk, 27 January 1908 for further descriptions of shebeens.

57. NA, PRB, report 4 July 1906.

58. NA, SNA, vol. 1/1/418, 3672/1908, report of the Chief Constable, 11 January 1908.

59. NA, SNA, vol. 250, 1445/1897, part I, Petition for Exemption from Native Law. For Gumede's attempts to purchase land, see NA, Chief Native Commissioner (CNC), vol. 240, 877/16. As an African exempted from Native Law, Gumede was also legally entitled to consume alcohol.

60. *Natal Advertiser,* 11 May 1908.

61. SANAC, Minutes of Evidence, vol. 3, p. 644, evidence of R. C. Alexander; and NA, DCL, no. 580, J. Hillier to Town Clerk, 5 January 1909.

62. In 1905 White Commercial Traders' Licenses could be broken down as follows: Wholesale Trade (262); Eating Houses (139); Bar (872); Hotels (8); Bottle (21); Hotels and Bars (18); Bakers (12); Hawkers (43); Butchers (19); Lodging and Eating Houses (25); Billiards (51); Mineral Oil (9); Clubs (50); Pawnbrokers (2); Wholesale Wine/Spirits (39); NA, DCL, no. 555, Inspector of Licenses to Town Clerk, 4 December 1905.

63. NA, PRB, no. 7, report 3 July 1905; and SNA, vol. 1/1/361, 197/1907, R. H. Arnold to Chief Magistrate. In January 1906 legislation was passed prohibiting the consumption of "meths" (methylated spirits); see NA, SNA, vol. 340, 1342/1906, Chief Constable to Chief Magistrate, 23 April 1906. Indians in Durban had free access to any alcohol provided it was consumed on

licensed premises. According to most official sources of that time, Indians were seldom arrested for drunkenness.

64. NA, DCL, no. 574, Chief Constable to Town Clerk, 15 April 1908; DCL, no. 579, extract from report by J. Stuart, December 1908; and *Debates of the Natal Legislative Assembly*, 2 August 1905.

65. Medick provides a valuable word of caution in relation to the linkage between the deprivations of proletarian existence, as determined by industrial capitalism, and the onset of the mass consumption of alcohol; H. Medick, "Plebeian Culture in the Transition to Capitalism," in *Culture, Politics and Ideology*, ed. R. Samuel and G. Stedman Jones (London: Routledge and Kegan Paul, 1982).

66. As magistrate of Mapumulo, H. C. Lugg had some interesting comments in this regard; CAD, K373, Assaults Commission, Minutes of Evidence, p. 2.

67. NA, PRB, no. 7, 30 November 1906.

68. Between October and December 1906 over 20,000 five-day passes were issued to African men and women. By 1907 it was reported that about 1,500 monthly contract workers, 1,500 togt workers and perhaps half of Durban's ricksha pullers were unemployed; NA, SNA, vol. 1/1/361, 197/1907, Det. R. H. Arnold to Chief Magistrate, 14 January 1907.

69. *Debates of the Natal Legislative Assembly*, 31 July 1906.

70. The relative success of this measure can be gauged from the fact that over half of the approximately one hundred eating houses catering for Africans in 1905 had closed down by January 1907.

71. NA, DCL, no. 547, report re Kafir Market, 13 February 1905. Previously, forty African tenants had paid an Indian property owner 1/- per month giving him an annual rent of £672.

72. NA, DCL, no. 547, petition by 940 Africans against the abolition of the market, 6 March 1905.

73. NA, SNA, vol. 1/1/361, 197/1907, R. H. Arnold to Chief Magistrate, 14 January 1907.

74. See correspondence in NA, SNA, vol. 1/1/365, 906/1907.

75. *Natal Mercury*, 25 March 1907; 26 March 1907.

76. See NA, SNA, vol. 1/1/375, 2447/1907, Chief Magistrate to Under SNA, 28 September 1907.

77. See, for example, T. L. Schreiner, *Government Liquor Monopoly in Russia and the Transvaal*, n.d. (1902). In Durban, Sweden's "Gothenburg system" was consciously invoked as an appropriate model. Of course there was a similar example in the Transvaal, where the Kruger government had

granted a liquor monopoly to a private distillery; van Onselen, "Randlords and Rotgut," pp. 48–67.

78. NA, SNA, vol. 1/1/375, 2447/1907, Draft Bill (no. 17) of 1907. The Bill introduced the principle of a beer monopoly, a principle which, in the words of James Stuart, was "quite foreign to the old native regime." Significantly, the Natal Native Affairs Commission of 1906 supported the principle of monopoly.

79. *Natal Mercury,* 15 October 1907.

80. *Reports of the Decisions of the Full Court of the Native High Court,* Ambulozi v. Durban Corporation, January 1908.

81. For the survey that revealed seventy-six shebeens in Durban see NA, DCL, no. 574, Chief Constable to Town Clerk, 15 April 1908.

82. *Natal Mercury,* 19 May 1908.

83. For the government's discussion of the Bill, see *Debates of the Natal Legislative Council,* 8 and 9 September 1908.

84. *Natal Government Gazette,* No. 3710, 10 October 1908, Act to amend the law relating to Native Beer.

85. NA, SNA, vol. 1/1/416, 3514/1908, Chief Constable to Chief Magistrate, 18 January 1909.

86. NA, DCL, no. 580, petition of 116 traders to Mayor, 13 January 1909; DCL, no. 579, A. Mbambo and J. M. Shezi to Mayor, 7 December 1908; and SNA, vol. 418, 3818/08, Petition of M. Gumede, January 1909.

87. Interview with G. Zungu, Umlazi, Durban, 5 June 1987; interview with S. B. Borquin, Westville, Durban, 23 January 1982.

88. NA, Durban Town Clerk's Files (DCTF), vol. 48, file 91, W. Wanless to Town Clerk, 3 September 1915.

89. See Hemson, "Dockworkers of Durban," p. 133. For Hemson's useful discussion of the beer monopoly, see pp. 124–42.

90. The continuing conflicts over the historical origins and social significance of *utshwala,* insofar as they underpinned particular positions on liquor supply to Africans, are reflected in J. M. Orpen, *Natives, Drink, Labour: Our Duty* (East London: Crosby and Sons, 1913). Orpen, a fierce opponent of the beer monopoly, claimed that far from being enjoyed by Africans since "time immemorial," Kaffir beer was "an invention which was introduced at some not very distant period from the north" early in the nineteenth century. According to Orpen, the argument that *utshwala* was a "national food" was a "false contention."

91. NA, SNA, vol. 1/1/401, 1692/08, meeting between Mr. Jas. Stuart and the mayor of Durban, R. Jameson, and Chief Constable Donovan, 27 May 1908.

92. Swanson, "Durban System," p. 174.

93. CAD, Assaults Commission, Minutes of Evidence, p. 33.

94. *Durban Mayor's Minutes,* 1911, p. 23.

95. Union of South Africa (S.C. 7–'26), "Report of the Select Committee on the Liquor Bill," appendix K.

96. The number of Africans charged with drunkenness dropped from an average annual figure of 1,042 between 1902 and 1908 to 350 between 1909 and 1914; *Durban Mayor's Minutes,* 1902–1915. For reports on the decrease in African drunkenness after 1909 see DCTF, vol. 48, file 91, Chief Constable to Town Clerk, 14 November 1916.

97. In 1913 stevedoring companies succeeded in lobbying local government to open beerhalls at 10 A.M. (as opposed to 8 A.M.) and to close the outlets between 2 P.M. and 4 P.M. This was in reponse to observations that workers were frequently in "a stupid and dazed condition as to be unfit for work" due to consumption of municipal beer; see NA, DCL, no. 637, Chief Constable to Town Clerk, 1 April 1913.

98. CAD, Assaults Commission, Minutes of Evidence, p. 37.

99. NA, DCTF, vol. 48, file 91, Statememt of a Deputation of the Native Branch of the WCTU, 14 September 1914.

100. *Izwe la Kiti,* 22 October 1913.

101. Hemson, "Dockworkers of Durban," p. 157, n. 156.

102. CAD, Assaults Commission, Minutes of Evidence, p. 7.

103. NA, *Report of the Deputation sent to Durban by the Municipal Council of Johannesburg to Enquire into the System of Housing Natives and the Sale of Kaffir Beer to Natives,* 1916, p. 24.

104. NA, CNC, vol. 236, 550/16, Prayer of the Natal Native Congress, Pietermaritzburg, 1916.

105. When a boycott of Durban's beerhalls was initiated at a time of increasing unemployment and decline in real wages in 1948, protest centered on the price of beer and not the system itself.

106. P. la Hausse, "The Message of the Warriors: The ICU, the Labouring Poor and the Making of a Popular Political Culture in Durban, 1925–1930," in *Holding Their Ground: Class, Locality and Culture in 19th and 20th Century South Africa,* ed. P. Bonner et al. (Johannesburg: Ravan Press, 1989), pp. 19–58.

107. NA, Durban Magistrates Correspondence, vol. 494, D. 4/280/1914, Chief Magistrate to CNC, 5 May 1914.

108. In order to protect the municipal beer monopoly, Act 23 prohibited the sale of beer within approximately five miles of the town. Rural Africans were still allowed to brew beer with the permission of the local magistrate.

No doubt this provided cover for many peri-urban brewers. Between 1912 and 1917 there was a steady increase in the number of offenses relating to the possession of quick-fermenting and highly intoxicating drinks such as *isishimeyana, skokiana,* and *ikali.*

109. Various correspondence in NA, DCTF, vol. 48, file 91.

110. NA, J. Hope Redford, *Report on Enquiry into the Durban System of Control of Native Beer,* 30 April 1921.

111. NA, *Report of the Deputation Sent to Durban by Municipal Council of Johannesburg.*

CHAPTER FOUR

THE "DURBAN SYSTEM" AND THE LIMITS OF COLONIAL POWER IN SALISBURY, 1890–1935

Richard Parry

INTRODUCTION

THE STRUGGLE OVER the control of alcohol manufacture, sale, and consumption by Africans in Salisbury illustrates two central and complementary principles about the practical operation of an administration in a small colonial town. First, it shows that the extent of direct control over the subordinate black population depended fundamentally on the resources available to the colonial authority. Second, it reveals that in practice colonialism was based on a series of implicit compromises, not so much between colonizer and colonized but between ideology and reality in the minds of the colonizers themselves. Faced with the central problem of creating a population subservient to colonial interests, administrators in Salisbury were unable to perform much more than an untidy and uncoordinated holding operation using maximum violence at particular moments and ignoring African transgressions at others. In "creating" the colonial town they created an ideology that obscured the real powerlessness of their position and the existence of autonomous ideological, cultural, and social patterns outside their perception as well as their control.

Consequently, the history of the administrative efforts of the Salisbury municipality is one of inadequate means, frustrated actions, and limited goals. It began with the efforts to establish a "colonial space" that would provide the economic and ideological base for the exploitation of the town's black populace. That endeavor involved limiting the social relations between black and white, as well as the physical separation of the black population, and met with limited practical success. The problem then arose of financing the operation of "colonial space." The municipality's solution was to charge Africans for the cost of their own control, to be paid though location rents and beer profits. Even that limited goal, however, almost proved beyond the capacities of the colonial state as embodied in the Salisbury municipality. By setting low targets and deploying minimal resources, the municipality managed to maintain the system, but at maximum human cost to the black population.

ALCOHOL, HOUSING, AND
THE LOCAL AUTHORITY, 1890−1912

In 1890 Cecil Rhodes's Pioneer Column finally disbanded at Fort Salisbury on the Makabusi plain. Administrator Archibald Colquhoun proclaimed the tiny settlement as the administrative capital of the territory between the Zambezi and Limpopo Rivers that had earlier been granted to the British South Africa Company under Royal Charter.[1] Established in order to attract capital into Mashonaland, the village was an entirely artificial creation, a crucible for the generation and extension of political and economic power imposed upon, rather than arising out of, the local economy. The company anticipated that the discovery of a "Second Rand" would draw capital into the territory and finance both local development and an infrastructure and dividends for its shareholders. They quickly realized, however, that the territory's mineral resources were modest and that spin-off capital from the Witwatersrand was limited.[2] Consequently, for the first thirty years of its existence the town experienced severe stagnation and remained both geographically isolated and economically peripheral within the subcontinent. It was not until the 1920s that the growth of the tobacco industry woke the sleepy colonial village. But that was to usher in a period of economic upheaval, a succession of boom and bust cycles, that followed developments on the international gold and tobacco markets and did not stabilize until after the Second World War.

The character of the town was molded by the precariousness of its economy, and that uncertainty fundamentally influenced the culture and administration of alcohol consumption. Before 1905 Salisbury was populated by white civil servants, traders, and adventurers and lacked the substantial white working class that had quickly developed on the Witwatersrand. It therefore depended heavily on skilled and semiskilled black immigrants and unskilled migrants from Portuguese East Africa, Nyasaland, and the Zambezi basin. Limited raw materials and demand meant that the local economy lacked medium or large-scale extractive industries, and production processes remained rudimentary. Skilled black workers found employment as smiths, builders, leather workers, carpenters, cooks, touts, transport riders, and overseers, while semiskilled and unskilled migrants worked in domestic service or in the municipal road-building and sanitation services. The preponderance of local commercial interests over industrial capital (particularly in the "kaffir truck" trade) created a certain ambivalence toward the question of African administration, since the economy depended on black buying power as well as black labor.

The high cost of living that resulted from the absence of local industry and geographical isolation initially meant that wages were unrestrained by the specific cost constraints of any particular productive process. This situation led to a degree of economic fluidity and prompted the local administration to lay less emphasis on controlling labor and enforcing work discipline. Instead they focused on entrenching the colonial spatial order, integrating the town into the imperial economy, and delineating space as an ideological construct. Administration therefore began with a survey of the town in 1891, the subdivision of plots and streets, and the delimitation of a ring of townlands or commonage totaling approximately 8,150 hectares (see Figure 4.1).[3] The basic purpose of this spatial reordering was to generate revenue

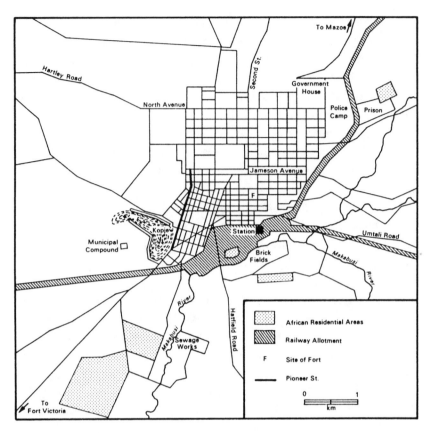

4.1 Street map of Salisbury, c. 1920

by establishing and enforcing ownership rights. The survey was swiftly
followed by a proclamation that a cluster of huts on the southeastern
part of the commonage was to function as a "native location."[4]

The commoditization of urban space provided a framework for the
exercise of administrative power, but it could not conceal the tenuous
nature of colonial power itself. The struggle over alcohol was of central importance in reflecting the priorities of the municipality and the
extent to which it was able to realize them. The struggle was waged
on two fronts. First, the state reacted to the demands of white workers
for the deskilling of black immigrant workers by seeking to curtail the
complex informal economy and the extensive social interaction between black and white traders, touts, gamblers, and drifters in the

Pioneer Street area. It did this by outlawing the consumption of wine and spirits by blacks. Second, the municipality moved against black brewers of traditional beer as a means of limiting their economic independence within the urban area. Both those campaigns had strong ideological and social as well as economic dimensions. Their lack of success, however, demonstrated clearly the contradictions and inadequacies of colonialism.

Black immigrants from the Cape and Natal congregated in the cheap lodging houses, stables, and brothels that sprang up around Pioneer Street. Like their white counterparts, the black immigrants had a long tradition of alcohol consumption, particularly of Cape and Madeira wines and brandy. In the Western Cape alcohol had played an important role in the workplace as a number of employers operated under the "tot" system.[5] The centrality of alcohol in social and cultural interaction was reinforced by the relative absence of women and alternative recreational facilities in Salisbury. In 1896 the sale of "European" liquor to Africans and Indians was subject to a fine of £25 or three months' hard labor—without much result. In 1898 the penalties were increased to a staggering £300 fine or six months' hard labor for a first offence.[6] "People must live," declared the *Rhodesia Herald*, "but not at the expense of debauching the native population on whose sobriety and labour the industries and comfort of the white community almost wholly depend."[7]

The campaign to suppress the liquor trade was led by a group of merchants known as the Kopje establishment. The trade was a triple irritant to the Kopje merchants. First, in the stagnant economic conditions of 1898 the liquor sellers cut deeply into their share of the legitimate African market. By driving the smaller trader-liquor sellers out of business, the merchants hoped to gain control over a market that was seriously overtraded.[8] Second, as property values began to rise in Manica Road and the Causeway, the Pioneer Street property owners sought to "clean up" the street. That attempt culminated in an offensive against prostitution in 1910. Finally, the area's social, economic, and racial heterogeneity was profoundly threatening, since it offended middle-class sensibilities (which wished to throw a cordon sanitaire around the contaminating influence of the dangerous classes) and South African racial ethics (which stressed the bad example such behavior had on African employees).

The nature of the liquor trade made detection and proof by ordinary police methods almost impossible, so the "establishment" onslaught was spearheaded by members of the black South African working class, which also provided the majority of customers. Volunteer trappers were sent out by the police after careful briefing and instructed to buy a drink from a particular target. Evidence was obtained by means of a small piece of sponge concealed in the mouth of the volunteer trapper. The seller was then confronted by the trap in the company of a regular policeman.[9] Such a system inevitably conferred a great deal of power on the trap himself. As he often provided the initial information about the dealer and had a free hand in the methods he used to get the dealer to supply him with a drink, there was a great deal of scope for African traps to use the law enforcement machinery of the colonial state to square their personal accounts. As a trap at the trial of Sydney Davis explained, "I have a grudge against Davis because he searches my parcels if I buy scoff [food] at other stores. . . . Cornelius and I arranged the trap before we saw the police about it."[10] That did not save Davis from a £50 fine or six months' hard labor.

Once trapping became standard practice, no one queried the motives of traps, but many undoubtedly recognized the vulnerability of certain whites and used the colonial system against them.[11] Before the 1898 amendment of the 1896 regulations, statutory rewards were given to traps when convictions were procured, but later, as their role expanded in the policing of the town, an informal system of rewards and favors for informers seems to have operated.[12] While opposition to the consumption of "European liquor" by black workers came mainly from white settlers and the Pioneer Street merchants, the local authority also had its objections. It considered that the use of *doro* or *mhamba* (traditional *rapoko* or grain-based beer) reduced the quality of labor performed and the size of the potential workforce by allowing African beer producers and vendors an alternative source of income within the urban economy.

Although clause 27 of the 1895 Location Regulations prohibited the possession or sale of beer in the vicinity of the location, there were no specific provisions for its enforcement.[13] The 1898 Town Location Regulations attempted to remedy this deficiency. They provided for the appointment of an Inspector of Native Locations empowered to apprehend "idle or disorderly" persons and search the property of persons suspected of possessing intoxicating liquor.[14] The agitation that produced restrictions on the sale of beer in the 1895 regulations was primarily directed at the effect beer sales had on the labor supply. But colonial consciousness linked the labor issue to an appeal to the "public order." As a white colonist complained in 1894,

[It is] a shame to see, day after day, crowds of these lazy niggers coming into town with calabashes of the vile stuff, and after disposing of it for cash, they clear home to their kraals. The brutes are too lazy to work, and not only do they find this an easy way of obtaining money but invariably under cover of darkness takes [sic] other people's property home with them too.[15]

The 1898 regulations were aimed at those Africans residing in the location who inhibited the labor supply by following an alternate economic route and simultaneously provided a recreational enclave that encouraged absenteeism and insubordinate behavior. But the state had no desire to stamp out beer altogether, recognizing its nutritional value as well as its ubiquity. In the end, the state compromised by allowing Africans to possess alcohol for their own use. That concession effectively hamstrung the operation of the law. To prove that individuals possessed beer for sale rather than for their own use was often beyond the ability of the police, who doubled as public prosecutors in the Magistrate's Court. In one case, for example, the defendant pleaded guilty to the charge of possession and the ranger testified to having found four large buckets of beer in a state of fermentation in his hut. The magistrate found him not guilty, however, noting that the prosecution had produced no evidence to prove that the beer in question was an intoxicating drink nor that the quantity of beer found was more than he required for his personal use.[16] The town council responded by enacting a further bylaw prohibiting the manufacture of "kaffir beer" for sale.[17]

The issue of alcohol consumption was closely connected with the debate over housing, specifically the extent to which the municipality should take responsibility for both black housing and social control. At the turn of the century, the municipality was responsible for a handful of huts on the commonage, over which it had no legal and little practical authority.[18] Before 1906 the location had less than fifty occupants and most blacks either squatted at the brickfields (or in various "private locations") or lived on their employers' plots or as tenants in the Pioneer Street area.[19] Following the passage of the 1905 Urban Locations Ordinance, a new location was laid out a mile or so south of the railway line, and fifty-six corrugated-iron rondavels and a four-room brick barracks were erected. By the end of 1907, however, there were still only a dozen tenants, and a massive police drive began to fill all available accommodation. The municipality experienced only temporary success, as the workers began to abandon the overcrowded, expensive, and repressive location for accommodation in the town, on the commonage or on the farms beyond. Four months later, ten huts were unoccupied and a year later half were empty.[20]

The municipality then launched unsuccessful attacks on the Wesleyan Location and the Railway Reserve, which were "in a very dirty state" and were venues for "a good deal of beer brewing and drinking."[21] The unauthorized settlements on the brickfields, however, constituted the major impediment to the council's efforts to rationalize the pattern of black residence. Once again they were thwarted by their lack of full jurisdiction over the area. The ranger reported that "it is a frequent occurrence for idle and mischievous natives to take refuge on the brickfields, where they seem to be harbored by the natives employed there. This gives rise to a good deal of trouble, beer drinking, gambling and other vices being carried on and the police appear unable to exercise any control."[22]

The struggle to fill the location began again in the dry season of 1909 as the police stepped up their raids on the stores and yards of Manica Road and Second Street. By the end of October, before the arrival of the rains, the situation had deteriorated further and monthly revenue from the location had dwindled to less than £10. It was another year before the Inspector of Locations was finally able to report that the location was full. This achievement reflected increased municipal powers over the commonage and intensified police activity, particularly on the brickfields, but it was mainly the result of population increase and a serious accommodation shortage during the boom of 1910–1911.[23]

The location was a manufactured colonial space, an essential precondition for the exercise of a degree of control over the economic and social lives of a black semipermanent working class. The effectiveness of such control depended, however, on the resources of the impecunious municipality, who were always more conscious of their balance sheet than the nature of the social order. The implicit relationship between finance, housing, and alcohol was made more explicit with the passage of the Kaffir Beer Act of 1912, which gave the council a de jure monopoly over the sale of *doro* and provided a clear financial incentive for tackling the issue of beer brewing.

THE BEER MONOPOLY AND THE LIMITS OF COLONIAL POWER, 1913–1923

Before 1913 the efforts of the municipality to curb the trade in *doro* were sporadic and ineffectual. While they drove some brewers onto the commonage or to the private locations beyond they appear to have had little effect on the quantity brewed or consumed. By 1912 a steady increase in population meant that brewing had become a thriving industry. Trading stores in the vicinity of the location supplied a preparation of *rapoko* already sprouted, crushed, and cooked ready for beer making, thus cutting down the time the brewer needed to spend preparing the grain prior to fermentation.[24] In the location, the headman made regular (and predictable) Saturday night inspections. The headman was himself responsible for a large proportion of the illegal brewing and consistently turned a blind eye to the trade. On Mondays the location superintendent visited the area. Outside the location, the beer trade flourished on the brickfields and freehold plots (where a hundred or so workers would congregate for weekly drinking parties), and Africans from outside the town came in daily to hawk beer at their customers' places of work.

In 1909 the "Durban system," based on the monopolization of the production and sale of beer in town, was introduced by the Durban municipality.[25] The experiment was closely monitored by administrators throughout the subcontinent. Two years later, the 1911 Native Affairs Commission, keenly aware of the financial constraints on "native" administration, recommended the adoption of the Durban system in Southern Rhodesia. The commission supported their recommendation with a characteristic reference to the effect of unregulated beer selling on the social and moral fiber of the black population:

> Immorality of women, both married and single, in the vicinity of mines and other industrial centres is a growing danger to the future moral and physical welfare of the native races. . . . husbands allow their women to take beer for sale to natives employed at these centres . . . this leads to prostitution and . . . the former share the proceeds. The sale of beer is contrary to all native traditions and is largely the cause of moral decline.[26]

In contrast to the extended delay over the passage of the 1905 Locations Ordinance, the Kaffir Beer Ordinance was passed in the same year and permitted the Salisbury and Bulawayo municipalities to implement a similar system.

The Durban model was followed in most respects with one important difference. The council did not manufacture its own beer but retailed supplies bought in bulk from the Salisbury Brewery. The town council was consequently able to make a large profit without major capital investment. They bought beer for between 10d and 1 shilling per gallon and sold it in the beerhall for 2 shillings a gallon.[27] The municipality justified the high profit margin on the monopoly trade on the grounds that a reduction in beer prices would lead to an increase in drinking and drunkenness. From the mid-1920s it also argued that large profits were necessary to counterbalance the supposed tendency for the rest of the native affairs account to run a "deficit." As table 4.1 illustrates, beer profits between 1914 and 1930 amounted to £22,554, while expenditure on the location exceeded revenue by £53 for the same period. The council reported a deficit on the location account every year between 1925 and 1930.

A canteen for the sale of *doro* opened in the location in 1913. If the system had worked smoothly the town authorities would have had every reason to congratulate themselves. By introducing the monopoly they anticipated being able to solve all the key problems of colonial administration simultaneously. They would be able to control brewing, which provided an alternative source of income for blacks in the white man's town. They could reduce the volume of drinking, and thus would have more control over absenteeism. And they could eliminate drunkenness, by strictly controlling the alcohol content of the beer sold. In addition, the operation of the monopoly would allow the authorities to keep a finger on the pulse of popular culture. Most appealing of all, the profits from the venture looked like they would support the whole of Native Affairs expenditure, thus exonerating employers and ratepayers from all future financial responsibility.

In practice, the system did not work smoothly and received its first challenge within three days of the opening. Drinkers unanimously condemned the beer as sour and the canteen had to be shut.[28] By acting as retailers only, the municipality guaranteed itself a profit of 1s 2d on each gallon sold, but had no control over the product. Beer from the major supplier, South African Breweries, was erratic in both quality and quantity. It remained so until the municipality took over brewing operations in August 1936. Much of the difficulty over the quality of the beer seemed to stem from the attitude of Mr. Samuels, longtime manager of the brewery, toward the holders of the monopoly. When, for example, Kanzulila took over as beer maker from Isaac, who had returned to Nyasaland in October 1929, Samuels (known as *kanyandura*, or a "man not right in the head," by his workers) refused to supply him with sufficient yeast and in consequence the beer was bad. As Kanzulila noted, the brewery was less interested in selling good beer to the municipality than in retailing yeast directly to Africans engaged in the growing hop beer trade.[29] Samuels countered all criticisms by blaming the inexperience of the location superintendent or the prevalence of private brewing which made the canteen less attractive.[30]

Successive location superintendents confronted other obstacles in their quest to maximize profits from the monopoly. Immediately after the canteen opened, the barman saw his chance to share the profits of the system and began adding a gallon of water to every three and a half gallons of beer.[31] Not surprisingly, few drinkers were tempted to spend 3d per small cup or 6d per large cup on watered-down, unpalatable beer, particularly when they had access to alternative sources.

The location superintendent countered by launching a series of nightly raids on the location, the railway station area, and the brickfields; he also employed a number of informers.[32] Those efforts had some success, but the pressure could not be sustained, and soon the location residents, both brewers and drinkers, fought back. After six months, sales had fallen off considerably as the location brewers under the headman, Makubala, had managed to intimidate most informers and enforce a boycott of the canteen.[33]

In order to sell his diluted and undesirable product, the superintendent had to close down competing sources of supply both inside and outside the location. When he tried to stifle brewing inside the location he met opposition from an unexpected quarter. The magistrate, E. A. Brailsford, refused to convict those charged, upheld the right of Africans to possess beer for their own consumption, and challenged the authorities to prove that the beer had been for sale. Makubala, the location headman, was acquitted when he argued that the four gallons of *qilika* (beer mixed with the hallucinogenic juice from a crushed root) found in his possession were for his personal use.[34] In 1915 the superintendent faced steadily declining profits and attempted to counter the ubiquitous trade in the location by taking the law into his own hands. But he recognized that he could not be "too strict" with the residents, otherwise they would move out of the location and so deprive the council of both rent and beer revenue.

He suggested that part of the solution lay in prohibiting squatting within a certain radius of the town and refusing to grant private location licenses within that area. Unless that was done, he argued, it served no good purpose to prohibit brewing in the location itself.[35] The town ranger reported that large numbers of squatters congregated around the brickfields, the old rifle range, and the Native Commissioner's Messengers Camp, but that most of the large-scale brewing took place at Epworth Mission and in private locations on farms.[36] When Epworth was placed under quarantine as a result of a smallpox outbreak in August 1915, beerhall profits increased to record levels. But the effect was temporary and raids on the squatter camps succeeded only in redistributing the residents to different parts of the same area.

By the end of 1916 neither the squatting issue nor the problem of brewing in the location had come any closer to resolution. The legal position was further complicated by the council's realization that its licensed monopoly to sell beer in an urban area did not extend to the location.[37] In March 1917 this was regularized by the promulgation of a regulation prohibiting the possession of beer within the common-age and over a two-mile radius outside the commonage boundary, but excluding the location.[38] But the council continued to receive adverse judgments from Mr. Brailsford in the Magistrate's Court, who refused to convict anyone arrested in his own hut for drunkenness or other similar offenses unless the arresting officer had previously obtained a warrant. Brailsford continued to apply the principle of a "reasonable quantity" for an individual's own consumption, allowing up to twelve gallons on some occasions.[39] The reasons for Brailsford's insistence on using legal loopholes to thwart the municipality's effort are not all that clear, but it seems likely that his aim was to maintain the inde-pendence of his court against the executive arm. On a personal level, he was a prickly character, not given to suffering fools lightly, and may have enjoyed resisting the ham-fisted efforts of the local admin-istration to enforce their questionable monopoly.

The effect, as the town clerk complained, was "to considerably di-minish the authority of the representatives of the council in the eyes of the black inhabitants." The attorney general suggested that the matter could be resolved by bringing prosecutions forward under section 13(2) of the 1906 Native Urban Locations Ordinance, that is, for pos-sessing intoxicating liquor without a permit. In August 1918 a case was brought under this section but the accused, Annie, was acquitted. The magistrate held that the section "did not apply to natives."[40] The administrator responded by promulgating regulations under section 9 of the 1906 ordinance, which prohibited the possession of beer or any other intoxicating substances in the location.

The African population of the location, many of whom had been following this long-running legal wrangle with a great deal of inter-est, sent a deputation to the Superintendent of Natives asking him to repeal the new regulations on possession. They pointed out that the new restrictions were intolerable and if they were not lifted, or rents were not halved to allow them to buy beer, then fifty-seven families would leave the location.[41] The council refused to budge but the legal saga was not yet over. Two weeks later, a woman named Jofina was charged under the new regulations with the possession of fifteen gallons of beer. The magistrate acquitted her on the grounds that the regulations were ultra vires, since section 9 of the 1906 ordinance did not empower the administration to make them.[42] The location superintendent noted that as soon as the decision had been printed in the *Herald*, brewing openly recommenced, and in 1920 he remained unable to prosecute brewers. Hence he reported that his "methods of limiting this industry [were] therefore somewhat illegal." Finally, a Kaffir Beer Ordinance was passed in November 1920, which resulted in a movement out of the location when the brewers lost a series of test cases.[43] As a result, social tensions increased in the location and the 1921 dry season saw a dramatic series of fires in the location as brewers took revenge on informers by setting fire to the thatched roofs of their huts.

It had taken the municipality almost ten years to establish a legal foundation on which to enforce its monopoly. That delay was partly the result of slipshod legal work in the Law Department and a magistrate who, on some issues at least, tenaciously asserted his independence from the bureaucratic requirements of the town. It is important, therefore, to avoid overestimating the efficiency and single-mindedness of the colonial state in pursuing any particular course. Even on an issue as close to the pocketbook as the beer monopoly, both the local and territorial authorities were capable of repeatedly shooting themselves in the foot. It does not necessarily follow that the state was unable to exert a strong grip whatever the niceties of the legal situation many have been, but even in practice the efforts of the location superintendent were usually easily evaded.

From the point of view of the local authority, the position was made no easier by endemic corruption and violence within the location itself. None of the location superintendents between 1900 and 1923 escaped the attention of the courts. The first superintendent, John Smith, was fined for seriously assaulting a resident named Thomas (who later took his revenge by stabbing Smith's horse).[44]

Smith's successor, H. S. Winter, was found guilty of assaulting a municipal employee who requested that he be signed off at the end of his contract.[45] Winter died in the influenza epidemic of 1919 and was replaced by R. H. B. Mason, who was soon under investigation for illegally demanding "premiums" on location rents, failing to live in the location (as required in his contract) and allowing rent to "go astray."[46]

The record of the location headmen was no better. Mordecai was convicted of extortion in 1908. His successor, Julius Mawasa, absconded with £16 in pass fees and rent in 1912, and two years later Makabula was dismissed for "inciting the people not to use the canteen" and "aiding and abetting the brewing of kaffir beer."[47] The council had no better luck with Makabula's successor, James Manda, a major figure in the Watchtower Church during the 1917 alarm. He was dismissed and deported.[48] A few years later Gatsi, who was installed as headman by Mason, was described by the town clerk as a "notorious gambler" who "had infected more than one young native girl with V.D. and . . . [whose] conduct generally was a menace to the wellbeing of the residents."[49]

The location brewers exercised a high degree of cunning, struggling as they were for economic survival. But after 1920, as the legal tide turned against them, many moved to the farms bordering the commonage. The Kaffir Beer Act of 1920 prohibited brewing within two miles of the commonage boundaries and the Williams, Hilton, and Willow Bank farms, which lay just outside the limit, became the center of lively weekend parties. In 1927 the exclusion zone was extended to five miles, but its increased size made it correspondingly difficult to police.[50] Many brewers developed a more effective means of challenging the council monopoly by brewing large quantities of legal, and supposedly nonalcoholic, "hop beer" out of a blend of hops, yeast, and sugar with the addition of tobacco, methylated spirits, or *rapoko* beer to provide extra "kick." Hop beer was not covered by the 1920 Act, and sales of yeast at the brewery rocketed in the latter part of 1922 as the drink caught on.

Despite the mushrooming of the hop beer industry after 1922, the beerhall was able to make a handy profit of between £2,400 and £2,800 per annum between 1925 and 1929, although this must have been a small fraction of the money that went into the pockets of hop beer brewers and "Native Eating House" proprietors. In 1929 the superintendent tried to halt the brewing of hop beer. The predominantly female brewers responded with a beerhall boycott that totally emptied the canteen of customers, and within three days the superintendent was forced to give in.[51] Between 1930 and 1936 sales fell from an average of £4,000 to £500 per year as the hop brewers expanded their share of the market by offering a more convenient service and a cheaper, more powerful product while the quality of the beer received from the Brewery continued to decline. In one fifty-three-day period, a reliable tester reported that the beer was "bad" on twenty-nine days and "good" on only five. The location superintendent recommended that the council take over brewing and employ women to do it as in Durban and Bulawayo. He experimented with 12s 6d worth of *rapoko* and produced saleable beer at about 3d per gallon, after allowing for labor costs and firewood.[52] As a result, the contract with the brewery was not renewed and in February 1937 a brewery next to the beerhall was erected at a cost of £1,800. Profits for the year ending in June 1938 rose to £4,307.[53]

Consequently, the Durban system, which envisaged municipal control of both brewing and marketing, was not fully implemented in Salisbury until 1937. There appear to be two main reasons why it was not begun earlier. First, the fiscal conservatism of the municipality showed in its marked reluctance to spend any more than was necessary within the location. Even though the profits of the monopoly were shared with the brewery, the town councillors preferred not to risk further capital on brewing plant and supervision charges as long as there was no guarantee of increased sales. They were highly realistic about the competition they faced from black brewers and were aware of their inability to enforce the monopoly on the ground. Second, the "Native Location" income and expenditure account showed a profit of £22,501 between 1913 and 1930 without showing a deficit in any year (see table 4.1). The surplus was taken to the general account and used on roads and other amenities in the white areas. In short, the situation was satisfactory. Africans paid for their own administration and housing with minimal effort on the part of the

Table 4.1: Location and beerhall profits, Salisbury location, 1914–1930

	Location			Beerhall		
	Revenue	Expend.	Profit	Revenue	Expend.	Profit
	£	£	£	£	£	£
1914	1,093	577	516	778	448	330
1915	1,092	475	617	1,885	448	1,134
1916	939	622	317	1,554	642	912
1917	1,023	590	433	1,411	1,006	405
1918	1,210	616	594	891	717	174
1919	1,244	1,260	−16	1,227	776	451
1920	1,346	981	365	1,593	977	616
1921	1,423	1,065	358	2,109	1,287	822
1922	1,511	1,084	427	2,579	1,488	1,091
1923	1,566	1,481	85	2,173	1,375	798
1924	1,819	1,709	110	3,815	2,202	1,613
1925	2,373	3,100	−727	5,202	2,459	2,743
1926	2,863	3,506	−643	4,846	2,356	2,490
1927	3,478	4,085	−607	4,791	2,314	2,477
1928	3,812	4,574	−762	4,912	2,286	2,626
1929	4,859	5,128	−269	4,414	1,993	2,421
1930	6,069	6,920	−851	2,957	1,506	1,451
Total	37,720	37,773	−53	47,137	24,583	22,554

Source: Municipality of Salisbury, "Mayor's Minutes 1908–9 to 1938–9."

council bureaucracy. Only when the account showed a deficit of over £500 in 1936 did the council give serious consideration to a more profitable scheme.

BREWING, GENDER,
AND THE SOCIAL FORMATION

The economic struggle between canteen and brewers over the alcohol market was only one facet of a multidimensional network of relationships involving alcohol in Salisbury. For blacks, as for white workers, the consumption of alcohol was a central cultural reference point. As with the sharing of food, the sharing of beer was preeminently a social experience, a means of situating oneself within a social order that had been fractured at various points by the demands of the colonial political economy.

The use of alcohol by blacks in colonial society was, on one level, an essentially subversive action, an implicit denial of personal subservience in the search for individual and social gratification. This was true even though the colonial administration was inherently ambivalent toward alcohol use, encouraging it as the central means of financing African administration while simultaneously condemning its effects on the efficiency of the workforce. In ideological terms, alcohol tended to break down the barriers of fear and restraint that individuals felt toward their oppressors, thus subverting the elaborate pattern of colonial controls. But, in general, alcohol and *dagga* (marijuana) provided an escape from the tedium of everyday reality, allowing individuals to forget their circumstances rather than change them. The use of alcohol also provided powerful linkages—both emphasizing the continuity between town and countryside, and cementing urban-based bonds. On that level, the growing consumption of hop beer meant a shift in the cultural framework through which material reality was mediated, toward a new positive formulation of urban culture, with its emphasis on hard living and continual improvisation as reflected in a shebeen and jazz band subculture that was to encompass much of the permanent working class in Salisbury in the 1930s and 1940s.

Alcohol was equally significant for the operation of gender relations in the location. Until the tobacco boom of the mid-1930s, when women began to be used to undercut male wages in the tobacco-processing barns, economic opportunities for females in the formal sector were few. Consequently, most women survived by providing basic services such as cooked food, beer, and sex for the male population. The trade in sex had its own structure and hierarchy. Sexual relationships ranged from *mapoto* marriages, stable informal relationships lasting several months or years, through liaisons lasting a couple of weeks (until the male migrant's money had run out), to encounters with "grass women," who charged a flat rate of 2s 6d a time.[54] The crucial factor in a woman's position in the sex trade was her relationship to the brewing network. Although a substantial number of women who operated as prostitutes in Salisbury tended to be mobile, traveling between the major towns and mining centers, many became permanent residents of the location. New arrivals in town without any means of support were obliged to sell themselves to gain food and shelter. Later they might be taken under the control of an older woman or "storekeeper," who operated a brewing and prostitution business, before finally gaining full independence and operating a shebeen themselves.

The jump to independent status came when a woman was able to accumulate sufficient resources to allow her to set up her own brewing business, attract customers, and thus encourage other women to operate as prostitutes under her control. The career of Mary Nyrenda, for example, began on the mine circuit and ended up in the Salisbury location from where she supplied women to whites as well as blacks.[55] She developed powerful connections and proved almost untouchable by the authorities, in one case persuading witnesses brought before the Magistrate's Court to deny sworn statements they had previously made to the police.[56]

The attitude of those women toward the municipal beerhall was generally pragmatic. While it was a direct competitor for drinking customers, the beerhall was a particularly good place for soliciting custom. The established class of beer brewers saw it as a threat to their business, but for many less established women it provided an opportunity to operate semi-independently, outside the direct control of "storekeepers." In September 1922 the superintendent attempted to reduce the most blatant soliciting and banned a number of women from the canteen after 5 P.M. The women responded with a boycott and persuaded the male clientele to leave with them—as a result, the banning order was rescinded.[57] A further total boycott proved successful in 1929 when efforts were made to clamp down on the production of hop beer.

When questions of "morality" were concerned, the municipality was never less than pragmatic. In 1932 the Southern Rhodesian Missionary Conference requested that segregation between the sexes be introduced in the beerhall. The Chief Native Commissioner advised the town council that this was "the correct thing to do" but that "such a step will result in a falling off of revenue from the Beer Hall as the bachelors will spend less money there than they do at present." The council refused the request.[58]

Although the location women showed their powers of organization in 1922 and 1929, they were ignored by male activists seeking to weld the black working class into a coherent political movement. The Southern Rhodesian Industrial and Commercial Workers Union began operations in Salisbury in 1929 but was hamstrung by a petit bourgeois ideology of self-improvement that was not only alien to the vast majority of the permanent working class but prevented them from tapping preexisting grassroots organization within the location. Charles Mzingeli, the organizer of the Salisbury branch, condemned the beer monopoly but not the consumption of alcohol itself. The branch secretary Aaron Tobolo, however, addressed a meeting during which he deplored beer drinking, gambling, and the money spent on European clothes.[59] Only five people turned up at the next meeting.

In essence, neither the town council nor the ICU showed any sign of understanding the reality of black urban life or the economic importance of beer brewing and prostitution for a large proportion of the black residents of Salisbury. The authorities, however, were content merely to accept that social control and the potential from beer sales were unobtainable without the introduction of expanded resources. The failure of the ICU was more stark. By failing to target their constituency and empathize culturally with the concerns of urban blacks, both male and female, they remained an elitist movement without a popular base and had disintegrated by the mid-1930s after constant pressure from the state.

CONCLUSION

The implementation of the Durban system in Salisbury was, in essence, a case study of the limits of colonial power. Faced with the perennial problem of balancing the "Native Location" account, the municipality seized on the idea of a monopoly over the production and sale of beer. The system promised a measure of social control through housing provision, without the administration having to draw on revenue from white taxpayers (and voters).

However, the town authorities were not prepared to gamble on their suspect ability to enforce their legal monopoly. Rather than producing the beer themselves, they preferred to retail beer produced by the South African Brewery. By means of numerous, but usually ineffectual, campaigns against independent brewers they managed to maintain a small annual profit on the "Native Location" account. Only when the account began to show a deficit did they fully implement the Durban system by taking control over brewing themselves.

Colonialism in a small town like Salisbury was characterized not by its coercive power but by its inadequacies. Alcohol policy was expressed in the language of grand segregation, but it had to be implemented by harassed and corrupt officials. Insofar as the authorities even understood the dynamics of popular culture in the town they fondly believed they had "created," they were aware that control was an unobtainable ideal. Most of the time, however, they were content to drift along, reacting to crises as they arose, ignoring the social and human consequences of inadequate wages, appalling living conditions, monotony, and violence.

NOTES

1. A. Keppel-Jones, *Rhodes and Rhodesia: The White Conquest of Zimbabwe, 1884–1902* (Kingston and Montreal: McGill-Queen's Press, 1983), p. 172.

2. R. Churchill, *Men, Mines and Animals in South Africa* (London: Sampson, Low, Marston and Co., 1892), chap. 15 and 17.

3. G. H. Tanser, *A Scantling of Time* (Salisbury: Pioneer Head, 1965), pp. 54–117.

4. National Archives of Zimbabwe (NAZ), Local Government Archive (LG), 47/1, Sanitary Inspector to Chairman, Board of Management, Salisbury, 17 March 1892.

5. P. Scully (in this collection).

6. NAZ, S235/383, Government Notice no. 134, 1896; no. 240, 1898.

7. *Rhodesia Herald,* 6 September 1898.

8. *Rhodesia Herald,* 9 March 1898.

9. NAZ, D3/5/1, R. v. J. Buckley, 17 September 1898.

10. NAZ, D3/5/1, R. v. Davis, 8 June 1898.

11. NAZ, D3/5/40/32, R. v. Strydom, and R. v. Maruta.

12. NAZ, D3/5/1, R. v. George Cohen, 3 May 1898. Among the numerous examples of the activities of "professional" informers see the careers of Harry Edwards and Freddie Jeneker in NAZ, D3/5/26/821, 991, 1085; and D3/5/27/760, 872, 907, 908.

13. NAZ, LG47/4, Town Clerk to Chief Inspector, Municipal Police, 30 July 1897, 11 January 1898; and LG47/5, Town Clerk to Secretary to the Administrator, 28 January 1898, 24 November 1898.

14. NAZ, S235/383, Government Notice no. 181 of 1898.

15. *Rhodesia Herald,* 30 November 1894.

16. *Rhodesia Herald,* 26 September 1899.

17. *Rhodesia Herald,* 3 February 1900; Municipality of Salisbury, *Mayor's Minute 1899–1900,* p. 7.

18. NAZ, LG47/11, Town Clerk to Chief Secretary, BSAC, Salisbury, 5 June 1902; 9 January 1903; 26 August 1904; LG47/13, p. 499; Municipality of Salisbury, *Mayor's Minute 1906–1907,* p. 9.

19. Municipality of Salisbury, *Mayor's Minute 1905–1906;* NAZ, S138/11, Application for Private Location, Jowala's Plot, Salisbury, 13 January 1920; NAZ, LG52.6/1, Town Ranger to Town Clerk, 25 January 1905.

20. NAZ, LG47/16, Town Clerk to Chief Inspector, Southern Rhodesia Constabulary, 2 May 1908; LG52/6/1, Inspector of Locations to Town Clerk, 7 August 1908; Municipality of Salisbury, *Mayor's Minute 1908–1909,* p. 19.

21. NAZ, LG52/6/1, Inspector of Locations to Town Clerk, 25 September 1908.

22. NAZ, LG47/17, Town Clerk to Sub Inspector, SRC, 26 August 1909; *Rhodesia Herald,* 11 June 1909, 27 July 1909.

23. NAZ, LG52/6/1, Inspector of Locations to Town Clerk, 13 October 1910.

24. Municipality of Salisbury, *Mayor's Minute 1910–1911,* p. 17.

25. P. la Hausse (in this collection).

26. Emphasis in original. Southern Rhodesian Government, *Report of the 1911 Native Affairs Commission,* p. 2.

27. *Rhodesia Herald,* 25 August 1916; NAZ, S86, Southern Rhodesian Government, *Report of the Native Affairs Commission Enquiring into the Salisbury Municipal Location, 1930* (Jackson Commission), pp. lx–lxi.

28. NAZ, LG 52/6/1, Location Superintendent to Town Clerk, 1 October 1913.

29. Municipality of Salisbury, Town Clerk's Papers, Harare (MS/TC), 12/7 J1, Location Superintendent to Town Clerk, 19 November 1929.

30. MS/TC, 12/7 J1, South African Breweries to Town Clerk, 15 November 1929.

31. NAZ, LG 52/6/1, Location Superintendent to Town Clerk, 13 November 1913.

32. NAZ, LG 52/6/1, Location Superintendent to Town Clerk, 9 October 1913, 13 October 1913.

33. NAZ, LG 52/6/1, Location Superintendent to Town Clerk, 1 April 1914.

34. Ibid.

35. NAZ, LG 52/6/1, Location Superintendent to Town Clerk, 13 May 1915.

36. NAZ, LG 52/6/1, Town Ranger to Town Clerk, 17 May 1915.

37. NAZ, LG 52/12, Town Clerk to Secretary, Department of the Administrator, 24 November 1916.

38. NAZ, LG 52/12, Secretary, Department of the Administrator to Town Clerk, 28 March 1917.

39. NAZ, LG 52/12, Location Superintendent to Town Clerk, 7 September 1917; Town Clerk to Secretary, Law Department, 26 July 1918.

40. NAZ, LG 52/12, Town Clerk to Location Superintendent, 30 July 1918; Town Clerk to Secretary, Department of the Administrator, 13 August 1918.

41. NAZ, N3/20/2, Chief Native Commissioner to Town Clerk, 4 January 1919.

42. NAZ, LG 52/12, Location Superintendent to Town Clerk, 21 January 1919.

43. NAZ, LG 52/6/3, Location Superintendent reports, 31 December 1920, 31 January 1921.

44. NAZ, LG 52/6/1, Town Ranger to Town Clerk, 21 November 1905.

45. NAZ, D3/5/34/1725, R. v. H. S. Winter, 1 October 1913.

46. NAZ, LG 52/23, Town Clerk to Secretary, Department of the Administrator, 24 February 1923, 21 April 1923; Town Engineer to Acting Town Clerk, 14 June 1923.

47. NAZ, D3/5/21/1032, R. v. Mordecai; LG 52/6/1, Location Superintendent to Town Clerk, 20 February 1912, 3 March 1914.

48. NAZ, N3/5/8, Chief Native Commissioner to Town Clerk, 23 Oc-

tober 1917; Assistant Superintendent, CID to Chief Native Commissioner, 10 December 1918.

49. NAZ, LG 52/23, Town Clerk to Secretary, Department of the Administrator, 21 April 1923.

50. NAZ, LG 52/6/4, Location Superintendent Report, 30 May 1922; S 138/11, CID Report on Hilton Farm, 30 March 1926; Staff Officer, British South African Police to Chief Native Commissioner, 8 December 1928.

51. NAZ, S85, Jackson Commission, evidence of Rusiti and Munyoma (location residents) and Rev. Holmon-Brown (Epworth Mission), pp. 61–62, 73.

52. MS/TC, 12/7/2, Location Superintendent to Town Clerk, 4 June 1936.

53. MS/TC, 12/7/2 J1, Town Clerk to Secretary, Rhodesia-Nyasaland Royal Commission, 6 July 1938.

54. L. Vambe, *From Rhodesia to Zimbabwe* (Pittsburgh: University of Pittsburgh Press, 1976), pp. 185–88.

55. NAZ, D3/5/51/2001, R. v. Wernberg.

56. NAZ, LG 52/6/2, Location Superintendent to Town Clerk, 1 October 1920; Assistant Superintendent Morris, CID to Location Superintendent, 11 October 1920.

57. NAZ, LG 52/6/4, Location Superintendent reports, 31 August 1922, 30 September 1922.

58. MS/TC, 12/7/21, Chief Native Commissioner to Town Clerk, 13 September 1932; Town Clerk to Secretary, Southern Rhodesian Missionary Conference, 21 September 1932.

59. NAZ, S138/22, Detective Sergeant Clark to Assistant Superintendent, CID, Salisbury, 28 October 1929.

CHAPTER FIVE

PROHIBITION AND ILLICIT LIQUOR ON THE WITWATERSRAND, 1902–1932

Julie Baker

INTRODUCTION

THE RAPID DEVELOPMENT of the Witwatersrand, following the discovery of gold in 1886, led to a massive influx of black mine workers and profit seekers (fig. 5.1). Alcohol quickly became a profitable commodity within that booming industrial environment. In his classic study of the rise of the liquor industry in the Transvaal, and the evolution of alcohol regulation on the Witwatersrand, Charles van Onselen showed how the Randlords and their allies successfully lobbied the Kruger government for restrictive measures against African alcohol consumption.[1] While mine owners initially used alcohol to secure and control black workers, by 1895–1896 their attitudes had shifted. Drunkenness, alcohol-related deaths, and "faction fights" among black workers became more prevalent. Many workers continually failed to show up for work; between 15 and 25 percent of black miners were incapacitated by alcohol each day. Because the industry needed to boost production by bringing absent workers back into the mines, it, along with other temperance advocates in the Transvaal, persuaded the Kruger government to implement a policy of "total

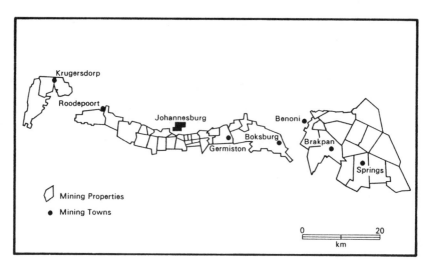

5.1 Witwatersrand mining towns and mine properties, c. 1910

prohibition" for black workers. Subsequently, the liquor laws of 1896 and 1898 prohibited the possession of alcohol by all blacks.

Van Onselen concluded that, in the aftermath of the South African War, the British administration under Sir Alfred Milner dealt a further blow to the liquor trade by strengthening prohibition through Ordinance no. 32 of 1902: "The British administration . . . passed legislation to prevent any further distilling, deported undesirable immigrants, smashed the illicit liquor syndicates, and then rendered the entire black workforce on the Witwatersrand more productive and efficient."[2] However, the evidence for the period from 1902 to 1932 indicates that the 1902 prohibition law certainly did not solve the alcohol problem on the Witwatersrand.

It was one thing to declare prohibition; it was quite another to enforce it. Mine owners continued to experience lost shifts due to drunkenness, smaller but numerous liquor syndicates continued to operate, and mine managers still perceived alcohol as a useful recruiting device. Contemporaries regarded prohibition as a failure. The proliferation of illicit alcohol on and around mine properties helps put in perspective claims by some historians that mine owners and managers exercised "total control" over the mining environment. Workers, liquor dealers, and compound managers all had their reasons for sabotaging prohibition. The end result was a fragmented and ineffectual prohibition amid a thriving liquor trade.

THE FAILURE OF PROHIBITION

The stringent provisions of Ordinance no. 32 of 1902 prohibited the supply of liquor to any black person in and around the urban centers of the Transvaal. But the Milner administration and the mine owners were well aware of the Kruger government's failure to effectively enforce a policy of total prohibition in the 1890s. Mine owners and managers were pragmatists. They certainly wanted to control the consumption of alcohol within the vicinity of mines in order to raise work productivity, but they needed a continuous flow of labor and wanted workers to renew their contracts. Mine managers knew that access to alcohol was an important element of a mine's popularity. In such circumstances, the mining industry opted to control alcohol with alcohol. The government tried to solve the industry's dilemma by allowing mine managers to issue beer to their workers. The 1902 ordinance (and all liquor legislation thereafter) allowed any employer with more than fifty black laborers to brew and distribute low-alcohol beer rations to their employees.

Known as *utshwala, boyaloa,* or *joala* in Zulu, Tswana, or Sotho respectively, sorghum beer issued by the mines could not contain more than 3 percent alcohol. The mines issued the beer free of charge after a worker came off shift on condition that it was consumed on mine property. This offered the mine owners total prohibition outside the mines and controlled consumption on them. Within six months of passage of the 1902 ordinance, at least sixty-six gold mines had licenses to brew sorghum beer. In 1905 beer was included in the first regulated diet scale on the mines as part of the weekly rations. By distributing their own beer, mine management sought to reduce the appeal of illicit stronger drinks, secure a more sober and disciplined workforce, and attract labor to the mines.

Management also believed that sorghum beer possessed antiscorbutic properties that would improve the diet of the workforce and lead to greater work productivity. The medical officer of health for the Witwatersrand Native Labour Association (WNLA), Dr. George Turner, argued: "I am perfectly convinced, although I cannot prove it scientifically, that Kaffir Beer is a nourishing thing. It is as good as a meal to me. Eggs and milk are nothing compared to the value of Kaffir beer as a pick me up."[3] Turner's effective lobbying on behalf of the mining industry ensured continued government support for the brewing of beer on the mines. Other experts agreed with Turner, and the nutritional value of the beer ration became accepted wisdom in the mining industry.

The government and the industry paid little attention to those who claimed that the beer had few, if any, positive dietary qualities. In 1907 J. M. Orpen, an expert on the diet of black laborers, raised several objections to its use and supported instead the distribution of a widely used and nonintoxicating sour beverage known as *leting* or *marewu*.[4] The District Medical Officer of Health for the Witwatersrand had an equally negative view of "alcohol as a food." He questioned the notion that the beer was antiscorbutic, when scurvy was so prevalent on the mines. Early scientific studies noted that an improvement in the mine diet would have produced even better results against scurvy.[5]

During the 1920s and 1930s more thorough scientific testing of sorghum beer continued to call its dietary value into question.[6] The mining industry preferred to ignore those studies as well as the results of several prominent international studies that concluded that even moderate quantities of alcohol (one quart of beer) could have a deleterious effect on the human body. These studies maintained that alcohol consumption could impair coordination, nervous stability, and the ability to think clearly and rapidly. Alcohol "tots" could lead to industrial wastage through the cycle of accidents, damaged machinery, lost shifts, ill health, and death. The studies emphasized the importance of replacing alcoholic stimulants with other nourishing beverages. The nutritive value of those substitutes further helped reduce the craving for alcohol. Some mine doctors maintained that the majority of black workers drank because their system craved a stimulant after severe physical exertion, not necessarily because they had a preference for liquor. As long as their diet failed to provide the necessary substitutes, workers would continue to crave alcohol.[7]

Irrespective of any negative arguments against the beer ration, its distribution suited the needs of the industry. The amount issued varied from mine to mine. Some mines allotted one gallon per worker per month while others averaged four gallons per month, distributed two or three times a week. Most mines brewed between 2,000 and 5,000 gallons each month. In May 1913 the sixty-four member mines of the Chamber of Mines, employing 181,000 workers, brewed a total of 258,000 gallons of beer. By 1926 the average beer issue approximated eight and a half quarts per worker per month.[8] Contrary to industry expectations, however, mine beer did not serve as an effective substitute for stronger alcoholic beverages in a climate of prohibition. Workers were rarely placated by mine beer and seemed able to obtain or manufacture stronger alcoholic beverages almost at will.

Although by law mine beer was supposed to contain less than 3 percent alcohol, in practice, the alcohol content varied considerably and often exceeded the legal limit. Workers easily adulterated and fortified the weak beer through storage and additives that prolonged fermentation. By adulterating the brew in various ways they were able to hasten the process. Workers produced a variety of other strong alcoholic beverages which acquired names like "kill me quick." A concoction like *qedeviki* or *motopa* resembled the traditional, nonalcoholic drink *marewu* and was extremely difficult to detect. Other drinks— such as *gwebu* and "Palestine Bee Wine"—could be produced at great speed with yeast and sugar. One extremely popular drink known as *skokian* or *khali* contained water, golden syrup, and a root (known as *ntsema*). The alcohol content of *skokian* was actually quite low but the root had narcotic properties. The Rand compounds provided a major market for purveyors of golden syrup (a mixture of molasses, invert sugar, and corn syrup). Between 1910 and 1913, 45 million pounds (weight) of syrup were sold in the Transvaal, much of it to make *skokian*. Piles of empty syrup tins often littered the mine compounds and their environs.[9]

Workers usually found it easier to obtain these and other drinks from illicit liquor brewers and traders who did not live on the mine properties. The illicit drinks often contained more dangerous additives such as methylated spirits, patent medicines, or calcium carbide. Dealers obtained methylated alcohol from grocers or pharmacies and mixed it with cheap Cape brandy for a tidy profit.[10] In 1903 the manager of the New Unified Main Reef Gold Mine found 1,020 empty cologne bottles that had been sold to the workers by a Reef storekeeper. Analysis revealed a "pernicious looking liquid" of 66 percent proof.[11] The legislation always seemed to be trying to catch up with the appearance of new drinks. As soon as one was prohibited, another appeared.

The failure of prohibition became evident to the mine owners, who continued to complain about loss of shifts due to drunkenness. A report in 1910 found that on most gold mines, the period from Saturday to Tuesday was plagued by absenteeism. The percentage of workers incapacitated by alcohol ranged from 1 to 15 percent per day—as many as 500 workers on a single mine.[12] In the five years between 1913 and 1917 the mines lost a total of 132,360 shifts through drunkenness—an average of 2,206 per month or 1.35 percent of the workers employed.[13] In 1926 the Transvaal Mine Medical Officers' Association described its perception of the subversive effect of alcohol on labor productivity: "[The Association] views seriously the amount of alcoholic excess amongst Mine Natives. This has resulted in many cases of assaults, and in the loss of shifts, with serious effects on the work of the mines."[14]

Contemporaries repeatedly pointed to the failure of prohibition in curbing alcohol consumption on the mines. According to the report of the 1908 Transvaal Liquor Commission, prohibition was undermined by an enormous and continuous illicit trade in liquor. The commission concluded that "unless . . . some definite method of improving the administration of the law . . . can be discovered, it must be admitted that a large illicit trade is, in practice, a necessary concomitant of the attempt to enforce prohibition upon large masses of natives assembled together for industrial purposes."[15] Between 1903 and 1909 there were 55,856 alcohol-related convictions in the Transvaal; the vast majority were on the Witwatersrand.[16] In the Johannesburg district, liquor offenses accounted for almost a quarter of all convictions among blacks in 1917. Some argued that the number of people actually convicted represented no more than a third of those who made their living from the illicit traffic.[17]

In 1918 the government explicitly recognized that its policy of prohibition had failed when it appointed a select committee to examine the operation of the liquor laws. The committee pointed to the existence of a vast liquor trade whose policing was a major drain on the public purse:

> The state of affairs existing on the Witwatersrand, as disclosed by the evidence, cannot be described as otherwise than appalling. . . . No less than 168,521 persons were convicted for contraventions of the Liquor Laws on the Witwatersrand and in Pretoria during the years 1903–1917. . . . The direct cost to the state in connection with the enforcement of the Transvaal Liquor Laws for the last 16 years must have run into millions of pounds sterling.[18]

Some years later, the 1926 Select Committee on the proposed new liquor bill issued an equally negative appraisal of prohibition: "the policy of total prohibition inaugurated by the Ordinance of 1902 has to a large extent broken down. . . . It is an absolute failure."[19] The 1930–1932 Native Economic Commission also pronounced prohibition a failure that had "brought in its train many evils."[20]

BLACK WORKERS, POOR WHITES, AND REEF TRADERS

The fundamental explanation for the failure of prohibition was the determination of black workers to drink and the willingness of a sizable class of men and women to risk fines and jail to obtain the considerable profits that participation in the alcohol traffic could bring. Excessive alcohol consumption among black workers was in part a by-product of industrial boredom and stress. The migrant labor system, an impersonal compound life, rapid and disorganized urbanization, the appalling conditions in the locations, an unjust, racially stratified social system, and the unhealthy and dangerous mining environment, all fostered escapist drinking. Just as important, however, was the role of alcohol in the formation of a drinking culture outside the comprehension or control of mine management. Few of the migrants who came to the mines were abstainers and some, such as the Mozambicans, had a long history of liquor consumption.[21] Alcohol was a necessary accompaniment of sociability, reinforcing kinship and other networks and helping to insert the worker into the social networks of the compound and the locations.[22]

As black mine workers asserted their desire to drink without sanction, so the mine compounds provided a large and thriving market for the purveyors of illicit liquor. At the industry level, the mine owners had lobbied vigorously for prohibition and regarded the illicit liquor trade with dismay. They constantly urged tighter controls, more police raids, and harsher penalties. But the activities of poor whites, impoverished blacks, avaricious traders, and corrupt medical practitioners constantly undermined the ability of the state to enforce prohibition. A basic contradiction, and flaw, in the liquor legislation was its attempt to bar blacks but not whites from using alcohol. That opened the door for extensive involvement in the illicit liquor trade by poor whites.

In the aftermath of the South African War (1899–1902), thousands of "poor whites" flocked to the Rand. Finding it difficult to compete for jobs with both skilled white tradesmen and unskilled, poorly-paid blacks, they congregated in industrial slumyards (fig. 5.2).[23] In search of a livelihood, many turned to illicit liquor dealing with adjacent mine compounds. Between 1903 and 1917, the courts convicted 8,214 white men and women for trading in liquor. Between 1917 and 1922 another 1,414 whites were convicted.[24] Even the threat of a jail sentence failed to deter the liquor dealers. Most employed blacks as go-betweens and paid them for any time spent in jail. In association with their clients, the dealers used a variety of ingenious methods to circumvent the law. Illicit liquor was brought into the compounds through broken windows, through the latrines, or simply thrown over the walls. Outdoor lighting was frequently broken so that liquor could be brought into the compounds under cover of darkness.[25] In many compounds African liquor syndicates operated in associaton with the dealers. They paid off clerks, police, and even compound managers. By 1915 newspapers depicted the South African Police Department as "powerless" in its fight against liquor and dubbed the detectives "Weary Willies."[26]

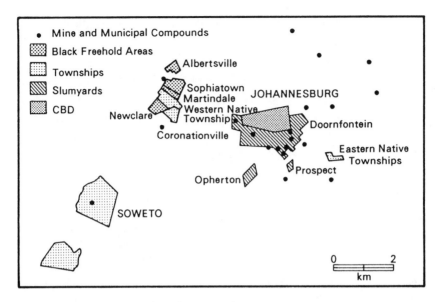

Legend:
- ● Mine and Municipal Compounds
- ▓ Black Freehold Areas
- ▢ Townships
- ▨ Slumyards
- ▦ CBD

Albertsville
Sophiatown
Martindale
JOHANNESBURG
Newclare
Western Native Township
Coronationville
Doornfontein
Eastern Native Townships
Ophernton
Prospect
SOWETO

0 ————— 2
km

5.2 Johannesburg's slumyards and compounds

White dealers in illicit liquor took advantage of several loopholes in the legislation. It was lawful, for example, for farmers to manufacture liquor for their own use. When challenged in court, some dealers used this clause to escape prosecution. For its part, the mining industry had always opposed the clause: "there are hardly any Boer Farmers who are likely to take advantage of it and in the past the only persons who have been known to have availed themselves of this privilege have been some of the illicit liquor dealers."[27] Under another clause, individuals could sell small quantities of alcohol to blacks for medicinal purposes. One patent medicine, known as "witte dulcis," contained 79 percent alcohol.[28] Unscrupulous doctors and pharmacists also took advantage of the clause. In 1924 a Benoni doctor, William Glucksman, and a pharmacist, M. S. Katzen, were tried for establishing a profitable medical partnership based on dispensing "medicinal" liquor. Over a six-month period, Glucksman issued more than 500 prescriptions for 800 bottles of assorted alcohol. Katzen, who handled the prescriptions, received more alcohol from Johannesburg's wholesale liquor merchants than the two nearest bottle stores. In 1926 the Transvaal Medical Council found Glucksman guilty of "infamous conduct" and removed his name from the Register of Medical Practitioners.[29]

The control of the illicit liquor trade was inconceivable without the application of more fundamental social remedies. In the absence of a solution to the urban poor-white problem, prohibition was basically unworkable. But whites were not the only suppliers of illicit alcohol. Blacks in overcrowded municipal and mine locations thrived on profits from illicit beer sales. Women residents, in particular, found themselves marginalized in the urban labor market and turned to illicit liquor production as a means of survival.[30]

Municipal regulations demanded that all black migrant workers not housed on the premises of their employers had to reside in designated areas known as locations. Many of the mines established their own locations to accommodate the small percentage of black miners who were accompanied by their families. By 1904 there were at least 108 locations in the Transvaal; the mining companies controlled about sixty-one of them. Because they were meant as "temporary" accommodation for migrant labor, locations did not have to comply with municipal housing regulations. Consequently, most were slums. Yet, the municipalities and mining companies charged rent. Much of the rent was paid from the proceeds of illegal beer and liquor selling. That prompted the municipalities to tolerate a certain amount of "crime." Black female residents in the locations gained considerable notoriety as the suppliers of liquor to workers in adjacent mining compounds. As one Native Affairs official pointed out, "locations along the Reef are a great source of revenue to their respective municipalities and those concerned in the supervision do not worry too much about the manufacturing and consumption of liquor for fear of driving away revenue."[31]

After the First World War, as the black housing crisis in Johannesburg became more acute, the town council began to investigate the possibility of introducing municipal beerhalls in order to raise more revenue. A similar system had been in operation since 1909 in Durban, where the municipality had a profitable legal monopoly on the sale of sorghum beer. In 1921 one Johannesburg municipal councillor argued that £400,000 was needed to provide basic housing for 140,000 African residents: "(White) ratepayers should insist on the Government . . . empowering the Municipality to brew and distribute Kaffir Beer. The proceeds could be earmarked exclusively for Native development."[32] The majority of Native Affairs Department inspectors, however, viewed the system as contrary to the welfare of black workers, though it had powerful supporters. The Medical Officer of Health for Johannesburg, Dr. Charles Porter, argued that the scheme was proper and desirable.[33] In 1918 the Select Committee on the Working of the Native Liquor Laws, as well as the Chamber of Mines added their weight. The Natives (Urban Areas) Act of 1923 and the 1928 Liquor Bill (Act no. 30 of 1928) granted municipalities the right to establish beerhalls, though it was some years before the first beerhalls appeared on the Rand.[34]

Throughout this period, the policing of the illegal alcohol trade was made more difficult by the countervailing interests of numerous reef traders. Mine storekeepers and other traders supplied most of the key ingredients—golden syrup, yeast cakes, and corn malt—used in the manufacture of alcoholic beverages. The traders represented a political lobby of some power and influence, and the government moved against them only during periods of unrest. In January 1914, for example, when martial law was proclaimed during a strike on the Rand, all compound inspectors and mine managers were given the power to prohibit the entry of golden syrup and pearl barley into the compounds.[35] The Transvaal Traders Association and the Chamber of Commerce launched a counter attack over the next two years to regain the highly profitable golden syrup trade. The lobby groups argued that the state had no right to prohibit a legitimate trade and forced the government to rescind the order in March 1916.[36]

WET AND DRY COMPOUNDS

The effectiveness of prohibition was also seriously compromised by contradictory labor policies on the mines themselves. At the group level, mine owners lobbied vigorously for total prohibition. However, there is sufficient evidence to argue that, during the day-to-day operation of a mine, individual managers actively connived to undermine prohibition. A basic task of the mine manager was to maintain a full complement of workers. The managers knew that the popularity of a mine among black workers was affected by its alcohol policy. Competition for labor made mine and compound managers less than determined to curtail illicit activities.

For much of the period of prohibition, the Rand gold mines were faced with perennial labor shortages and competed fiercely with one another to obtain labor. That competition eased somewhat after 1912 with the formation of the Native Recruiting Corporation. But black migrants remained extremely sensitive to working and living conditions and showed distinct preferences for certain mines. As the twentieth century progressed, a growing proportion of the mine workforce were "voluntaries" (migrants who made their own way to the Rand and once there shopped around for the best employment conditions).[37] Most migrants were aware how closely a mine monitored and controlled leisure activity, including drinking and access to alcohol. "Wet" mines (where prohibition was not enforced) were infinitely preferable to "dry" ones. Competition for labor made compound managers loath to acquire the reputation of running a dry compound.

Mine labor recruiters had always been aware of the connection between the availability of alcohol and the success of their recruiting efforts. They argued that workers accustomed to drinking at home were unlikely to shun alcohol while on the Witwatersrand:

> A properly controlled supply of liquor to these natives [Mozambicans] would lead to an increased supply coming forward. This stands to reason when one considers the fact that these natives have unrestricted access to any liquor in their own country, where undoubtedly it demoralizes them, whereas if properly controlled here in the compounds a moderate supply of good liquor would . . . prove a great inducement to the average East Coast Boy.[38]

Consequently, compound managers tended to be lenient with workers found in possession of alcohol. Few were actually prosecuted for alcohol-related offenses on the mines. Managers preferred to destroy the liquor rather than lay charges. Female residents of mine locations were often allowed to draw beer rations alongside their husbands. The managers argued that if that privilege was withdrawn, the women would simply revert to brewing their own illicit beer. On weekends many visitors to the mine shared in the beer ration.[39] Mines belonging to the Johannesburg Consolidated Investment Group were particularly notorious for their relaxed attitude toward alcohol. New Primrose, Government Areas, Witwatersrand, New Rietfontein Estates, and Van Ryn Deep mines were all harshly criticized in 1914 for the proliferation of illicit liquor on their properties. One observer described those mines as "swimming in liquor," while the compound manager at New Rietfontein was accused of profiteering by selling liquor to his own workers.[40]

The daunting task of supervising the drinking practices of thousands of workers fell to the compound managers and mine police. The duties of the compound managers were often too onerous for them to devote much time to curtailing all illicit liquor activity. Yet the compounds were certainly easier to police than slumyards and townships, and a vigilant compound manager ought to have been able to exercise considerable control over on-mine drinking. As the Native Grievances Inquiry pointed out in 1914, "A compound manager who, personally and by his compound police exercises proper supervision over his compound, can almost entirely prevent the use of this stuff within its walls and many of them do so."[41] But compound managers were not there simply to control for alcohol. They were also supposed to attract and keep labor on the mine.

Mine management could have full labor complements or a sober workforce, but not both. The Native Grievances Inquiry highlighted the dilemma:

> The difficulty is that this action [enforcing prohibition] is necessarily taken at the expense of a certain amount of popularity among the natives, and that this is a point upon which compound managers are naturally very sensitive, since their living largely depends upon the number of natives whom they can attract to their compounds. As a result there is a certain amount of underhand competition going on to make certain compounds attractive by winking at the manufacture and consumption of liquor.[42]

Officials from the Native Affairs Department routinely observed that certain compound managers countenanced or at least did not seem interested in preventing the illicit alcohol traffic. The managers were willing to curtail brewing in and around their compounds only if abolition was uniformly enforced across the Reef. Since it was not, illicit liquor had to be tolerated on mine property for fear of driving labor to a less vigilant competitor.

Compound managers and state officials regularly clashed over the issue of illicit liquor control. Municipal police, concerned about the threat posed to social order, constantly demanded that mine management pay more attention to the alcohol that flowed in and around mine properties. Although the policing of compounds was usually the preserve of mine employees, the adjacent municipal police had the authority to raid compounds. When they did so, they invariably uncovered large caches of illicit liquor. During one such raid at Spes Bona Mine in March 1914, the police destroyed over 400 gallons of intoxicating liquid and found twenty-two empty brandy bottles in the possession of a compound policeman. Liquor brewed at Spes Bona was also sold at other compounds.[43] An indication of the sheer volume of liquor confiscated can be gained from a partial list of raids conducted by police between 1911 and 1921 (table 5.1).[44]

The police maintained that such enormous quantities of liquor could not have been brewed without the knowledge or consent of the compound managers:

> There is no doubt that the presence of large quantities of illicit liquor was well known all along the Reef and was openly winked at by the mine authorities for the reason that it was thought that a large supply of beer would make the compounds popular and would prevent the white illicit trader from introducing more harmful liquor.[45]

One police inspector recommended that the authorities transform compounds into virtual prisons. He wanted a high barbed wire fence around each compound, powerful lights, and a guard at all times. Other members of the police force recommended the establishment of penal colonies for all those convicted under the liquor legislation.[46]

Under pressure from the police department, the Department of Native Affairs introduced measures to curtail illicit liquor production and consumption. In 1914 it issued a circular warning all compound managers that they would be held strictly responsible for liquor found in the compounds. Compound managers soon learned that they could

Table 5.1: Liquor raids on mine compounds, 1911–1921

Date		Gold Mine or Location	Liquor Found (Gallons)	
March	1911	Driefontein Deep (Location)	5250	beer
			50	khali
2 July	1911	Brakpan (Location)	1500	beer/khali
3 Sept.	1911	Wit Deep (Location)	1500	beer
8 Oct.	1911	E.R.P.M. (Location)	3000	beer
19 Oct.	1911	Cinderella (Location)	650	beer
9 Nov.	1911	Ginsberg (Location)	2000	beer
10 Dec.	1913	Gov't. Areas State Mine	400	liquor
October	1914	Central Comet (Location)	200	khali
			150	beer
Jan.	1915	Geduld Compound	60	khali
August	1920	Crown Mines (Location)	568	beer
August	1920	Simmer East Compound	3000	beer
August	1921	Simmer East Compound	3280	beer

Source: Various[44]

expect several warnings before anything was done. Police raided the Modder West Gold Mine in January 1920, for example, and destroyed 350 gallons of beer and *skokian*. They warned the compound manager to be more vigilant. A month later he received a similar warning. Another raid in October 1920 netted a further 400 gallons of illicit liquor. At the end of the month the police found still more liquor. The Native Affairs Department wanted to withdraw the compound manager's license but that was not possible without a full magisterial enquiry. He received yet another warning instead.[47]

Mine managers who ran wet compounds still faced a major dilemma since a total absence of control raised absentee rates and reduced worker productivity. Mine records also indicate a strong correlation between alcohol and accidents underground. Work with explosives, machinery, and trucks left little room for error. The underground environment of deep-level mining was hazardous enough without the additional complication of intoxication. The annual reports of the Government Mining Engineer regularly carried gruesome details of underground accidents involving inebriated workers.[48] Nor were alcohol-related accidents restricted to working hours. Intoxicated workers frequently fell off bunks onto concrete floors and seriously injured themselves. Mine violence between groups of workers also tended to be more common where alcohol flowed.[49]

Under prohibition, the alcohol consumed by mine workers was often highly intoxicating and sometimes extremely dangerous. Traditional sorghum beer took longer to make and gave off a distinctive strong odor that deterred many from brewing it illegally.[50] Spirits and home concoctions were faster to make, often odorless, and harder to detect. Most of the illegal liquor was consumed quickly and in large quantity for fear of discovery. In those conditions, black miners became easy targets for unscrupulous dealers who served up dangerous brews containing a variety of unknown and poisonous substances—concoctions "coloured by additions of copper and the smell masked with tobacco juice."[51]

Management clearly believed that the beer ration was a powerful aid to maintaining sobriety and productivity. During the proceedings of the Mining Regulations Commission (1907–1910), mining companies were asked directly whether their beer had any ill effects on the health or general efficiency of their black workforce. Of fifty-nine respondents, only one answered in the affirmative. The rest claimed that there were no ill effects and even that the beer was "very beneficial" to the health of workers.[52] The reality was somewhat different. Prolonged storage of mine-brewed sorghum beer led to the formation of fusel oil. Classed as a brain and nerve poison, its side effects were easily confused with those of excessive drinking.[53] Workers hiding their beer rations to raise the alcohol content were in real danger of fusel oil poisoning.

Mine beer was often manufactured and consumed in very unhygienic circumstances. Some mines erected separate beer brewing huts of corrugated iron. The huts were filthy and neither they nor the receptacles were flyproof. The water used in the brewing process was often impure, and the beer was usually strained by hand. Investigations in 1916 revealed that the companies used whatever containers they had at their disposal. Paraffin tins, iron and steel drums, galvanized iron vessels, and wooden vats and barrels were all used. The Medical Officer of Health in Johannesburg found traces of metallic zinc in the iron containers sufficient to produce chronic zinc poisoning. Tins with traces of carbide and petrol were commonly used in the cooling process, further endangering the health of the consumers.[54] Mine managers either did not know or did not care. The beer ration may well have helped to draw labor to the mines and to curb the worst excesses of the illicit liquor trade, but it did so at the expense of the health of black miners.

CONCLUSION

The failure of prohibition on the Witwatersrand was a result of complex and contradictory social forces. The racist discourse of the early twentieth century justified prohibition for blacks but not whites, claiming that employers and white society generally had to be protected from the evils of black excess. At the same time, the major employers of black labor—the Witwatersrand gold mines—needed alcohol. Mine management was aware that access to some alcohol would make mine life more bearable, discourage the illicit liquor traffic around the mines, and provide an important advantage in a highly competitive labor market. The mine owners therefore supported the distribution of sorghum beer to all mine employees. They did this aware that alcoholic consumption might work against the growth of a healthy, stable, and productive workforce. By controlling the size and alcohol content of the beer ration, the mines sought to resolve this contradiction.

In the sense that black mine workers continued to drink, and to drink often and a great deal, the attempt to impose partial alcohol prohibition failed. During the first three decades of this century, men and women of substance, both black and white, officials and nonofficials, testified repeatedly to the failure of efforts to curb the alcohol trade and drinking. That failure, they argued, encouraged the consumption of more potent and dangerous drinks, it bred crime, and it nurtured an ominous disrespect for the rule of law.

The entire strategy of prohibition was doomed from the start. In practice it was impossible to create "black" islands of prohibition surrounded by "white" pools of unrestricted liquor. Partial prohibition left the way open for segments of the population to engage in a lucrative illicit liquor trade. Black workers fiercely resisted the attempts to control their drinking, devising many ingenious and covert ways to circumvent the controls of capital and state. Opinion, as well as practice, was divided within the ranks of mine owners and managers. Officially committed to controlling alcohol availability and consumption, those who actually ran the compounds were caught in a bind. The tighter the controls over alcohol, the greater the likelihood that a mine would suffer labor shortages. The looser the controls, the greater the chance of absenteeism, workplace inebriation, and mine accidents. Compound managers played a delicate balancing game with varying degrees of success. It is clear, however, that there were powerful pragmatic forces within the mining industry subverting prohibition.

NOTES

1. C. van Onselen, "Randlords and Rotgut 1886–1903," in *Studies in the Social and Economic History of the Witwatersrand* (London: Longman, 1982), 1:96.

2. Transvaal Archives Depot, Pretoria (TAD), Government Native Labour Bureau (GNLB), vol. 181, file 815/14/D54, "List of Licences to Brew Kaffir Beer," 1903; Ordinance no. 32 of 1902 (assented to 27 October 1902), Regulations outlined in Government Notice no. 710 of 1902.

3. TAD, Secretary for Native Affairs (SNA), vol. 379, file 3241/1907, Dr. George A. Turner, Statement on Alcohol prepared for the Mining Regulations Commission, 1907.

4. TAD, Governor General (Gov.), vol. 1092, file 50/56/07, J. M. Orpen, "Native Labourers and Diet," and "Natives and Beer," in *Natal Mercury*, 25 and 27 July 1907; Gov., vol. 1151, file 50/13/08, J. M. Orpen to President, S.A. Federal Medical Congress, Pretoria, 8 October 1907.

5. TAD, Gov., vol. 1151, file 50/13/08 and SNA, vol. 395, file 524/1908, Dr. Charles Lane Sansom, District Medical Officer of Health for the Witwatersrand, to Director of Native Labour, 11 February 1908; SNA, vol. 780,

Ethel M. Doidge, "The Flora of Certain Kaffir Beers 'Leting' and 'Joala,' " Transvaal Department of Agriculture, Agricultural Science Bulletin no. 5, 1910.

6. E. M. Delf, "Studies in Experimental Scurvy—With Special Reference to the Antiscorbutic Properties of Some South African Food-Stuffs," *South African Institute for Medical Research Publication* 2/14 (1921); F. W. Fox and W. Stone, "The Anti-Scorbutic Value of Kaffir Beer," *South African Journal of Medical Science* 3 (1938); F. W. Fox and L. F. Levy, "The Antiscorbutic Value of Some South African Foodstuffs as Measured by their Indophenol Reducing Power," *South African Medical Journal* 9 (1935).

7. Central Archives Depot, Pretoria (CAD), Mines and Works (MNW), vol. 324, file 1307/16, Memorandum by Dr. A. J. Orenstein, Superintendent of Sanitation, Rand Mines to Safety First Committee, Rand Mutual Assurance Co., 12 December 1914.

8. TAD, GNLB, vol. 294, file 238/18/D54, List of "Mines Authorized to Issue Kaffir Beer to their Employees"; Chamber of Mines Statistics, "Kaffir Beer Brewed and Drunkenness Amongst Native Labourers"; GNLB, vol. 181, file 815/14/D54, Native Affairs Department, Circular Minute "A"20/17, "Monthly Consumption of Beer," 11 December 1917; Union of South Africa, (S.C. 7–'26), "Report of the Select Committee on the Liquor Bill," Minutes of Evidence, p. 289.

9. TAD, GNLB, vol. 272, file 127/17/D54, Inspector, Native Affairs Department (NAD) Germiston West to Director of Native Labour, 16 March 1917; GNLB, vol. 136, file 2756/13/54, NAD to all Mine and Compound Managers, 27 January 1914; South African Police, Johannesburg to Director of Native Labour, 11 December 1922; GNLB, vol. 367, file 62/26/54, Magistrate, Kimberley to Director of Native Labour, 9 February 1926; GNLB, vol. 137, file 2756/13/54, "Memorandum on Cali or Skokian," n.d.; U.G. 37–'14, "Report of the Native Grievances Inquiry 1913–1914," pars. 515, 516, 524. *Skokian* was declared an intoxicating substance by Proclamations 19 and 60 of 1906; see GNLB, vol. 135, file 2756/13/4, H. Payne, Inspector, NAD Germiston to Director of Native Labour, 28 March 1916.

10. CAD, MNW, vol. 671, file 2338/23, H. C. Bredell for Commissioner, South African Police to Secretary for Justice, Pretoria, 4 September 1916. The use of methylated alcohol was restricted under Transvaal Ordinance no. 8 of 1906, sec. 14.

11. TAD, SNA, vol. 176, file 2437/1903, Report by Dr. Charles L. Sansom, District Medical Officer of Health for the Witwatersrand, September 1903.

12. *Transvaal Mining Regulations Commission, Final Report, vol. 1,* 1910, p. 83.

13. TAD, GNLB, vol. 294, file 238/18/D54, Transvaal Chamber of Mines, Drunkenness amongst Native Labourers for May 1913 and May 1917, and Shifts Lost through Drunkenness, 1913–1917.

14. TAD, GNLB, vol. 137, file 2756/13/54, Executive Committee of the Transvaal Mine Medical Officers' Association to Acting Director of Native Labour, 26 June 1926.

15. TAD, TKP, vol. 183, Transvaal Report of the Liquor Commission 1908, Pretoria, 1910, Chap. 2, par. 2.

16. Ibid., Annexure no. 9, Contraventions of Transvaal Ordinance no. 32 of 1902, 1 July 1903–30 June 1909.

17. TAD, GNLB, vol. 177, file 701/14/D243, Convictions in the Transvaal, 1912–1913; GNLB, vol. 294, file 238/18/D54, "Natives Discharged from Gaol and Sent to Johannesburg Pass Office and Natives Who Were Convicted in Johannesburg of Being Drunk, 1917"; *Transvaal Mining Regulations Commission, Final Report, vol. 1,* 1910, p. 79

18. Union of South Africa (S.C. 2–'18), "Report of the Select Committee on Working of Transvaal Liquor Laws" (Cape Town, 1918), pp. ix–x.

19. S.C. 7–'26, "Select Committee on the Liquor Bill," pp. 442–45.

20. Union of South Africa (U.G. 22–'32), "Report of the Native Economic Commission 1930–1932," pars. 756–58.

21. P. Harries, "Labour Migration from Mozambique to South Africa," (Ph.D. diss., University of London, 1983).

22. For a more detailed discussion of mine drinking culture see D. Moodie (this collection).

23. On the poor white influx see C. van Onselen, "The Main Reef Road into the Working Class," in *Studies in the Social and Economic History of the Witwatersrand* (London: Longman, 1982), 2:111–70.

24. S.C. 2–'18, "Select Committee on Transvaal Liquor Laws," p. x; TAD, Department of Justice (JUS), vol. 368, file 3153/23, Convictions for Sale of Liquor to Natives in the Magisterial Districts of the Witwatersrand During 1922 and Previous Five Years, 1923.

25. TAD, GNLB, vol. 195, file 1356/14/D97, Superintending Engineer, East Rand Proprietary Mine (ERPM) to E. C. Meyer, General Manager, ERPM, 21 August 1914; GNLB, vol. 135, file 2576/13/54, H. Payne, Inspector, NAD Germiston, to Director of Native Labour, 28 March 1916.

26. "Liquor Trade with Natives: Police Powerless," *Rand Daily Mail,* 5 October 1915.

27. Barlow Rand Archives, Johannesburg (BRA), H.E., vol. 132, p. 37, Samuel Evans to Wernher, Beit & Co., 3 November 1902.

28. TAD, Law Department (LD), vol. 986, file AG285/05, Public Prosecutor to Resident Magistrate, Pretoria, 13 November 1908.

29. TAD, JUS, vol. 395, file 3/20/25, Report by Magistrate and Chairman, Benoni Liquor Licensing Court, December 1924.

30. P. Bonner, "'Desirable or Undesirable Sotho Women?' Liquor, Prostitution and the Migration of Sotho Women to the Rand, 1920–1945" (Paper presented at African Studies Institute, University of Witwatersrand, Johannesburg, 1988).

31. TAD, GNLB, vol. 40, file 515/12/D102, Inspector, NAD Boksburg to Director of Native Labour, 12 December 1914.

32. G. Kretzchmar, addressing Johannesburg Federation of Ratepayers' Association, 4 April 1921, as quoted in *Rand Daily Mail,* 5 April 1921.

33. TAD, GNLB, vol. 272, file 127/17/D54, Replies to Circular "A"5/17, 27 February 1917; GNLB, vol. 293, file 191/18/103, Dr. Charles Porter to Parks and Estates Committee, Johannesburg, 9 September 1924.

34. TAD, MNW, vol. 341, file 2315/16, E. A. Wallers, President, Transvaal Chamber of Mines, Address at Annual Meeting, 25 March 1918; GNLB, vol. 137, file 2756/13/54, Acting Director of Native Labour addressing meeting of the Transvaal Mine Medical Officers' Association, 15 July 1926.

35. TAD, GNLB, vol. 136, file 2756/13/54, S. M. Pritchard, Director of Native Labour, to all Inspectors, 7 January 1914, 27 January 1914. For an extended discussion of the *"khali* crisis" see D. Moodie (in this collection).

36. TAD, GNLB, vol. 294, file 238/18/D54, H. S. Cooke, Acting Director of Native Labour to Inspectors, 24 March 1916.

37. A. Jeeves, *Migrant Labour in South Africa's Mining Economy* (Montreal and Kingston: McGill-Queen's Press, 1985).

38. TAD, SNA, vol. 52, file 1866/02; Gov., vol. 119, file 474/02, Official of the Native Labour Association to C. Vincent, 28 August 1902, as quoted by Commissioner for Native Affairs, 5 September 1902.

39. TAD, GNLB, vol. 181, file 815/14/54, Inspector, NAD Boksburg to Director of Native Labour, 11 October 1915.

40. TAD, GNLB, vol. 198, file 1504/14/D80, Inspector, NAD Germiston West to Director of Native Labour, 21 October 1914; B. B. Betts, Sub-Inspector, SAP Germiston to District Inspector, SAP Boksburg, 2 October 1914; Inspector, NAD Benoni East to Director of Native Labour, 6 October 1914; Inspector, NAD Benoni West to Director of Native Labour, 8 October 1914.

41. U.G. 37–'14, "Native Grievances Inquiry," par. 517.

42. Ibid.

43. TAD, GNLB, vol. 136, file 2756/13/54, B. B. Betts to District Commandant, SAP Boksburg, 10 December 1913; Compound Manager, New Goch G.M. to Inspector, NAD Johannesburg East, 9 March 1914; Director of Native Labour to Management, New Spes Bona, 24 March 1914.

44. TAD, GNLB, vol. 38, file 196/1912, Memorandum in Regard to Illicit Liquor amongst the Labourers on the Reef, 20 December 1911; Memo on Kaffir Beer, Boksburg District, 12 December 1911; GNLB, vol. 136, file 2756/13/54, B. B. Betts to District Commandant, SAP Boksburg, 10 December 1913; Inspector, NAD Benoni East to Director of Native Labour, 10 December 1913; Inspector, SAP Boksburg to General Manager, ERPM, 16 October 1914; W. C. Loftus, Sub-Inspector, SAP Benoni to District Commandant, SAP Boksburg, 18 January 1915; GNLB, vol. 137, file 2756/13/54, Memorandum on "Kaffir Beer," n.d.; "Raid on a Mine Compound," *The Star,* 29 August 1921; "Compound after a Raid: Interrupted Orgy at the Simmer East," *The Star,* 30 August 1921; "Detectives' Clever Ruse," *Rand Daily Mail,* 30 August 1921.

45. TAD, GNLB, vol. 38, file 196/1912, Memorandum in Regard to Illicit Liquor amongst Mine Labourers on the Reef, 20 December 1911.

46. TAD, GNLB, vol. 136, file 2756/13/54, Memorandum on Better Supervision of Native Compounds and Locations along the Reef for the Purpose of Checking Illicit Liquor Dealers, n.d.

47. TAD, GNLB, vol. 197, file 1440/14/48, Inspector, NAD Benoni to Director of Native Labour, 11 February 1920; A. S. Brown, Head Constable, SAP, to Sub-Inspector, SAP Benoni, 17 October 1920; Director of Native Labour to Inspector, NAD Benoni, 21 October 1920; H. Hamel, Mining Commissioner, to General Manager, Modder West Gold Mining Co., 27 October 1920; Inspector, NAD Benoni East to Mining Commissioner Boksburg, 28 October 1920.

48. TAD, TKP, vol. 218, Transvaal Mines Department: Yearly Report of the Government Mining Engineer, 1903, table 22a.

49. TAD, GNLB, vol. 88, file 18/1913, Director of Native Labour to Portuguese Curator, Johannesburg, 21 November 1913; GNLB, vol. 267, file 628/15/12, part 3, Director of Native Labour to Dr. Orenstein, 19 December 1919, and to Public Prosecutor, 22 December 1919; Director of Native Labour to all Inspectors, 22 December 1919; Inspector, Western District Johannesburg to Director of Native Labour, 21 January 1920.

50. TAD, GNLB, vol. 137, file 2756/13/54, Acting Director of Native Labour addressing meeting of Transvaal Mine Medical Officers' Association, 13 July 1926.

51. TAD, TKP, vol. 146, Transvaal Administration Reports for 1905–1906, Transvaal Public Health Department's Annual Report, Annexure B, Conditions of Living in the Native Compounds, September 1906, p. B63.

52. *Transvaal Mining Regulations Commission Final Report, vol. 1*, 1910, p. 83.

53. Ibid., p. 315; C. F. Juritz, "Kaffir Beers, Their Nature and Composition," *Agricultural Journal* 2 (1906).

54. TAD, GNLB, vol. 86, file 3672/12/54, NAD to all Inspectors, 10 February 1916.

CHAPTER SIX

ALCOHOL AND RESISTANCE ON THE SOUTH AFRICAN GOLD MINES, 1903–1962

Dunbar Moodie

INTRODUCTION

DESPITE THE SOUTH African state's policy of total prohibition for Africans before 1962, black miners tenaciously clung to alcohol as a necessary accompaniment of informal sociability. Even those who otherwise insisted on their faithful adherence to mine rules, cheerfully admitted to illegal drinking. Whatever the regulations, consumption of alcohol was seen as a right for adult men. The avoidance of prohibition became a game for mine workers and the source of innumerable entrepreneurial rackets both on and around compounds.

While the brewing and serving of liquor was traditionally a female pursuit, and men always preferred to drink alcohol produced and served by women, a blurring of gender lines occurred around alcohol, as with sexuality.[1] On the compounds men brewed liquor for themselves and for sale to their fellows. Since gold mine compounds were never closed, however, more adventurous souls could venture forth to farm and town shebeens to drink illicit liquor produced and served by "town women."

In 1962 pressures from South African liquor interests finally led the state to lift all controls on the sale of alcohol to Africans. Within a year or two virtually all gold mines had constructed "liquor outlets" (compound bars). Although this brought an end to compound brewing rackets, some men still preferred to drink in neighboring shebeens, where prices were higher but women served. Before 1973 there seems to have been little change in sociable patterns of alcohol consumption by migrant peasant proprietors who had come to the mines to supplement homestead production.

Radical change to a more proletarian "South African" labor force in the late 1970s, however, introduced a new breed of black miner for whom "alcoholism" was a serious problem.[2] Whereas black mine workers for years had resisted state and management efforts to impose prohibition, members of the National Union of Mineworkers in the 1980s began to condemn drunkenness as demoralizing to worker solidarity. Management, on the other hand, now insisted on the more traditional black workers' "right to drink" in the face of union liquor outlet boycotts. The meaning of alcohol for miners and management had taken a sharp turn with recruitment of a different work force in the 1970s.

This chapter looks at the organization of illegal drinking among African miners themselves and the place of alcohol in their lives during the long prohibition period. Prohibition never stopped African workers from imbibing stronger stuff than the watered-down compound issue. Compound brewing and alcohol purchased from illicit shebeens and municipal beerhalls near the mines were always an important part of mine life. Illegal drinking represented an important ingredient in the moral economy of the mine and helped support ethnic solidarities sustaining resistance to proletarianization.[3]

THE "KHALI" SCANDAL

Beginning in 1903, the state permitted mines to serve allegedly nutritive low-alcohol beer to their workers. Most mines served such "kaffir beer" once or twice a week right up until the 1960s, and this was regarded as a basic right by workers.[4] In November 1922, for example, when visiting Shangaan dancing teams were issued compound beer at Randfontein Estates (see fig. 6.1), there was a shortage for regular workers. Mpondo miners rushed the beer kitchen in a group and five of the combatants required hospitalization.[5]

Since gold mine compounds were "open," the brewing policies of local administrations affected mine drinking. After 1924 municipalities could adopt one or a combination of policies on "kaffir beer" for urban Africans. They could choose total prohibition (as in Johannesburg), municipal beerhall monopolies (as in Durban), domestic brewing (as in Bloemfontein and Kroonstad), or a combination of domestic brewing and controlled local sales (as at New Brighton in Port Elizabeth). After 1937, unless municipalities established monopolistic beerhalls or licensed individuals to sell African beer, they could not prohibit domestic brewing.[6] When the state took control over urban African affairs from the municipalities in the 1950s, beerhalls (more euphemistically, "beer gardens") proliferated in urban areas.

Missionaries and other advocates of prohibition tended to confuse temperance with total abstinence or advocated total abstinence for "primitives," who could not hold their liquor. In contrast, both management and black workers held more nuanced and ambivalent attitudes toward alcohol. Management, of course, deplored the absenteeism

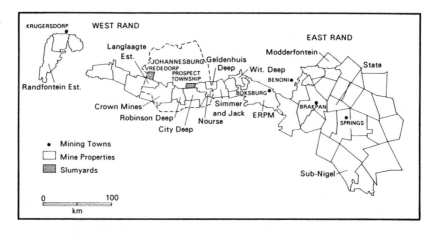

6.1 Witwatersrand gold mines, 1936

that followed drinking bouts but recognized worker demand for alcohol as a basic requirement of migration to the mines. Compounds that turned a blind eye to brewing were more popular with workers, so management had to walk a delicate line between the advantages of attracting employees and the risks of high absenteeism and Native Affairs department revocation of compound managers' licenses.[7]

For many workers, the insipid compound beer issue was quite insufficient. The *khali* scandal turned up by the Buckle Commission in 1913 and 1914 was a clear illustration of the character of mine drinking and the dilemmas that haunted management on this issue. In December 1911 acting Police Commissioner Theo Truter pointed out that:

> Large quantities of kaffir beer, khali and skokian are being brewed in the different compounds and married quarters attached to the compounds. . . . there is no doubt that the presence of large quantities of illicit liquor was well known all along the reef and was openly winked at by the Mine Authorities [because] it was thought that a large supply of beer would make the compounds popular.[8]

In a raid on State Mines in 1913, a police report noted that "a river of skokian ran out of the gate whilst the Police were engaged in emptying the barrels, drums and other receptacles."[9]

The great attraction of *khali* or *skokian* for workers was that it fermented very fast, being ready for consumption within an hour (according to one source), and certainly within two or three.[10] Compound managers giving evidence before Commissioner Buckle sounded the alarm on *khali*. Both A. Spencer Edmunds of Geldenhuis East and G. A. Tandy of Princess Estate reported indiscriminate, virtually universal brewing of *khali* on compounds along the Rand.[11] "One has only to look at the thousands of empty Golden Syrup tins strewn about in the vicinity of any Compound or Location and they tell their own tale," said Tandy. Mozambican mine workers (who were the major brewers) insisted on using imported Lyle's golden syrup rather than the local Natal variety because it produced a stronger brew.[12] Edmunds reported stamping out *khali* in his compound, but "at great cost to the Mine—in 12 months my East Coast labour fell from 1233 to 703, a difference of 530 natives of the very best class."[13] According to M. Smith, the Native Affairs inspector on the East Rand,

> Liquor making . . . is a means of enticing East Coast natives especially to a Compound to allow promiscuous brewing of "Khali." Compounds that try to put down the practice are victimised by the other Compounds, whose policy it is to entice the drink loving labourers to leave the service of the former when time expired.[14]

Smith reported that despite several Chamber of Mines circulars warning the mines to put down the liquor making with a strong hand, mine managers were reluctant to act since "the ones who try to obey the instructions lose their natives and thereby incur the displeasure of their superiors."[15]

In the countryside, recruiters feared that restrictions on brewing would affect their trade.[16] But industrial unrest on the Rand in 1913 and early 1914 gave the state a chance to try to stamp out *khali* brewing. In the interests of "public safety," the Director of Native Labour, S. A. M. Pritchard, prohibited the importation of golden syrup into the compounds. Mine worker drunkenness and absenteeism plummeted—as did sales of golden syrup in the concession stores and stores around the mines. Pritchard was delighted and took steps to entrench his state of emergency regulations.

Although he could not prohibit the sale of golden syrup in normal times, Pritchard sent a circular on 17 February 1914 to all mine managers threatening to suspend their compound managers' licenses if they did not immediately end all brewing on their compounds.[17] At that point, virtually all compounds tried to stop workers bringing golden syrup onto their premises. Many also disallowed any large (ten- to twenty-gallon) tins on their compounds. The earlier abrupt drop in the sale and import of golden syrup continued, and the Transvaal Mines Traders' Association was up in arms.[18]

Workers went off-mine to get their illicit brews, and for a while police raids on compounds turned up surprisingly little of the substance. The ban on the sale of golden syrup was lifted in 1916, however, and compound brewing surged as issues of compound popularity still continued to haunt the managers. An East Rand police report in January 1926, thirteen years after the *khali* scandal, claimed that apparently every endeavour must be made by the Compound Manager to make his compound popular amongst the natives. . . . I am informed that where a Compound Manager is exceptionally keen in putting down the liquor traffic in his compound and it becomes unpopular in consequence, he is told by those controlling him what is happening and he must take steps to make it more popular.[19]

Khali was still being brewed in certain compound rooms or on nearby farms and townships under the alternative name *skokian*. Black miners also reverted to brown sugar and other additives to doctor compound beer. The records mention a range of additives, including cologne, concentrated essence of Jamaica ginger, methylated spirits, carbide, sorghum malt, sprouted grain, and yeast.[20]

DRINKING NETWORKS ON THE MINES

Despite state legislation and missionary admonitions, most African males used alcohol as an essential adjunct to sociability. At the time, senior males recognized excessive drinking as a problem, especially as migratory labor saw it spreading to women and young men, the most productive members of African societies.[21] Traditionally, fairly heavy but socially controlled drinking was integral to rural sociability.[22] In the 1930s Monica Hunter captured the rich fabric of Pondo social interaction and the subordinate but crucial role of alcohol:

Meat feasts, dances and beer drinks are frequent between the harvest and ploughing seasons. During five winter months—June to October—I heard of seventy-three beer drinks, eight girls' initiation dances, three weddings, two feasts for the initiation of diviners, and a number of other ritual killings, within five miles of nTibane store. Many of the feasts lasted for two to three days. There was a young people's dance practically every weekend. Every festival is open to all who care to attend, and some travel ten miles to a beer drink or dance.[23]

She observed that men and their *amadikazi* (lovers) often went from one beer drink to another, sometimes not returning to their own homes for a week. Between November and May, when there was a great deal of work to do in the fields and grain for beer was becoming scarce, there were few ritual feasts but frequent planting and weeding parties. Everyone, even pagans, tended to celebrate Christmas with a beer drink or fight.

This intense Mpondo sociability carried over into the mine compounds, as one miner, Nyovela Manda, pointed out:

> On Saturdays, miners were allowed to visit their home friends from other mines, or we were visited on our mines. We bought them beer and meat and sat in a semi-circle and talked about home events and our girl friends as all the young men always talked. . . . That's how we enjoyed ourselves on the mines.[24]

Sakhile Mdelwa told a similar story:

> On the weekends I used to visit other mines. Every miner would visit his home friends in his free time. We talked about girl-friends and our families. If there were recent arrivals (new ones) from home, we were curious to know what was happening at home when they left. Sometimes we asked if our girl-friends had new boy-friends as we were away all those months. But no one would be cross about a girl-friend. They bought each other beer and sat in a circle, usually home friends alone.[25]

Kent McNamara's meticulous study, in which he tracked drinking networks photographically at an East Rand Proprietary Mines' (ERPM) beerhall, confirmed that persons from the same region and language group tended to drink together—indeed half the drinkers were from the same home village or rural location.[26]

However, drinking friendships with work mates could extend beyond ethnolinguistic boundaries. McNamara found that most wider drinking sets included Mozambican workers (Shangaans). Although the Mozambicans were quite popular, these drinking groups were not as intimate as groups of home friends. "They had friends of other tribes, whom they had met at work," said Ndleleni Makhilane.[27] "They visited each other on the weekends in the hostels. But their deepest friendships were with home friends."

According to Sakhile Mdelwa:

> We had friends from other tribes with whom we drank beer. We talked about the different customs and laws of our respective home lands and discovered if each other were married. Our greatest pride was our girl-

friends and how many we had. We inquired whether our friends had their own *umzi*'s and if their parents were still alive. We also discussed our work and what had brought us to the mines.[28]

Mine drinking sets were never as closed to outsiders as the closely knit networks of traditionalist Xhosa (*amaqaba*) in East London.[29] Like the *amaqaba*, however, the Mpondo home friend networks were most exclusive among newcomers to the mines. Experienced workers, like Mpotsongo Mde, reported that Mpondo who roomed together were not necessarily from the same home area, but from all over Pondoland.[30] Furthermore, their friends were often not home friends or even Mpondo, but underground work mates:

> At first we would speak Fanagalo, but as the friendship continued we would learn each other's languages—especially Shangaans in this case. With home friends we would speak of home, but with work mates we spoke of how hard or how easily the work was going underground. We drank the beer supplied by the mines, supplemented by brown sugar. If we were found out, we would be punished.[31]

Mozambicans were not the only work friends. Sandiso Madikizela, for example, observed that:

> I was friendly with people from Basotho and other tribes who were work mates from the same team. We used to visit each other on weekends. When I went to a Basotho room, I was the guest of my Basotho acquaintance who would go to the kitchen and fetch food and meat and beer for me. . . . When we discussed our work, we spoke of the cruelty of the boss boy or the white man. We also talked about work if we were working in a very dangerous place and were scared.[32]

Whatever the informal networks on the compound—and boundaries were fluid not fixed—drinking was an integral component. For most miners the consumption of alcohol was indispensable to compound social life. Yet as we have seen, except for rations of low-alcohol compound beer twice a week, drinking on the mines, as well as in town and even in the countryside, was forbidden by law. Resistance to prohibition was a fact of life for both workers and management.

BREWING RACKETS
AND RESISTANCE TO PROHIBITION

Mpondo informants never hesitated to acknowledge that supplementing the compound issue of beer with brown sugar was not allowed. Nevertheless, it was common practice to doctor the beer supplied by the mine and to store it for several days until it had "ripened" in containers that were buried either in the rooms or around the compound. Periodically, police raided compound rooms and the drains would run with beer.[33] Yet it was difficult for the mine police to pin the act of brewing on any one individual when rooms housed from fifteen to forty inmates.

Generally, black miners did not dispute that the law obliged mine authorities to raid their rooms for liquor. Such arrangements, they said, were the rules (*mteto*) of the mine. One or two reports, however, imply that in certain periods of tight labor supply or of mine worker militancy against management, workers took action to broaden the terms of the implicit contract about brewing. One case occurred within six weeks of a successful wage strike on Van Ryn Deep (fig. 6.1). On 31 January 1916 on the neighboring New Modderfontein mine, about 300 Mpondo held a meeting to plan a boycott of meat and beer and to picket the kitchen in protest against the compound managers' long-established practice of throwing out beer stored in rooms. According to the Director of Native Labour, a number of workers actually boycotted the beer issue for a couple of days until "their natural inclinations overcame their resolution and the matter adjusted itself."[34]

Another example occurred on 10 January 1943 during a full-scale riot at Nourse Mines. About 150 Xhosa workers demanded "the right to brew beer in the compound" along with "an increased wage in lieu of rations." When Gilchrist, the compound manager, denied their request they threw stones at him, marched to the kitchen, and assaulted the cooks and the assistant compound manager, Davidson. They pulled Davidson "towards a pot of beans which [they] said were not fit for human consumption. [A worker] held him with one hand and with the other tried to force some of the beans in his mouth."[35] The workers proceeded on to the beer room only to be met by the South

African Police, who arrested them. Compound brewing settled back into the old cat-and-mouse game with its accompanying rackets.

Before 1930, and to some extent thereafter, Mozambican workers, with their many generations of migrancy, were among those most deeply involved in the informal sector of compound life. This was especially the case with liquor, since Mozambicans had acquired a taste for strong liquor at home and hence were particularly dissatisfied with the weak compound issue (whose alcoholic content varied from 5.6 percent to 0.87 percent, with an average of 3.12 percent).[36] It had long been Portuguese practice to sell cheap metropolitan wine to its Mozambican subjects. Pinto Coelho's 1904 report on high mortality among Mozambican mine workers in fact advocated that they be supplied with wine for their health and to teach them moderation, for otherwise they would "seek oblivion in drunkenness, and . . . descend to the level of an animal."[37] Mozambican recruiters pushed for a similar concession, but the Transvaal authorities refused to countenance such special pleading.

Historically, Mozambican miners were canny entrepreneurs. "East Coasters" migrated early to South Africa—to the sugar fields in Natal before the opening of the gold mines—and they seem to have appreciated the value of cash and consumer goods from very early on.[38] Mpondo interviewees reported that their Mozambican friends laughed at them for investing their earnings in cattle. *Khali* was not brewed by all workers' groups, nor was it brewed merely for personal consumption. At least until 1930, Mozambicans predominated both in brewing "hard stuff" on the compounds and in selling it. For example, an East Rand police report on a December 1913 raid on Knight Central stated that "in four rooms occupied by Shangaans in the Compound about 1100 gallons of khali was found and 31 arrests made, no beer was found in any of the other rooms and there is no doubt that khali and skokian is brewed by the Shangaans and sold by them to the other natives in the Compound."[39] In a couple of faction fights involving alcohol, workers had gone to the room of a Mozambican to get the liquor.[40] Another worker, testifying about his friend who died as a result of a fall while inebriated, said they had gone with two other Xhosa-speaking drinking friends to a "Shangaan" room to buy adulterated "native liquor."

Certain mine compounds enjoyed distinct periods of popularity as centers for the supply of liquor: for example, Spes Bona Compound in Johannesburg East, and West Driefontein and New Primrose on the East Rand before World War I; Langlaate B on the Central Rand in the late 1910s; and Witwatersrand Deep compound in the early 1920s (fig. 6.1).[41] Although not all reports specify the ethnic origins of compound dealers, whenever they do they mention Mozambicans. As often, the reports mention that brewers had positions as mine police or cooks on the compound. Compound rackets, profitable entrepreneurial sidelines for Mozambican workers and black compound officials alike, frequently involved the sale of illicit liquor.[42]

In his evidence to the Economic and Wage Commission in 1924, A. W. G. Champion, who had recently been employed as a mine clerk, alleged that the compound manager himself took a cut of the profits in liquor dealing: "He permits this kaffir beer to be brewed and he gives what may be termed unstamped licenses to brew kaffir beer. . . . they make more than their salaries by selling jobs as boss boys and police boys."[43] Such charges were difficult to substantiate, since the state and management acted only in the most egregious cases. Yet Compound Manager G. A. Tandy testified to the Buckle Commission in 1914 that "in many cases police boys are in collusion with the brewers and get paid at the rate of about one pound for every tin of, say, 10 gallons brewed, and that is often the reason why some boys are so anxious to get police jobs."[44]

If so, it would have been in the interests of prospective mine policemen to bribe compound managers. Most evidence is indirect. For example, on New Primrose Mine in 1914, Compound Manager Bodley rehired as mine policeman a certain "Waistcoat" who had just completed six months' hard labor for selling liquor.[45] Within months, a police raid found Waistcoat gambling in his room, in which was stored eighty gallons of *khali*, obviously for sale. On several mines, the head cook or a mine policeman was given the key to the brewing room and permitted to issue beer without supervision. On many mines access to beer was a perquisite of the mine police force and their cronies. As recently as the mid-1970s, when liquor was freely available at the mine bar, black compound police turned a blind eye to illegal activities such as *dagga* (marijuana) dealing in certain rooms. In fact, it was precisely the tendency toward favoritism on the part of mine police that caused groups of workers early on to demand that mine police be appointed from their own "tribe." Generally, black workers did not contest the right of indunas and mine policemen to brew liquor or to delegate the right to brew to particular rooms. Such arrangements, winked at if not actually delegated by their white bosses, assured the availability of liquor.

Occasionally resentments over liquor supplies spilled over into ethnic conflict, however. On 31 January 1928, for instance, Portuguese workers refused their food and marched to the manager's house to demand the dismissal of the chief induna, a Xhosa-speaking Hlubi.[46] Mozambican boss boys led the demonstration. They apparently resented "the destroying of liquor in certain East Coast rooms." The compound manager himself reported that their protest "was a deliberate attempt to master the liquor control" and that the majority of the leaders "came from rooms in which persistent attempts are made to carry on the manufacture of liquor concoctions." It appears that the chief induna had decided to break the Mozambican brewing racket by raiding rooms previously immune to mine police searches. A Native Affairs Department review criticized the compound manager for permitting the induna to raid the rooms for liquor without being accompanied by a white. The review noted that the Mozambicans, "who are particularly addicted to Skokian," resented anyone entering their rooms and "upsetting their liquor."[47] Clearly "rights" to brewing rackets were a delicate matter on the compounds.

The compounds were not the sole sites for brewing rackets aimed at mine workers, however. Mine location, farm and township shebeens, and municipal beerhalls were quite as important at different points in time. Before 1920 a few skilled and trusted workers were housed by the mines (with their women—not necessarily their wives) on "locations" adjacent to the compound.[48] Compounds which were well known for their liquor rackets were often also associated with infamous mine locations. These were raided along with the compounds by zealous South African policemen.[49]

Before urban townships sprang up around new mines, farm shebeens enjoyed privileged access to the large mine worker market. In 1914 Jacobus van der Walt, member of parliament for Pretoria South, reported to the Natives Land Commission that

> there are thousands of natives in my constituency, they mostly come from locations in the bushveld. They live in the neighbourhood of the gold-fields from 6 to 8 miles away. They sow lands mostly on the half share system. The lands belong mostly to companies and rich people. It is very easy for a native to make a living there and that is why they congregate to a very great extent in that area. As a rule on Saturday nights the mine labourers go out on their bicycles to these lands and stop there during the week-end when they have beer drinks.[50]

Such rural shebeens long outlasted sharecropping on South African farms.

Enforcing prohibition in the countryside was beyond the resources of the thinly scattered rural police force:

> This area is not protected by the town police and the rural police are too few in number to look properly after these natives, and numerous cases of stock thefts and even murder take place. Not only sheep and poultry are stolen but also the cattle given out by the Government to poor whites have been taken by these natives and slaughtered for these meetings.[51]

Besides, the police argued, mine management bore the rightful responsibility for controlling forays of mine workers into the countryside. Indeed, on 19 August 1916 the Commissioner of Police wrote to the Secretary for Native Affairs urging that passes for mine workers state their destination so that they could be kept away from "certain farms in the East Rand district which are hotbeds of illicit liquor traffic [where] liquor is buried on the veldt away from the houses."[52]

New regulations did little to help, however. The manager of Sub-Nigel mine on the East Rand, for instance, reported in 1934 that even though his mine refused the workers permission to visit Spaarwater farm, they went to shop at the store there.[53] From that point local "touts" would lead them to nearby settlements ("they spring up of their own accord like mushrooms, as soon as the boys come over with their money"), where abounded "a good deal of illicit Native Liquor, and prostitution, and other evils."[54] The manager's investigations revealed that women came from Nigel township on Thursday to the farm huts, where they brewed for the weekend, and returned to town on Monday or Tuesday.

Other rural shebeens on the Rand may likewise have been integrated quite early into the urban system, a system dominated in the 1930s by "regular Native skokiaan queens" from Basutoland.[55] Graham Ballenden of the Johannesburg municipality noted that a "skokian queen" formed temporary attachments with mine workers so that they would bring their friends to drink at her place.[56] Links between social networks and drinking were equally significant in country and town.

For mines in established urban areas, township shebeens provided attractions similar to the *skomplas* (married quarters) and the farm shebeens. However, there were more of them to choose from. Furthermore, they spawned greater risks because of their urban clientele. Experienced mine workers, especially voluntaries, who signed on again and again, sought out the urban milieu. Such workers tended to congregate around the mines in the Johannesburg municipality. Robinson Deep and City Deep, Nourse Mines, Simmer and Jack, and certain Crown Mines shafts tended to attract such proletarianized (or lumpen proletarian) workers. On those mines the boundaries between compound and township were quite permeable, with many workers choosing to live in town and many more opting to drink there.

Two townships—Prospect in central Johannesburg and Vrededorp in the west of the city—were renowned during and after World War I as places where mine workers both dwelt and drank. In 1919 a police report described Vrededorp in the following terms:

Large numbers of natives are residing in this location. They are chiefly employed on the neighbouring mines. These natives keep women here for the purpose of making and trading in illicit liquor. They are constantly being arrested and convicted, but as soon as one Liquor Den is closed others are opened. On Saturdays and Sundays large numbers of natives visit these dens and are a nuisance to the European residents of Mayfair North, Fordsburg and Vrededorp. I would estimate the number of natives, mostly mine natives living here at about 1200. The residents of Mayfair North . . . object very strongly to the large number of natives continually passing to and from the Crown Mines to the location. They are in many instances under the influence of liquor and insulting.[57]

The success of the Native Affairs Department in obliging the mines to control compound brewing in 1914 pushed mine workers out into the surrounding townships, especially on weekends.[58] Township drinking confronted mine managers with a new set of problems. Not only were many workers drunk or hung over when they reported for work Monday morning, others did not show up at all, having been arrested in town for liquor offenses. Conscientious policing of Prospect township in November 1916, for instance, so "seriously depleted Monday morning shifts" at Wolhuter Mine that the manager refused to allow his workers out without a special pass and then apparently "obstructed" the issue of such passes. This in effect incarcerated many Wolhuter workers. At once a deputation from trading stores around the mine visited the Native Affairs Department inspector to demand the workers' legal rights to patronize their shops and their eating houses.[59] Unlike Kimberley, Johannesburg was not a company town, so market pressures on commercial interests, along with worker resistance, combined to keep the compounds open.

In 1934 mine management still faced the same dilemma. R. Develing, the compound manager of ERPM, wrote that "mine natives trek from here daily, especially over weekends and pay days, and in many cases absent themselves from work for several days. Others return to the compounds unfit for work either from assaults or being under the influence of liquor."[60] The manager of Sub-Nigel related despairingly how "they come back, especially at weekends, drunk, and there are a tremendous number of assaults, also convictions for liquor and so forth."[61] Police attempts to prevent drinking by arresting mine workers in the townships created as many problems for mine managements as did the after effects of the alcohol itself. It is hardly surprising that mine and compound managers chose to wink at brewing rackets in their compounds or even at some adulterations of compound issue beer in worker rooms.

At the same time, gold producers took every opportunity to attack municipalities for failing to control brewing in their townships.[62] By the late 1920s and 1930s, as mines closed down or combined in Johannesburg and began developing on the Far East Rand, centers of illegal liquor shifted to the East Rand townships of Benoni, Boksburg, and Brakpan. Boksburg fenced off its location and ordered mine workers not to enter, but Benoni location, the Benoni Indian Bazaar, and Power Street in Brakpan became latter-day Vrededorp and Prospect townships.[63] In the words of Leonard Cheeseman, an East Rand retailer giving evidence to the Trading on Mining Grounds Commission in 1934:

> Power Street is a business street with approximately thirty eight shops. They are in close proximity to State Mine and also to the Brakpan Location, and not very far from the municipal compound. Their idea of trade is entirely Native trade. Wherever there is Native trade of course you naturally get the skokiaan woman and so on—the illicit liquor selling.[64]

Mine managers reporting to the same commission said they found the urban locations "very undesirable."[65] Nonetheless, they were unable to prevent workers "wandering about" on weekends. H. Wellbeloved of the Native Recruiting Corporation summed up the problem:

> They issue a large number of special passes over the weekend; but if a boy really wants to go away, and you don't give him a special pass, he will go without it. He will take the risk of being caught. We don't really restrict the issue of special passes. Take the Brakpan location: that is out of bounds. As far as the compound managers are concerned, they will not give their boys specials to go there, but they get there all the same. The restraint is so slight that if any attempt were made to effect further control by the refusal of special passes [the workers] would not stand for it.[66]

Municipalities were hard-pressed to control mine workers coming to drink, even in well-policed townships, such as Orlando (part of what later became Soweto). In fact, Graham Ballenden, Manager for Municipal Affairs in Johannesburg in 1933, discovered that at least sixty mine workers had been rented houses in Orlando by claiming to be married to their "concubines," women from the slumyards in the center of town. This arrangement benefited both the women, who were not entitled to a house unless they were married, and their mine worker companions, who obtained the comforts of home life, a social center for drinking with their cronies, and possibly extra income. As Ballenden noted, "the woman would make the liquor, and the [man] would go back to the mines and bring his friends—probably twenty or thirty of them over the weekend."[67]

Supporting this account, several Mpondo interviewees mentioned

Sotho friends in the 1950s and 1960s who had set up their lovers in town houses. Even in 1982, the social worker in the Welkom Anglo-American mine township (called Las Vegas by the locals) reported that many of the "wives" were in fact urban mistresses of the workers, rather than wives from the country. The pattern had apparently not changed in the fifty years between Orlando in 1933 and Welkom in 1982, despite changes in the drinking laws.

CONCLUSION: AFTER 1973

A 1982 survey of mine shebeens on one Thabong (Welkom) street revealed that among those who came to drink, at least one client would have close links with the shebeen owner.[68] Shebeens had more to offer than simply alcohol. Drinking was located in a social context, and part of that context was certainly access to women. Men visited the shebeens for more than the alcohol. They came because those drinking places were convivial opportunities to get away from the work place. Traditional mine workers seldom drank alone or with strangers. Drinking beer, preferably prepared by women, was an important aspect of sociability.

When prohibition ended for Africans in 1962, the gold mines at once established bars on the compounds. This action brought the demise of the long-established brewing rackets and more informal adulterations of compound issue beer. Men no longer brewed beer. Drinking groups no longer met in compound rooms. Miners could choose between management-supervised "liquor outlets" or shebeens outside the compound. Shebeens, although more expensive, continued to draw miners because of their intimacy and the attractions of attentive women.

A dramatic increase in wages after 1973 (with the rise in the price of gold), and a conscious policy by the Chamber of Mines to hire workers from within South Africa created a fundamentally different labor pool. These mining industry policy changes, which coincided with depopulation of the white farms and resettlement in the bantustans, all served to make a more stable, more skilled, better educated, fully proletarian migrant work force. The new breed of miners had greater preference for manufactured "European" beer and more money for hard liquor. Gradually even the shebeens stopped brewing and merely retailed mass-market beer and liquor, marked up 50 to 100 percent.

Only one of seven shebeens surveyed in Thabong in 1982, for instance, brewed traditional beer, and its clientele was older men from Lesotho. Furthermore, drinking networks decreasingly shared a common commitment to peasant proprietorship. Men from pitifully overpopulated rural or urban slums could no longer discuss and plan their building of the homestead as they drank together. With no productive future in the countryside, migrants saw their numerous dependents "eat their earnings." Men anticipating no future reward for the drudgery and alienation of mine work and painful separation from loved ones, would more likely find drink a means of escape and less a seal of solidarity.

One management study reported in 1978 that the hospital admission rate of men under the influence of alcohol at one of the mine hospitals in the Orange Free State had increased from 1.12 per 1000 per year in 1973 to 10.7 per 1000 in 1977.[69] According to the study, that was only the tip of the iceberg. In 1976, a participant observer on a Welkom mine reported:

There is a beer-hall in the middle of the compound which is full of people from Monday to Monday. Some people use more than R3 (Rands) a day, and the people drink in groups. The ordinary people drink Sotho beer while some few people who are a bit educated use brandy, which really absorbs the whole money from [them]. Some of these people who always drink use most of the money [so] that by the end of the week they have no money in their pockets and they forget to write letters to their families. On Sundays the miners pay a visit to their friends who are in the other mines nearby. There they discuss matters relating to their homes. Some never talk about their homes. They just visit their friends in order to drink or to visit with them in towns where they can see [their] women.[70]

Youth protest that originated in Soweto in 1976 spurred condemnation of the widening toll of escapist drinking that spread to the mines in the 1970s and 1980s. Radical youth publicly denounced the alcoholic excesses of their elders as undermining the liberation struggle.

Young people targeted beerhalls and bottle stores as prime symbols of their parents' capitulation to white exploitation.

In the mid-1980s some of these tactics eventually spread to the mines in the form of liquor outlet boycotts, led by militant young unionists. The 1985 liquor outlet boycott at Vaal Reefs No. 1 compound is a case in point.[71] For both tactical and moral reasons, the local union chose alcohol as one of its rallying points. Because boycotting a liquor outlet did not directly affect production, management could not declare it illegal and seek a court injunction. The workers believed that the boycott would nevertheless deal a blow to management profits. Furthermore, the new breed of workers tended to see alcohol as a strategy for whites to keep blacks in submission. Supporters of the boycott insisted, "We are not here to drink, but to earn money for our families!" Such arguments won unanimous approval at the union meeting.

The first day of the boycott, 5 November 1985, the bar was empty. The next day a group of Xhosa-speaking workers, mostly Mpondo, marched into the liquor outlet clad in sheets and heavily armed and sat down to drink. By closing time the bar was as busy as ever, with all the regulars back at their customary stations. The boycott was over. Two weeks later, on 19 November, a second attempt aborted when the union apparently ignored informal terms negotiated with the strikebreakers. At the meeting enthusiasm for the second boycott ran so high that union leaders failed to allow a day to lay in a stock of liquor to tide the heavy drinkers over. White-sheeted men bearing arms broke the boycott again.

Once more the new militants underestimated the importance of alcohol in the migrant culture of the mines and the effectiveness of local management and mine security support for the conservatives. Mine police had twice condoned the serving of liquor to men carrying weapons. In retaliation, someone threw a petrol bomb into the liquor outlet. For several days thereafter the strikebreakers roamed the compound and *skomplas,* allegedly in full view of management and accompanied by mine police, seeking to attack any union shaft steward. They succeeded in seriously wounding one and killing two others. The shaft stewards had seriously disrupted their drinking, they said, and management had given permission to root out these union leaders. Compound management clearly took advantage if divisions within the workforce over the issue of alcohol.

Drinking patterns were no longer a common ground for migrant solidarity and resistance to management. More traditionalist workers, including the Mpondo dance team, continued to assert their right to freely imbibe. More proletarianized workers, with their activist leadership, protested the evils of management-orchestrated alcoholic excess. Alcoholic consumption, which for decades had brought migrant miners together, was now driving a wedge between the two groups. Sociable drinking, which once had represented protest against management, could now signify collaboration with the enemy.

NOTES

1. On sexuality, see T. D. Moodie, "Migrancy and Male Sexuality on the South African Gold Mines," *Journal of Southern African Studies* 14 (1988): 228–56.

2. H. J. Kruger and G. P. Rundle, "A Report on the Problems Associated with Excessive Drinking amongst Black Mineworkers," *Association of Mine Managers of South Africa: Papers and Discussions, 1978–1979* (Johannesburg: Chamber of Mines, 1981). For changes in drinking patterns after 1973, see annexure C.

3. On moral economy see T. D. Moodie, "The Moral Economy of the Miners' Strike of 1946," *Journal of Southern African Studies* 13 (1986): 1–35; J. Crush (in this collection). For resistance to proletarianization and mine migrant culture see Moodie, "Migrancy and Male Sexuality"; and T. D. Moodie, "Social Existence and the Practice of Personal Integrity" (Paper presented at Center for the Humanities, Wesleyan University).

4. For the situation in the 1940s, see Cory Library, Rhodes University, Lansdown Commission Evidence, Statement by African Mine Workers Union, 25 June 1943, p. 23. In 1964 the gold mines brewed a total of 37 million gallons of beer; 27 million gallons was issued free to mineworkers, the remainder was sold in liquor outlets under the terms of the 1962 act; see J. Crush and A. Jeeves, "The Politics of Migrancy" (Paper presented to Canadian Association of African Studies Annual Meetings, Kingston, 1988).

5. Transvaal Archives Depot, Pretoria (TAD), GNLB, vol. 197, file 987/13/68, Native Affairs Department Inspector, Randfontein to Director of Native Labour, 17 November 1922.

6. See A. Lynn Saffery, "The Liquor Problem in Urban Areas," *Race Relations Journal* 7 (1940): 88–94.

7. For further details see J. Baker (in this collection).

8. TAD, GNLB, vol. 38.

9. TAD, GNLB, vol. 136, file 2756/13, Sub-Inspector, Benoni to District Commandant, Boksburg, 8 December 1913.

10. TAD, GNLB, vol. 136, file 2756/13/54: E. Meyer, Manager of ERPM to SA Police District Comdt., Boksburg, 27 April 1916; Johannesburg Public Library, Buckle Commission, Evidence of S. A. M. Pritchard, Director of Native Labour (DNL), 2 February 1914; see also Central Archives Depot, Pretoria (CAD), K358, p. 67; and Dominions Royal Commission, 6 April 1914, pars. 2496ff. and 2555ff.

11. CAD, K358, Evidence of Edmunds, 30 January 1914, pp. 2–4, and Written Statement and Evidence of G. A. Tandy, 3 March 1914, pp. 1–6; and GAT 1 and 2 (see also evidence of Joseph Winter, Langlaagte Estate, 27 October 1914, p. 26 and Donald Walter Robertson, Geldenhuis West, 30 January 1914, pp. 11, 130).

12. CAD, K358, Evidence of G. A. Tandy, 3 March 1914, p. 3.

13. Ibid., Written Statement of Edmunds.

14. TAD, GNLB, vol. 136, file 2756/13, Smith to Director of Native Labour, 9 December 1913.

15. Ibid.

16. CAD, K358, Evidence of C. W. de Villiers, Native Recruiting Corporation, 4 March 1914, pp. 87–89.

17. TAD, GNLB, vol. 136, file 2756/13.

18. Ibid., Correspondence regarding the sale of Golden Syrup and the Director of Native Labour's legal right to ban it, 6 March 1914, 26 March 1914, 22 April 1914; file 2756/13/54, Native Affairs Department Inspector's responses to a Director of Native Labour circular asking if the sale of Golden Syrup should be permitted again on the mines, 18 April 1916. Permission was granted; see J. Baker (in this collection).

19. TAD, GNLB, vol. 136, file 2756/13, District Comdt., SAP, E. Rand, Boksburg to Deputy Commissioner, Witwatersrand, 29 January 1926.

20. TAD, Secretary for Native Affairs (SNA), vol. 176, file 2437/03, T. Trevaille-Williams, Manager, New Unified Main Reef Gold Mine to J. Harry Johns, Consulting Engineer, 29 September 1903; *Rand Daily Mail*, 26 Sep-

tember 1916; TAD, GNLB, vol. 136, file 2756/13/54, Director of Native Labour Circular, 22 August 1921, and Responses; GNLB, vol. 367, Conference of NAD, Municipalities, and Location Superintendents Regarding Urban Areas Act, 5 September 1924, pp. 11–12; see also GNLB, vol. 366, file 45/26/110, Circular from SA Police, Brakpan/Springs to all Compound Managers of Far East Rand Mines, 23 February 1926.

21. M. Hunter, *Reaction to Conquest,* 2d ed. (London: Oxford University Press, 1961), p. 357; CAD, Native Economic Commission, Minutes of Evidence, pp. 3273, 3607, 3782. By the 1970s, people in Lesotho cited the temptations of alcohol as the most important of three reasons why migrants absconded (went *tsipa*). The others were "town women" and "homosexuality"; see Agency for Industrial Mission, Theological Student Journals, 1976.

22. P. Mayer and I. Mayer, *Townsmen or Tribesmen* (Cape Town: Oxford University Press, 1961), pp. 111–21.

23. Hunter, *Reaction to Conquest,* pp. 356–59.

24. Vivienne Ndatshe (henceforth VN), interview with Nyovela Manda, Mcela Location, 20 November 1982. Ms. Ndatshe's notes on miners' life histories in 1982 are housed in the African Studies Institute, University of Witwatersrand, Johannesburg.

25. VN, interview with Sakhile Mdelwa, Mfundzeni, 27 November 1982.

26. J. K. McNamara, "Brothers and Work Mates," in *Black Villagers in an Industrial Society,* ed. P. Mayer (Cape Town: Oxford University Press, 1980), pp. 310–20.

27. VN, interview with Indleleni Makhilane, Mantlaneni, 16 September 1982.

28. VN, interview with Sakhile Mdelwa, Mfundzeni, 27 November 1982.

29. Mayer, *Townsmen or Tribesmen,* pp. 90–165.

30. Dunbar Moodie (DM) and VN, interview with Mpotsongo Mde, 4 October 1984, tape 11. Interviews I conducted in Pondoland with Ms. Ndatshe as interpreter are housed in the African Studies Institute, University of Witwatersrand.

31. Ibid.. Fanagalo was the lingua franca on the mines.

32. DM and VN, interview with Sandiso Madikizela, 30 September 1984, tape 3.

33. See, for example, DM and VN, interview with Temba Gqumeni, 20 August 1988, tape 1988/25.

34. CAD, NTS, vol. 210, file 277/16/473, Sub-Inspector W. C. Loftus, SA Police, Benoni to District Cmdt., Boksburg, 4 February 1916; Acting Director of Native Labour to Commissioner of Police, Pretoria, 11 February 1916.

35. *Star,* 10 January 1943 and 23 January 1943; CAD, NTS, vol. 7675, file 103/332, Kotze, Native Affairs Department Inspector to Director of Native Labour, 11 January 1943.

36. TAD, GNLB, vol. 158, file 274/14/245, Extract from George Albert Turner, M.B., C.H.B., "The South African Coloured Miner in his Kraal."

37. TAD, SNA, vol. 244, file 2912/04, 30 June 1904.

38. See P. Harries, "Kinship, Ideology and the Nature of Pre-Colonial Labour Migration" in *Industrialisation and Social Change in South Africa,* ed. S. Marks and R. Rathbone (Harlow: Longman, 1982).

39. TAD, GNLB, vol. 136, file 2756/13, Sub-Inspector, SA Police to District Cmdt., Boksburg, 10 December 1913.

40. TAD, GNLB, vol. 207, file 1721/14/48, W. Walker, Sub-Native Commissioner, Krugersdorp to Director of Native Labour, 17 December 1925; GNLB, vol. 184, file 1169/14/48, Native Affairs Department Inspector, Johannesburg West to Director of Native Labour, 9 July 1914.

41. TAD, GNLB, vol. 136, file 2756/13, F. A. D. Edmeston, Native Affairs Department Inspector to Director of Native Labour, 18 March 1914, 25 March 1914, 28 November 1914; Inspector, SA Police, Boksburg to Manager, New Primrose Mine, 15 June 1914, and Replies (for similar situations on other "Barnato" (JCI) Compounds see GNLB, vol. 198, file 1504/14/80. JCI mines were notorious for illicit liquor at this time; see also Inspector, SAP Boksburg to General Manager ERPM regarding Driefontein Compound, which was on ERPM); GNLB, vol. 135, file 2756/13/54, Sgt. T. Bridgewater, SA Police to Sub-Inspector, Western Area, 10 August 1917; and GNLB, vol. 136, file 2756/17/54, SA Police Report, 31 October 1922, and ensuing correspondence.

42. For an interesting variant on the involvement of compound officials in mine brewing rackets, see J. Crush (in this collection), which demonstrates the involvement of Swazi state appointees in Swaziland compound brewing.

43. CAD, Economic and Wage Commission, ICU Evidence, pars. 7790ff., 7851ff., and 7955ff.

44. CAD, K358, GAT 2.

45. TAD, GNLB, vol. 136, file 2756/13, Inspector, SA Police, Boksburg to Manager, New Primrose Mine, 15 June 1914.

46. TAD, GNLB, vol. 197, file 987/13/68, W. Walker, Sub-Native Commissioner, Krugersdorp to Director of Native Labour, 6 February 1928, and other correspondence on West Rand Consolidated disturbance.

47. The malcontents raised other issues against the induna, complaining

that their own induna was under his thumb. However, after wavering on the issue, management stood firm and arrested and repatriated eleven highly paid and experienced "East Coast Natives," not least because the compound manager feared collective violence from the "Cape workers" on behalf of "their" induna.

48. S. Moroney, "Mine Married Quarters: The Differential Stabilization of the Witwatersrand Workforce, 1900–1920," in *Industrialisation and Social Change,* ed. S. Marks and R. Rathbone (Harlow: Longman, 1982). Such mine townships continue to this day to have a reputation for heavy drinking and access to women.

49. Moroney mentions Witwatersrand Deep Location; he might equally have written of Van Ryn Estates or Langlaagte Royal Locations.

50. Union of South Africa (U.G. 22–'16), "Report of the Natives Land Commission," vol. 2, p. 267.

51. Ibid., Evidence of Van der Walt, p. 267.

52. TAD, GNLB, vol. 210, file 1875/4/72, 29 August 1916.

53. CAD, Trading on Mining Ground Commission (TMGC), Minutes of Evidence, 1934, pp. 334ff. The farm store owner's right to trade apparently could not be infringed upon.

54. CAD, TMGC, Evidence of Wellbeloved, Native Recruiting Corporation, p. 905.

55. See P. Bonner, "'Desirable or Undesirable Sotho Women?' Liquor, Prostitution and the Migration of Sotho Women to the Rand, 1920–1945" (Paper presented at African Studies Institute, University of Witwatersrand, Johannesburg, 1988).

56. CAD, TMGC, pp. 602–3.

57. CAD, Confidential Police files (SAP—Conf.), file 6/757/20/1/A, F. V. Lloyd, Sub-Inspector Western Area to Deputy Commissioner of Police, Johannesburg, Report on "Malay Location, Vrededorp," 3 September 1919. See also *Rand Daily Mail,* 2 March 1920; CAD, Minister of Justice (JUS), vol. 291, file 3/215/20, Vrededorp Riots, 19 March 1920; TAD, GNLB, vol. 309, file 125/19/48, Minutes of Meeting, 4 March 1920, Meeting with black residents, 25 March 1920, and Director of Native Labour to Secretary of Native Affairs, 1 December 1920. The latter file details the fruitless efforts to move black residents from Vrededorp. As late as 1931, "native traders" from the western suburbs of Johannesburg around Crown Mines were complaining that liquor sales were cutting into their sales of legitimate merchandise (see CAD, JUS, vol. 538, file 7934/29/1 and following correspondence).

58. See, for example, TAD, GNLB, vol. 136, file 2756/13, Correspon-

dence between Manager, City Deep and Director of Native Labour, regarding Prospect Township and mine workers drinking and living there, 9 April 1914, 17 June 1914, 8 July 1914, 17 July 1914; GNLB, vol.40, Native Affairs Department Inspector, Boksburg, 12 December 1914; GNLB, vol. 137, file 2756/13/54, Native Affairs Department Inspector, Johannesburg-West to Director of Native Labour on "Drunkenness among [Mine] Natives," 1 June 1915.

59. TAD, GNLB, vol. 210, file 1875/14/72, Native Affairs Department Inspector, Johannesburg-East to Director of Native Labour, "Police Vigilance in and about Prospect Township," 25 November 1916.

60. TAD, T240, Benoni Town Council Archives, R. Develing to Municipal Location Superintendent, 22 August 1934.

61. CAD, TMGC, p. 320.

62. See, for example, CAD, JUS, vol. 538, file 7934/29/1, General Manager, Gold Producers' Committee to Secretary for Justice and ensuing correspondence regarding illicit liquor trade in Johannesburg, 17 September 1929.

63. For Benoni and Brakpan locations, see CAD, JUS, vol. 538, file 7934/29/2, Commissioner, SA Police to Secretary for Justice, "Illicit Liquor Selling: Benoni and Brakpan Locations." For Power Street, see GNLB, vol. 136, file 2756/13, V. Acton to Assistant Magistrate, Brakpan, 18 December 1927, and ensuing correspondence; TMGC, pp. 108ff.

64. CAD, TMGC, p. 142.

65. Ibid., pp. 345, 375ff.

66. Ibid., pp. 904–5.

67. Ibid., pp. 595–96.

68. Information from Thabong town women study that I directed in 1982.

69. Kruger and Rundle, "Report on Problems," p. 4.

70. Agency for Industrial Mission, "Student Observer Report," n.d. In this study, theological students from Lesotho worked on the mines and kept journals under my direction—the quote is from one of the journals.

71. This account of events on Vaal Reefs No. 1 draws on evidence to the Anglo-American Commission of Enquiry on Vaal Reefs Exploration and Mining Co., Johannesburg, 1987 (D. A. Bregman, Commissioner). A copy of the evidence to this commission is housed at Sterling Library, Yale University.

CHAPTER SEVEN

THE ROLE OF ALCOHOL IN LABOR ACQUISITION AND CONTROL ON THE NATAL COAL MINES, 1911–1938

Ruth Edgecombe

INTRODUCTION

AFTER 1911 THE Natal coal-mining industry developed a new policy aimed at settling a significant proportion of its black labor force with their families in the vicinity of the mines. The main instrument for transforming transient migrant workers into permanent colliers was the notorious token system, a form of debt peonage practiced on some 85 percent of Natal coal mines.[1] Through the token system, mine management offered unlimited credit to workers in mine stores and manipulated traditional beer-drinking practices by providing beer on credit in colliery beer halls.

From their inception in the 1880s, the coal mines of Natal (fig. 7.1) had always needed a permanent core of labor. Although superior in quality to Transvaal coal, Natal coal's higher mining costs and a less favorable geographical location excluded it from the lucrative and expanding Rand market. Natal's own domestic market was limited, and characterized by cutthroat competition, forcing the coal owners to turn to the bunker and export trades—a precarious base on which to

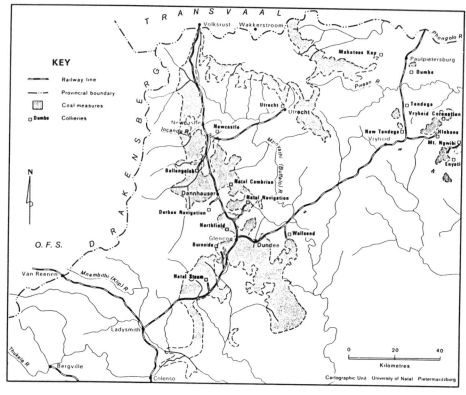

7.1 Coal mining region of Natal

build an industry. Natal coal had to compete in the eastern market
with superior northern-hemisphere coal, and with eastern producers
such as India and Japan. When the other coal producers suffered misfortune, such as strikes or wars, the Natal coal trade experienced
some degree of prosperity. The only sustained periods of profitability
occurred during the years of the two world wars. As the fortunes of
the industry fluctuated, so did its labor needs. Enough labor had to be
kept on hand to cater to sudden upsurges in demand.

The coal mines also faced severe local constraints, including distance
from the port of Durban, an inadequate transportation infrastructure,
and a chronic shortage of railway trucks. Natal coal was particularly
friable and could not be stockpiled at the mine. The companies had to
work straight from seam to truck. Trucks were often not available, so
the mines stood idle, sometimes for days at a time. Those conditions
meant that periods of labor retrenchment alternated with intense

labor demand. The companies found it impossible to compute labor requirements in advance, and had to decide what to do with their workers during times of enforced idleness. The lack of sustained profitability, and the knowledge that good times were invariably succeeded by bad, made the coal owners intensely cost conscious. This consciousness influenced all facets of mining policy, including labor, and the provision of adequate facilities for workers.

Robert Campbell, the general manager of the Natal Navigation Group, remarked that "the rich coal deposits in the Transvaal have brought the profits of the Natal coal mines to a very fine point with the result that the Natal mines are unable to finance a proper recruiting system."[2] Apart from the cost, the mines found it virtually impossible to establish an efficient, centralized recruiting system along the lines of that developed by the gold mines of the Transvaal. The gold mines took over thirty years to perfect the instruments needed to recruit and control migrant labor effectively.[3] The Natal coal owners did not set up a centralized recruiting system until as late as 1943, after the abolition of the token system, and in response to increased labor demand to meet a massive wartime market for coal.[4]

The coal owners could always draw some labor from the immediate vicinity of the mines. Most collieries in Natal were situated on farms that the coal owners had bought or leased for mining operations. Many of the original black inhabitants continued to live on the farms and worked for the mines. The coal-bearing region of northern Natal had the largest concentrations of privately owned black land in the province. Many collieries were located close to such land and to mission-owned farms. Black landowners readily provided rental accommodation for black workers. Some white farmers also permitted such tenants on their farms. Several companies actually bought land for the specific purpose of attracting and settling labor. These attempts were neither extensive nor very successful.[5] The mines were forced to look elsewhere for their permanent core of labor.

The Natal coal mines were plagued by labor shortages in their early years. From the 1890s they turned increasingly to indentured Indian labor. By 1911 they employed 6,000 Indians in addition to 7,000 Africans. The Indians provided the continuous, cheap, and controllable core of labor demanded by the circumstances of the Natal coal trade.

The Indian government's decision in July 1911 to end indentured Indian labor was a serious blow to the Natal coal industry. The announcement came in the wake of the terrible explosion at Glencoe Colliery in 1908, which had seriously disrupted the flow of black recruits from the Cape. Its effect was further exacerbated by political developments in 1910. The coming of Union deprived the coal industry of the protective legislative cocoon spun round the labor supplies of Natal and Zululand by the Natal colonial government. The panic-stricken coal owners responded to the Indian decision with wild schemes, including the recruitment of labor from as far afield as Japan. More realistically, they worked to replace the diminishing core of Indian labor with black labor held on the mines by the "token system."[6]

THE TOKEN SYSTEM

The Natal Native Beer Act of 1908 provided employers and the state with the means to control, if not eliminate, African alcohol consumption. The backbone of the act was provided by the "license system" and the principle of monopoly. Under the act, the Licensing Board could grant a license to sell beer at mines with the approval of the Secretary for Native Affairs.[7] Only the licensee could make or keep beer at a mine, apart from the specified quantities that the Native Labour Regulation Act allowed to be brewed and kept in mine married quarters. Privately owned mine concession stores provided credit and ran mine beerhalls and stores. The provision of beer on credit in mine beerhalls became a potent means of chaining indebted colliers to the mines. Through the token system, the coal owners manipulated African drinking customs to their own advantage. In so doing, they created a labor pattern that was unique in South Africa.

The token system worked in the following way. When a new recruit arrived at the mine he was already in debt for cash advances and his rail fare. He immediately needed to purchase a blanket, billycan, and boots. The mine storekeeper issued him with tokens to pay for the goods. These were known as *skillivaans* ("trash money"). The tokens came in denominations of 3 pence, 6 pence, and 1 shilling (with no intermediate values), and would be used by the new recruit to purchase his requirements. The recruit also had to use tokens to purchase his other needs: bread and meat from the store, items such as soap, matches, and tobacco, and beer from the beerhall. The supply of tokens was unlimited. The storekeeper recovered these advances on payday, when the recruit had completed his ticket of thirty shifts. Typically, little or nothing of his pay was left by this stage. To see him through the next ticket of his contract of six to nine months, he had to acquire more tokens. Recruits thus stepped onto a treadmill of debt. They had little or no money to remit home, or to buy a beast for *lobola* (bride wealth). They had no funds for their rail fare home, or to provide food for the journey, and tended to remain on the mine.

One miner, T. Nzimande, described the effect of the system at Northfield Colliery near Glencoe: "I did work on the mine since I was a small boy, but I could not leave the mine to go and look for work elsewhere because I would have starved on the road. I had no cash on me."[8] Reverend D. J. Kambule of the African Ethiopian Church alleged that "by reason of the temptation afforded by the Token-credit system, the Natives, who are recruited from all parts of the Union, are unable to save a penny either for themselves or their dependents. Nor do a majority of them ever see their homes again."[9] Wives and children left behind became "widows when their husbands are alive" and "orphans while their fathers are yet alive."[10]

In one case on record, the Inspector of Native Labour for Dundee received inquiries from the family of a miner who had been gone eleven years, and who had never once remitted any money home.[11] Miners often formed new liaisons with women residing near the mines. Lucy Vilakazi married her husband when he was working at the Durban Navigation No. 2 Colliery: "My husband always buys in tokens. I have never seen cash."[12] Some wives followed their husbands to the mines. Elias Mkwanase explained that "some of the Native's wives have come to reside in the neighbourhood of the mines where their husbands work to try and get a little money from their husbands because in their kraals they do not receive anything."[13]

Samuel Lazarus, who founded Mines Stores (Natal) Ltd. in 1911, with branch stores on several Natal mines, is credited with devising the token system.[14] But its subsequent development and refinement was the result of close collaboration between mine managements, storekeepers, and local government officials. In 1919 Ignatius de Jager (Inspector of Native Labour for the Dundee district) improved the efficiency of the system by having token issues endorsed on the work tickets of the colliers and entered in store books. This practice removed the possibility of further disputes about the degree of indebtedness of a worker.[15]

Coal owners and mine managers assiduously supported the storekeepers by allowing them to establish trading monopolies and providing them with facilities for the recovery of debts. The deduction of cash from laborers' wages to a third party was technically illegal. Management devised methods to circumvent the prohibition. On payday the mine secretary handed over the full cash wage to the worker. The worker in turn handed it over to the storekeeper or his representative, sitting at an adjacent desk. He deducted the amount owed to the store, and gave what was left back to the worker. Managements and storekeepers claimed that the repayment of debts was voluntary, but a miner had little option in the matter.[16]

With the token system, keeping concession stores on the Natal collieries was a highly profitable undertaking. Robert Shapiro, who bought Mine Stores (Natal) Ltd. in 1919, noted that the token system "means our business was practically on a cash basis—no bad debts." He estimated that of the 9,500 black workers employed on the Natal collieries in 1935, some 60 to 70 percent availed themselves of the token system.[17] Monopoly conditions, and the use of tokens, meant excessive profits for the storekeepers. A blanket costing 5s in token money at a mine store could be bought for 3s 6d at an Indian store.[18] Boots issued at the Natal Cambrian Colliery (where the token system was not used) cost 9s 9d. On other mines they cost double that amount in tokens.[19]

Such was the support given by mine management and compound managers to storekeepers that government officials suspected them of getting a "side cut."[20] But the government officials clearly recognized the value attached to the system by management:

These permanent Natives are regarded as the "backbone" of the coal mining labour force; and the expressed and obvious desire of the mine managements is to increase that permanent source of manpower by turning this "floating" worker into the path of detribalisation as quickly as possible. Any scheme, therefore, which will train for the future a colony of skilled colliers, living with their families on the mines, is favourably regarded by the mine owners.[21]

Robert Campbell argued that "credit . . . is responsible for us being able to retain our trained men." In his view the token system anchored the family on the mine and enabled them "to live a settled, contented life."[22] Given the conditions of the Natal coal trade, when it could take from five to as many as twelve weeks to earn a ticket of thirty shifts, the token system did make it possible to retain labor.[23] This was particularly true when on most collieries no rations were provided for children, and mealie meal (maize meal) only was issued to women.[24] By 1938 an estimated 60 percent of the labor force on the larger Natal collieries consisted of permanent workers. On some collieries in the Natal Navigation Group, the figure was as high as 75 percent.[25]

The token system operated by exploiting the improvidence of workers. Easy credit was thrust upon them: "When a boy goes to a mine office and asks for money he is not welcome . . . but at a Jew store, if he asks for 10 shillings they give him a pound [20 shillings]."[26] A collier at the Durban Navigation mine noted, "I have been here for 6 years. That is all I have got (pointing to the clothes that he was wearing). I am the first to be there for tokens. I am mesmerised by this thing; I can just tear it off and get what I want."[27] Refuting arguments that the token system was entirely voluntary, Archdeacon Lee of Rorke's Drift remarked that "every man is a free agent in the matter of life and death, but he does not have much choice. He either lives or dies, and in this case he either goes to the mine and falls in with the system, or he does not go."[28]

BEER ON CREDIT

Under the token system, beer was freely available on credit in colliery beerhalls. This credit was a major source of indebtedness and a critical factor in the success of the system in stabilizing labor. In the late 1920s, new draft legislation threatened to cancel the beer-licensing system in Natal and bring the province into line with legislation elsewhere by allowing the mines to brew and supply beer to their labor free of charge. Those proposals were strongly opposed by Natal coal owners and mine managers.

When the new Liquor Act was finally passed in 1928, the Minister of Justice allowed the collieries to continue with the old system.[29] Although the regulations prescribed cash sales only, the minister assured the storekeepers that he did not intend to interfere with the token system.[30] Joel Maduna, induna at the Dundee Coal Company's By-Products Works, described the seductive lure of beer on credit: "If they spent cash on drinks he would not spend so much money as they do with the skillivaans because when all their money had been spent each one will say: I will drink on pay-day. With the token system he drinks even when he has no money."[31] On most collieries the beerhalls were strategically located between the mine shaft and the compounds. Dundee's Inspector of Native Labour observed that workers coming off shift "throng these places, animated doubtless to some extent by a sense of temporary loss of vitality and a conceivable desire for companionship and conviviality."[32] The warmth of beerhalls, where winter fires were sometimes provided, attracted workers from the "uninviting, comfortless and unhygienic" compounds that characterized most of the Natal collieries.[33]

The law prescribed that the alcoholic content of beer sold at the halls should not exceed 2 percent. But the alcoholic content of beer could only be scientifically tested in Johannesburg—a logistical difficulty compounded by the fact that beer was sold and consumed in a state of active fermentation.[34] In practice the brews were often more potent. Black workers referred to the beer as *isipiliti* (spirits). Witnesses to the Kaffir Beer Committee of 1938 alleged that the manufacturers added carbide to the brew to increase its potency. Aloe ash was also added, supposedly to induce greater thirst so that more beer would be drunk.[35]

Unlike urban beerhalls in Natal, those on the mines did not exclude women, a factor that spared mine canteens from demonstrations by women when protests against municipal canteens swept the northern Natal countryside in the latter months of 1929.[36] The presence of women provided an added inducement to workers to patron-ize beerhalls.[37] A characteristic of the colliery beerhalls was the large number of women, many of whom were prostitutes, who thronged round them at all hours of the day. One observer noted how workers coming off shift were immediately collared by women and "whipped into the beerhall."[38]

In the late 1930s, the Kaffir Beer Committee denounced the beer-halls as "an evil, a public nuisance and menace to natives, both mor-ally and physically."[39] But storekeepers and mine managers defended the "law-abiding manner" in which they ran the beerhalls. They claimed that by supplying beer in reasonable quantities under strict supervision and control, they were performing a public duty, by inhib-iting excessive drinking and assisting the authorities to cope with the selling and brewing of illicit liquor.[40] Most mine managers supported the beerhalls as a means of controlling labor over the weekends and reducing absenteeism. Robert Campbell claimed that before the ad-vent of beerhalls, a colliery employing 600 to 700 men would be short 50 to 100 workers every Monday morning. With the token system, the workers tended to stick to the mines and were usually available for work on Monday.[41]

Local officials often staunchly defended the system. In the 1920s the Inspector of Native Labour at Dundee and an architect of the sys-tem, I. W. de Jager, claimed that he saw nothing irregular in the token system, which he deemed to be an efficient method of accounting. He viewed the provision of beer as a "native right" and the beerhall as "a means of saving the natives from reckless squandering of their earn-ings."[42] His counterpart in the Vryheid district, C. R. Eagar, dismissed the claims that all wages were wasted at the mine stores and beerhalls as "frivolous."[43]

A few mine managers opposed the system. Robert Ferguson of the Natal Cambrian Colliery saw the beerhalls as the root of the trouble on the collieries, and favored total abolition and the issue of free beer rations.[44] Another dissenting voice was that of Fred Steart, general manager of Northfield Colliery. He also favored beer rations but commented that "the sale of beer through the beerhalls on the collier-ies has been so firmly established in Natal [that] the labor position at this colliery might be seriously affected if laborers are unable to purchase beer here when they could do so at a neighbouring colliery." In 1931, when the mine's stores license came up for renewal, he still imposed stricter conditions such as the exclusion of women from the beerhall, the prohibition of credit, and reduced hours of sale.[45] Those restrictions fell into abeyance when the owners sold the colliery to the Natal Navigation Group. The new general manager, Robert Campbell, was an ardent supporter of the system. Nonetheless the number of critics of the system was on the rise.

ENDING THE TOKEN SYSTEM

Serious criticism of the token system by workers first surfaced during the depression in the early 1930s. Before this they seldom openly criticized the system for fear of dismissal or victimization.[46] Public criticism began to mount. Opposition was spearheaded by farmers attempting to sell produce to colliers. By the 1930s, tokens had become a medium of exchange in the coal-mining districts, and farmers could get nothing else for their produce. Convicted criminals tried to pay their fines in tokens. Tokens appeared in church collection plates and were offered as admission fees to concerts.[47] Amidst the hardships of the depression years, mine storekeepers grew fat. Outside traders complained bitterly of the unfair competition from the mine stores' monopoly.[48] There was a strong strain of anti-Semitism to some of the opposition to storekeepers, obscuring the fact that non-Jewish coal owners and mine managers had made the token system possible.[49]

Farmers' associations in the Vryheid area protested and appealed against the "absolute monopoly between the mine bosses and the storekeepers."[50] The congress of the National Party condemned the token system, as did the Joint Councils of Europeans and Natives in the Vryheid and Dundee districts, and the Natal Indian Congress. So did the Native Economic Commission of 1930–1932. Organizations ranging from the South African Institute of Race Relations to the Pietermaritzburg Society for the Welfare of Natives, pleaded for action against the system.[51] Government officials, coal owners, and storekeepers squared up for a long and laborious fight over tokens and beerhalls.

At first, attempts were made to negotiate with storekeepers. In 1932, after a court ruling that trading in metal discs was illegal, storekeepers promised to do away with the token system by 1 April 1932. But they interpreted this promise as merely one to discard metal discs, which they replaced with embossed paper tokens.[52] Regulations were then framed under the Native Administration Act of 1927, which prohibited the use of tokens, and the presence of storekeepers in mine pay offices, after 1 September 1934.[53]

Many mines did not observe the new regulations.[54] Robert Shapiro deliberately courted arrest at Northfield Colliery. In the ensuing court case, the magistrate ruled that the regulations were ultra vires in that it did not lie within the power of the Governor General to make such regulations.[55] The case went on appeal to the Supreme Court, which ruled that the wording of the regulations was "bad for uncertainty," but failed to clarify the quesiton of the powers of the Governor General.[56] This failure in effect meant that legislation would be required to end the token system.[57]

In the meantime, officials of the Native Affairs Department negotiated various compromise arrangements with the storekeepers concerning the operation of the token system.[58] In 1934 C. L. Cope and B. Gildenhuys replaced de Jager and Eagar as inspectors of Native Labour in the Dundee and Vryheid districts respectively. Although both were strongly opposed to the token system and did their best to enforce the agreements, it soon became clear that the storekeepers were ignoring them.[59] The storekeepers' position was further strengthened when Cope was succeeded by W. N. Engelbrecht, who was described by the Chief Native Commissioner as "a very weak reed."[60]

The Chief Native Commissioner was then deputed to conduct a personal investigation of the token system in April 1937. His report argued strongly that the token system should be abolished and beer licenses removed from storekeepers. Legislation could not, however, be enacted because the session of Parliament was almost over. Instead, the Native Affairs Commission was instructed to conduct yet another enquiry into the token system.[61] The commission's report of June 1938 echoed the findings of the Chief Native Commissioner and recommended banning the selling of beer for profit. The commission also found that the operation of the token system had caused such widespread aversion throughout the reserves of Zululand and Natal that it was no longer functioning effectively as a means of acquiring and retaining labor.[62] The Deputy Inspector of Mines observed that the mines "are cutting their own throats; the boys are no longer going to the mines."[63]

Although most mine managers had argued consistently that the token system was a means of combating desertions and attracting labor, the case of Enyati Colliery showed those claims to be fallacious by the later 1930s. The token system had been abolished at that colliery in 1934. Although neither living nor working conditions were any better there than at the other mines, the colliery had enough voluntary labor coming forward to work, notwithstanding the widespread labor shortages of the late 1930s.[64] In 1938 the rate of desertion at Enyati was 5 per month, compared with 6 per day at Hlobane Colliery, where the token system continued to operate.[65]

Desertions were one way of showing opposition to the system, strikes were another. The demand for the abolition of the token system featured prominently in a strike involving 600 workers at the Vryheid Coronation Colliery on 3 December 1935.[66] The token system had clearly outlived its usefulness by 1938. Some managers recognized this by doing away with it in advance of the Native Administration (Amendment) Act of 1939, which finally ended the token system in Natal.[67] Three years later, coal owners at last brought a centralized recruiting organization into being, and began to pay much more attention to improving living and working conditions on the collieries in an attempt to make its recruiting agency more effective in a booming market for labor.

At the eleventh hour of the passage of the Native Administration (Amendment) Act through Parliament, the clauses relating to beer were withdrawn, thanks to the intervention of the member of Parliament for Newcastle, who represented powerful vested interests in northern Natal.[68] A new committee was appointed to investigate the question of the supply of beer on the coal mines. Its recommendations were along similar lines to those of previous enquiries: the existing system of beerhalls should be abolished, and mine management should provide beer at cost under strict conditions.[69]

The Minister of Justice, however, decided to give the beerhalls "a final probationary test." New conditions governing the operation of beer licenses were introduced, such as the exclusion of women from the beerhalls, limiting hours of sale, and fixing prices.[70] At first, those provisions seemed to reduce drunkenness and rowdiness somewhat. But mine managers asserted that they also increased illicit brewing.[71] Robert Campbell complained that mines were once again experiencing labor shortages on Mondays, and those who came to work were "stupid and unreliable," if not drunk.[72] Mine management and storekeepers were soon disregarding the conditions governing beerhall licenses.[73] In 1949 the agent for the High Commission territories described a payday visit to the beerhall at D.N.C. no. 3 mine: "I could not get within 10 yards of the entrance due to men, women and children. It was not a nice sight."[74]

In the 1940s there was growing concern about the relationship between drunkenness and mine accidents. After a series of such accidents, the manager of D.N.C. No. 3 Colliery remarked "as long as we have privately controlled 'Beer Halls' with the profit motive behind it, we will never stop drunkenness."[75] In 1951 the Secretary for Mines criticized the Natal system because it was impossible to ensure that too much drink was not being given to the workers. He urged that profit-making beerhalls should be done away with.[76] The impact of drunkenness on labor productivity was also noted by a branch of the National Party in northern Natal, which urged that greater controls be exerted over beerhalls because white miners had to take the responsibility for the inability of black miners to perform their work.[77]

Growing criticism prompted the drafting of a new liquor bill aimed at eliminating profit-oriented beerhalls and giving mine managers the right to manufacture free beer for their employees.[78] Inevitably, the old arguments that this would encourage illicit brewing resurfaced.[79] The Deputy Commissioner for Police pointed out that while the Native Labour Regulation Act catered for the beer needs of married workers, beerhalls remained necessary to meet the needs of single men. Illicit brewing would be far more troublesome to the police than beerhalls.[80]

That argument gathered strength in 1956 when the government

ordered coal owners to restrict the permanent quota of the black labor complement to 3 percent at each mine.[81] While the implementation of that order was intended to be gradual, it was clear that the Natal coal industry would henceforth have to look to migrant labor to meet its main labor requirements.[82] When the Liquor Act was finally passed in 1961, not only was the beerhall system left intact, but the sale of European beer, wine, and spirits to blacks was permitted for the first time in Natal since 1878.[83]

CONCLUSION

The beerhall token system, which evolved out of the Native Beer Act of 1908, was of fundamental importance to labor control on the Natal collieries. In contrast to the more urbanized mining conditions of the Transvaal, illicit European liquor dealing appeared to be entirely absent in the more rural mining areas of Natal.[84] But a major problem confronting Natal coal owners was the counterattraction of traditional beer drinking parties, which drew labor away on weekends and often well into the working week. The introduction of beerhalls, where workers could purchase beer on mine premises, was designed to control excessive drinking and to ensure that the bulk of the work force was available for work on Mondays. The beerhall system accorded with state policy "to legalise the supply of Kaffir Beer under conditions of proper control."[85]

Unlike the Transvaal mine owners, coal owners in Natal were unwilling to undertake the brewing and supply of beer as a free ration, or for sale, and so this function was handed over to concession storekeepers. The involvement of private interests, and the profit motive, would in time lay the system wide open to abuse, particularly when associated with excessive credit under the token system.

The linking of beerhalls with the token system was a critically important element in extending the supply of permanent black labor in the vicinity of the mines. The volatile conditions of the Natal coal trade before the 1950s required a core of stabilized labor, particularly since lack of sustained profitability precluded cost-conscious coal owners from developing efficient recruiting structures, as well as the concomitant elements of attractive living conditions and sporting and social amenities. By the 1930s the token credit system had proved successful in achieving a permanent labor supply, although certain ethnic groups, such as the Xhosa and the Basotho, proved quite resistant to easy credit. But the abuses inherent in the involvement of private interests had generated such widespread public and worker aversion against the system by 1938 that the credit system was clearly doomed as a means of building up further labor supplies.[86]

Between 1939, when the token system was officially abandoned, and 1956, the proportion of permanent labor on the Natal collieries declined from 60 percent to 28 percent.[87] With coal owners having to rely increasingly on migrant labor, a central recruiting organization was finally brought into being in 1943, and much greater attention was paid to the provision of social amenities, other than beerhalls, on the mines.[88] The process of transition from stabilized to migrant labor was assisted by the changing circumstances of the Natal coal trade in the 1950s. The inability of the South African Railways to meet the transport requirements of the South African economy had all but destroyed Natal's coal export trade by 1954. The industry acquired a much stronger domestic orientation, assisted by the expanding coal requirements of the developing South African economy, especially coking coal, of which Natal was then the only known source of supply. With a steadier demand base, the labor requirements of the industry became more predictable.

Notwithstanding the demise of stabilized labor, the central requirement of liquor legislation—the control of labor—remained. The question of control assumed greater urgency as the shape of the Natal coal industry's labor force gradually changed from one in which permanent workers living with their families in the vicinity of the mines was dominant, to one of single, migrant men living in open compounds, dominated by a male culture of beer and prostitutes, however much mine management might seek to develop diversionary activities such as sport, music, and bioscopes. The need to control labor explains why the essential features of legislation relating to beer in Natal remained unchanged from the pioneering act of 1908.

NOTES

1. Central Archives Depot, Pretoria (CAD), Department of Native Affairs (NTS), vol. 7046, file 63/322, Native Affairs Commission: Report of Investigation into the Token System, 1 June 1938.

2. CAD, NTS, vol. 2120, file 227/280, A. S. Dunlop to Secretary for Native Affairs, 30 September 1935.

3. A. Jeeves, *Migrant Labour in South Africa's Mining Economy: The Struggle for the Gold Mines' Labour Supply, 1890–1920* (Montreal and Kingston: McGill–Queen's Press, 1985).

4. Natal Coal Owners' Society Minutes, Talana Museum, Dundee (NCOS), 22 January 1943.

5. See *Natal Native Affairs Commission 1906–7 Evidence* (Pietermaritzburg, 1907), evidence of Sir B. W. Greenacre, J. Livingston and R. P. Gilbert; Colonial Secretary's Office, Natal Archives Depot, Pietermaritzburg (NAD), 7282, Indian Immigration Commission 1909, 10–11 February 1909, pp. 565–77, 596–97.

6. Transvaal Archives Depot, Pretoria (TAD), Government Native Labour Bureau (GNLB), Pretoria, vol. 81, file 3154/12/77D, Rough notes of meeting between the Director of Native Labour and representatives of Sugar Planters; see also CAD, NTS, vol. 2067, file 138/280, Notes of a meeting between the Minister of Native Affairs and the NCOS executive, 22 August, 1911; Memorandum on Native Labour, Natal and Zululand (1911); Notes of an interview between the Minister of Native Affairs and the Natal Indian Immigration Trust Board, 22 April 1911.

7. Married households were not allowed to possess more than three gallons of beer at any one time. NAD, Secretary for Native Affairs, 1/1/418, file 3765/1908, Minutes by James Stuart, Magistrate, Native Affairs Department, 22 December 1908; NCOS Minutes, 18 February 1926, appendix B, Shepstone and Wylie to Natal Navigation Collieries, 16 February 1926.

8. CAD, NTS, vol. 2120, file 227/280, Verbatim Notes of Evidence, Native Affairs Commission, Dundee, 28 January 1938.

9. Ibid., D. J. Kambule, "Scandalous Exploitation of Natives on Natal Coal Mines."

10. Ibid., Verbatim Notes of Evidence, Native Affairs Commission, Dundee, 28 January 1938.

11. Ibid., Token System. Documents submitted to Enquiry, Evidence, Rex v. Shapiro, 1934.

12. Ibid., Verbatim Notes of Evidence, Native Affairs Commission, Dundee, 28 January 1938.

13. Ibid.

14. Ibid., Token System. Documents submitted to Enquiry, Evidence, Rex v. Shapiro, 1934.

15. CAD, NTS, vol. 7046, file 63/322, Report by H. C. Lugg on Token System, 15 April 1937.

16. CAD, NTS, vol. 2119, file 227/280, V. H. M. Barrett to Inspector of Mines for Natal, 2 August 1937.

17. CAD, NTS, vol. 2120, file 227/280, Token System. Documents submitted to Enquiry, Evidence, Rex v. Shapiro, 1934.

18. Ibid., Evidence of government officials: P. L. Hatting to Native Affairs Commission, 27 January 1938.

19. Ibid., Evidence submitted by Robert Ferguson to Lugg Enquiry, April 1937.

20. Ibid., Evidence of D. Harland Bowden, Native Affairs Commission, 27 January 1938.

21. CAD, NTS, vol. 7046, file 63/322, Native Affairs Commission: Report of Investigation into the Token System, 1 June 1938.

22. Ibid., Token System. Documents submitted to Enquiry, Evidence, Rex v. Shapiro, 1934.

23. CAD, NTS, vol. 2119, file 227/280, Records of proceedings of a meeting held at Dundee, 21 June 1935.

24. CAD, NTS, vol. 2120, file 227/280, Record of enquiry into Token Credit System, April 1937, annexure D, evidence of W. N. Shum.

25. Ibid., annexure D.

26. CAD, NTS, vol. 2119, file 227/280, Evidence of D. Harland Bowden, Native Affairs Commission, 27 January 1938.

27. Ibid.

28. CAD, K26, Native Economic Commission, vol. 4, Evidence given at Vryheid, 18 September 1930.

29. NCOS Minutes, 18 February 1926, appendix B. Shepstone and Wylie to Natal Navigation Collieries, 16 February 1926.

30. CAD, NTS, vol. 2119, file 227/280, R. Shapiro and J. N. Glutz to E. G. Jansen, 9 July 1931.

31. CAD, NTS, vol. 2120, file 227/280, Verbatim Notes of Evidence, Native Affairs Commission, Dundee, 28 January 1938.

32. CAD, NTS, vol. 7046, file 63/332, Inspector of Native Labour, Dundee to Chief Native Commissioner, 21 April 1928.

33. Ibid., Report of the Committee concerning the supply of Kaffir Beer on the Natal Coal Mines, 27 November 1938.

34. CAD, NTS, vol. 7046, file 63/322, Acutt and Worthington, Memorandum Kaffir Beer Licences (Natal Coal Mines), 23 May 1955.

35. CAD, NTS, vol. 7046, file 63/322, Report of the Committee concerning the supply of Kaffir Beer on the Natal Coal Mines, 27 November 1938.

36. H. Bradford (in this collection).

37. CAD, NTS, vol. 2120, file 227/280, Evidence submitted to Lugg Enquiry, April 1937.

38. CAD, NTS, vol. 2120, file 227/280, Evidence of D. Harland Bowden, Native Affairs Commission, 27 January 1938.

39. CAD, NTS, vol. 7046, file 63/322, Report of Committee concerning the supply of Kaffir Beer on Natal Coal Mines, 27 November 1938.

40. CAD, NTS, vol. 2119, file 227/280, R. Shapiro and J. N. Glutz to E. G. Jansen, 9 July 1931.

41. Ibid., Interview between R. Campbell and Inspector of Native Labour, 20 September 1934.

42. Ibid., Inspector of Native Labour to Chief Native Commissioner, 31 August 1928; I. W. de Jager to E. G. Jansen, 14 July 1931.

43. Ibid., Inspector of Native Labour, Vryheid to Director of Native Labour, 11 October 1932.

44. CAD, NTS, vol. 2120, file 227/280, Evidence submitted to Lugg Enquiry, April 1937.

45. De Beers Archives, Kimberley, S4/NC2, F. A. Steart to the Secretary, De Beers Consolidated Mines Ltd., 3 February 1931.

46. CAD, NTS, vol. 2120, file 227/280, C. L. Cope to Director of Native Labour, 19 February 1934.

47. Ibid., Native Commissioner, Vryheid to Chief Native Commissioner, 22 November 1937; Evidence given by William Mtimbulu and Alfred Kumalo to Lugg Enquiry, April 1937; NTS, vol. 2119, file 227/280, P. H. Kritzinger to Minister of Justice, 25 July 1932.

48. See CAD, NTS, vol. 2119, file 227/280, Biggermans to Secretary for the Minister of Justice, 10 June 1932.

49. CAD, NTS, vol. 2120, file 227/280, D. J. Kambule, "Scandalous Ex-

ploitation of Natives on Natal Coal Mines"; Evidence of Government Officials, B. Gildenhuys, Native Affairs Commission, 27 January 1938.

50. See CAD, NTS, vol. 2119, file 227/280, Senator P. J. Wessels to General Smuts, 30 January 1935; W. Birkenstock to Minister of Finance, 30 January 1934.

51. Ibid., Secretary for Native Affairs to J. J. van Schalkwyk, 12 November 1931; Rheinallt Jones to Secretary for Native Affairs, 24 September 1934; NTS, vol. 2120, file 227/280, P. F. Williams to Minister of Native Affairs, 4 December 1936; L. E. Hall to Attorney General, Natal, 16 October 1936; Verbatim Notes of Evidence, Native Affairs Commission, Dundee, 28 January 1938.

52. CAD, NTS, vol. 2119, file 227/280, Chief Clerk of Attorney General, Natal to Public Prosecutor, Vryheid, 25 November 1932; Secretary for Native Affairs to Secretary for Finance, 29 April 1935; Magistrate, Vryheid to Chief Native Commissioner, 21 March 1933.

53. Ibid., Secretary for Native Affairs to Secretary for Justice, 6 June 1933; Acting Secretary for Native Affairs to Secretary for Finance, 13 June 1934.

54. Ibid., C. L. Cope to Director of Native Labour, 6 September 1934; B. Gildenhuys to D. L. Smit, 3 November 1934.

55. Ibid., Rex v. Shapiro and B. Mandelstam, Criminal Case, Dundee, no. 1466 of 1934.

56. Ibid., Attorney General, Natal, to Secretary for Native Affairs, 18 April 1935.

57. Ibid., Record of Proceedings of a Meeting held at Dundee, 21 June 1935.

58. Ibid., D. L. Smit to Minister for Native Affairs, 2 February 1939.

59. CAD, NTS, vol. 2120, file 227/280, Evidence of D. Harland Bowden, Native Affairs Commission, 27 January 1938; NTS, vol. 2119, file 227/280, C. L. Cope to Ben Gildenhuys, 5 February 1934.

60. Ibid., H. C. Lugg to D. L. Smit, 19 March 1937.

61. CAD, NTS, vol. 7046, file 63/322, Report by H. C. Lugg on Token System, 15 April 1937.

62. Ibid., Native Affairs Commission: Report of Investigation into Token System, 1 June 1938.

63. CAD, NTS, vol. 2119, file 227/280, Evidence of D. Harland Bowden, Native Affairs Commission, 27 January 1938.

64. Ibid.

65. Ibid., Evidence of J. A. L. de Lange, January 1938.

66. Annual Report of the Inspector of Mines for Natal, 1935, Inspector of Mines Office, Dundee.

67. CAD, NTS, vol. 2119, file 227/280, Inspector of Native Labour, Vryheid to Secretary for Native Affairs, 30 September 1938; Chief Native Commissioner to Secretary for Native Affairs, 4 October 1938.

68. CAD, NTS, vol. 7046, file 63/322, D. L. Smit to Secretary for Justice, 20 July 1939.

69. Ibid., Report of the Committee concerning the supply of Kaffir Beer on Natal Coal Mines, 27 November 1938.

70. Ibid., Secretary for Justice to Secretary for Native Affairs, 21 June 1940.

71. CAD, NTS, vol. 7033, file 31/322(6), Kaffir Beer Enquiry, Glencoe, 27 September 1941; NTS, vol. 7034, file 31/322(6), Report of Native Affairs Commission to enquire into the provisions of Natives (Urban Areas) Act concerning the use and supply of Kaffir Beer, 1941; NTS, vol. 7035, file 31/322(6), statement by Willie Shum.

72. Ibid., R. Campbell to Chairman, Native Affairs Commission, 24 September 1941; NTS, vol. 7033, file 31/32(6) Kaffir Beer Enquiry, Glencoe, 27 September 1941.

73. CAD, NTS, vol. 7046, file 63/322, Chief Native Commissioner to Secretary for Native Affairs, 21 November 1949.

74. Ibid., G. E. Pott to Government Secretary, 11 August 1949.

75. Inspector of Mines for Natal Accidents, Inspector of Mines Office, Natal, 769/49, Durban Navigation Colliery No. 3, 12 September 1949; Mines Department Accidents, 204/43, D.N.C. No. 2, 27–28 April 1943.

76. CAD, NTS, vol. 7046, file 63/322, Secretary for Mines to Secretary for Justice, 1 February 1951.

77. Ibid., Provinsiale Sekrataris, Herenigde Nasionale Party to C. R. Swart, Minister of Justice, 13 November 1950.

78. Ibid., Minute 63/322, 17 March 1951 to Secretary for Native Affairs.

79. CAD, NTS, vol. 7046, file 63/322, Chief Native Commissioner to Secretary for Native Affairs, 11 April 1951.

80. Ibid., I. C. van Rooyen to Chief Native Commissioner, 28 March 1951.

81. NCOS Minutes, 13 September 1956, J. F. Barnard to NCOS, 17 August 1956.

82. Ibid.

83. Ibid., 17 October 1961; Natal Mine Managers Association Minutes, Talana Museum, Dundee, 20 September 1961.

84. CAD, NTS, vol. 7066, file 63/322, Inspector of Native Labour, Vryheid to Chief Native Commissioner, 14 April 1928.

85. Ibid., Director of Native Labour to Secretary for Native Affairs, 7 November 1938.

86. CAD, NTS, vol. 2120, file 227/280, Evidence of D. Harland Bowden, Native Affairs Commission, 27 January 1938.

87. NCOS Minutes, 13 September 1956.

88. Annual Report of the Inspector of Mines for Natal, pp. 29–30.

CHAPTER EIGHT

"WE WOMEN WILL SHOW THEM": BEER PROTESTS IN THE NATAL COUNTRYSIDE, 1929

Helen Bradford

INTRODUCTION[1]

"IT IS SURPRISING to me that action should be taken by the women, and that the men have kept in the background. It . . . points to the fact that an agitator is at the back of the whole affair," declared an uncomprehending magistrate in the South African village of Weenen in September 1929.[2] A beer boycott supported by thousands of workers in the harbor city of Durban had exploded into the Natal countryside. During the spring and summer of 1929, African women marched down village streets, chanted war songs, raided beerhalls, and assaulted male drinkers. They also transformed the boycotts. A campaign initially supported mainly by male migrant laborers was sustained by female nonworkers. A symbol of the exploitation of black male workers (the beerhall), came to embody the oppression of women by men. Instead of "agitators" mobilizing females, women taught leaders that the two sexes had distinctive experiences of capitalism and the state, gender-specific relations to political and social organizations, and different reactions to patriarchal oppression.

"A woman had no time for liquor. It was the man who went to drink," recalled Linah Mhlongo of her experiences in Natal in the

1920s. "Women worked harder than men. . . . We worked, we bred children, everything done by a woman. You worked even when pregnant. You couldn't rest."[3] Nor could you engage in many other activities. By law, a black Natal female had no right to private property; throughout her life all her assets and earnings legally belonged to a male guardian. Women's reproductive powers were often exchanged for cattle in marriages arranged by patriarchs; proverbs celebrated the taming of shrews by patrilocal, patrilineal households. As perpetual minors, women were largely excluded from black political processes and were even denied information about the male-dominated public domain: "No Zulu man will discuss anything of importance with a woman."[4]

Androcentric wisdom suggests that in a broader political economy based on capitalist exploitation and racial oppression, African women have displayed little, if any, feminist consciousness. In particular, female beer protests have often been regarded as backward-looking resistance by nonfeminist women defending "a traditional domestic function of women."[5] Yet feminists have long insisted that the family is a key site of female oppression—and certainly homesteads were racked by gender conflict in the 1929 Natal boycotts. Because women experienced the cheap-labor system and the racist state through the mediating structures of patriarchy, issues relating to female oppression permeated their economic and political struggles. Thus demonstrators frequently showed an awareness of and an antagonism to their subordination as a sex. They resisted discriminatory practices by black and white men, acted on the belief that women could be a political force in their own right, and usurped male identities, male practices, and male violence. They also broke through the boundaries of nationalist, class, or "traditionalist" categories: to confine women who struggled against beerhalls to these straitjackets is to transform "herstory" into "history."

GENESIS OF THE BEER PROTESTS

For capitalists, alcohol has historically been a contradictory commodity—it has both accelerated proletarianization while undermining labor power itself.[6] But as ever more blacks were pried off the land, Natal colonialists increasingly believed that beer and brewers were the ruin of the African male working class. After "an 'overdose' of Native Beer" (sorghum-based *utshwala*), men turned up late or were unfit to work. After drinking beer with a "kick"—*utshwala* mixed with methylated spirits, or sugar-based *isiqataviki* ("kill-me-quick"), or *isishimiyana*—men allegedly stole, fought, killed, or "ran amok."[7] Black females who drank beer were at least as destructive; if allowed access to alcohol in the same place as men, they supposedly became prostitutes and spread venereal disease. Indeed, women drinkers contaminated the future as well as the current generation of cheap laborers. They neglected domestic labor "to go routing about the country to these beer-drinkings," "even use the drink to wean their children," and hence "little children have as great a craving for the drink as the grown-up people."[8]

One link in this chain connecting beer, women, and workers was snapped in Natal in 1908. The Native Beer Act enabled the establishment of municipal beerhalls that both monopolized the sale of *utshwala* in urban areas, and also admitted only adult African men. If exploitation was easier when the quality and quantity of alcohol sold to workers was circumscribed, social control was cheaper when paid for by the oppressed buying beer at four to five times its cost. By 1929 eleven Natal municipalities were channeling the profits from *utshwala* into bleak barracks for migrant workers, matchbox houses in segregated locations, unserviced Town Lands for informal settlement, and inflated salaries of bureaucrats.[9]

The state's monopoly simultaneously involved effectively proscribing all Africans from selling nutritious *utshwala,* and prohibiting brewing in urban areas. The system rested on a bedrock of force. In midnight blitzes, police broke down doors, dug up floors, and seized beer vessels; they sexually harassed women, smashed household goods, and destroyed thousands of gallons of alcohol. They also met with resistance. As a weary Dundee constable complained in 1928, "Kaffir Beer is now very seldom found at the kraals, the Natives hide it away from the kraals in holes and in long grass, consequently raids cannot be conducted at night time."[10]

South African legislators, however, were often impervious to the problems of enforcing their edicts. Since uncontrolled access to alcohol was increasingly opposed by rural employers—and because the newly elected Pact government was more sensitive to this constituency—the 1928 Liquor Act extended urban controls over beer to the countryside. From January 1929 the brewing and drinking of *utshwala* in the reserves was prohibited. On private land, the consent of a white occupier was essential. (Permission was promptly granted by managers of coal mines struggling to attract labor; it was withheld by many farmers clearing their lands of "surplus" tenants, and technically impossible to obtain on African-owned plots.) In all other areas—including peri-urban Town Lands, where brewing had previously occurred relatively freely—every beer drink required the blessing of the magistrate. At a time when the development of agrarian capitalism was already impoverishing rural blacks, the Liquor Act clearly laid the basis for a broad alliance against a further turn of the economic and political screws.

Yet if liquor legislation united town and countryside, it affected women and men differently. Females suffered most as consumers. At least in towns where beerhalls existed, men could "drink in a cage," while women were forbidden access to alcohol. Females were also hit hardest when brewing became a criminal offense, since the established sexual division of labor (sometimes reinforced by male violence) allocated this illegal task largely to them. Crucially, too, it was female livelihoods that were at stake. Although a Vryheid man could still argue that the beer brewed by a woman "would belong to the husband," he was fighting a rearguard battle. By the 1920s ever more black women had wrested control over beer-derived incomes from men, and were carving out beer selling as their own economic domain.[11]

Not all women, however, were equally affected by the Liquor Act. First, female demonstrations erupted only in towns where beerhalls compounded the effects of the law. These establishments barred women as drinkers and competed with them as brewers; they also siphoned male earnings into oppressive structures, underlay vicious enforcement of beer restrictions, and provided a rallying point for females. Second, the act was difficult to implement away from the towns.

Hence the peri-urban women who dominated the demonstrations were drawn mainly from the African-owned plots and Town Lands surrounding the villages. These protesters were close enough to suffer both from enforcement of the new legislation and also from increased male patronage of the beerhalls. Third, women who had been subject to restrictions for decades were among the demonstrators. As the Newcastle magistrate said tartly to a deputation of farm and urban women, the ban on brewing within a five mile radius of the town "has been the same for twenty years in Natal. Why do you complain now?"[12] Officials were partially correct in alleging that protest eight months after the act came into effect was not entirely spontaneous.

In 1928 a nationwide black political movement had fragmented when the 100,000-member Industrial and Commercial Worker's Union (ICU) had been replaced in Durban by the ICU *yase* (of) Natal. Under the leadership of A. W. G. Champion, this splinter body recruited female beer sellers to combat waning finances. Perhaps with an eye to these new members—and aware of popular beer campaigns in the past—the opportunistic Champion began to coordinate resistance to the building of a beerhall in an area where shebeens proliferated. But resistance was transformed into a boycott with mass appeal only when it attracted the support of migrant dock laborers, resentful of paying for "barracks which are full of bad laws" with every overpriced beer they bought.[13]

By May 1929 members of the ICU's Women's Auxiliary, armed with sjamboks, were marching through the streets of Durban to Union meetings promoting home brewing. As the boycott gathered momentum, rank-and-file militants outstripped their leaders, stoned beerhalls, and clashed with police. In June 6,000 Africans battled with 2,000 whites who had besieged the ICU Hall. A Women's Auxiliary organizer, Ma-Dhlamini, "dumbfounded" male ICU leaders as she ferociously fought the vigilantes: she "was the woman in the man who stood before the forces . . . in military attire," and released many males from "the jaws of the lion." But there was bloodshed as well as bravery during the "Durban massacre." Six Africans and two whites were killed, 120 people were injured, and ICU *yase* Natal gatherings were promptly banned.[14]

The boycott, however, not only continued with astounding success for the next eighteen months but also spread to the rural areas (fig. 8.1). Upheavals in Durban frequently reverberated in the countryside. The tens of thousands of migrant laborers who sluiced through the port city also flowed back to the rural areas with tidings. On this occasion, however, these male "Secret Agents throughout Natal" were reinforced by women.[15] Uncharacteristically—since both the ICU and its secessionist offshoot were heavily male-oriented—Champion dele-

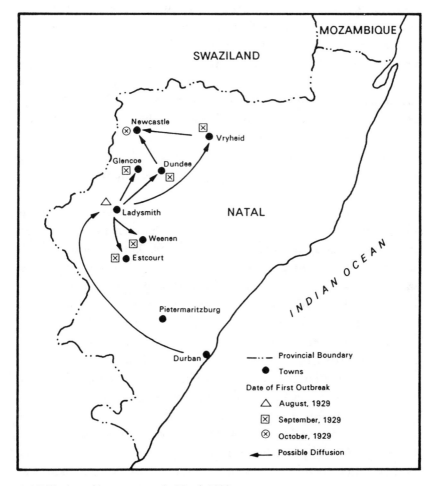

8.1 Diffusion of beer protests in Natal, 1929

gated to females the tasks of extending the boycott to the countryside. In mid-September, after collecting funds at both Union and Communist Party meetings, members of the Women's Auxiliary left Durban. Led by the indomitable Ma-Dhlamini, they headed for Weenen, Estcourt, Ladysmith, Glencoe, and Dundee "for the purpose of marshalling the Kaffir Beer agitation."[16]

The villages for which they embarked were minute—adult black populations often numbered in the hundreds—but they were far from sunk in rural idiocy. Indeed, demonstrations had already erupted in Ladysmith, Weenen, and Pinetown. Undoubtedly inspiration for the protests frequently derived from the outside: "in planning their raid on the canteen," Weenen women declared, "they were following the example of Durban and Ladysmith." Women's Auxiliary members probably added precept to precedent, although they maintained the low profile typical of female leaders in this period. Thus, by late September, all their target towns had been caught up in the campaign, and geographically separate demonstrations had acquired a relatively unified ideology. In all but one of the villages ultimately affected by the protests, ICU-derived demands surfaced for closure of the beerhalls and legalization of brewing.[17]

Why did the ICU *yase* Natal campaign have such resonance among village women? For one thing, as the economic vice tightened, beerhalls drained away desperately needed funds. The earnings of male workers had long failed to cover family subsistence needs. But household budgets were even more unbalanced when men spent 25 to 50 percent of their daily wage on a sixpenny quart of *utshwala*, which women could brew for sixpence a gallon.[18] Moreover, the 1928 drought in central Natal had swept northward. By mid-1929 harvests were poor or disastrous in most areas caught up in the spring protests. "We complain of the famine. We are starving," cried Glencoe women to the magistrate as they demanded the right to brew.[19]

While drought had spawned hunger since preindustrial times, the development of rural capitalism and urban townships now compounded its effects. According to Estcourt women demanding closure of the beerhall, they were poverty stricken because farmers had compelled reduction of livestock. Similarly, spokeswoman Matobana Mjara complained bitterly to the magistrate of attempts to whittle away herds on the Weenen Town Lands: "I have come here to ask what we are to eat. . . . We lived on our stock and now we have to reduce it." Here as elsewhere, women did not merely request the right to brew. Weenen demonstrators also demanded an end to stock limitations, a halt to evictions, and a reduction of rent. The laboring poor were rooted in regional political economies—and women infused their protests with a host of demands related to local struggles for survival.[20]

But poverty—like the Liquor Act and the ICU—affected men and women differently. Not only were female wages usually considerably less than those of males: placing food on the table was also primarily a female responsibility. There may well have been a "hierarchy of hunger" as women went short to feed men and children.[21] Stock limitations were certainly skewed sexually. In both Weenen and Estcourt, goats on which women survived "while the husband is away" were being far more vigorously reduced than the cattle owned by men.[22]

As significant, perhaps, was the impact on women of longer-term changes in relations of production and reproduction. As men were stripped of land—and increasingly supported themselves from pittances rather than from the labor of women and children—so wives and offspring were being transformed from assets to burdens. "They are not feeding me," explained an aggrieved husband who had failed to support his family; "I go to town and go and work for myself because I am starving."[23] But for women, the decreasing value placed on children by men was exacerbated by the increasing importance of female sexuality in male eyes. Many protesters were not only responsible for hungry children, they were also shabbily dressed and hence disadvantaged in the struggle to retain male support. They pointed to their old clothes and cried, "We wear sacks because our husbands spend their money and time at the beerhalls."[24]

There was already a female tradition of invoking white authorities against black males who sloughed off their families. "They do not trust the father; they do not trust the husband," complained an outraged male member of the black elite. "The court is the husband of the wife; the court is the father of the daughter. They run up there for their food and clothing."[25] Most women, however, appealed not to judges but to sons for the necessities of life. But youths were also breaking away from patriarchal households—and as they won their own freedom they further marginalized mothers. In Newcastle females were protesting precisely because youths had joined elders in squandering their money at the beerhall.[26]

It was not only food and clothing for the family that was subordinated to drink for men. Shelter was also at risk. In Estcourt, women raided the beerhall when "the houses were under arrest because of liquor. The man takes money for beer, and then he says, 'Whew, I am dying.' Then the white man would come and he would lock the door."[27] Females, their survival often structured around the home, were more directly imperiled as rent money was spent on *utshwala*. Spokeswomen calling for closure of the Weenen beerhall were under threat of eviction from the Town Lands, while "men sold their stock and are spending the proceeds at the beer canteen."[28] Small wonder that black women did not primarily perceive beerhalls as places where African workers paid for their own oppression. For rural women, they symbolized instead female subordination in a world that was ruled by men.

CLASS, CULTURE, AND CONFLICT

The 1928 Liquor Act underscored female oppression by precipitating ever more family men into the beerhalls. These establishments had long been dominated by rougher laborers made single by migrancy— a "floating population and of a promiscuous character"—whose "incessant fighting" and "bad language" frequently transformed the halls into foci of an aggressive male subculture.[29] But now that home brewing was prohibited, complained the wives of farm tenants, their husbands were also patronizing the beerhalls and "coming home drunk and ill-treating them." "We want our husbands," shouted many other peri-urban demonstrators as they marched on the beerhalls; married men, they insisted, were now leaving their wives "hungry and naked" as they spent all their earnings on municipal *utshwala*.[30]

Officialdom, however, was far from convinced that women were mobilizing merely as aggrieved wives. One magistrate dryly noted that the local beerhall was not patronized by family men from the Town Lands.[31] Others were well aware that images of a nuclear family with a dependent wife jarred with reality. Cohabitation with lovers was increasingly common and illegitimate births were "becoming quite the fashion nowadays" among "the Christianized class." Urban men bewailed the fact that "our womenfolk are getting out of hand and they are leaving us."[32] Furthermore, as male control over female productive and reproductive capacities was eroded, so procreators of children were becoming petty traders of commodities. Or as a policeman sourly expressed it,

> Undoubtedly a number of the protesting native women are genuinely concerned, but attached to each party of native female demonstrators is a very large sprinkling of women who want not only liberty of action in brewing of native beer and other intoxicating concoctions, but license to make and sell as much as they like to the detriment of industry and farming operations.[33]

Women also sought license to survive in a patriarchal world. Black female populations in these villages often doubled or trebled in the 1920s, and few legal jobs were open apart from extremely ill paid domestic service.[34] For many of the demonstrators with infants, the sexual division of labor was constricting their choices at precisely the time when financial needs were expanding—but brewing could be combined with child care. Moreover, for wives who lacked economic and emotional security—in exogamous marriages, in a society where wages revolved around single men—a petit bourgeois escape route was singularly attractive. Throughout South Africa, black brewers displayed a stubborn pride in their independent contributions to household budgets: "That's right—that is how a woman does it; look at us, we do not sit and look up to our husbands or fathers to work alone; we have sent our children to school with money from beer selling."[35]

Females whose procreative powers had long been marketed by patriarchs could also sell their own sexuality at shebeens. As in the American South, this often constituted "an improvement, however grim, for women too frequently forced to submit to sexual exploitation without even the demeaning recognition of the independent existence reflected in a cash payment."[36] The sale of sex may often have been more lucrative than the retailing of liquor, and the two trades were certainly intertwined. Thus, demonstrators in Newcastle came mainly from African-owned plots notorious as both "hotbeds of vice" and as centers of brewing. As the ex-manager of a colliery beerhall sententiously remarked, "Home brewing is invariably associated with women of bad repute. It serves as an attraction to draw the native to these women for other purposes."[37]

It was hardly surprising that brewers-cum-prostitutes had impinged on his consciousness. In northern Natal several colliery beerhalls were run by a company, the Mines Stores (Natal) Ltd., that had come to an amicable understanding with mine owners at the expense of shebeens. Since mine managers struggling to attract permanent workers to the collieries held that "men must have women in the same way as they must have beer," the Mine Stores allowed females—including prostitutes—into its beerhalls.[38] Moreover, since mine owners sought to shackle indebted laborers to the collieries, the trading company issued credit only in the form of metal tokens—and simultaneously throttled shebeens. When the protests against municipal beerhalls swept through Natal, some women seized the opportunity to challenge colliery practices as well. Thus 400 Glencoe women gathered on a mission farm situated between two coal mines and supporting a population that allegedly lived from the sale of beer and sex. They demanded the closure of "the Jews Canteen" and the end of the "trash money" that channeled male wages to merchant capital.[39]

Although they also threatened to destroy beer in the Dundee municipal hall, neither they nor any other demonstrators marched on the colliery beerhalls, "where the best customers are the women." Significantly, then, females raided only beerhalls that practiced sexual discrimination. Indeed, some emphasized their demand to consume *utshwala* on equal terms with men. Females were neither served at the municipal beerhall nor allowed to brew, argued Newcastle protesters; while "the men wasted their money at the canteen the women had to go dry." Ladysmith demonstrators substituted action for words: one raid consisted solely of gate-crashing the beerhall and seizing alcohol.[40]

Only a minority of peri-urban females—and an even smaller proportion of those in the countryside—participated in such demonstrations. Did social factors distinguish the Amazons from fearful females who rushed to the police for protection against these viragos? Certainly, females in effective control of their families were prominent among spokeswomen in Weenen. They included a widow, as well as Matobana Mjara, whose husband was a migrant in distant Cape Town.[41] Female assertiveness also tended to increase as the authority of males decreased with the fission of the homestead, and most Weenen demonstrators derived from a chiefdom characterized by households much smaller than usual. In Estcourt, where some three-quarters of adult African women were married, five unmarried women were at the fore of the protests. If in their personal lives they lacked attachments to men who frittered away money, in public they had attempted to win sympathy as distressed wives. The magistrate was not amused: "They had deceived him about their husbands and sons squandering their money, and the five before him had no husbands or children."[42]

They may not have had husbands or sons, but they were certainly enmeshed in a mutual-aid network composed of women. Females who were largely excluded from male society, and who were sardined together in locations and Town Lands, could hardly avoid developing an informal ethic of solidarity. Like their counterparts on the Rand, Natal brewers probably exchanged information about the credit ratings of customers, coordinated prices and parties, kept a wary eye out for the police, and supported one another when arrested.[43] Patrilocal patterns of settlement facilitated the flow of other women's movements over considerable distances and may have been just as significant as ICU activists in developing remarkable regional solidarity. Thus, Dundee women helped organize the Newcastle protests, and females based in villages where boycotts were already in progress participated in demonstrations elsewhere.[44] Even generational barriers were partially overcome. Young, middle-aged, and old participated in the Weenen demonstrations. In Dundee elderly women were left behind in the first rush on the beerhall only because they ran too slowly.[45]

The church—somewhat contemptuously termed *ibandla labesifazana* ("congregation of women") by Zulu-speaking men—also welded females together.[46] By the 1920s women formed the backbone of both mission and separatist churches. Largely excluded from many other organizations, they flocked to join institutions that sanctified the female sphere of the family, celebrated female rites of passage such as birth and marriage, and simultaneously undermined older forms of patriarchal oppression. Thus, many brides were nominal church members: Christian weddings barred husbands from taking a second wife, and improved women's chances of holding men legally responsible for maintenance. To the distress of a white male minister, many black females clearly perceived religion less as a spiritual defense against the forces of evil than as a secular weapon in their struggle against men.[47] To the delight of a white female missionary, a 1926 Natal conference of black women's prayer unions was infused with "delicious feelings of Woman's rights. . . . I believe our Zulu women will show the men how to do it yet. Wouldn't that be a joke?"[48]

Three years later, she may have been less amused by the use made of the organizational infrastructure created by weekly hymn-singing, banner-bearing services. According to Charles Kumalo, rural and urban women could unite in the Estcourt beer campaign because "in church they congregated to pray, and it was there where they sat and discussed these things."[49] The symbols and rhythms of the religious week also imposed themselves on the protests. The Newcastle women invariably approached the magistrate on a Thursday, precisely the day devoted to women's prayer activities. They carried several homemade flags and a green banner on their first march and a large white flag on the second.[50] In addition, black women flaunted their adherence to an ideology positing justice transcending that of the state. When females marched on the Dundee magistrate from colliery and peri-urban properties, they solemnly sang a hymn and prayed before entering the town. In Weenen before the trial of the first batch of demonstrators, a large procession of women—all dressed in black—stood in front of the magistrate's court, "sang a Doxology, and then marched on to the court singing hymns."[51]

For all this, the marriage between Christians and beerhall boycotters was not without conflict. Among poor women in working class or rural communities, economic reality, patriarchal authority, and long-standing custom all thwarted acceptance of the mission church tenet that teetotalism was next to godliness. In every center except Vryheid—where deputations reputedly consisted largely of ladies "of a good type" who may well have belonged to white-run churches—females demanded the right to brew.[52] Moreover, the issue of the consumption or sale of alcohol was a rock upon which the alliance between black preachers and protesters could founder. Although Champion tried to weld together the interests of churches, temperance associations, and beer boycotters in Durban, African ministers preaching teetotalism at ICU meetings were "only extricated with some difficulty from an enraged audience."[53] The relationship between village females and black preachers was as strained. Far from supporting the women, a black minister in Newcastle preferred to help police arrest brewers who followed "the non-Zulu custom of selling beer."[54] Far from accepting the refusal of a separatist preacher to join their protest, militant women in Weenen threatened to wreck his house.[55]

They also mobilized a constituency broader than Christians alone. When the Weenen magistrate gave suspended sentences to the forty-two women charged with rushing the beerhall, "raw natives" joyfully congregated outside the church as their Christian compatriots gave thanks to the Lord.[56] In Estcourt, Kumalo recalled that the rioters wore traditional dresses, and that leaders came mainly from the farms, "because they knew how to fight with sticks. . . . They also chose people who knew how to sing praises. As it was clear that people wanted war. They sang battle songs when they went to attack."[57] Both female and rural worlds were relatively resilient in the face of capitalist inroads, and symbols from an older setting undoubtedly resonated among many women who had but recently left the farms.

That was perhaps particularly true of Weenen, a laggard district as regards the development of capitalist agriculture and urban industry. When women in this tiny town challenged racial and sexual geography by invading whites' public domain, they appropriated male accouterments and female rituals of precolonial days. Three days after the first raid on the Weenen beerhall—carried out by some two hundred domestic servants, washerwomen and others wearing dresses largely of Western style—the shocked magistrate met a deputation of four carrying assegais. Ten days later, sixty to seventy women confronted the local authorities. Many defiantly carried sticks, wore feathers and cow tails, and repeated their threats to give their husbands "a good thrashing." By the time of the second raid, most had repudiated bodily symbols that defined them as colonized people and sexual inferiors. "The majority of these women were wearing cow tails '*Mtshokobezis*' and feathers and some were even wearing men's loin coverings."[58] This subversive role reversal was redolent of ceremonies surrounding a Zulu goddess associated with beer—and may similarly have been intended "to compel the assistance of the Unseen by some flagrant outrage on decency."[59] But the women left nothing to chance intervention by supernatural forces. Wielding two sticks each, they chased all the men out of the beerhall, and vigorously assaulted the police.

In a society where militarism was the prerogative of males, the bellicose overtones of the protests electrified both white and black men. Even before the colonial state suppressed black military activities, Zulu-speaking women were divorced from the weapons, the marching, and the fighting associated with war. By the 1920s the syncretic culture that had emerged sanctioned "faction fighting" among males, while socially constructing women as submissive. Female bodies, in particular, were straitjacketed. As the vector of women's reproductive powers, they were the site that best symbolized subordination to men. To be feminine was to be clad in clothes that signaled marital status, restricted to dance steps that were demure, excluded from the stick fighting once practiced by girls, and confined to an argot shorn of words disrespectful to male elders. Violence, outspokenness, audacity— all these were masculine traits.[60]

In the beer protests, however, women assumed identities from which they were barred both as females and as members of a conquered nation. They mustered in marching formation, paraded in threes, chanted war songs, brandished weapons, and generally behaved "in a riotous manner, dancing, shouting and striking their sticks on the ground."[61] They picketed beerhalls and forcibly prevented men from buying alcohol; they marched through beerhalls, smashed their windows, assaulted male drinkers, and tried "to take possession of the canteen."[62] Nor were settlers exempted, as women defied every norm of feminine behavior. By preference, protesters confronted white magistrates en masse. When forced to elect representatives, they contemptuously rejected men or chiefs. "We are now the men," declared Matobana Majara in a statement pregnant with meaning, "we don't want any chiefs speaking for us." In Estcourt, women refused to give their names: some called themselves Drink or Trouble. Their spokeswoman rudely informed the magistrate that her name was *Hluphekile* ("Worried") and her husband's name was *Dakwanjalo* ("Always Drunk").[63]

These aggressive confrontations in the offices of power frequently culminated in furious melees on the streets. After the failure of two deputations in Newcastle, females attacked the beerhall with sticks, bit and stoned the police, broke the nozzle of the fire hose directed at them, and violently resisted arrest.[64] Two days after Estcourt women had been "captured" following the first raid on the beerhall, a female "army" marched on the prison to take it by storm. Fearful white residents near the jail could feel the ground shake as stamping, dancing, and singing prisoners demonstrated solidarity with the women outside.[65] In Weenen too, both passive and active resistance to settler sanctions was the order of the day. Females still at large "demanded to be sent to the Gaol with the others," while women imprisoned for a raid "were singing and shouting and would not listen to the Gailer."[66]

The battle over beer was most intense in Ladysmith, perhaps because it coincided with conflicts over the creation of a segregated township next to the sewerage works.[67] On a mid-September afternoon, after four deputations and three demonstrations had not secured any lasting redress, women were picketing the beerhall. Violence erupted when about thirty police tried to arrest the forty or so pickets. As bruised and bleeding women "were thrown into the lorries like bags," others thronged round the white head constable, "poking their sticks past his head and in front of his face" and "simultaneously attacking other members of the Force with sticks and stones."[68] After arresting thirteen women, the police doggedly raided dwellings near the beerhall for liquor. They were forcibly tackled by females as they loaded the trucks with saucepans and casks containing about two hundred gallons of beer.[69]

That evening, some one hundred and fifty incensed females, followed by "a few men" and children, marched on the jail and demanded that they too be arrested. "*Voetsak!*" ("Bugger off!") shouted the head constable and began assaulting the women; "*Bulala!*" ("Kill!")

yelled the crowd and hurled bottles of kerosene against the prison walls.[70] All available policemen were rushed to the scene. The women "used sticks, stones and bottles furiously attacking," and tried to break open the jail. After a fierce battle, in which several police were injured, twenty-six more women and two men were arrested, while the rest threw missiles at the forces of law and order as they fled. Not that the conflict was over. Protests simmered on for months and an attempt was made to burn the beerhall in December.[71]

Unlike their Ladysmith compatriots, some females benefited from the social condemnation visited on men who physically beat up women in public. Fire hoses were the preferred method of control in battles outside beerhalls: hitting women with jets of water was apparently more acceptable within male morality than clouting the "weaker sex." There were times, too, when black police "evidently did not relish fighting with Amazons."[72] Because they were outnumbered, and perhaps feared being defeated by females, or because they "were not fools to beat up [their own women]," they frantically blew their whistles for white support, or pretended incompetence with the fire hose, or simply ran away. In South Africa, as elsewhere, riotous females could clearly sap male forces of direct repression.[73]

What, however, of white officials less involved in conflicts on the streets? Undoubtedly, many magistrates perceived females through sexist lenses. Almost by definition, women could not be a genuine threat to law and order; almost as a reflex action, some tried to shore up cracks in patriarchal authority before committing the women to prison. Thus, magistrates initially imposed a plethora of suspended sentences, and sternly ordered "the men to control their women folk."[74] Many were also uneasy about the Liquor Act's interference with customary rights—and could be pressured into concessions. In both Weenen and Ladysmith, beerhalls were temporarily closed. In Pietermaritzburg the hasty issue of brewing permits to women on African-owned plots averted a threatened picket of the beerhall and kept the capital city quiescent throughout the year.[75]

Central state officials, however, were wrenching local authorities into line with a more starkly repressive and segregationist policy. In November several hundred Transvaal policemen descended on Durban to enforce payment of taxes, eradicate illicit brewing, and end the spread of "Communist propaganda" from town to countryside. Deploying machine guns and bayonets, and using tear gas for the first time in South African history, they arrested several thousand male workers and destroyed thousands of gallons of alcohol. The Minister of Native Affairs also ordered the dissemination of a blunt message to Africans in Natal villages characterized by "turbulent and riotous conduct": "it is for the European population to indicate to the Government whether there shall be facilities for the brewing and sale of liquor."[76]

Confronted by obdurate women, and facing financial crisis if the protests were successful, village authorities were not slow to pick up such cues. They threatened Town Land tenants with eviction, and warned female demonstrators that their sticks would soon be countered with guns. As women with suspended sentences reappeared in courts, magistrates all over the countryside imposed even harsher sentences of one to three months without the option of fines. To the relief of white residents, and the dismay of black females, there were limits to paternalism when women acted like men.[77]

PARTICIPATION OF BLACK MEN

Ironically, the removal of wives from the sphere of the home to the confines of prison at last galvanized males into action. Child care suddenly loomed uncomfortably large for many working-class men. When fifty-one Estcourt women were imprisoned, their husbands "threatened to lodge the babies in the Magistrate's garden for him to look after."[78] In Newcastle angry men armed with sticks joined women waiting for eight female convicts to be transferred. Although mounted police prevented the attempt to free the prisoners, one man broke through the cordon, struck at the police, and was promptly arrested. In Weenen the magistrate had to make elaborate plans to move fifteen convicted women to the larger Pietermaritzburg jail, since "the men had decided to rescue the women," and "were going to cause trouble even if it resulted in bloodshed."[79]

Yet the men failed to fulfill their threat, just as most rural males failed to mobilize in support of the women's earlier demands. Undoubtedly, numerous men boycotted beerhalls for months; female pickets presumably concentrated minds already aware that municipal *utshwala* was politically objectionable or simply "bad beer." But if beer sales fell temporarily, there were few signs of enthusiastic male support for the campaign. In no rural town did males overtly organize or support the initial protests; only one man was arrested in the clashes outside beerhalls. Certainly the ICU *yase* Natal scathingly concluded that "from Weenen to Newcastle women fought well, but they could not succeed because their men were in collusion with the Government and Local Authorities."[80]

Many males might have leveled a similar accusation at the Union. Thousands of tenant households had been evicted from farms in 1927–1928 for associating with ICU-inspired struggles. Blacklisted by farmers and frequently unable to settle in overcrowded reserves, these evictees had poured into the slums and Town Lands of neighboring villages. Perhaps their womenfolk responded to the ICU *yase* Natal campaign—few had joined the ICU and brewing was undoubtedly one route to survival. But many men were extremely hostile to the Union. A year before the beer boycott erupted in Dundee, the ICU branch secretary was almost murdered by infuriated evicted males who believed the Union was "in league with the Dutch farmers."[81] Insofar as it was unable to persuade men to protest against rural beerhalls, the ICU *yase* Natal may well have been reaping the whirlwind sown by the male-dominated ICU in the countryside.

There were further distinctions between Durban and the villages that underpinned differential male participation in the protests. Both gender roles and political controls had changed faster in the industrializing and populous port city. Here women without men were carving out lucrative careers as "shebeen queens" while many of their rural counterparts merely eked out an existence. Here men without women had already "descended" to brewing and were directly affected by new restrictions related to the Liquor Act.[82] Moreover, the connections between beerhalls and barracks were patent to thousands of male migrant laborers in the metropolis; the links between leisure and oppression were blurred for the hundreds of laborers in villages where segregated townships and compounds were in their infancy.

Hence the vibrant alliance forged between brewers and migrants in Durban was tenuous or nonexistent in the countryside. Brewers had not the power of their city counterparts, while male workers had not the grievances. Village men did not merely fail to participate in the protests—some actively opposed the boycotts. In Ladysmith "the men got angry because they were not allowed to get the beer." In Estcourt, migrants "complained that if the canteen were closed, where would they drink?"[83]

Men radicalized by state repression took the initiative in the city, while women angered by male oppression set the pace in the countryside. Even if village males could overcome sexist prejudices, they still had to vault over material obstacles related to differential incorporation into the working class. Even sympathetic male laborers would have found difficulty in participating in demonstrations that usually occurred during working hours on weekdays. Even supportive male workers were often less militant than women who were neither full-time wage laborers nor subject to passes in a period of deepening recession. And even defiant males often regarded employers and day-to-day political controls as far more immediate targets than beerhalls. By late 1930 these gender differences had at last torn even the Durban campaign apart. The focus of male resistance here had shifted from beerhalls to passes, and females were bitterly echoing the battle cry of the countryside: "the men have failed and we women will show them what we can do."[84]

CONCLUSION

The time for successful protests had passed. Many husbands, lovers, and sons were prepared to boycott beerhalls only briefly. They often compared favorably with shebeens situated in unheated lean-to's where the stench was unbearable, where typhus from contaminated water was a constant threat, and where large families were crammed into one or two rooms. As appealing was drinking in an all-male domain, where men accustomed to sexually segregated existences could evade the pressure of discontented women and consolidate their positions as the dominant gender. If the price of a beer in a municipal hall enabled men to escape the stifling confines of domestic life, evade the police and prisons of settler society, and relax after arduous work into a masculine subculture, then it was a price many were only too willing to pay. But if abolition of the beerhalls and legalization of brewing allowed females to escape patriarchs, police, and economic pressures, then small wonder the history of black women's struggles has been so intimately entwined with beer.

NOTES

1. An earlier version of this paper appeared as "'We Are Now the Men': Women's Beer Protests in the Natal Countryside, 1929," in *Class, Community and Conflict*, ed. B. Bozzoli (Johannesburg: Ravan Press, 1987).

2. Natal Archives Depot (NA), Correspondence of Weenen Magistrate (CW), file 2/3/4, Weenen Native Commissioner (NC) to Chief Native Commissioner (CNC), 11 September 1929.

3. University of the Witwatersrand (UW), African Studies Institute (ASI), Oral History Project (OHP), Vusi Nkumane (VN) and Helen Bradford (HB), interview with Linah Mhlongo, Vryheid, 24 November 1981.

4. E. Krige, *The Social System of the Zulus* (Pietermaritzburg: Shuter and Shooter, 1981), p. 126. One proverb—referring to the dress adopted by married women—is *akuqhalaqhala lahlul isidwaba:* "no defiant woman ever defeated a leather skirt."

5. T. Lodge, *Black Politics in South Africa since 1945* (Johannesburg: Ravan Press, 1983), p. 148. See also C. Kros, *Urban African Women's Organizations, 1935–1956* (Johannesburg: Africa Perspective, 1980), pp. 2–3, 45–49; J. Yawitch, "Natal 1959—the Women's Protests," in *Collected Papers of Conference on the History of Opposition in South Africa* (Johannesburg: 1978), p. 219.

6. C. van Onselen, "Randlords and Rotgut, 1886–1903," in *Studies in the Social and Economic History of the Witwatersrand* (London: Longman, 1982), 1:52, 62.

7. UW, Church of the Province of South Africa Archives (CPSA), evidence to the Native Economic Commission (ENEC), AD 1438, box 10, summary by F. Lucas of Natal magistrates' opinions of "Kaffir Beer," and box 12, "Native Custom" by V. Makanya; *Natal Witness*, 23 September

1929; P. la Hausse, *Brewers, Beerhalls and Boycotts* (Johannesburg: Ravan Press, 1988), p. 47.

8. UW, CPSA, ENEC, box 8, Detective A. Hoffman, p. 7652; P. la Hausse (in this collection).

9. P. la Hausse (in this collection). The municipalities, with the dates when their beerhalls were established, were Dundee (1912), Durban (1909), Estcourt (1915), Greytown (1910), Howick (1929), Ladysmith (1912), Newcastle (1908), Pietermaritzburg (1909), Pinetown (1925), Verulam (1924), and Vryheid (1913).

10. Central Archives Depot (CAD), Native Affairs Department (NTS), vol. 2081, file 200/280, Inspector, District Commandant of South African Police (SAP), Dundee to Dundee magistrate, 9 May 1928; NTS, vol. 7054, file 110/322, District Commandant, Dundee to Deputy Commissioner, Pietermaritzburg, 25 September 1929.

11. CAD, ENEC, box 4, Evidence of W. Ndhlovu, p. 1561; P. la Hausse, "The Struggle for the City: Alcohol, the Ematsheni and Popular Culture in Durban, 1902–1936" (M.A. diss., University of Cape Town, 1984), p. 140. In the early twentieth century, Durban men sold the *utshwala* produced by women. By the 1920s, females here—as in many villages and reserves—were themselves selling beer, although some first had to ask permission from patriarchs.

12. *Star,* 1 November 1929.

13. P. la Hausse, "Struggle for the City," p. 25. For more details about these two mass movements, see H. Bradford, *A Taste of Freedom: the ICU in Rural South Africa, 1924–1930* (New Haven: Yale University Press, 1987).

14. CAD, NTS, vol. 7606, file 49/328, CNC to Secretary of Native Affairs (SNA), 8 November 1929, enclosing *Igazi ne Zinyembezi; Natal Witness,* 12 November 1929. Ma-Dhlamini perhaps looked like a man because she was wearing the ICU uniform.

15. CAD, NTS, vol. 7054, file 110/322, A. Champion to CNC, 14 October 1929.

16. Ibid., Sub-Inspector CID, Durban to Divisional CID Officer, Pietermaritzburg, 21 September 1929.

17. NA, CW, file 2/3/4, undated newsclipping written on 6 September 1929. Female activists often mobilized door-to-door rather than at mass meetings. The Women's Auxiliary members were perhaps particularly difficult to discern because numerous black police turned in "utterly useless" reports on the ICU *yase* Natal.

18. CAD, ENEC, Evidence of P. Armstrong, Vryheid, p. 1519 and J.

Farrer, Durban, p. 6568. Many men working in these villages averaged thirty to forty shillings a month; Newcastle women complained that at wages of a shilling a day, African males were unable to buy both beer and food.

19. CAD, NTS, vol. 7054, file 110/322, Minutes of meeting at Dundee, 19 September 1929.

20. *Star,* 26 September 1929; NA, CW, file 2/3/4, Minutes of meeting between Weenen NC and female deputations, 6 September and 9 September 1929.

21. The phrase derives from O. Hufton, "Women in Revolution 1789–1796," *Past and Present* 53 (1971): 93.

22. NA, CW, file 2/3/4, Minutes of meeting between Weenen NC and female deputation, 6 September 1929; U.G. 37–'28, *Agricultural Census no. 10, 1927,* (Pretoria: Government Printers, 1928), p. 52; U.G. 12–'32, *Agricultural Census no. 13, 1930* (Pretoria: Government Printers, 1932), pp. 42, 48. Since goats were regarded by whites as destructive animals and by blacks as poor men's cattle, their chances of survival were slim when male homestead heads were ordered to reduce their holdings.

23. UW, CPSA, ENEC, box 7, Evidence of Mr. Nyongwana, Pietermaritzburg, p. 6772e; *Star,* 26 September 1929.

24. P. la Hausse, *Brewers, Beerhalls and Boycotts,* p. 5. For the growing importance of female sexuality over fertility, compare J. Guy, "Analysing Pre-Capitalist Societies in Southern Africa," *Journal of Southern African Studies* 14 (1987) with L. Longmore, *The Dispossessed* (London: Jonathan Cape, 1959).

25. UW, CPSA, ENEC, box 7, Evidence of Mr. Nyongwana, Pietermaritzburg, p. 6722e.

26. *Star,* 1 November 1929.

27. UW, ASI, OHP, VN and HB, interview with Jacob Mchunu, Mooi River, 1 December 1981.

28. NA, CW, file 2/3/4, Minutes of meeting between Weenen NC and female deputation, 6 September 1929.

29. *Natal Witness,* 20 September 1929; CAD, ENEC, box 16, H. Mtetwa and C. Kumalo to Commissioner, Vryheid, 18 September 1930. It is difficult to discern the outlines of these migrants in the villages: they included sewerage workers in Estcourt and probably incorporated many laborers in construction, transport, and heavy industry (such as iron and steel in Newcastle).

30. *Star,* 26 September 1929; CAD, NTS, vol. 7054, file 110/322, District Commandant, Dundee to Deputy Commissioner, 25 September 1929.

31. NA, CW, NC Weenen to CNC, 11 September 1929.

32. CAD, ENEC, box 4, Evidence of Dundee Agricultural Society, Dundee Farmers' Association and Glencoe Farmers' Association, pp. 1267–68; UW, CPSA, ENEC, box 7, Evidence of J. Gumede, Pietermaritzburg, p. 6780.

33. CAD, NTS, vol. 7054, file 110/322, District Commandant, Dundee to Deputy Commissioner, 25 September 1929.

34. Due to both rural and gender struggles, black female populations in these villages often increased some sixfold between 1921 and 1936. In Newcastle, for example, numbers rose from 459 to 3,055 women.

35. E. Mphahlele, *Down Second Avenue* (London: Faber and Faber, 1980), p. 41.

36. E. Fox-Genovese and E. Genovese, *The Fruits of Merchant Capital* (Oxford: Oxford University Press, 1983), p. 140.

37. S.C. 3–'23, *First Report on the Select Committee on Native Affairs* (Pretoria: Government Printers, 1923), p. 144.

38. R. Edgecombe (in this collection).

39. CAD, NTS, vol. 7054, file 110/322, Minutes of meeting at Dundee, 19 September 1929; NTS, vol. 2081, file 200/280, Sub–NC, Benoni and Acting Divisional Inspector, Natal to Secretary of Labour, 31 October 1927; NA, CNC, 22/484, N2/2/2(6), Compound Manager, Burnside to Manager, Burnside Colliery, 8 October 1935. Jewish capitalists founded the Mine Stores.

40. CAD, NTS, vol. 7054, file 110/322, District Commandant, Dundee to Deputy Commissioner, 25 September 1929; ENEC, box 4, Evidence of P. Armstrong, Vryheid, p. 1520; *Star,* 1 November 1929.

41. NA, CW, 2/3/4, Minutes of meeting between Weenen NC and female deputation, 9 September 1929, and Weenen NC to CNC, 16 October 1929. Mjara had recently sent her husband the vast sum of £40 when he was convicted on a *dagga* charge in Cape Town—perhaps brewing was not the only string in her bow.

42. *Star,* 26 September 1929.

43. See, for example, E. Hellman, "Rooiyard: A Sociological Survey of an Urban Native Slum Yard" (Ph.D. diss., University of Witwatersrand, 1935), pp. 77–78.

44. *Star,* 28 October 1929; W. Beinart, "*Amafeladawonye* (the Die–hards): Popular Protest and Women's Movements in Herschel District in the 1920s," in W. Beinart and C. Bundy, *Hidden Struggles in Rural South Africa* (London: James Currey, 1987), p. 240.

45. NA, CW, file 2/3/4, undated newsclipping written on 6 September 1929; CAD, NTS, vol. 7054, file 110/322, District Commandant, Dundee to Deputy Commissioner, 25 September 1929.

46. B. Sundkler, *The Christian Ministry in Africa* (Upsala: Swedish Institute of Missionary Research, 1960), p. 171.

47. UW, CPSA, ENEC, box 12, Statement by Rev. J. Dewar; Hufton, "Women in Revolution," p. 108.

48. D. Gaitskell, "Female Mission Initiatives: Black and White Women in Three Witwatersrand Churches, 1903–1959" (Ph.D. diss., University of London, 1981), p. 172.

49. UW, ASI, OHP, VN and HB, interview with Charles Kumalo, Mooi River, 28 November 1981.

50. *Star,* 1 November 1929 and 22 November 1929.

51. NA, CW, file 2/3/4, undated news clipping written on 9 September 1929; CAD, NTS, vol. 7054, file 110/322, District Commandant, Dundee to Deputy Commissioner, 25 September 1929.

52. CAD, NTS, vol. 7054, file 110/322, Vryheid NC to CNC, 26 September 1929.

53. CAD, NTS, vol. 7599, file 46/322, CNC to SNA, 31 August 1929.

54. *Natal Witness,* 7 December 1929.

55. NA, CW, file 2/3/4, Weenen NC to CNC, 28 September 1929.

56. CAD, NTS, vol. 7054, file 110/322, District Commandant, Dundee to Deputy Commissioner, 25 September 1929.

57. UW, ASI, OHP, interview with Kumalo.

58. NA, CW, file 2/3/4, Weenen NC to CNC, 26 September 1929; see also undated news clipping written on 6 September 1929, Weenen NC to CNC, 12 September 1929 and Weenen NC to CNC 19 September 1929.

59. L. Samuelson, *Zululand, Its Traditions, Legends, Customs and Folk-Lore* (Pietermaritzburg: Marianhill Mission Press, 1911), p. 166.

60. M. Gluckman, "Zulu Women in Hoecultural Ritual," *Bantu Studies* 9 (1935): 261–62; H. Tracey, *Zulu Paradox* (Johannesburg: Silver Leaf Books, 1948), p. 73. For comparative insights on the significance of women's bodies in female subordination and protest, see C. Ifeka-Muller, "Female Militancy and Colonial Revolt," in *Perceiving Women,* ed. S. Ardener (London: J. M. Dent, 1977), p. 135.

61. CAD, NTS, vol. 7054, file 110/322, District Commandant, Dundee to Deputy Commissioner, 26 September 1929.

62. *Natal Witness,* 9 October 1929; see also NA, CW, file 2/3/4, Weenen NC to CNC, 11 September 1929; *Natal Witness,* 23 November 1929, 28 November 1929.

63. NA, CW, file 2/3/4, Minutes of meeting between Weenen NC and deputation of women, 6 September 1929; *Natal Witness,* 10 September

1929; *Star*, 26 September 1929. Journalists' versions of the husband's name—*Nagwa Njolo, Nanwa Njalo*—have been corrected; *isidakwa* was a common term for drunkards.

64. *Star*, 22 November 1929.

65. *Star*, 26 September 1929.

66. NA, CW, file 2/3/4, Weenen NC to CNC, 11 September 1929.

67. *Natal Witness*, 16 September 1929.

68. CAD, NTS, vol. 7054, file 110/322, District Commandant, Dundee to Deputy Commissioner, 25 September 1929; *Natal Witness*, 28 November 1929.

69. *Star*, 18 September 1929.

70. CAD, NTS, vol. 7054, file 110/322, District Commandant, Dundee to Deputy Commissioner, 25 September 1929; *Natal Witness*, 18 September 1929, 28 November 1929.

71. CAD, NTS, vol. 7054, file 110/322, District Commandant, Dundee to Deputy Commissioner, 25 September 1929; *Natal Witness*, 28 December 1929; *Star*, 1 February 1930.

72. NA, CW, file 2/3/4, undated news clipping written on 6 September 1929.

73. Ibid., Weenen NC to CNC, 11 September 1929; UW, ASI, OHP, interview with Kumalo.

74. NA, CW, file 2/3/4, Weenen NC to CNC, 1 October 1929.

75. CAD, NTS, vol. 7054, file 110/322, District Commandant, Dundee to Deputy Commissioner, 25 September 1929, and CNC to SNA, 4 November 1929; *Natal Witness*, 19 September 1929.

76. NA, CW, file 2/3/4, CNC to NCs Durban, Pinetown, Ladysmith, Weenen, Estcourt, Dundee, 5 October 1929; *Natal Witness*, 16 November 1929; P. la Hausse, "Struggle for the City," pp. 27–28.

77. NA, Dundee Town Council Minutes, August 1929–July 1930, meeting on 26 September 1929; CAD, NTS, vol. 7054, file 110/322, District Commandant, Dundee to Deputy Commissioner, 14 October 1929; *Star*, 23 November 1929.

78. CAD, NTS, vol. 7054, file 110/322, District Commandant, Dundee to Deputy Commissioner, 25 September 1929.

79. NA, CW, file 2/3/4, Weenen NC to CNC, 28 September 1929; *Star*, 23 November 1929.

80. CAD, NTS, vol. 7606, file 49/328, booklet "Dingiswayo," produced by the ICU *yase* Natal; P. la Hausse, "Struggle for the City," p. 163.

81. G. Coka, "The Story of Gilbert Coka of the Zulu Tribe of Natal, South

Africa," in *Ten Africans,* ed. M. Perham (London: Faber, 1936), pp. 311–12.

82. D. Hemson, "Class Consciousness and Migrant Workers" (Ph.D. diss., University of Warwick, 1979), pp. 132, 209.

83. UW, ASI, OHP, interview with Kumalo; *Natal Witness,* 28 November 1929. By 1929 the only villages with both beerhalls and segregated townships were Estcourt and Vryheid.

84. D. Hemson, "Class Consciousness," p. 258. A women's leader elsewhere in the country also claimed that females were more militant: "Men are cowards! They are afraid of losing their jobs."

CHAPTER NINE

BEER BREWING IN UMTATA: WOMEN, MIGRANT LABOR, AND SOCIAL CONTROL IN A RURAL TOWN

Sean Redding

INTRODUCTION

BEER BREWING AND consumption, an integral part of rural African culture in South Africa, became a major concern of urban government officials in the late nineteenth century. The action of beer brewing itself was rarely under scrutiny. Instead it was the brewing and sale of beer by black women to black men in urban areas that became the focal point of official disquiet. In Umtata, in the Transkeian area of the Cape Colony, beer brewing began as a minor local nuisance to the white authorities, developed into a far more volatile issue, and eventually became part of a broader national discourse about urbanization and social control. The gradual transition in how officials conceived of the problem clearly reflected the growing integration of the Transkeian region into the economy and society of greater South Africa.

In the 1860s, before the Cape Colony annexed the Transkei, white traders and farmers established a settlement on the banks of the Umtata River. When the Transkeian region was finally annexed in 1884, Umtata was the largest town in the region and ideally situated to be the administrative capital (fig. 9.1). The town became the headquarters of a predominantly white government ruling an overwhelmingly black population. The Cape government severely restricted the private ownership of land within the Transkeian Territories. In Umtata, however, those restrictions did not apply. Both whites and blacks could buy lots and settle with freehold tenure.

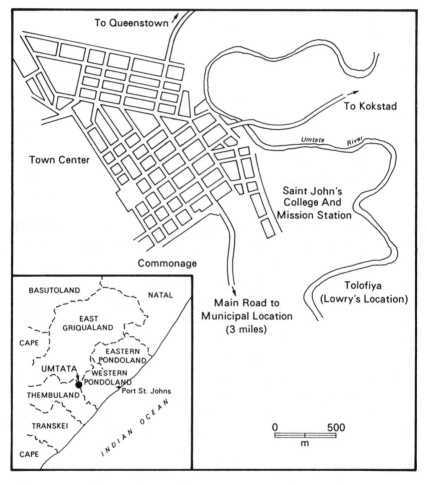

9.1 Location and street map of Umtata, Transkei

Annexation accelerated the intrusion of markets in livestock, wool, hides, and to a lesser extent grain. In addition, the government imposed a hut tax. These new economic opportunities and costs initiated a process of complex social change, involving shifts in the sexual division of labor and increasing dependence on markets as a source of cash and vital staples.[1] In the 1890s persistent droughts crippled agricultural production in the district. In 1897 rinderpest destroyed 95 percent of the cattle population. This devastation set the stage for greatly increased labor migration from the Umtata district. In destroying cattle, rinderpest simultaneously destroyed a source of food, draft power, income, and credit. Increasingly, when Africans needed money or credit they went to the white trader or labor recruiter, who were often one and the same.[2]

Although agriculture rebounded early in the twentieth century, as the proceeds of migrancy were reinvested in the rural economy, few households were able to reestablish themselves as independent producers capable of surviving without recourse to wage labor. Unable to sustain themselves in the rural areas, first men and then women migrated to seek wage-earning employment. For men, job seeking often took the form of traveling to the Transvaal gold mines or to the larger urban areas of the Cape Colony.

Labor migration from the Transkeian territories to the Transvaal gold mines soared between 1906 and 1916.[3] In 1906 the mines lost their access to indentured Chinese laborers and set their sights on the "native reserves" instead. Competitive recruiting intensified, contributing to the increased number of Africans leaving for work. Recruits were offered larger advances and better transportation to and from the mines, although mine wages actually declined in real and nominal terms between 1897 and 1911.[4] By the 1930s most African homesteads in the Umtata district were thoroughly dependent on migrant labor for their livelihood. The Reverend Hoadly of Umtata noted that African men "must go to the labor centres in order to ease their position."[5]

With the coming of the railroad in 1916, Umtata swiftly became the largest entrepot in the Transkei for migrants on their way to and from the Johannesburg gold mines, a function it still performs today.

As a way station for migrant laborers, Umtata offered significant new opportunities for single black women from the countryside. The floating population of unattached African men with money to spend became a lucrative source of income for dealers in beer. There was a massive increase in the brewing and consumption of beer in the town. The brewing of beer, which in the rural areas each household did primarily for itself, became a booming commercial enterprise in Umtata's black neighborhoods, where most people were wage earners who had no time to brew.

For white officials, the production of beer by single women and its sale to migrants represented a double threat. Not only did it challenge the maintenance of social order in the town, but the presence of so many female brewers from the countryside was symptomatic of the breakdown of the rural family and with it the erosion of the migrant labor system itself. Yet official perceptions of beer brewing were only one side of the story. For the migrants, beer drinking provided a link to the countryside, with its rituals and social gatherings, as well as a rejection of white norms of propriety, sobriety, and "civilization." It also blurred the drinkers' fears, frustrations, and boredom. Those emotions were very real for men traveling for the first time to the mines, or returning home after several months or even years away.

BEER BREWING AND WOMEN IN TOWN

Before the entrenchment of migrant labor, rural Transkeian life for the majority of women had been one of agricultural labor and family maintenance. These tasks included raising children, cooking, gathering wood, tending crops, and brewing beer. Men did much of the preparation necessary for cultivation, they tended cattle, built huts, and occasionally hunted. When men became migrants many left the rural areas, never to return. Others stayed away for long periods and sent insufficient money home. Agricultural output, already devastated by environmental disaster, declined in their absence. Male labor migration sometimes forced women to migrate to town themselves in search of wage labor and money to support their families. Rather than following the men to the larger urban centers, many chose to work in nearby Umtata. Migration to Umtata allowed for short-term employment, involved relatively little risk or commitment, and permitted continued close contact with rural kin.

In the rural areas, beer brewing was women's work, important for both social and nutritional purposes.[6] Women soaked the grain, ground it, cooked it, and mixed it with sprouted sorghum to make the mash which then fermented into thick beer (*utywala*). When brewing for a large party, such as a wedding or the initiation of adolescent boys, many women from several homesteads gathered to brew the beer together. Beer was also a necessary part of rural hospitality and a way to celebrate the end of a good harvest. Low in alcohol content, beer provided some variety in a diet otherwise consisting overwhelmingly of grain and milk, with occasional meat. Socially, beer brewing was often the catalyst for social events and provided the opportunity to entertain friends and demonstrate a successful harvest.

Like other aspects of rural culture, the role of brewing and consumption of beer changed over time, even in the nineteenth century.[7] The intrusion of agricultural markets into the countryside implicitly increased the "cost" of *utywala* since grain used to make it could have been sold or the land used to grow the grain could have been used for grazing instead. In addition, women without access to grain could purchase sorghum for brewing. It was in the urban setting, however, that beer itself became a commodity to be bought and sold. In town, beer brewing retained much of its social importance while simultaneously developing into a commercial enterprise. Women were still the ones who brewed the beer, but no longer as part of their familial tasks. People still drank beer at parties and ritual events, but in town they usually paid for it. While the techniques of beer brewing were essentially unchanged, the act of selling the beer was a substantial change from rural practice.

With few marketable skills and little in the way of resources, black women in Umtata faced a narrow range of options for earning a living. Most domestic servants in the town were women, the exceptions being "garden boys," "herd boys," and cooks in the three major (white-owned) hotels. Most manual laborers and government or office clerks were men. This urban division of labor consistently relegated women to the lowest paying jobs. The skills they did use in town—such as the washing of clothes or brewing of beer—were those used in rural family life. Domestic service was most commonly available, but the hours were long, the wages low, and the working conditions often intolerable. Domestics usually received food and lodging but were not allowed to have their children with them.[8] Living on the employer's premises also meant a much longer workday. Servants had little security of tenure and were frequently dismissed at a moment's notice, while those servants who attempted to leave on their own were often prosecuted. Given the conditions of domestic service, earning a living by illegal means was an appealing alternative.

Beer brewing for sale was lucrative and allowed women the independence of self-employment. Some became full-time brewers, while others supplemented their income from wage employment with beer selling. Still others were short-term migrants who came to Umtata to earn a little cash and then return home. In October 1901, for example, a woman named Yeliwe Mashuba testified about why she had brewed beer for sale:

> On the 30th day of September I was engaged to make some Kafir beer by one Meyisi at the brickfields near the Mission Station Umtata. I had come from home for the purpose of obtaining employment, and undertook to make a barrel of beer . . . for two shillings. I received two large paraffin tins . . . of Kafir corn from Meyisi and made the beer, I did not know that I was making it for sale. On the 2nd [October] I was instructed by Meyisi to sell what I could.[9]

Mashuba had come to town to earn money using her knowledge of beer brewing. She was a country woman using a country skill. Even the fact that she was hired by a man reproduced country practices—Meyisi provided the raw materials, the place and the customers; he was in a sense throwing a beer party, although the guests had to pay for what they drank.[10]

From the official point of view, beer brewers like Mashuba were always a potential nuisance. The white name for *utywala*—kaffir beer—exemplified white denigration of the place of beer in African culture and of African culture more generally. But in the countryside beer brewing was so widespread and so obviously an integral part of society that officials rarely tried to control it. Officials and missionaries disapproved of beer drinks, just as they disapproved of many expressions of African culture. But officials simply could not enforce the antibeer legislation that existed. What concerned them more was when rural brewers—in the form of single, unmarried women—came to town.

Initially, white officials were not overtly hostile to the presence of black women in Umtata. Their numbers were small and they were in demand as domestic servants. Although some whites in municipal government wished to restrict brewing activity as early as 1884, the resident magistrates, chief magistrates, and the Department of Native Affairs resisted such restrictions before 1910. When the municipal council tried to pass a bylaw in 1888 restricting the production of "any Kafir Beer, Karee, or other intoxicating liquor whatsoever, within the Location or within the Municipality," the chief magistrate of the Transkei, H. G. Elliot, and the Native Affairs Department successfully recommended its rejection.[11] The magistrates were certainly not supporters of beer; in fact, they frequently stressed the correlation between beer drinks and criminal assaults and murder.[12] But in 1888 they did see beer brewing and drinking as integral facets of African family life, and therefore as indications of the stability of rural culture. In addition, because beer brewing was so common, the enforcement of a total ban even in town would have been beyond the capability of the administration.[13] The sale of beer within Umtata was illegal, but brewing was not, and there was no limit on the amount an individual could brew.

The laxity of the municipal laws on beer made the arrest and prosecution of brewers difficult. Umtata's rural setting also created enforcement problems for the police. Women with the makings of beer and beer itself moved easily across the largely imaginary rural-urban boundary.[14] In one civil case in 1901, a rural women, Janet Tyopo, sued an urban man, Ngwanya Mpidwa, for ten shillings, the "price of one pocket of kafir corn sold and delivered" to Mpidwa. The "kafir corn," or sorghum, had been malted, preparatory to its use for brewing. Janet

Tyopo had brought the grain into town to sell to another client, but it had been refused because it was not up to standard. She then sold it to Mpidwa, who never gave her the money. Despite her participation in the beer trade, she won her suit in the magistrate's court.[15]

The Umtata police force, whites as well as blacks, were frequent customers of beer sellers, which suggests that they did not take the ban on beer sales all that seriously. The fact that they were recognized customers, however, did allow them to carry off the occasional sting operation.[16] A policeman with marked money would make a beer purchase and then arrest the seller. In 1899, after one such operation, a white police sergeant, Edwin Goldsmith, testified at the trial of a woman named Lekata that he had bought beer from her:

> I bought 6d. worth myself from the accused and paid the money. . . . I took the beer to Soyise's room. . . . I then sent for the accused to come to Soyise's room. . . . She said it was not her beer but Makwash's beer. Makwash came and said that it was not his but the room in which it was sold was his [and that the] accused made it to enable her to get a little coffee and sugar.[17]

Goldsmith added that he was in uniform when he bought the beer. The very fact that Lekata freely sold beer to a white man whom she knew to be a policeman indicated the lax state of law enforcement in Umtata.

BEER SELLING AND LABOR MIGRATION

In the period up to 1908, white officials saw the issue of beer brewing for sale as primarily a problem of drunkenness and public disorder and not an issue with larger social significance. By 1908 there was much less confidence among white officials in the stability of African rural society or in the ability of the African family to control its own members. In that year, A. H. Stanford, chief magistrate of the Transkei, submitted a proposal to the Cape attorney general that would have placed restrictions on beer brewing in town. The proposal tried to control both the brewing of beer and the presence in town of those women who did the brewing. But Stanford's blueprint was not approved.

The attorney general would not approve what he considered to be a sweeping proclamation, stating: "the whole thing is too prohibitory when one remembers that it is the national drink which is being dealt with."[18] Instead he suggested that the municipality issue permits to legal location residents to brew limited quantities of beer.[19] The Umtata town council adopted the policy, making it illegal for an African household to be in possession of more than five gallons of beer at one time. Individual households were to do all their own brewing, since the sale of beer was still illegal. In addition, urban households outside the municipal location had no legal right to be in possession of beer.

Stanford's attempt to outlaw brewing was aimed at halting the movement of single African women and families to town. By putting a limit on how much beer could be on hand, the municipality made the task of enforcing the ban on beer sales easier. By making beer more difficult to market, the authorities hoped to restrict economic opportunities for women and to impede their townward migration. White concern over the growing numbers of women in town was partially rooted in fears that the black population of Umtata would soon outstrip the white and that crime would become endemic. More fundamentally, white officials were concerned that women brewers and all single women living in town were part of and contributed to a cycle of family breakdown that ultimately threatened the system of migrant labor.

In the decade after 1910 the permanent and floating population of Umtata grew rapidly as the town became a central collection point for migrant workers bound for and returning from the Rand mines. As single women and migrant laborers flocked into town, the illegal sale of alcohol became more pervasive and visible to whites. Public drunkenness and crime rates inevitably soared. The main sites for the brewing and sale of beer became Lowry's Location (Tolofiya), a group of shanties on white-owned property on the edge of town, and the municipal location (fig. 9.1). A police officer described conditions in Tolofiya in 1920 as being: "occupied 'mostly' by women, the majority of whom are prostitutes and females of the most degraded type. Other women, who possibly do not practice prostitution, hire rooms or huts on this property for the special purpose of making kaffir beer for sale to natives, men who are returning home from the mines."[20] On arrival in Umtata, returning miners picked up their deferred pay from the Native Recruiting Corporation or Mostert's Labour Organization and made for the "dens" at Tolofiya "where they obtain kaffir beer and even stronger liquor and when reduced to a drunken condition are robbed of their earnings."[21]

The tenor of that description of the commerce at Tolofiya clearly revealed the growing official intolerance of women and beer brewing. First, officials disapproved of drinking and drunkenness for the threats they supposedly posed to order and decorum in the town. Second, they no longer saw *utywala* drinking as a necessary component of African social life. Beer was now lumped into the same category as "stronger liquor" (distilled spirits), which it had been illegal for Africans to consume since 1878.[22] Finally, beer brewing skimmed off the wages of male migrants—wages often badly needed by rural families.[23] Unless male migrants contributed financially to the support of the rural homestead, those homesteads risked becoming destitute, forcing more family members to migrate to urban areas in search of wage labor. Unrestrained alcohol consumption in town threatened to undermine the rural homestead and, ultimately, the migrant labor system itself. Single women made and sold the beer, and their growing presence in town was symptomatic of the disintegration of the rural homestead.[24]

White officials were not the only ones who drew a strong connection between the perpetuation of migrancy and the beer trade in the urban areas. Rural white traders, for example, feared a loss of revenue if wages failed to reach the countryside.[25] Although the number of independent trader-recruiters declined as the Native Recruiting Corporation exerted its influence after 1912, traders did not lose their interest in labor migration. It was the traders who promoted the system of deferred pay whereby a mine worker automatically remitted part of his wages back to the family in the reserves. This ensured that the worker would help support his rural family, and that the family would spend some of the money in the traders' shops. It also meant that the worker would not spend all his wages on beer and prostitutes in way stations like Umtata.

In addition to attacking the beer trade, the municipal government moved to control the influx of women into town. Before 1913 the government allowed women to live in the municipal location regardless of their marital or employment status. As long as a woman could pay the site rent (in 1905 it was ten shillings every six months) she could live there.[26] That policy was revised as officials became more concerned about the numbers of single black women living in town. In 1919 the site rent in the municipal location increased to ten shillings per quarter. By the early 1920s, for a woman to live lawfully in the location she either had to be married or steadily (and legally) employed. But police enforcement did not keep pace with municipal legislation: even in 1929, roughly one-third of the 150 women in the location were unmarried or widowed, and twenty-five were not legally employed.[27]

Black women also had other living options outside the municipal location. Throughout this period there was a severe housing shortage among Umtata's poor of all races. The shortage was such that the privately owned Tolofiya settlement never wanted for tenants, most of whom were black. The monthly rent was much higher than in the municipal location, but it was closer to the town center and was not under the surveillance of a municipal headman (who was really a black policeman). This meant that beer could be brewed and sold with scant regard for the law. One police raid in 1929 netted 800 gallons of illegal beer at Tolofiya. At the time, there were ninety-four women living in the location.[28] White residents complained incessantly about Tolofiya. In 1918 the Reverend Hoadley, warden of St. John's College in Umtata (just across the river from Tolofiya), complained to the Resident Magistrate that "the behaviour there is scandalous, particularly on Sundays. It is notorious as the worst spot near Umtata."[29] He went on to demand the removal of "this plague spot" from the town.

Police harassment remained the major form of control in both Tolofiya and the municipal location. The number of prosecutions and convictions for the sale of beer rose steadily from the early 1930s (table 9.1), but they were not effective deterrents. After serving their

Table 9.1: Beer selling convictions in Umtata, 1896–1951

Year	Average No. of Convictions per annum	Approximate African Population[1]	Conviction rate (per 100 residents)
1896–1901	2.20	550	0.40
1915–1922	14.90	830	1.80
1930–1931	62.00	1,713	3.62
1939–1941	64.33	2,696	2.38
1949–1951	123.33	5,028	2.45

[1]Population figures are estimates for the years 1901, 1921, 1930, 1929, and 1949.
Source: Municipal records, Umtata

sentences, women convicted of selling beer simply returned and began to brew and sell again. The municipal council therefore began to look to national legislation as a way of dealing with the problem. The 1923 Natives (Urban) Areas Act would have been the perfect instrument to use against these women, since the law made it illegal for African women without wage employment to live in those urban areas proclaimed under the act. It also provided for three separate systems of controlling the brewing and sale of *utywala* in proclaimed municipalities: home brewing with permits, licensed commercial brewing by blacks for sale, and the municipal monopoly system of brewing and sale (the so-called Durban system).

The Umtata municipal council was unable to proclaim the town until 1943, since the act also stipulated that urban areas had to provide housing in segregated townships for a substantial proportion of blacks living in town. In 1931 the municipality built a new location but was still unable to meet the requirements of the act. Regardless, the municipality followed the spirit of the 1923 act and refused to rent dwellings to unmarried women who were not legally employed. Also in the spirit of the act, the town clerk in the late 1930s considered adopting the Durban system of beer brewing. But to the clerk's dismay, the Department of Native Affairs refused the application to build a beerhall and brewery.[30] There were three reasons behind the refusal. First, on the basis of a simple cost-revenue analysis of the clerk's plans, the brewery and beerhall could not have made a profit in a relatively small town like Umtata.[31] Second, in order to make a profit the beerhall would have had to lure additional customers from the countryside, the exact opposite of what was intended.[32] Finally, a beerhall run on a commercial basis by whites patently contradicted the paternalistic official image of the Transkei as a native reserve where "custom" and "tradition" were upheld.[33]

In 1943 the application of the act facilitated a severe crackdown on African women in Umtata.[34] Enforcement of the law began to change the population of the locations. By the 1940s (and through the early 1950s), the large proportion of adult women living in the Umtata municipal location were married; the municipal council had achieved its goal of controlling the presence of single black women in the locations.[35] This did not mean that the officials had reversed the inexorable tide of rural disintegration and family breakdown. Rural women in search of wage employment, like their male counterparts, now went much further afield to the major urban centers of the Witwatersrand, the Cape, and Port Elizabeth.[36]

CONCLUSION

Changes in official attitudes toward the control of beer production and consumption in Umtata clearly paralleled the emergence of the Transkei as the major migrant labor reservoir in South Africa. After 1910 white officials and residents increasingly deplored the presence of single women in town. The women contributed to and were supported by a booming beer trade with transient migrant workers passing through Umtata. Their presence, and the beer trade that supported them, indicated to officials that rural society was disintegrating. More than that, from the official point of view, women were "robbing" returning migrants of their savings. Thus, controlling beer became bound up with the desire to maintain the system of migrant labor and ensure the existence of viable African homesteads in the rural areas. Beer brewing came to be a political act, threatening the existence of white political and economic control.

The women who sold beer knew that their actions were illegal, but they continued to brew. Either the costs of being arrested and prosecuted did not seriously decrease the profits involved, or else the women were so poor that this was the only existence they could eke out. For buyers and sellers alike, the fact that their sometimes rowdy beer drinks took place directly across the river from St. John's College and Mission Station (one of the largest missions in the Transkei) may have provided a little extra enjoyment and satisfaction.

White officials, both local and national, and white traders worked to negate the potential erosion of the migrant labor system. Nationally, the mining companies began deferring the payment of wages until the migrants returned home to the rural areas. Deferred wages were supposed to forestall further black migration to the towns. At the local level, officials attempted to control the potential threat posed by commercialized beer brewing in rural towns such as Umtata. Various national laws existed to restrict beer brewing and sale either explicitly (for example, through the imposition of the Durban system) or implicitly (by outlawing the presence of single, unemployed women). In Umtata, after 1908, watchful tolerance gave way to a systematic verbal and legal assault on beer and the brewers. Unable to harness national legislation to operate a municipal monopoly over beer, the local government used harassment and evictions to limit the trade. Finally, by the 1940s, the increased impoverishment of the countryside forced women to migrate further than Umtata in search of wage labor. By that time, beer had become a minor side issue in that Transkeian town.

NOTES

1. In other areas of the Transkei these trends have been documented by C. Bundy, *The Rise and Fall of the South African Peasantry* (Berkeley: University of California Press, 1979); and W. Beinart, *The Political Economy of Pondoland* (Cambridge: Cambridge University Press, 1982); see also J. Lewis, "The Rise and Fall of the South African Peasantry: A Critique and Reassessment," *Journal of Southern African Studies* 11 (1984): 1–24.

2. A. Jeeves, *Migrant Labour in South Africa's Mining Economy* (Montreal and Kingston: McGill-Queen's Press, 1985), pp. 87–89; Records of the

Chief Magistrate of the Transkeian Territories, in Cape Archives Depot (CMT) 3/681, file 175, Blue Book Report for 1907, by A. H. Stanford; CMT 3/882, file 670, Letter 15041, Chief Magistrate Transkei (CMT) to Secretary for Native Affairs (SNA), Pretoria, 12 September 1911. Usury was widespread throughout the territories; see CMT 3/148, RM (Resident Magistrate) Nqamakwe to CMT, 1 September 1899; CMT 3/280, Letter 2115/98, CMT Elliot to Superintendent of Native Affairs, Cape Town (Walter Stanford), 1 April 1898; and CMT 3/171, Letter 597, RM Umtata to CMT, 8 September 1899.

3. Bundy, *Rise and Fall,* p. 121; Jeeves, *Migrant Labour,* appendix 1.

4. F. Wilson, *Labour in the South African Gold Mines, 1911–69* (Cambridge: Cambridge University Press, 1972), p. 45.

5. Records of the Town Clerk of Umtata (henceforth 3/UTA) 66, file 48g, preface, n.d. (probably 1930–1932).

6. See 1/UTA 2/1/1/6, 17 October 1884, Gobizembe v. Ncubela.

7. P. McAllister (in this collection).

8. See, for example, 1/UTA 1/1/1/14, case 403, R. v. Rebecca, 23 October 1893.

9. 1/UTA 1/1/1/30, case 647, R. v. Meyisi, 8 October 1901.

10. Ibid. Other cases included CMT 3/190, Memo, S. Emslie, Inspector of Licenses to CMT, 18 October 1901; 1/UTA 1/1/1/30, case 758, R. v. Benelwa Mhlati, Sarah Ann Nkonzeni, and Nontozake Sangongo, 5 December 1901; 1/UTA 1/1/1/40, case 741, R. v. James Meseti, alias Xegwana, 31 December 1907.

11. 3/UTA 1, minute book 2, Meeting of Municipal Council, 14 December 1888.

12. CMT 1/84, Annual Report for 1890, 8 January 1891, CMT to SNA; CMT 3/170, letter 927, RM Umtata to CMT, 21 December 1894; CMT 3/170, letter 12, ARM UTA to CMT, 7 January 1897.

13. This did not prevent them from trying to control the trade; see 1/UTA 1/1/1/12, case 143, R. v. Rosie Mafuna, 9 June 1892; case 225, R. v. Jack and Sarah, 22 August 1892; case 240, R. v. Nomjwara, 30 August 1892; 1/UTA 1/1/1/24, case 412, R. v. Tom, 24 July 1899; 1/UTA 1/1/1/23, case 34, R. v. Nomiya, 26 January 1899; case 225, R. v. Matches and Madhlameni, 3 May 1899; case 227, R. v. Nokimberly, 3 May 1899; 1/UTA 1/1/1/29, case 147, R. v. Maqarana, 26 February 1901; 1/UTA 1/1/1/30, case 642, R. v. Mangati, 4 October 1901; case 643, R. v. Ncandana, 4 October 1901.

14. For examples of beer (or the makings) entering the town and leading to prosecution see 1/UTA 1/1/1/12, case 356, R. v. Tom Nyeko, 9 December 1892; 1/UTA 1/1/1/29, case 147, R. v. Maqarana of Umtata, 26

February 1901; case 148, R. v. Sanna Marapukana, 26 February 1901; *Territorial News,* 15 January 1910.

15. 1/UTA 2/1/1/47, case 275, Janet Tyopo v. Ngwanya Mpidwa, 24 October 1901.

16. 1/UTA 1/1/1/24, case 412, R. v. Tom, 24 July 1899; 1/UTA 1/1/1/29, case 147, R. v. Maqarana of Umtata, 26 February 1901.

17. 1/UTA 1/1/1/24, case 431, R. v. Lekata, 1 August 1899.

18. CMT 3/798, file 461, "Subject: Transkeian Territories: Regulation of the Sale of Kafir Beer in Townships and Villages; Report of the Attorney General," 30 June 1908.

19. Ibid.

20. 3/UTA 18, file 49, Report dated 3 November 1920, SAP to the Municipal Council.

21. Ibid.

22. 1/UTA 6/1/216, file 14A, Reverened A. A. Hoadley to RM Umtata, 27 August 1918.

23. 3/UTA 18, file 49, Sanitary Inspector's Report for Week Ending 27 June 1923; 3/UTA 66, file 50, Health Inspector, Municipality of Umtata, Health Dept. to Town Clerk, 23 March 1938.

24. In the late 1920s, public health officials and the Resident Magistrate initiated a strident campaign against prostitution and venereal disease in Umtata. The campaign was also directed at the presence of single women. Venereal diseases supposedly disabled the migrant laborer and prostitution, like brewing, skimmed off his wages; see 1/UTA 6/1/38, file 13/6/2, Detective Sgt. J. C. Naude to RM Umtata, 27 May 1929; 1/UTA 6/1/38, file 13/2/4, RM Umtata to Sec. for Public Health, Pretoria, 5 June 1929; and 1/UTA 6/1/38, file 13/2/4, E. H. Cluver to Sec. for Public Heath, Pretoria, 21 August 1929.

25. 1/UTA 2/1/1/83, case 563, Nokoyi v. Henry Mbodlela and Jackson, 28 October 1913; 3/UTA 66, file 50, Health Inspector, Municipality of Umtata, Health Dept. to Town Clerk, 23 March 1938.

26. Anon., *Transkei and the Danger Ahead* (printed for the Transkei Lookout Club, 1914), 7pp.; Natal Archives Depot, Chief Native Commissioner (CNC), vol. 342, file 1541/18, circular minute d.1/18, H. S. Cooke to Native and Sub-Native Commissioners, 23 January 1918; 1/UTA 6/1/2, file 2/2/5, "Remittances, 1924."

27. In practice, as long as a woman was living steadily with one man, the location superintendent usually presumed that she was married; 1/UTA 6/1/38, file 13/6/2, Acting RM Umtata to Sec. for Public Health, Pretoria,

30 October 1929, enclosing "List of Widows and Unmarried Women Living in Municipal Location"; 3/UTA 18, file 48E, Location Superintendent Strachan to Town Clerk, 21 October 1929.

28. 1/UTA 6/1/38, file 6/13, RM Umtata to Secretary for Public Heath, Pretoria, 11 December 1929.

29. 1/UTA 6/1/216, file 14A, letter, 27 August 1918.

30. 3/UTA 66, file 50, RM Umtata to Town Clerk, 7 December 1944.

31. CMT 3/1097, file 13/24/9, CMT to SNA, Pretoria, 26 October 1944 and 27 November 1944; 3/UTA 66, file 50, Town Clerk to Chairman and Members of Native Affairs Committee (of the Municipal Council), 4 September 1940; Town Clerk to Sec. Native Affairs Board, 5 May 1944.

32. 3/UTA 64, file 48A, Rev. James Mariner, Methodist Church to Location Superintendent, 21 January 1943; 3/UTA 66, file 50, RM Umtata to Town Clerk, 25 May 1944.

33. See S. Dubow, "Holding 'A Just Balance between White and Black': The Native Affairs Department in South Africa c. 1920–33," *Journal of Southern African Studies* 12 (1986): 217–39.

34. See the eviction notices served in 3/UTA 64, file 48A, letters dated 26 February 1943. Many of these women had been previously convicted of beer selling.

35. 3/UTA 66, file 48H, Health Inspector to Town Clerk, Umtata, 17 April 1944; Town Clerk to Chairman and Members of Native Affairs Committee, Municipal Council of Umtata, 26 October 1938; 3/UTA 64, file 47D, "Report for August 1949," Location Superintendent to Town Clerk, 9 September 1949; 1/UTA, 6/1/98, file N9/23/2, Department of Native Affairs Questionnaire, completed by Town Clerk, dated 28 July 1954.

36. P. Bonner (in this collection).

CHAPTER TEN

BEER DRINKING AND LABOR MIGRATION IN THE TRANSKEI: THE INVENTION OF A RITUAL TRADITION

Patrick McAllister

INTRODUCTION[1]

ONE OF THE most striking features of social life among the Xhosa inhabitants of Willowvale district, Transkei, is the large number of beer drinks that punctuate daily existence.[2] Beer is brewed for cooperative work parties and ploughing groups, to celebrate the harvest, and in honor of the oxen that labored. Beer drinks may be held to mark changes in status such as the establishment of a new homestead or the freeing of a widow from the restrictions of mourning, or they may be held for no apparent reason other than to provide hospitality. Beer is brewed in conjunction with ancestor rituals, and sometimes as a substitute for such a ritual, and large quantities of it are required for the large festive occasions accompanying events such as male initiation. In order to raise money, homesteads sometimes brew beer for sale.[3]

Beer brewing as well as the formal distribution and consumption of commercial liquor (mainly brandy) is also central to the various rituals connected with labor migration.[4] These rituals represent an example of what Hobsbawm and Ranger refer to as "the invention of tradition"—the innovative modification and use of existing cultural resources to grapple with new social situations. This chapter attempts to explain how the most elaborate of these rituals of labor migration—a large beer drink called *umsindleko*—arose, in terms of the older ritual from which it developed and the changing socioeconomic context of the people concerned.

THE TRANSITION

In the Transkei and Ciskei (fig. 10.1), from at least the 1930s onward, the return of a migrant worker to his home and community has been marked by the ritual killing of an animal. This practice seems to have evolved from earlier rituals that were held to mark safe return from a long journey or from war, and Xhosa speakers in the Transkei still refer to going out to work as being *etorhweni* ("on an expedition") and as *emfazweni* ("at war").[5] Among the Pondo the ritual for a returned migrant was called *ukubulela* ("giving thanks").[6] Among the Bhaca a beast was slaughtered as *umbuliso* ("a special thanksgiving") when a young man returned from his first spell at work, to thank the ancestral shades for keeping him safe.[7] Return from subsequent work spells was marked by the killing of a goat. In the Keiskammahoek district this ritual was known as *ukubulela abadala* ("giving thanks to the ancestors").[8] Among the Xhosa of Willowvale district, Transkei (see fig. 10.1), the return of a migrant worker was marked by a killing, referred to simply as *umhlinzeko* (from *ukuhlinza,* "to slaughter"). As one informant put it, the killing was held "because when you return home there should be the smell of meat, it should be clear to all that you have returned."

In the past the procedure involved in the killing varied considerably. Some say that it took place inside the cattle byre, that the "spear of the home" was used, that it was necessary for the goat or ox to cry out, and that the returned migrant ritually tasted a special portion of the meat.[9] These features indicate a ritual killing in the full sense of the word, involving communication with and an invocation to the ancestors. But it is clear that it was a small, domestic affair. Close kin who

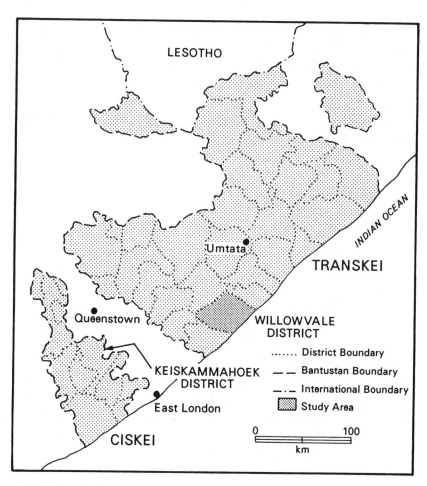

10.1 Willowvale District, Transkei

lived nearby would attend, as would close neighbors, but it was not a community occasion. Others say that it did not matter what kind of animal was killed, that it was killed outside the cattle byre simply by having its throat cut and that there was no ritual tasting. Such variations are probably associated with different households or clans, but it is also possible that informants were referring to different time periods.

To the extent that *umhlinzeko* still occurs, it is of no religious significance. A man simply kills a sheep, goat, or pig for himself or for his son, usually next to the cattle byre, without any ceremony and without calling kinsmen to be present. The meat is consumed by the family concerned, though portions may be sent to neighbors and nearby kin. The *umhlinzeko* killing has largely been replaced with a beer drink called *umsindleko*. The two terms—*umsindleko* and *umhlinzeko*—are used interchangeably to refer to either a beer drink or a killing, a practice facilitated by what is possibly the original meaning of *umsindleko*—"food which a woman prepares and keeps for her absent or traveling husband" in anticipation of his return.[10] *Umsindleko* is a relatively large affair in contrast to its predecessor, and may be attended by up to two hundred people, who come from neighboring wards as well as the local subwards. It is held to mark the return of a migrant worker, not every time he comes home, but after every four or five (or more) spells at work:

> If my son has been to work, has been obedient and loyal to me and has worked well in that he has sent money home and asked me to buy cattle for him, and if he has brought money home with him when he returned, I will instruct his mother to brew beer for him. People will come to partake of the beer. It will be explained to them that this beer has been brewed because my son has been to work, has worked satisfactorily and has done great things. It will not be said openly that he has bought cattle. At the beer drink the ancestors will be called upon and addressed . . . if there are people here drinking beer, then the ancestors will also be doing so.[11]

The consumption of beer at an *umsindleko* ceremony centers on the migrant whose return is being celebrated. If he is a boy or a young man who is not yet old enough to be permitted to drink with his seniors, he is initially seated at the back of the hut where the beer drink is being held. This spot is called *entla* and it is closely associated with the ancestors. The first beaker drawn from the cask of beer is taken over to him by his father or senior kinsman and he drinks a few mouthfuls from this beaker. The ritual tasting serves to focus attention on the young migrant and on the reason for brewing. At the same time, it symbolically incorporates him into the ranks of the seniors. Words are then addressed to the migrant before he is allowed to leave and to join his peers in another hut, where a portion of the beer has been put aside for them.

A more senior man remains in the company of others. He is not asked to sit in the *entla* position but takes full part in the beer drink. As the head of the homestead he is likely to assist with the distribution of beer, to give special gifts of beer to certain categories of close kin, important people, and "beer friends." He makes announcements occasionally about the purpose of the event, and receives and responds to words said by others. As at any beer drink, the five-liter beakers of beer move freely, and the returnee is called over to receive mouthfuls from others, reciprocating when the beaker reaches him and it is his turn to drink. He is thus symbolically incorporated back into the community through the commensality and conviviality of the occasion.

More formally, *umsindleko* involves, firstly, a public recognition of the migrant's efforts on behalf of his homestead. He is formally praised for his success at work and urged by the men of the community to continue in this vein. Secondly, the ceremony has a religious character. The participants see it as a thanksgiving to the ancestral shades for protecting the migrant at work and ensuring his safe return. It is due to the shades that the migrant suffered no misfortune, and *umsindleko* is thought to ensure their continued blessings and protection so that future trips to work will also be successful. It is through the attendance of people at the beer drink, and especially through the words spoken by them, that the attention of the shades is drawn to the homestead and their presence and blessings secured.[12] In the *umhlinzeko* killing, on the other hand, it was through the invocation to the shades by the migrant's father or senior lineage members that communication with the shades occurred.

Umsindleko involves elaborate speech making, in which members of the community address the migrant. The speakers are senior representatives of the community, and their speeches are an attempt to ensure that the migrant interprets his spell at work "correctly"—that is, in the terms laid down by the speakers. The speakers stress the importance of working for the rural home and the importance of returning home (return in itself is seen as a moral good). They say that the money earned at work should be spent on things that build the home and not be wasted on prostitutes, fine clothes, and transistor radios. They emphasize rural values and the importance of being part of a community, while decrying urban values and individualistic behavior. In the case of young men particularly, the speakers refer to the social dependence of the migrant on his seniors. In effect, the speakers provide an ideological framework within which to interpret the migratory experience, by publicly proclaiming the norms and values of the community regarding the expected behavior of the labor migrant and by placing these expectations within a broader perspective—that of the relationship between labor migration and rural social life. The speeches represent the authority of the elders, the community, and the ancestors and constitute an attempt at social control. *Umsindleko* says that the migrant's efforts at work have meaning and legitimacy only insofar as they benefit his rural home and community and that he depends on the community for success at work and for successful building of his rural homestead.[13]

INTERPRETING THE TRANSITION

Some informants spoke of *umsindleko* as an old, well-established custom, something that had been done by their fathers and grandfathers. In doing so they may have been fusing the killing (*umhlinzeko*) with the beer drink, apparently unaware of the fact that *umsindleko* is of relatively recent origin. That *umsindleko* is something that was "invented," rather than an established tradition, emerged in a speech by Dwetya, a man of about seventy-five years, at one *umsindleko* beer drink:

> Here is the point, Dombothi! Modi [the previous speaker] has finished speaking. Dombothi [the returning migrant], when I grew up it was said that when one comes back from service [work] a slaughtering is done. This was changed. It was said: "*Thyini!* This person has come home with a snake," and this custom was discarded. I myself was slaughtered for by Tela [the speaker's father]. He discarded that practice. And you were slaughtered for by Poni [Dombothi's father]. You have returned from service; from the business of serving Poni's homestead. And with me, I was building Tela's homestead. It has been like that since I was born. I am speaking to say we fell down [changed]. It was said: "*Hayi bo!* He has

bought it!" We came to this, Dombothi, to this that has been done by your wife in cooking [brewing] for you, child of my grandmother, on your return from work. This thing, Dombothi, that is being done by your wife, I commend it, notwithstanding that it was not so at the beginning; it was a goat slaughtered by your father. He used to say: "My child, I am slaughtering for you because you are from service." This was changed; people said: "No! He has bought a snake!" Child of my grandmother! Dombothi! I say engrave these words in your mind. It is fine, Dombothi, when they say this wife of yours is cooking for you. I wish you good health always. Go back again to work for Poni's homestead. I say so, I, Mbambushe [a praise name]. I am going to speak the truth. She should cook for you again while you are back. We are happy because of your return. Even if you do not return with anything, you yourself in person are all right. I have stopped.

Some informants went on to speak of sons being able to purchase "wisdom" (*ubulumko*) at work: "This wisdom lives on blood, and fathers, in slaughtering for their sons, did not know if they were providing blood for wisdom or not, since they did not know if their sons had bought it or not." The allusion was to the well-known witch familiar *umamlambo,* usually associated with male witchcraft and conceived of as a magical snake:

> A son goes out to work and he buys a snake there. If you slaughter here for your son you are slaughtering for a snake that is going to ruin your homestead. . . . They say that this snake is a medicine. You put it in your pocket and keep it there while you move around. At night it becomes a beautiful girl and the owner must sleep with her. There are seven vaginas and you have to use them all that night. The next thing that people hear is that your son is a witch and that he kills people. They will then go and burn down your homestead.[14]

It seems then that people stopped slaughtering for their migrant sons because of the fear of *umamlambo,* acquired for the purpose of killing their fathers and inheriting the latter's position and property. Since a father could not know if his son had indeed "bought a snake" or not, he refrained from doing *umhlinzeko* for him, and returned migrants, anxious to avoid suspicion, stopped asking for this killing to be performed. Older men, too, are supposed to be able to become witches in this way and to have stopped slaughtering for themselves on their return home, but this belief is usually associated with young, unmarried men.

So much for the widely held folk explanation of the change from the killing (*umhlinzeko*) to the beer drink (*umsindleko*). What are we to make of it? Clearly, any sociological "explanation" of the change from the killing to the beer drink must include reference to all or most of the dramatic features of both these rituals. This leads away from simple but plausible explanations such as a decrease in stock holdings coupled with increased maize yields during the period when large-scale labor migrancy was becoming institutionalized. Such an essentially materialist explanation might make sense of the substitution of maize beer for meat, in accordance with a general trend toward increased agricultural production and decreased livestock holdings. As an explanation for the substitution of *umsindleko* for *umhlinzeko,* however, it would be incomplete. Certainly, we might expect some "spiritual" rationalization for the change, although a beer drink is regarded as just as effective a means of communicating with the shades as a killing. However, this explanation does not tell us why the change was conceived of in terms of witch beliefs; why a small, fairly private ritual was replaced by a large, public one; or why the participants in the latter address formal speeches that often have the characteristics of admonitions to the returned migrant, a feature, according to informants, that did not occur in conjunction with the killing. These are crucial questions, and need to be answered in accounting for the ritual change.

The most appropriate starting point is the likelihood that the change was conceptualized in terms of witch beliefs because such beliefs constitute attempts to cope with ambivalence and strain in social life and enable people to place within a recognized idiom conflicts they could not otherwise express. In this sense witch beliefs both reflect social structure and are attempts to explain social reality and social change.[15] In the case of *umhlinzeko-umsindleko,* it seems that the belief in *umamlambo* was used to justify and make intellectual sense of the switch from a killing to a beer drink. The switch itself resulted from certain ambiguities and strains in social life due to changing material and social conditions. The killing became inappropriate as a vehicle for reincorporating returned migrants and for making statements about the relationship between migrant labor and rural society. *Umsindleko* took its place because, as a beer drink, it was more appropriate for this purpose.

What were these changing conditions? What sorts of conflicts and strains did they generate? We need to look first at changes in homestead (*umzi*) size and composition, which were linked in turn to changes in social practice, especially in the social organization of production and features associated with production, of which labor migration was one.

From the late nineteenth century the size and composition of Transkeian homesteads changed quite radically. Formerly, homesteads were much larger (ten to forty huts each) and consisted of an extended family—man and wives, unmarried sons and daughters, married sons and their wives and children, and often other kin.[16] Homesteads were relatively self-sufficient and the available resources were under the control of the homestead head. His sons depended on him for their subsistence and for wives, since he controlled the cattle holdings. Sons remained in the father's homestead until he died or until they became senior men.[17]

By the 1930s homesteads had declined markedly in size and were situated more closely together than before, due to a number of related factors. Among these was land shortage and increased population pressure as a result of the appropriation of Xhosa land. Since a man with his own homestead would have had a greater claim to a field than one living in his father's home it was to the advantage of the family for sons to establish independent homesteads soon after marriage. Homesteads may also have become smaller because there was no longer any need to concentrate for defensive purposes.[18] Factors such as the growth of individualism and the decline in the incidence of polygyny were no doubt also important.[19] Migrant labor played a significant role in this process. It provided sons with an alternative source of cattle (through wages). They became less economically dependent on their fathers, they could provide their own bridewealth, and they were able to establish independent homesteads earlier in life.

Those changes were accompanied by a change in the organization of rural production. The smaller homestead cultivated less land and grew maize rather than sorghum (previously both crops were raised). Beinart argues that this suited the smaller homestead because it was less labor intensive and it allowed for extensive intercropping. Day-to-day labor in the field was not required. Instead, cultivation became oriented toward intensive inputs of labor at crucial but widely spaced intervals in the agricultural cycle—plowing and planting, weeding, and harvesting.[20]

The switch to maize and the widespread introduction of plows raised agricultural output.[21] Individual homesteads pooled their resources in order to perform the required tasks, and work parties and cooperative plowing groups became very important. The expansion of production also depended on the cash earned through migrant labor. First, the money earned at work allowed people to buy plows, fertilizer, and other agricultural inputs. Purchase of oxen provided the homestead with bargaining power in its cooperative relationships with other homesteads and thus also contributed to the welfare of the community as a whole. Later, as homestead heads became increasingly involved as migrants, dependence on neighbors grew. The head's absence meant that an *usipatheleni* ("caretaker") had to be delegated (if he had no grown sons) to look after the affairs of the homestead. That task usually fell to a neighboring agnate, but any good neighbor would do.[22]

The growing dependence on periodic, intensive, cooperative inputs helps to explain the strong emphasis on neighborliness in rural Transkei and the specific ritual change from *umhlinzeko* to *umsindleko*. It can be seen that the series of social and economic changes outlined above involved a paradox. The growth of individualism and increased economic independence, accompanied by increased labor migration and the change in rural production, led to a greater dependence on other homesteads and neighbors, on the community as a whole. Adjoining homesteads, now closer together than when homesteads were larger, provided the basis for socioeconomic interaction. Those homesteads congregated within a particular geographical area became important as such—as neighbors rather than as kinsmen. As Hunter observed in the 1930s, "The more *imizi* [homesteads] subdivide the more kinship bonds tend to be replaced by ties binding neighbours."[23] Neighborliness did not arise as a *new* social principle, but it became more important as the kinship system weakened.

The change to *umsindleko*, probably gradually from about the 1940s onward, coincided with, reflected, and provided normative or ideological support for the changing nature of rural production as outlined above.[24] Ancestor rituals such as *umhlinzeko* are not community affairs and limit full participation to close blood kin. In a situation where homesteads were economically interdependent, and where migrant labor brought the required agricultural inputs, the migrant laborer became, in a sense, public property. His proper incorporation back into rural society, and the success or otherwise of his work efforts, became a matter of communal concern. The *umhlinzeko* killing became inappropriate as a vehicle for reincorporating the migrant. A beer drink became more suitable, because beer drinking in the Transkei is a communal, public affair, as it is throughout Africa. Furthermore, there is evidence that beer drinking became much more widespread in the Transkei from the turn of the century onward.[25] One of the reasons for this was probably that communal work was usually concluded with a beer drink organized by the benefiting homestead. From a ritual that correlated return from work with the unity and independence of the agnatic cluster or extended family, emerged one where the importance of the local group and of the community as a whole was recognized.

However, in order to grasp the logic of the change and to understand why it was conceptualized in the idiom of witchcraft one has also to consider it from another point of view—the nature of the relationship between father and son and between elders and juniors in general. Those relationships were subjected to strain and underwent certain changes with increased independence and access to wage earning on the part of sons, and they involved, among other things, a struggle for control of the son and his earnings. Previously, control over juniors turned largely on the question of bridewealth. A man obtained *lobola* cattle from his father or senior kin such as father's brothers and mother's brother, and this practice gave seniors power over their juniors. It was also possible to obtain *lobola* through raids and *ukubusa* (labor service for chiefs or wealthy men). The growth of a money economy first replaced raiding and *ukubusa* as a means of obtaining cattle, and later it replaced the other two (primary) sources of *lobola*—father and senior kin.[26] The process probably occurred much earlier among the Xhosa proper—whose cattle holdings never fully recovered from the cattle killing in 1857 and among whom labor migration became institutionalized at an earlier stage—than it did elsewhere in the eastern Cape and Transkei.[27]

To be sure, the son's growing independence was tempered by the fact that cattle bought by him were regarded as belonging to the father (as is still the case in conservative parts of Transkei today), and he still depended on his father and senior agnates in the marriage process and in ritual. But his bargaining power was improved. From a position of total dependence on the father, the son became someone on whom the father depended for the cash inputs needed to enable his homestead to survive. This dependence weakened the father's authority and the political and economic power of seniors in general. Access to wealth that could be had without their agency was a threat that, it is suggested, was manifested in the belief that sons could become witches at work. Sons could *buy* a snake with their earnings as labor migrants. The belief that *umamlambo* sometimes takes the form of a beautiful girl with whom the son has sexual relations also makes sense, in view of the threat to the seniors' role as provider of bridewealth, on which much of their authority rested.

It is suggested that the *umhlinzeko* killing was stopped partly as a result of the change in the father-son relationship, that its cessation was symbolic of an attempt by fathers as a group to retain control over their sons and to guard against the possibility of suspected witchcraft. But the father's homestead remained dependent on the son's earnings in order to retain its place in the organization of production. The *umhlinzeko* killing emphasized the bond between father and son and the son's status within the local agnatic group. Father slaughtered for son, emphasizing the son's dependence on the father and on agnates. By brewing *umsindleko* beer, on the other hand, the father avoided the possibility of "feeding" the "snake" but still acknowledged the son's role in contributing to the homestead and, through this, to the community. This is quite clear in the speech by Dwetya, cited above.

Brewing beer for the community as a whole indicated that the father was still the head of the homestead and that his homestead, through the efforts of the son, was being "built up" and was a good one to cooperate with. The power of the son was thereby channeled and made relevant to a wider principle, that of neighborhood, rather than that of the jural relationship between father and son. *Umhlinzeko* involved the direct father-son relationship, *umsindleko* the relationship between homestead head and other homesteads, through the son's efforts. The son as independent wage earner was essentially ambiguous and disorderly—a threat to structure. By relating his role as migrant more strongly to the emerging principle of community or neighborhood (in *umsindleko*), a clearer definition of the son's role in structure developed and his potential disorderliness was controlled.[28] The ambiguous social position of juniors and their threat to seniors was reflected in the belief that they had access to a form of mystical power that rivaled the power of the shades available to elders. Resolution of the ambiguity, of the conflict between senior and junior, and of the threat of the uncontrolled power of witchcraft was achieved through substituting the drinking of beer for the killing of a beast or goat, the authority of the elders of the neighborhood for that of the individual father.

CONCLUSION

As indicated earlier, the conflict (or potential conflict) between elder and junior turned on the question of who would control the junior's migrant earnings and, through this, his ability to marry and establish his independence. Such conflict was widespread in colonial Africa, where elders took various measures to try to keep their sons economically dependent on them.[29] In the case of Willowvale, the measure was a religious one in which the elements of an established ritual tradition, *umhlinzeko,* itself adapted to the purpose of migrant labor, were combined with witch beliefs, themselves modified through participation in a migrant labor economy, in an innovative way. The innovative combination of these elements in accordance with changed rural relationships of production created a new ritual, *umsindleko*, through which the elders tried to contain the new-found power of juniors.

As Mary Douglas argues, ritual harnesses disorder and turns it into a force for good. But this transformation could not be achieved by the *umhlinzeko* killing. The very blood being offered to the ancestors in the *umhlinzeko* killing was serving to feed the snake, which symbolized the potential disorderliness of the migrant, his potential to disrupt established authority patterns and to challenge the power of the elders. Blood itself thus became an ambiguous symbol, standing not only for the *umamlambo* snake and the disorderly forces of witchcraft, but also for the orderliness of society, represented by the shades and their earthly representatives, the elders of the kin group. Substitution of beer for blood solved this problem. The symbolic ambiguity of blood is also the likely reason why, when killings for returned migrants do occur today, which is seldom, they do not involve an invocation to the shades and they are not performed in the sacred cattle byre. They are not religious. As Victor Turner often pointed out, symbols lose and gain meaning over time, and ritual must be seen as part of a *process* of adaptation, through which people come to terms with changes in their environment and realign their religious life with external realities.[30]

To put it more simply, the *umhlinzeko* killing, with its emphasis on agnation, became inappropriate in the context of migrant labor and the cooperation of neighbors, and it stated a principle that was being challenged and contradicted by the very subject of the ritual. The switch to *umsindleko* accommodated both these contradictions. It realigned the father-son relationship in terms of the nature of the relationship between homesteads, and it related migrant labor to the changed organization of production. It did so, however, by drawing on certain cultural resources of a "traditional" kind and putting them together in a new way, as an accommodative response to new circumstances.

1. An earlier version of this paper appeared as "Beasts to Beer Pots: Migrant Labour and Ritual Change in Willowvale district, Transkei," *African Studies* 44 (1985).

2. Fieldwork was conducted in Willowvale district in 1976 and 1977, when I spent eight months in Shixini Administrative Area. Annual field trips of shorter duration have been made since 1978.

3. For a detailed account of Xhosa beer drinking see P. A. McAllister, "Xhosa Beer Drinks and their Oratory" (Ph.D. diss., Rhodes University, Grahamstown, 1986).

4. See P. A. McAllister, "The Rituals of Labour Migration among the Gcaleka" (M.A. diss., Rhodes University, Grahamstown, 1979); and P. A. McAllister, "Work, Homestead and the Shades: The Ritual Interpretation of Labour Migration among the Gcaleka," in *Black Villagers in an Industrial Society,* ed. P. Mayer (Cape Town: Oxford University Press, 1980), pp. 205–253.

5. See McAllister, "Rituals of Labour Migration," p. 224; and M. Hunter, *Reaction to Conquest,* 2d ed. (Cape Town: Oxford University Press, 1961), p. 251.

6. Hunter, *Reaction to Conquest,* pp. 251–52.

7. W. D. Hammond-Tooke, *Bhaca Society* (Cape Town: Oxford University Press, 1962) p. 240.

8. M. Wilson, S. Kaplan, T. Maki, and E. M. Walton, *Social Structure,* vol. 3, Keiskammahoek Rural Survey (Pietermaritzburg: Shuter and Shooter, 1952), p. 197.

9. Every homestead has a special spear, called the spear of the home (*umkhonto wekhaya*), which is used to immolate the sacrificial animal on ritual occasions.

10. Rev. A. Kropf, D.D., *A Kafir–English Dictionary,* 2d ed., ed. Rev. Robert Godfrey (Lovedale: Lovedale Press, 1915), p. 391.

11. McAllister, "Rituals of Labour Migration," p. 152.

12. For a full discussion of the religious nature of Xhosa beer drinks and the role of public oratory at these events see McAllister, "Xhosa Beer Drinks."

13. See P. A. McAllister, *Umsindleko: A Gcaleka Ritual of Incorporation* (Institute for Social and Economic Research, Rhodes University, Grahamstown, 1981).

14. Some men are thought to acquire *umamlambo* unwittingly, having

bought what they believed to be medicine (*iyeza*) or a charm (*ikhubalo*) which would help them to become wealthy, attract women, or whatever. See Wilson et al., *Social Structure*, p. 189; and Hammond-Tooke, *Bhaca Society*, pp. 285–86.

15. P. Mayer, *Witches* (Rhodes University, Grahamstown, 1954); W. D. Hammond-Tooke, "The Cape Nguni Witch Familiar as a Mediatory Construct," *Man* n.s. 9 (1970); and W. D. Hammond-Tooke, *The Bantu-Speaking Peoples of Southern Africa* (London: Routledge and Kegan Paul, 1974), pp. 335ff.

16. M. Wilson, "The Nguni People," in *The Oxford History of South Africa*, ed. M. Wilson and L. Thompson (Cape Town: Oxford University Press, 1969), 1: 111.

17. See Hunter, *Reaction to Conquest*, p. 25; W. Beinart, *The Political Economy of Pondoland* (Cambridge: Cambridge University Press, 1982), pp. 94ff.

18. Hunter, *Reaction to Conquest*, p. 59.

19. Many other factors probably also contributed to the decline in homestead size: Pax Britannica and the decline in chiefly power; education and missionary activity, which were linked to the growth of individualism and the decline in polygyny; and the introduction of concepts like that of individual property. See Hammond-Tooke, *Bhaca Society*, pp. 35–36; W. D. Hammond-Tooke, *Command or Consensus* (Cape Town: David Philip, 1975), pp. 82–83; Wilson et al., *Social Structure*, pp. 52–59; and M. Wilson, "Xhosa Marriage in Historical Perspective," in *Essays in African Marriage in Southern Africa*, ed. E. J. Krige and J. L. Comaroff (Cape Town: Juta, 1981).

20. See Beinart, *Political Economy of Pondoland*, pp. 99–100.

21. Ibid.; and Hunter, *Reaction to Conquest*, p. 357.

22. McAllister, "Rituals of Labour Migration," pp. 44–46.

23. Hunter, *Reaction to Conquest*, p. 60; see also C. Meillassoux, "From Production to Reproduction: A Marxist Approach to Social Anthropology," *Economy and Society* 1 (1972); and "The Social Organisation of the Peasantry: The Economic Basis of Kinship," *Journal of Peasant Studies* 1 (1973).

24. Men seventy years old and older claim that the *umhlinzeko* killing was held for them when they were migrants but that the practice gave way to a beer drink by the time their sons became migrants. This would place the change at around 1945.

25. See McAllister, "Xhosa Beer Drinks," pp. 47ff. Although the consumption of beer in the Transkei fluctuated according to such factors as the availability of grain and cattle, a turning point seems to have been reached in

the late 1920s or soon thereafter, when the decline in cattle population became irreversible, after which beer drinking remained a prominent feature of rural life.

26. Wilson, "Xhosa Marriage," pp. 140–41.

27. In Pondoland in 1931 and 1932 only 17 percent of men in 115 marriages examined by Hunter had provided all their own marriage cattle, but this was at a time when "almost every homestead owned cattle and was largely self-supporting in food" (see Wilson, "Xhosa Marriage," pp. 140–41). Later, in Pondoland as elsewhere, sons became relatively independent of their seniors with regard to finding *lobola* cattle.

28. The role of migrant labor in fostering conflict between elder and junior has been widely documented; see for example Hunter, *Reaction to Conquest,* p. 60; P. Harries, "Kinship, Ideology and the Nature of Pre-Colonial Labour Migration" in *Industrialisation and Social Change in South Africa,* ed. S. Marks and R. Rathbone (London: Longman, 1982).

29. M. Douglas, *Purity and Danger* (London: Routledge, 1966).

30. See V. W. Turner, *From Ritual to Theatre: The Human Seriousness of Play* (New York: PAJ Publications, 1982), pp. 21–23.

CHAPTER ELEVEN

BACKS TO THE FENCE: LAW, LIQUOR, AND THE SEARCH FOR SOCIAL CONTROL IN AN EAST RAND TOWN, 1929–1942

Philip Bonner

INTRODUCTION

MANY REGARD THE industrialization and urbanization that took place in South Africa between the mid 1930s and the late 1960s as the key development of twentieth-century South African history, producing new political dispensations and new forms of political struggle. Much of the attention paid to the subject has been skewed toward the latter half of the period which permits it to ignore key aspects of the phenomenon. In this chapter I contend that major parts of the new urban and industrial configuration were present from the mid to late 1930s, eliciting a policy response (the 1937 Native Laws Amendment Act) that, in its efforts to create a framework for orderly urbanization, foreshadowed its far more effective successor, the 1952 Native Laws Amendments Act. The character of the urbanization that was taking place in this period, and which the policymakers were seeking to control, has been widely misunderstood inasmuch as it ignores the mining–migrant labor side of the phenomenon and concentrates solely on fully urban communities.

The juxtaposition of mining and urban communities on the Witwatersrand, and their close interaction, lay at the heart of the problems of social control with which the local authorities perceived themselves to be faced, and figured high on the agenda of those drafting successive pieces of urban areas legislation. These problems centered less on women and families joining breadwinners in the urban locations than on "unattached" women in the locations, who were often involved in the brewing of liquor, being joined by mine-laboring men. This situation engendered "disorderly" urbanization both in the sense of producing unstable families and uncontrolled youth, and in the sense of creating pervasive social disorder in the locations, ranging from individual robbery and assaults involving mineworkers to massed conflicts between factions of migrants and between them and the police. In this chapter I examine some of the dynamics and roots of these developments by studying the histories and activities of Basotho male migrants and Basotho women. Both illustrate a path toward urbanization that many others were subsequently to follow. I also examine the struggles surrounding the local authorities' attempts to reimpose control and show how small-scale and sometimes highly atomized resistance to those efforts, often through simple evasion or vandalism (as for example with the location fence), defeated the most orchestrated official plan. I conclude with an irony and contrast by noting that the more the authorities sought to close down loopholes and shut off space for informal resistance, the more they helped foster a more politicized and organized collective resistance, linked in this case to the Communist Party of South Africa (CPSA), and by highlighting the disparity between the achievements of the beer brewers, juvenile delinquents, and delinquent miners, and those of formal political organizations, primarily the CPSA and the African National Congress (ANC).

SLIPPING THE LEASH:
PAYNEVILLE LOCATION, 1929–1942

The essential backdrop to black urban life on the Witwatersrand prior to the 1950s was the close nexus between mining and manufacturing development. This had a particularly intimate character in the 1930s when manufacturing growth rode on the back of huge expansion of the gold mining industry, prompted by South Africa's departure from the gold standard in 1933. That much is well known. Less widely understood are the close interconnections between the sociopolitical consequences of this abrupt economic shift. Studies of black urbanization and political life tend to treat the mining and urban populations as discreet entities largely unrelated to one another, yet nothing could be further from the truth. In many areas of the Witwatersrand, mine compounds lay in close proximity to white suburbs and black locations and were far less insulated from outside contacts than is commonly supposed (see fig. 11.1). On Sundays and public holidays black miners were free to get permits to leave the mines, and often took this opportunity to visit neighboring African locations where they provided a clientele for "single" women beer brewers and "prostitutes" who had taken up residence in the towns. These weekend invasions of the towns were apt to end in explosions of violence which both mine managements and municipalities viewed with great alarm. Of equal concern to both parties, the miners who took part in such jaunts were liable to abandon the mines at the end of their contracts to establish unions with the "single" women of the towns. Such relationships were often unstable, producing offspring who lacked parental supervision, and who presented further problems of social control.

It was this kind of disorderly urbanization in which women attracted men, that the Reef municipalities became increasingly anxious to curb. Among the most vociferous advocates of new legislative measures and tighter administrative controls was the small and undistinguished East Rand town of Springs. Springs attitudes and experiences may be taken as archetypal of the Witwatersrand as a whole in the sense that they embodied these problems in perhaps their most extreme and distilled form. It was Springs member of Parliament, Colonel Stallard, who at least partly authored both the 1923 and 1937 Urban Areas Acts. It was also Springs that took the initiative in convening the Conference of Reef Municipalities in January 1935, which resuscitated the ailing Native Laws Amendment Bill, and which in turn inscribed many of the most important features of the 1937 Act.[1] The experiences of Springs serve both as a case study of the

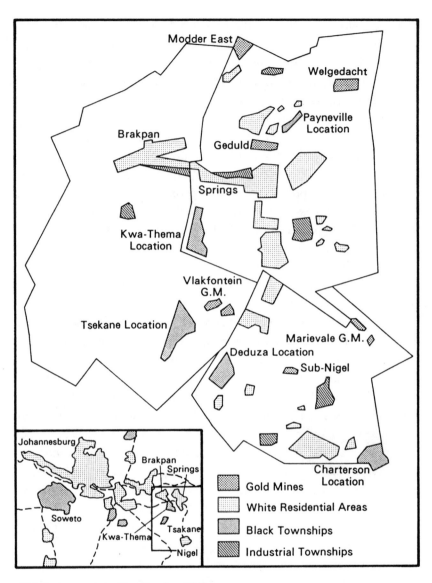

11.1 Springs and the East Rand, c. 1940

problems and pressures leading to the passage of the Native Laws Amendment Bill, and as an example of the obstacles that stood in the way of achieving its goals.

Complaints about the disorderly behavior of miners and the disruptive presence of "single" women on the Reef go back to the earliest years of the twentieth century. On the East Rand they became more intense immediately following the first World War. In 1921 the Transvaal Compound Managers' Association registered the first of several complaints about miners returning "hopelessly drunk," in this case from Benoni, and of the "serious assaults" that occurred in the compounds as a result.[2] Two years later the managers were demanding the fencing of locations (to keep mine laborers out), the proper administration of locations by full-time superintendents, and the monitoring, through special passes, of all mine laborers who entered these areas.[3] By the middle years of the decade, many municipalities had implemented the latter two suggestions and may have restored a measure of control, but this rapidly unraveled as the decade drew to a close.

In 1928 the new Liquor Act substituted the optional penalty of a fine for illicit dealing in liquor for the automatic terms of imprisonment that had previously been in force. At about the same time the Supreme Court declared ultra vires the location regulation that required the endorsement by location officials of special passes carried by visiting miners.[4] Even more ominously a new surge of women began to cascade into the towns. The female population of the Reef soared during the second half of the 1920s, at least partly in response to the first phase of secondary industrialization then occurring in the Union.[5]

Increasingly prominent in the ranks of these new immigrants were single Basotho women, who almost immediately acquired an extreme notoriety for the illicit brewing of liquor and for prostitution.[6] The compound managers, as a result, resumed their campaign for the more effective segregation of mine compounds and municipal locations, firing off protests and appeals in 1929 and again in 1934.[7]

The problems of Springs at this stage were nowhere near as acute as those at the neighboring towns of Benoni, Brakpan, and Germiston. As late as 1933, for example, the most serious difficulty the location had to face was an influx of farm laborers, including women who engaged in the small-scale brewing of liquor "as a sideline."[8] By the latter part of 1934 all that had changed. The first to draw attention to

the new state of affairs was the Location Advisory Board, who protested about being "overrun with mine natives at the weekend" and
about the escalation of "drinking and assaults with dangerous weapons."[9] In January 1935 the location superintendent expressed alarm
at the rapid expansion of the location's population, which he claimed
had doubled over the preceding three years, and at the influx of mine
laborers who came into the location "to settle their differences, especially over week-ends."[10] A major attraction for these visitors was the
substantial population of women, whose numbers had shot up in the
early years of the decade.[11]

A new and rapidly growing addition to the female population were
large numbers of "unattached" female immigrants from Basutoland,
who made a living through the illicit brewing and selling of liquor
and by entering more or less transient sexual relationships with men.[12]
These women very soon generated something close to a moral panic
among the municipal and mining dignitaries of Springs. A variety of
social maladies were attributed directly to their presence; others were
construed as being gravely aggravated by the activities in which they
engaged, so that Basotho women very quickly became symptomatic of
a multifaceted crisis of social control. It was for that reason the mines
and the municipalities placed such an exaggerated emphasis on this
issue in their evidence to countless select committees and official
commissions.[13]

The social problems with which Basotho women became associated
in the public discourse of Springs (and more generally on the Rand)
can be divided into four interlocking groups. The most obvious and
immediately pressing were the threats they were supposed to en-
gender to public order and security in the Payneville location (fig.
11.1). "Unattached" women, of whom the most numerous appear to
have been Basotho, served as a magnet for the rapidly multiplying
numbers of mine laborers in the immediate vicinity of Springs. In
May 1936 the Springs labor area already boasted an African population of 67,300—which included 50,000 miners, many of whom worked
on the closely adjacent East Geduld and East Daggafontein mines.[14]
Five years later Springs was the second largest labor district of the
Reef, with a population of 76,602, a similar proportion of whom

worked on the mines, and black mine workers were literally flooding into the location from three nearby newly opened mines.[15] This influx subverted order in two separate ways. The first was through the ordinary run of robbery and assault. In late 1936 the location manager penned the first of numerous reports lamenting the upsurge of crime in the location. "Hundreds of mine-boys" were invading the location every weekend, triggering a wave of "serious assaults."[16] Eighteen months later (and six months after three newly established gold mines on the outskirts of Springs began to produce) a note of desperation was entering his accounts of location affairs:

Crime in general is on the increase, and especially the illicit brewing and selling of liquor. I have experienced great difficulty with regard to the general lawlessness on week-ends. Natives pour into the location by the hundreds and by 5 or 6 p.m. most of these are intoxicated and start fights and brawls all over. Many accidents are being caused by drunken natives on pedal cycles and many are found lying drunk in the streets and passages and on sidewalks. There are also numerous occurrences of robberies. Certain gangs of robbers find their way into the location and concentrate on drunken natives. They pretend to be friends of these intoxicated natives and would assist them to a point where an opportunity is afforded to rob them of their money. If a victim offers resistance he is generally brutally assaulted.

He concluded with an appeal and a warning: "I beg again to draw your attention to the serious state of affairs and ask your assistance to tackle the problem before something similar to the Vereeniging riot occurs in the Springs location."[17] The reported incidence of serious crime in the location bears out the location manager's apprehensions (table 11.1). Between 1936 and 1938 the rate of serious crime in the location more than tripled.

Besides this pattern of low-level, relatively atomized anarchy, a different order of violence became increasingly common in the latter years of the decade. There were larger-scale confrontations between rival factions of mine workers from neighboring mines, or between visiting mine workers and location dwellers and police. More often than not the two kinds of conflict dissolved into one another: either

Table 11.1: Incidence of serious crime, Springs location, 1936–1938

	1 July 1936 to 30 June 1937	1 May to 31 August 1938
Murder	3	4
Culpable Homicide	4	3
Assault to Harm	63	98
Housebreaking and Theft	3	5
Robbery	10	10
Assault, Common	30	25
Theft, Common	25	12
Theft, Cycle	17	12
	155	169

Source: IAD, MSP, Minutes of PHC, 6 October 1937, 10 January 1939.

an attack on the police dissolved into a fight between miners or a fight between factions coalesced into a joint attack on the police. Occasionally, location dwellers would also be involved, sometimes on the side of the miners, sometimes on the side of the police. The confrontation that occurred on 15 September 1940 followed a fairly typical pattern.

At 3:00 P.M. that Sunday police were called out to deal with a faction fight (probably between Mpondo and Basotho miners) that had flared up in the location shortly before. By the time the police arrived the battling parties had drifted toward the fence on the east side of the location, which bordered on a plantation owned by the neighboring Grootvlei mine, where a much larger crowd of mine workers, some 2,000 strong, was congregated, some of them drinking, some fighting. As the police began breaking up the fights and destroying large quantities of liquor, women beer brewers on the inside of the location fence began urging the miners to "kill the police. Guns cannot hurt you," upon which a general offensive was launched by hundreds of visitors and location residents. So fierce was the onslaught that the police felt compelled to shoot their way out, leaving two of the crowd dead and two wounded by bullets. Six white and one African policemen were injured in the disturbance.[18] Mass conflicts of this kind occurred in June 1937, July 1938, April 1939, March 1940 (twice), September and December 1940, and April 1941 and had the location authorities wringing their hands in despair. The location seemed to be dissolving in a tumult of violence and disorder.[19]

The social matrix of these conflicts (as distinct from the social roots) was the illicit brewing of liquor and the presence of large numbers of "unattached," mainly Basotho, women. They were to be counted in their hundreds by the time the mass confrontations between factions of miners and police began to occur, and were held responsible, as the location manager repeatedly proclaimed, for "90% of the trouble in Payneville location."[20] This same group of unreclaimed women were also viewed as the root of a variety of other social ills. Several hundred mine workers were alleged to have established regular liaisons with Basotho women who had taken up residence in Payneville location, where the workers visited them on weekends. Once enmeshed in such relationships, miners were viewed as a total liability to the mines. Not only were they likely to be accompanied by friends when they visited their wives or lovers, thereby spreading ever wider the contagion of the towns, but it was also generally only a matter of time before they settled permanently inside the location, thereby "becoming detribalized and of no further use" as laborers in the mines.[21] Once known to be involved in such relationships, miners were never reengaged.[22]

The offspring of such relationships were viewed with equal disfavor. Compound managers insisted that "bastard families were becoming a serious menace, forming a class known as 'amalaita' who were absolutely useless for mining or manual labor of any kind."[23] The municipal authorities largely concurred. Relationships between miners and "unattached" women were often unstable and transient, leaving families of young children without paternal control.[24] Children reared in this environment were consequently even more likely than their fellows brought up in the town to drift into juvenile delinquency and crime, thereby aggravating the situation of acute social disorder that already prevailed. In this context, it is noteworthy that as early as 1937 the Payneville Advisory Board was drawing attention to the "many youthful criminals inside the location [who] paraded in blankets in the location at night and commit crimes for which mine boys are then blamed."[25]

Again the principal blame for this situation was attached to Basotho women, as were all manner of other social evils. At the beginning of 1939, the location manager leveled a series of other accusations:

> Besides being a menace to the peace and safety of the law-abiding residents of the location . . . [Basotho women] were responsible for the very unhygienic conditions, and must have been the cause of a lot of disease, since the place was hopelessly overcrowded. Stand-owners, realizing that accommodations were very much in demand, and that high prices were paid for rooms in their backyards are adding rooms on to their houses. . . . In many instances stand-owners receiving rent of 5 to 6 pounds per month from lodgers resigned from the service of their employers and lived an idle and unruly life, and for this reason also crime in general increased month to month.[26]

In this manner overcrowding, disease, the rising incidence of infant mortality and juvenile delinquency, social disorder, and the growth of parasitic and criminal classes were all laid directly or indirectly at the feet of the unholy trinity of Basotho women, illicit liquor, and visiting workers from the mines.

Seen from that perspective there was at least one obvious solution to the problem. Mine workers had to be stopped from visiting the location; "single" women and illicit liquor had to be kept out of their reach. Both mine managers and municipalities accordingly set about fashioning a set of legislative edicts and administrative controls to achieve those seemingly modest goals. The goals were both shortsighted and superficial inasmuch as they addressed symptoms rather than tackling or even recognizing the underlying causes. The authorities' working assumptions appear to have been that African women were naturally lascivious and immoral once deprived of "tribal restraints," and that fighting between miners was merely a reflection of age-old tribal hostilities and primitive atavisms.[27] Questions of why it was Basotho rather than other women who were primarily involved, or why "faction-fighting" between miners should suddenly have flared up in the late 1930s seem to have raised scarcely a flicker of interest in their minds. It is this deeper set of issues that I address next.

THE ROOTS OF DISORDER

The movement of Basotho women to the Reef amounted to little more than a trickle before the late 1910s.[28] Thereafter it rapidly swelled, becoming particularly brisk in the late 1920s. Initially the new immigrants clustered in the Nancefield location of Johannesburg, and around the East Rand towns of Benoni and Brakpan, where they rooted themselves with remarkable tenacity and resource. By 1930, for example, more than 250 out of 818 stands in Benoni location were "occupied by Native women, many of whom come from Basutoland."[29] Two years later Brakpan location was "teeming with people, principally from Basutoland who . . . have thrown up shacks all over the place and defied the authorities."[30] A second pronounced bulge in the volume of Basotho women's immigration to the Rand can be dated to 1934–1935, at which time the first large-scale movement of Basotho women to Springs and many other urban and peri-urban areas of the Reef occurred. As a result, by 1936, 22,669 Basotho women were recorded as being absent from their homes; the great majority of them were living on the Rand.[31] For the next fifteen years the rate of increase of Basotho women's immigration to the Rand slackened, but it still persisted on a scale unequaled by that from any other part of the subcontinent. By 1942 an estimated 20,000 Basotho women were living on the Reef, three-quarters of whom were considered to fall into the "undesirable" category of "unattached" women or those living in "irregular" transient unions, and the same pattern persisted for the next decade and a half.[32]

The movement of Basotho women to the Rand, while in many ways the outcome of the economic stresses to which Basotho society was subjected in the first three decades of the century, cannot be understood without also considering the migration of men. The single most salient sociological feature of that exodus was that the overwhelming majority of women swept along in it were then or had previously been married to Basotho men. Most fell into two distinct categories. They were either widows who rejected marriage to one of their deceased husband's male kin (under the levirate custom) and so came under pressure to leave their marital home, or they were married women who had been abandoned or seriously neglected by husbands who had taken a contract on the mines.[33] Both categories of women were the victims of the economic strains that afflicted Basotho society in the early to mid twentieth century—strains that came to bear on them both directly and indirectly through the intervening actions (or inactions) of men.

Basutoland's economic predicament is sufficiently well known to require only brief recapitulation here.[34] Land losses after the Free State war of 1867–1868, population pressure as a result of natural increases and the eviction of sharecroppers from the eastern Free State farms, exclusion from markets for agricultural products, and natural epidemics and blights all served to cripple Basutoland's previously thriving economy. Per capita incomes from agriculture dropped; levels of migrancy climbed. By 1911 approximately 25,000 Basotho nationals were working outside its borders. Despite the absence of so many people, Basutoland's economy retained a degree of viability until the late 1920s. Then depression and drought combined to break its back. In the 1932–1933 drought between 30 and 50 percent of cattle holdings were lost, and the cultivation of maize was temporarily extinguished.[35] Virtually every bit of ground cover was destroyed, and choking clouds of dust filled the air. Older Basotho still date key events in their lives by reference to the all-enveloping clouds of "red dust," and many even identify them as a turning point in their ability to win a daily subsistence from agriculture.[36]

Widows were among the most conspicuous casualties of the economic shocks. Once bereaved they were faced with two often equally unpalatable options: to be married to a male kinsman of their husband (the levirate) or to remain perpetually vulnerable to men.[37] Those choosing the latter option often fell prey to the opportunism of chiefs or to the greed of their husband's kin. A combination of land shortage and a proliferation of chiefs in Basutoland had pushed widows into an increasingly exposed position in the 1920s and 1930s. Under the system of "placing" chiefs in charge of newly-created chiefdoms (which had been started by Moshoeshoe), the number of chiefs had grown steadily in the late nineteenth and early twentieth centuries. As one Basutoland National Council member exclaimed in the early 1930s, "there are now as many Chiefs in Basutoland as there are stars in the heavens"—each of whom exercised authority over a steadily dwindling patrimony.[38] Their continually narrowing jurisdiction encouraged the chiefs to exploit more intensively their rights over the area that remained. Fines and tribute labor (*matsema*) for the chiefs' fields were extorted ever more remorselessly, with much of the burden falling on women. Widows, who lacked the protection of husbands and adult male children, were particularly vulnerable to those demands. Worse still, since widows were exempted from the payment of tax and the chiefs took a cut of the taxes collected in their territories, widows often found themselves arbitrarily deprived of their lands, which were then allocated to young male tax payers.[39] Other pressures, which might include the leveling of witchcraft accusations, could be applied by jealous in-laws, until the hapless widow was ultimately forced to leave. Such women often fled to government camps in Basutoland, where they engaged in the brewing of beer; alternatively they might proceed to the Free State or the Rand.[40]

Married women experienced the same economic privations primarily through the actions of their spouses. The chronic poverty of a growing section of Basotho society induced the husbands of Basotho women to migrate on labor contracts more frequently and for longer and longer periods of time. This often so shriveled their affective links to their families that they ceased to provide them with adequate material support or abandoned them altogether for life in the towns. Wives left stranded in this fashion constituted the main reservoir of the battalions of women that flocked to the Rand.[41]

Such problems and pressures were, however, not uniformly felt across all sections of Basotho society, and close scrutiny of precisely which men and women were most likely to succumb to economic hardships and sever their links with the land may help illuminate why it was Basotho women, rather than those from other parts of South

Africa, who were in the forefront of the move to the town. Practically all young Basotho men, of whatever economic circumstance, engaged in a spell of migrant labor on the mines, but it was younger brothers or those born into poorer households or households lacking in political influence who were liable to stay longer on the Rand.[42] The prevailing levels of bridewealth in Basutoland were exceptionally high compared to other parts of the subcontinent (twenty to thirty head of cattle for commoner marriages as compared with three to ten elsewhere), and in the absence of family support, even the initial downpayment of ten head of cattle required an extended spell of work on the mines.[43] Marriages as a result often had to be deferred until men reached their late twenties or older, a development that almost certainly spurred the immigration of bachelors to the towns.[44] For those facing that predicament, conventional marriage arrangements could be short-circuited by elopement with the bride—a practice that became increasingly common in the course of the 1920s and 1930s—but even that required the payment of six head of cattle as compensation to the family of the bride. Marriages contracted in that fashion, moreover, conferred fewer rights on the husband and were perceived to demand fewer obligations in return. In the face of the rival attractions of the towns, the bonds formed by such marriages were liable to prove appreciably more fragile and to have provided less incentive to return.[45] Deferred access to land also weakened men's attachment to their homesteads and lengthened the time they were likely to spend working in the towns. Even once married, poorer men or men from less influential families were often allocated one field out of the customary three and had to wait for the balance for an indeterminate period of time.[46] The barest elements of an autonomous homestead were thus denied to the heads of such households and that served further to weaken the resolve to return home.

A variety of other individually insubstantial, but collectively quite weighty, considerations also added to the drag on men's impulse to return home. In 1928 a new type of contract was introduced on the mines that progressively ousted other forms of labor recruitment. Known as the Assisted Voluntary Scheme (or AVS), it allowed prospective recruits a period of time to select a mine of their choice on arrival on the Rand, and provided for an advance of £2 in cash upon arrival at the mines.[47] The AVS provided a degree of personal latitude to the laborer that while small, had far-reaching effects. Advances in cattle and cash, which under the previous system had been furnished in Basutoland, now stood much less chance of finding their way back to the migrant's family at home. Similarly, the practice of deferring pay to be drawn at the end of a contract once a recruit had returned home from the mines was made fully discretionary. In practice, 90 percent of such recruits opted for the deferment of pay, but under the new system there was nothing to stop them from canceling this arrangement and drawing their pay as it fell due, or in a lump sum at the mine when their contract expired. A large number did, the British Agent for the High Commission territories reported, "especially the young and irresponsible type, and the money is spent or stolen before they leave the Reef." Having squandered their savings in this fashion, most were "too afraid or ashamed" to return home. Instead "they sign on again, and there is no mention of deferred pay in their contracts. They draw earnings every month and save nothing." Such "local" recruits, the British agent observed, had increased considerably during the last few years and "many [had] left wives and children uncared for and underfed." It was this type, he concluded, "who eventually develop into what is known on the Reef as the detribalized Basuto."[48]

THE SEARCH FOR SOCIAL CONTROL AND THE POLITICIZATION OF POPULAR STRUGGLES

From the mid-1930s a fresh solvent began to eat away at the already tattered fabric of Basotho society. For reasons that have yet to be adequately explained, Basotho miners either now or (more probably) at some earlier stage, acquired a virtual monopoly of shaft sinking and development work on the mines.[49] These were both more lucrative and more dangerous than other jobs on the mines but their availability fluctuated wildly according to the prosperity of the industry and the phase of expansion or consolidation that the industry found itself in. The mid- to late 1930s was a period of unprecedented expansion on the mines in which both shaft sinking and development were pressed ahead at a giddy pace. Basotho miners were among the principal beneficiaries of this period of expansion. A distinct new category of Basotho miner developed "wandering from one shaft sinking mine to another, earning good money, but remitting very little, if any earnings, home." Those increasingly "detribalized" Basotho, to use the British Labour Agent Elliot's somewhat misleading term, were subject to a rude shock toward the end of the decade. As new shaft sinking and development work slowed, many of the best-paying jobs on the mines came to an end.[50] It seems likely that a substantial proportion of Basotho miners affected by that change chose this occasion to take up employment in the rapidly expanding manufacturing sector, where wages stood two to three times higher than the average paid on the mines.[51]

Once cut adrift from the encapsulated world of the mines, such workers were a good deal more susceptible to the much-maligned forces of "detribalization" and urbanization. These could present themselves in a variety of forms. In one caricature, which one supposes was intended to be representative of a trend, the British Agent described the career of a Basotho ex-miner who, upon leaving the mines, established a relationship with a Basotho woman beer brewer, perhaps not insignificantly, from Springs. Having set himself up in family circumstances (to use the official language of the time) he was able to secure a house in the Payneville location of Springs, from which his wife was able to prosecute her beer brewing enterprises, upon whose earnings he was able to live a life of indolence and ease. With that the transformation from intrepid and industrious shaft sinker to "first-class loafer" was complete.[52]

Although overdrawn, Elliot's portrait does highlight a number of features of the changing character of the Basotho migrant's odyssey to the town. The most important of those were the propensity of Basotho miners to enter into liaisons or more permanent unions with urban women and the accelerating drift of Basotho women to the towns.

No corresponding tendency exhibited itself, at least nothing on nearly the same scale, among any other major group of African miners (or their womenfolk) who came to the Rand. Ever attentive to his duties, the British Labour Agent, Elliot, made extensive enquiries in the late 1940s as to why this was so; and flawed and partial though his answers were, they do provide some explanation. For Elliot, the root of the problem lay in the "unnatural conditions" under which miners were living on the Rand. As a consequence, "sodomy is very prevalent in the mine compounds." The most conspicuous exception to the pattern were Basotho miners: "They apparently do not approve of this type of entertainment, and prefer their women, which accounts, I think, for the large number of Basuto women on the Reef. Women from other tribes are very seldom found on the Reef, but sodomy is indulged in considerably by the Pondos, Swazis, Zulus and especially the East Coasters."[53]

Once Basotho miners secured employment in secondary industry a large proportion seem, like Elliot's archetypal figure from Springs, to have struck up or institutionalized a union with Basotho women in the towns. Since their larger, but still meager earnings from industry did not allow them to "keep a family locally" as well as maintain their families at home, a dwindling proportion of their earnings were remitted to their rural homestead and wives.[54] If, in addition, men failed to continue their payment of tax in Basutoland and paid it instead to the tax-collecting officers in the Union, as was increasingly common at this time, they fell more and more into arrears, which very shortly extinguished their right to the land. Under such circumstances, the temptation to sever all ties with their families became increasingly strong and the process of "detribalization" became complete.[55]

Basotho women abandoned in this way often traveled to the Rand in a last desperate effort to track their husbands down. Facilitating this exercise was the presence of large numbers of Basotho women of similar circumstances already in the towns and their ability to communicate by post. The vast majority of Basotho women received elementary education (a much larger proportion than men), and oral testimonies frequently tell of their seeking information or of announcing their arrival by letter.[56] If a wife finally made her way to the towns and found her husband installed in another residence with another wife "a family quarrel usually ensue[d]," after which "the man may set up a new home for her, or refuse to have anything to do with her—or she may not find him, in which case she may find another guardian for herself and the children who accompany her."[57] Once they found themselves in this situation, Basotho women often resolved never again to become wholly dependent on men, engaging instead in beer brewing and other informal income-generating activities to provide an independent income of their own. The unions that resulted were often transient and unstable, thus creating a self-reinforcing cycle in which husbands abandoned wives and abandoned wives courted the attention of other wives' husbands.[58]

The growing incidence of collective violence involving miners in the locations of the Rand is less easily explained but is also probably related to some of the developments outlined above. The massed conflicts that punctuated the life of the Payneville location in the late 1930s, while unusually frequent and severe, were an increasingly common occurrence inside and outside mine compounds all along the Rand. Dunbar Moodie, for example, notes a sharp rise in the numbers of "faction fights" inside mine compounds between 1938 and 1946, and an even greater intensity of ethnic and other conflicts involving miners may be discerned in the immediately adjacent locations along the Reef.[59] Moodie relates the changing incidence of collective violence involving miners over the whole sweep of the twentieth century to the changing composition of the mine labor force at particular times, but does not apply that insight systematically to the period from 1937 to 1946. In the course of his general discussion, Moodie also refers to a faction fight in Ventersdorp (on the West Rand) in 1938 that broke out when Basotho miners who had been engaged primarily in shaft sinking were suddenly swamped by new miners from other ethnic groups as the mine began to enter full-scale production.[60] Herein lies a key to the escalation of faction fighting along much of the East Rand.

The most intensive period of shaft sinking and development work followed South Africa's abandonment of the gold standard in 1933 and drew to a close toward the end of 1937, as mines became fully operational. Basotho miners, who for a brief interval had commanded most of the best-paid jobs in the industry, found their position of privilege comprehensively undercut. Not only did other groups of workers begin to predominate in their compounds, but the Basotho miners were also forced to accept other categories of labor at much lower pay.[61] Basotho miners sought to reconcile themselves to their altered positions by displays of arrogance and assertions of superiority and precedence vis-a-vis newcomers to the mines—behavior which when directed toward Mpondo miners often involved the assertion of superior masculinity because the Basotho were circumcised and the Mpondo were not.[62] The same attitudes and tensions were transported out of the compounds and into the neighboring locations. New groups of miners began to challenge Basotho miners' prior ascendancy in the weekend liquor culture of the location, which they had secured both by their numerical preponderance and their relative affluence. Since most of the women brewers and those providing sexual services to miners were "unattached" Basotho women, the rivalries that ensued often acquired a sharper ethnic definition. It is thus no accident that faction fights in Springs began in earnest in July 1938, six months after the new mines in its vicinity came fully on stream, or that every single conflict reported was between Basotho and Mpondo miners.[63] The dangers of analytically segregating the worlds of mining and manufacturing could not be clearer. The inhabitants and cultures of each world constantly flowed into and agitated the other, in a way that defied all official attempts at control.

"Faction fighting," narrowly defined, was only one part of collective violence on the mines. In Springs massed collisions between miners and police and miners and location dwellers were at least as common. Conflicts with police were almost invariably detonated by the raids they undertook in the locations for permits and liquor. These reached a new pitch of intensity in 1938. For the previous three years virtually every branch of the municipalities, the state, and the mining industry charged with managing African affairs had expressed mounting concern at the uncontrolled nature of the traffic in liquor in the locations and the collapse of social order that had ensued. A variety of initiatives were accordingly undertaken to segregate the compounds from the locations and to suppress the illicit brewing and selling of liquor. A number of those initiatives reached legislative fruition with the passage of the Native Laws Amendment Act, which came into effect on 1 January 1938 and which contained various measures to curb the activities of "unattached" women in the towns and staunch the seepage of mine laborers into secondary industry and the urban locations. One of the Act's most important provisions in this regard was to establish municipal monopolies for the manufacture of sorghum beer. The revenues that might accrue to municipal coffers from this source were potentially enormous and promised to furnish the wherewithal for ambitious programs of social welfare and urban renewal for the settled urban African population.

Before any of those objectives could be attained, however, "unfair" competition from illicit brewers in the location and the peri-urban areas had to be effectively suppressed. Until that was done municipal beerhalls would always be operating at a disadvantage. Beer sold on these premises generally retailed at four times the price charged by location women and was consumed in austere, regimented, antiseptic environments far removed from the heady and rowdy atmosphere of the shebeens, where female company was always close at hand.[64] Both police and municipalities therefore embarked on a campaign of unprecedented ferocity to eradicate the illicit liquor traffic once and for all.

The heightened intensity of raiding detonated explosions all over South Africa. In Vereeniging and Johannesburg's Western Townships effective boycotts of municipal beerhalls were mounted.[65] Elsewhere ugly confrontations developed between location residents and the police. In February 1938 twenty-nine police carrying out "the most extensive liquor raid . . . in years" in Middelberg location were attacked by "a mob of natives" and one policeman was seriously injured.[66] In April of the same year 100 Vrededorp residents retaliated against a police raiding party by belaboring them with stones and sticks.[67] The following month several hundred Africans stoned police who were raiding for beer on a vacant plot near Johannesburg's Bantu Sports Ground.[68] Two of the most violent centers of conflict were Benoni and Springs. In May 1938 arrests for permits in Benoni location led to a clash between a crowd of 800 men and women and the police. One person was killed and one other was injured before the incident "resolved itself" into a factional dispute between Basotho and Zulu.[69] In Springs four of the major collisions between municipal authorities and miners were precipitated by police raiding for liquor, yielding a toll of casualties that dwarfed all previous altercations between location inhabitants and their visitors and the police.[70] In this way official efforts to stamp out the sources of social disorder and conflict led to the escalation of violence to unprecedented levels.

BACKS TO THE FENCE

If the officials of Springs were profoundly uninquisitive about the deeper causes of urban social disorder, they made up for it with the extent and vigor of their attack on its effects. The attack was embarked on in earnest in 1936 and sometimes attained the character of a crusade. For much of the period that followed the municipality pinned its hopes on a combination of close policing, legislative restraints, and physical barriers to segregate the location from the compounds. Springs was in the forefront of the agitation for an amended Urban Areas/Native Laws Act and placed particular emphasis on securing curbs on the brewing of liquor and on the entry of miners and "unattached" women, either temporarily or permanently, into the location. The Council's awareness of the deficiencies of the existing legislation (to which the Reef municipalities had already drawn attention even before it was enacted into law) was heightened by its attempts to restrict the entry of women into the location in terms of clause 12 of the 1930 amended Native (Urban Areas) Act.[71] When the Council applied to the government at the end of 1936 to have the requisite powers conferred on it, it was informed by the Secretary for Native Affairs that both technicalities and practical objections made this section of the Act unenforceable, and it was advised to await the pending amending legislation (of 1937) for remedy.[72] Unable to evict what it saw as the principal source of its troubles, the Council now fell back on more crudely coercive controls and on the erection of a physical barrier to cut off the beer brewers from their principal sources of clientele. In mid-1936, following the example of many other municipalities on the Rand, the location's skeletal police force of five was considerably enlarged by the addition of a white location constable and twelve African police.[73] Up to that point the South African Police had been charged with controlling the illicit production of liquor and had met with scant success. Police raids were mounted once a week, usually on weekends. Although large quantities of liquor were destroyed, the brewers themselves were rarely apprehended:

> As soon as the police entered the location hundreds of unauthorized persons locked their rooms and cleared out into the plantation where the police had no authority to arrest them for permits. As soon as the police left they came back, and the same state of affairs would exist. . . . the liquor queens would then resort to the making of Skokiaan, Barberton, Hopana and other concoctions which would . . . be ready for consumption in less than 24 hours. These liquors, owing to the large quantities of yeast being used in the manufacture contain a very large percentage of alcohol—about 1 pint suffices to make a man drunk. And soon after a police raid there was as much liquor in the location as before the raid.[74]

With the expansion of the location police force, raids for permits and liquor took place much more regularly and to much greater effect. In the twelve months that followed, the location police force succeeded in making 3,442 arrests and in destroying over 11,000 gallons of liquor, and the overall level of crime and social disorder noticeably dipped.[75]

It was now that the Springs municipality played what it imagined to be its trump card. Ever since the far East Rand municipality of Brakpan had erected a fence around its location and successfully evicted 3,500 "undesirables," the idea of a fence had exercised an unnatural hold over the imaginations of most of the Springs councillors and officials.[76] Requests for the fencing of locations was one of the most prominent demands made at the conference of Reef municipalities convened by the Town Council of Springs in January and February 1935, and, in the face of fierce opposition from the residents of Payneville location, the Council went ahead with a plan for the construction of a ten-foot, "manproof" palisade early in 1937.[77] This deceptively simple solution to the location's manifold problems of control quickly rebounded on its somewhat ingenuous sponsors. Up to that point, as we have seen, the location police had achieved a modest measure of success in their efforts to contain the brewing of illicit liquor and the commission of crime. The erection of the fence almost immediately undid all those efforts. "Hundreds" of Basotho women residing in the location undertook an orchestrated demolition, employing gangs of youthful saboteurs, to break open selected parts of the palisade through which the brewers' mining clientele could secure entry.[78] As a result of these constant depredations a significant component of the location's police had to be reassigned to patrolling the fence. That duty meant that they were too thinly stretched either to maintain control over liquor and illegal residence in the location or to safeguard the fence effectively. Undermanned units patrolling the one-mile perimeter would no sooner reach one end of the fence than "palings [were] removed at the other." A dense plantation of trees on the Grootvlei mine side of the location further frustrated efforts at control, for "as soon as the mine natives see the police they retreat among the trees until such time as the police attempt to make an arrest, and then the hidden natives rush out from amongst the trees and attack the police with stones and other missiles." In the absence of reinforcements from the South African Police, the municipal patrols would usually beat an undignified retreat.[79]

Meanwhile the brewing of beer "and other strong concoctions" continued "wholesale" so that by May "control of the location" had been rendered "impossible."[80] In June a despairing location manager was predicting another Vereeniging riot, an eventuality that transpired exactly one month later after the first of the mass fights between factions of mine workers and location residents broke out. Here, in an ironic twist in the saga of the fence, mine workers who would normally have fled upon the appearance of the police now found themselves trapped on the inside of the fence, and so turned en masse to battle their pursuers.[81]

Thus were the high expectations of the Springs municipality cruelly dashed. One might have expected the Council to rue the day it ever heard of Brakpan's fence, which was the attitude quickly adopted by the location superintendent. Reviewing the first seven months of the operation of the fence, and noting that the number of assaults in the location had increased rather than been reduced, he concluded that from the point of view of administration, control, and expenses its advantages were outweighed by its disadvantages.[82] For the majority of councillors, however, that was an unpopular, well-nigh heretical view. Many had become fixated by the fence, elevating it to the status of a municipal fetish. Rather than considering that the whole idea might be misconceived, they interpreted its shortcomings as problems of faulty implementation. Thus a certain councillor Brink of well-known right-wing persuasions proposed digging a trench on the plantation side of the perimeter and electrifying the fence "to give a bit of a shock," while councillor Butler pitched in with suggestions that the palings be riveted or welded to the heavier bars.[83] Neither of those proposals were adopted, on moral or practical grounds. A recommendation made in the same spirit by the location's constable and superintendent—to augment the location police force with a further twenty-one new Zulu constables and with that expanded complement to prosecute a "clean-up" campaign—received a more favorable hearing and was scheduled for implementation in September 1938.[84]

One new development almost certainly helped stiffen the Council's backbone on the matter of the fence. The 1937 Native Laws Amendment Act virtually required municipalities to undertake the manufacture and sale of sorghum beer. If they had not created such a facility by 31 December 1937, the domestic brewing of sorghum beer was to be permitted, something that none of the Reef municipalities were prepared to countenance. Springs, like the rest of its municipal brethren along the Reef, jumped at the revenue generating opportunity that the Act offered and constructed a temporary facility that began production at the beginning of 1938.

In its early years the Springs beerhall can best be described as having a checkered career. Opening to great fanfare, it proved to be an instant and dismal failure. Beerhall sales steadily plummeted in the first six months of its operation, from what was in any case a pathetically low opening base.[85] Thereafter sales fluctuated upwards occasionally during periods of particularly severe harassment of illicit brewers, but not with major long-term effect. A report compiled by the Acting Medical Officer of Health in 1941 could have applied equally to more or less any point over the previous three years. Springs, with an African and "Coloured" population double that of its East Rand neighbors of Boksburg and Brakpan, had managed to generate a profit of £417 over the previous year, compared to £16,898 for the other two municipalities combined. From July 1940 to January 1941 the average daily takings in Springs were a paltry £8 10s. The acting M.O.H. concluded that "the disparity is almost absurd" and called for a "searching enquiry."[86] The production of more palatable beer in more accessible and congenial surroundings was one part of the answer, as council officials readily recognized, but the key to the difficulties, most continued to believe, was the effective insulation of the location from the neighboring compounds and the suppression of the illicit brewing of sorghum beer. It was this perception that stiffened the resolve of the location superintendent, who wavered briefly on the question of the viability of the fence, and it was this self-same understanding that provided the necessary justification for the very substantial expenditures he now requested for the (temporary) doubling of the location's complement of police.

Springs's much vaunted clean-up campaign was inaugurated in September 1938 with the aid of twenty Zulu policemen specially imported from Natal. After the first weekend the location superintendent was already cock-a-hoop, claiming a major advance in all aspects of social control. Large volumes of liquor had been destroyed, 110 "unauthorized" persons arrested, and "liquor queens" were alleged to be fleeing the location.[87] One month later 812 arrests had been made, serious crime had been slashed by 85 percent, the brewing and selling of illicit beer had been reduced by 65 percent, and municipal beerhall sales were shooting up. The location superintendent was even constrained to make the rash prediction (citing his location constable as source) that all Basotho women without rights to reside in the location would be prosecuted and those with rights of residence who continued to brew liquor would be prosecuted and deported in terms of section 17 of the amended 1937 legislation.[88] Even the fence was to acquire a new inviolability. Hexagonal-headed bolts, which one imagines were expected to confuse the location residents, were to be used to bolt the palings to their mounts.[89]

The same self-congratulatory attitude persisted into early 1939. The Christmas period in Payneville proved "the quietest on the Reef." Sales of municipal beer were up 600 percent. Crime continued to be down by three-quarters.[90] One distant cloud, however, could already be discerned hovering over the horizon. The twenty additional Zulu police had only been employed for a short-term blitz and were due to be laid off at the end of February 1939. The location manager therefore requested an increase in his permanent complement of police from nineteen to twenty-five once the temporary constables had been paid off.[91] The Council agreed, but the increase soon proved insufficient to the task. Almost from the moment the Zulu constables were retrenched the fence once again came under attack, control over the illicit brewing was lost, and the rate of serious crime soared.[92] Worse still, on Easter Friday clashes between massed battalions of mine workers and police, and between different factions of miners resumed— something that was to become almost a traditional part of the festivities in subsequent years.[93] From this point on the battle for the fence acquired an increasingly farcical quality. In May 1939 the Manager of Non-European affairs informed bewildered fellow committee members that patrols around the fence would now be issued with wrenches to reattach damaged or loosened palings, and he began to submit lost and damaged bolt and paling counts to the monthly meetings of his committee.[94] In August of the same year, two plainclothes constables were placed on duty to monitor the sale of illicit liquor through the fence—an assignment that proved unpopular and hazardous, as they were frequently recognized and then attacked.[95]

Such measures obviously touched only the fringes of the problem, and location authorities effectively relinquished control over the situation for the next two years. Miners broke through the fence at will, liquor was transacted across it with impunity, and mass clashes between miners became a regular occurrence. By the beginning of 1941 a dispirited acting M.O.H. was ready to throw in the towel: "It has been found that as soon as the palings which have been removed from the fence are replaced they are once again removed. . . . I consider no effective purpose is served by replacing palings which were no sooner replaced that they were again removed by offenders."[96] The redoubtable Councillor Brink was incensed at the expression of such a heretical view and swung the committee to his side.[97] The absurd charade continued until some time in 1942, when a new balance was struck by the contending forces. In that year a new beerhall was completed that produced a far higher quality product than heretofore and was much more conveniently and congenially situated than its predecessor.[98] At the same time the Grootvlei mining company cut back the plantation that had previously provided cover and sanctuary for miners intent on breaking into the location.[99] Such illegal entry did not end, nor did illicit liquor production cease, but production appears to have been brought down to more manageable proportions, thereby allowing the municipality a substantial slice of the mine workers' liquor consumption. Beerhall earnings climbed astronomically in the period, reaching £160,000 in 1945.[100] On the basis of this new balance of power and reward, both sides seem to have been content to declare a truce.

The council's efforts at controlling the manufacture of illicit liquor at the source met with only marginally more success in the period up to 1942. Women brewers evolved a variety of highly effective stratagems to avoid detection and prosecution, which they employed with great success. As the acting M.O.H. explained to one agitated meeting of the Public Health and Non-European Affairs Committee:

> Great difficulty exists in finding the actual brewing in progress. The first step in brewing is boiling the porridge. This is done with an ordinary domestic stove in the house and cannot be classed an offense. The subsequent steps consist of adding malt and cooling. These processes are carried out under the cover of darkness and are very difficult to detect. The whole process of adding malt takes but a few seconds, the resulting liquor being left unattended in some public roadway or in a plantation.[101]

Even when massed raids took place as on 16, 29, and 30 March 1941 and huge amounts of liquor were unearthed and destroyed, "it was noticed that after the raids took place large quantities were available in the plantation and were consumed by the mine natives." Indeed, such raids were more likely to accomplish the reverse effect, as they were almost always a component in the explosions of violence between miners and police that periodically rocked the Springs location. Thus, as the acting M.O.H. concluded, even "concerted activity . . . cannot be claimed to be having any serious deterrent effect."[102]

The redrafted section 17 of the new Native Laws Amendment Act, which ironed out a number of difficulties that had previously been experienced in the prosecution and removal of persons deemed "idle and disorderly," also proved seriously flawed, since

> proof of previous offenses for the possession of kaffir beer or intoxicating liquor, while bringing the native concerned within the terms of Section i(e) of the Act and giving jurisdiction to the Native Commissioner to hold an enquiry is not conclusive of the problem whether the native in question is an "idle and disorderly person" according to a recent Supreme Court judgement.[103]

Other changes introduced by the 1937 Act provided only limited succor to the beleaguered municipal authorities. The requirement that a woman entering an urban area for the first time should possess a certificate from the authorities granting her permission to leave turned out to be a dead letter, for, as anticipated by the Native Affairs Manager of Durban municipality, women simply claimed to have arrived in the urban area before the Act came into operation on 1 January 1938.[104] Likewise, the addition of a women's section to the prison farm labor colony at Leeuwkop, in which so much hope had been vested, failed to have the expected deterrent effect, because the courts were reluctant to consign women to the colony. As a result, over the next fifteen years, the section often had as little as two inmates, sometimes none, and never housed more than fourteen at the same time.[105] As became increasingly apparent with each passing year, only the issue of passes to African women and the official registration of African marriages would allow the authorities to reimpose their control and this, despite the municipalities' earnest entreaties in the discussions leading up to the passage of the 1937 Act, the Union government was too fearful to allow.[106]

CONCLUSION

The kind of politicization and organized opposition that official repression would evoke was signposted by the public response in the Payneville location to some of the Council's more draconian efforts to reassert its control, particularly in the clean-up campaign of late 1938. At this stage many township residents banded together to resist these impositions creating the nucleus of a more politicized oppositional culture that would have far-reaching repercussions. Already the erection of the fence and the planned municipal monopolization of beer had radicalized formal politics in the location and led to the forming of a Vigilance Committee.[107] Now the massed raids of September 1938 to February 1939 released a flood of complaints and raised the political temperature of the location to fever point.

Mass meetings were held in November 1938, and even Payneville's normally acquiescent Advisory Board members adopted a sullen and obstructive demeanor in their dealings with Council officials. Perhaps the most significant development of this period was the formation of a women's society known as the African Protection League.[108] Headed by Dinah Mayile, who twice led demonstrations on the office of the town clerk and who was "either directly or indirectly concerned in nearly every appeal against my [the Non-European Affairs Manager's] actions under the regulation," the league became the vehicle for a new kind of organized political consciousness that began to be distilled in the Payneville community.[109] It also became the point of entry of the Communist Party of South Africa, a development which proceeded to greatly widen the political horizons of Springs's African community to link them to more national political networks and concerns.

The link was made, as was so often the case in this period, by a Communist Party lawyer, V. Berrange, who represented the women beer brewers of the location in their various legal skirmishes with the municipality.[110] Building on this base the Communist Party soon became the most vocal and effective political force in Springs location. By the mid-1940s Party candidates were sweeping the advisory board elections, basing their appeal, as elsewhere on the East Rand, on the subsistence issues and local problems of the locations.[111] One of the principal outcomes of the Council's efforts to restore public order and social control in the location was thus the forging of a more coherent and radical political consciousness among its inhabitants, which promised to change the whole character and direction of class and popular struggles.

The task that now lay before the municipality and other local and central authorities was to fragment and disarm the political movement that was taking shape by denying it the issues around which to mobilize support, but this task went against the grain of imperatives toward rationalization and social engineering common to all industrializing societies. There is little sign that the authorities even perceived the dilemma with which they were faced. The task confronting the Communist Party of South Africa, and somewhat later the African National Congress, was to give appropriate direction to those stirrings and to link the localized grassroots radicalism into a nationwide political mobilization—a goal both organizations largely failed to achieve.

ACKNOWLEDGEMENTS

The financial support of the Richard Ward Foundation of the University of the Witwatersrand and the Institute of Research Development (IRD) of the Human Sciences Research Council (HRSC) toward this research is hereby acknowledged. Opinions expressed in this publication, and conclusions arrived at are those of the author and do not necessarily represent the views of either organization.

NOTES

1. Central Archives Depot (CAD), Germiston Municipal Archives (MGT) 114, vol. 1, file 42/9, Record of Proceedings of Conference held on 22 January and 14 February 1935.

2. CAD, Government Native Labour Bureau (GNLB), vol. 314, file 182/19/97, Minutes of meeting between the Transvaal Compound Managers' Association and the Native Affairs Department, 2 June 1921.

3. CAD, GNLB, vol. 314, file 182/19/97, Annual Report of the Executive Council of the Transvaal Compound Managers' Association, 30 June 1923.

4. CAD, MGT 114, vol. 1, file 42/9, Records of Proceedings of Conference, 22 January 1935, statement by Mr. Granger, representing the Transvaal Compound Managers' Association, pp. 7–10.

5. See D. Hobart Houghton, *The South African Economy* (Cape Town: OUP, 1976), 4th ed., pp. 106–7, 122–29; W. Freund, "The Social Character of Secondary Industry in South Africa: 1915–1945," in *Organisation and Economic Change,* ed. A. Mabin (Johannesburg: Ravan Press, 1989), pp. 78–119; W. Martin, "The Making of an Industrial South Africa: Trade and Tariffs in the Interwar Period," *International Journal of African Historical Studies* 23 (1990): 59–85. The percentage increases for four municipalities illustrate the magnitude of the change: Brakpan 58.6 percent (between 1921 and 1931); Germiston 158.9 percent (1921–1931); Kurgersdorp 99.0 percent (1921–1931); and Roodeport/Maraisburg 84.7 percent (1925–1931); see University of Witwatersrand (UW), Records of the South African Institute of Race Relations (SAIRR), AD 1715 S.7, "The Urban Native Memorandum," p. 11.

6. J. Cohen, " 'A Pledge for Better Times': The Local State and the Ghetto, Benoni, 1930–1938" (B.A. diss., University of Witwatersrand, 1982), pp. 26–27, 53–54; H. Sapire, "African Urbanisation and Struggles against Municipal Control in Brakpan, 1920–1958" (Ph.D. diss., University of Witwatersrand, 1988), pp. 92–94; P. Bonner, "'Desirable or Undesirable Basotho Women?': Liquor, Prostitution and the Migration of Basotho Women to the Rand, 1920–1945," in *Women and Gender in Southern African to 1945,* ed. C. Walker (Cape Town: David Philip, 1990), pp. 17–20; D. Moodie (in this collection).

7. CAD, MGT 114, vol. 1, file 42/9, Records of Proceedings of Conference, 22 January 1935, pp. 7–8.

8. Intermediate Archives Depot (IAD), Springs Municipal Archives (MSP), Minutes of the Public Health and Works Committee, 26 April 1932, p. 258.

9. IAD, MSP, Minutes of the Public Health Committee (PHC), 3 December 1934; Encl., Minutes of Payneville Advisory Board, 21 November 1934.

10. IAD, MSP, Minutes of PHC, 10 July 1936, p. 192.

11. By 1935 the female population of Springs was alleged to have overtaken that of males, an issue which formed the centerpiece of the mayor's opening address to the conference of Reef municipalities in January that year; CAD, MGT 114, vol. 1, file 42/9, Records of Proceedings of Conference, 22 January 1935, p. 2.

12. Bonner, "Basotho Women." First noted as a distinct social category in

1935, their numbers swelled into the hundreds in the next couple of years; IAD, MSP, Minutes of PHC, 12 August 1935, 10 May 1938; P. J. Smit, Location European Constable to Manager of Native Affairs, 5 May 1938, 9 August 1938; Report of Location European Constable, 8 July 1938.

13. Bonner, "Basotho Women."

14. IAD, MSP, Minutes of PHC, 10 July 1936, p. 192.

15. IAD, MSP, Minutes of Public Health and Non-European Affairs Committee (PH and NEAC), 15 September 1941, Memo to Native Affairs Commission enquiring into Kafir Beer.

16. IAD, MSP, Minutes of PHC, 8 December 1936.

17. IAD, MSP, Minutes of PHC, 7 June 1938.

18. IAD, MSP, Minutes of PH and NEAC, 14 October 1940, Encl., Chief Magistrate, Springs to Town Clerk, 20 September 1940; CAD, NTS, vol. 7676, file 6 110/332.

19. IAD, MSP, Minutes of PHC, 9 July 1937, 8 August 1938; Minutes of PH and NEAC, 11 April 1939, 11 April 1940, 6 January 1941; Report of Acting Medical Officer of Health (MOH), 15 April 1941.

20. IAD, MSP, Minutes of PHC, 9 August 1938, Report of Location European Constable, 8 July 1938.

21. CAD, NTS, vol. 7715, file 53/331(1), W. E. Gemmill, General Manager, Gold Producers' Committee to Secretary for Native Affairs (SNA), 8 November 1938; CAD, MGT 114, vol. 1, file 42/9, Record of Proceedings of Conference 22 January 1935, statement by Granger, Transvaal Compound Managers' Association, pp. 8–9.

22. CAD, MGT 114, vol. 1, file 42/9, Record of Proceedings, pp. 8–9.

23. CAD, NTS, 7715, file 53/331(1), Gemmill to SNA, 8 November 1938.

24. CAD, MGT 114, vol. 1, file 42/9, Record of Proceedings. For a similar perspective see Public Record Office (PRO), DO 35/1178/Y847/1/1, A. G. T. Chaplin, Agent for the High Commission Territories to Govt. Secretary, Maseru, 1 September 1942.

25. IAD, MSP, Minutes of PHC, 6 July 1936.

26. IAD, MSP, Minutes of PHC, 10 January 1939.

27. See, for example, T. D. Moodie, "Collective Violence on the South African Gold Mines" (Paper delivered to the Southern African Research Program Seminar, Yale University, 1990), p. 3.

28. *Star,* 24 June 1935.

29. CAD, NTS, vol. 7725, file 6 166/35, Director of Native Labour (DNL) to SNA, 12 September 1930.

30. Sapire, "African Urbanisation," p. 92.

31. PRO, DO 35/1178/Y847/1/1, Chaplin to Government Secretary, 1 September 1942.

32. Ibid.

33. Ibid., and J. Gay, "Wage Employment of Rural Basotho Women: A Case Study," *South African Labour Bulletin* 6(5) (1980): 42–44.

34. C. Murray, *Families Divided* (Cambridge: Cambridge University Press, 1982).

35. Ibid., p. 15.

36. Interview with L. Sefabo, Daveyton, 18 December 1987; interview with A. B., Daveyton, 8 May 1985.

37. J. Gay, "Basotho Women's Options: A Study of Marital Careers in Rural Lesotho" (Ph.D. diss., Cambridge University, 1980), p. 81.

38. Cmnd 4907, *The Financial and Economic Situation of Basutoland*, pp. 48–49.

39. R. Edgar, *Prophets with Honour: A Documentary History of Lekhotla la Bafo* (Johannesburg: Ravan Press, 1987), pp. 10, 130; Lesotho Archives (LA), Major Bell Tower Collection, box 71, 41st Session Bric 1945, item 44b; J. Kimble, " 'Runaway Wives': Basotho Women, Chiefs and the Colonial State, c. 1890–1920" (Paper presented to Women in Africa Seminar, University of London, 1983), pp. 15–16; and V. G. Sheddick, *Land Tenure in Basutoland*, Colonial Research Studies, no. 13 (London, 1954), pp. 163–64.

40. Kimble, "Runaway Wives," pp. 16–18.

41. Bonner, "Basotho Women."

42. PRO, DO 35/1178/Y847/1/1, Chaplin to Government Secretary, 1 September 1942; and H. Ashton, *The Basuto* (New York: Oxford University Press, 1952), p. 64.

43. Ashton, *The Basuto*, pp. 70–72, 174; Murray, *Families Divided*, pp. 125–26; L. Thompson, *Survival in Two Worlds: Moshoeshoe of Lesotho* (Oxford: Clarendon Press, 1975), pp. 52–69; P. Sanders, *Mosheshoe* (London, 1975), pp. 125–28; S. Poulter, *Family Law and Litigation in Basotho Society* (Oxford: Clarendon Press, 1976), pp. 90–95, 109; M. Wilson, "Xhosa Marriage in Historical Perspective," in *Essays in African Marriage in Southern Africa*, ed. E. Krige and J. Comaroff (Cape Town: OUP, 1981), pp. 161–62, 175; and A. Kuper, *Wives for Cattle: Bridewealth and Marriage in Southern Africa* (London: Routledge and Kegan Paul, 1982), pp. 136, 158, 167–68.

44. Ashton, *Basuto*, p. 79, n. 3; interview with M. N. Pukone and P. Tukisi, 20 October 1986 (Tukisi speaking).

45. Bonner, "Basotho Women"; and Ashton, *Basuto,* pp. 65–67, 259–62.

46. Ashton, *Basuto*, p. 145; and Sheddick, *Land Tenure*, p. 158.

47. PRO, DO 35/1178/Y847/1/2, Minutes of Resident Commissioners' Conference, 1943; and A. Jeeves, "An Account of the History of the Assisted Voluntary System on the South African Gold Mines," mimeograph (Queen's University, n.d.), pp. 1–4. My thanks to Alan Jeeves for this and related information.

48. PRO, DO 35/1178/Y847/1/1, H. J. D. Elliot, British Agent for the High Commission Territories, Memo on "Deferred Pay" (1939); DO 35/4110/Y3434/5, Sir E. Baring to Noel Baker, 25 May 1949.

49. J. Guy and M. Thabane, "Technology, Ethnicity and Ideology: Basotho Miners and Shaft-Sinking on the South African Gold Mines" *Journal of Southern African Studies* 14 (1988): 260–69.

50. PRO, DO 35/1178/Y847/1/1, Memo on "Deferred Pay" (1939); and Lord Harlech to Sir Eric Machtig, 30 December 1942.

51. PRO, DO 35/1178/Y847/1/1, Chaplin to Government Secretary, 1 September 1942, p. 5.

52. PRO, DO 35/1178/Y847/1/1, Memo on "Deferred Pay." There is some similarity here between the Springs example cited above and the statement made by Payne, location superintendent, Payneville location, to the Conference of Reef Municipalities held in Springs on 22 January 1935; see CAD, MGT 114, vol. 1, file 42/9, p. 6.

53. PRO, DO 35/1178/Y847/1/1, H. J. D. Elliot, British Agent for the High Commission Territories, Memo on "Native Women on the Reef" (1939). Elliot's analysis obviously begs a number of questions, the most notable being what happened to the large numbers of men from other than Basotho tribes who did not engage in these sexual practices? I have no ready answer to this puzzle. Suffice it for the moment to draw attention to the trend. For an analysis that confirms and contextualizes some of these points, see T. D. Moodie, "Migrancy and Male Sexuality on the South African Gold Mines," *Journal of Southern African Studies* 14 (1988): 228–56.

54. PRO, DO 35/1178/Y847/1/1, Chaplin to Government Secretary, 1 September 1942, p. 2.

55. PRO, DO 35/1178/Y847/1/1, Chaplin to Financial Secretary, Maseru, 18 May 1942.

56. PRO, DO 92/3, Annual Reports of Basutoland Department of Education, 1933, pp. 12–13; 1934, p. 11; 1936, pp. 11, 16; 1937, p. 16; 1945, p. 7; 1946, p. 15; 1947, pp. 15, 18; 1950, p. 20. See oral testimonies cited in Bonner, "Basotho Women."

57. PRO, DO 35/1178/Y847/1/1, Chaplin to Government Secretary, 1 September 1942, pp. 6–7.

58. Bonner, "Basotho Women."

59. Moodie, "Collective Violence," pp. 5–6 and table 2.

60. Ibid., p. 17.

61. PRO, DO 35/1178/Y847/1/1, Harlech to Machtig, 30 December 1942. For the Springs mines see IAD, MSP, Minutes of PHC, 10 January 1939.

62. Moodie, "Collective Violence," pp. 19–21.

63. See notes 18 and 19, above.

64. IAD, MSP, Minutes of PH and NEAC, 15 September 1941, "Memo to Native Affairs Commission enquiring into Kaffir Beer"; and Minutes of PHC, 11 August 1937, "Memo 27 July 1937 from Advisory Board."

65. *Star,* 3 August 1939; CAD, NTS 7032, 31/322/6, Minutes of Evidence of Native Affairs Commission appointed to enquire into the working of provisions of the Natives (Urban Areas) Act relating to the use and supply of Kaffir Beer, Evidence of O. J. T. Horak, pp. 67, 85; NTS, vol. 7036, file 31/332/6, Third Interim Report to the Ministry of Native Affairs, 10 February 1941.

66. *Rand Daily Mail,* 21 February 1938.

67. *Rand Daily Mail,* 12 April 1938.

68. *Star,* 23 May 1938.

69. *Bantu World,* 15 May 1937, p. 18.

70. See notes 18 and 19, above.

71. CAD, NTS, vol. 4149, file 11/313 (iii), Conference of Managers and Superintendents of South African Municipal Affairs, Johannesburg, 9–11 November 1927; NTS, vol. 8859, file 99/362 (unmarked file), M. Nicolson to SNA, 31 January 1930; IAD, MSP, Minutes of PHC, 16 November 1936.

72. IAD, MSP, Minutes of PHC, 8 December 1936 (SNA to Town Clerk, Springs, 16 November 1936). It appears there were two serious flaws in the act. First, the certificates of approval that were supposed to be obtained by women had to be granted by the urban local authority itself, and it was not entitled to delegate its powers in this respect to any of its officers. Second, women could be precluded even from passing through or visiting the area without bearing such a document, if the regulation was in force.

73. IAD, MSP, Minutes of PHC, 1 April 1936; 10 May 1938 (P. J. Smit to Manager of Native Affairs, 5 March 1938).

74. Ibid.

75. Ibid.

76. Sapire, "African Urbanisation," pp. 127–29; IAD, MSP, Minutes of PHC, 3 September 1934, 8 December 1936; MGT 114, vol. 1, file 42/9, Record of Proceedings of Conference, 22 January 1935.

77. IAD, MSP, Minutes of PHC, 6 July 1926.

78. IAD, MSP, Minutes of PHC, 10 May 1938 (P. J. Smit to Manager of Native Affairs, 5 March 1938).

79. IAD, MSP, Minutes of PHC, 15 November 1937.

80. IAD, MSP, Minutes of PHC, 10 May 1938.

81. IAD, MSP, Minutes of PHC, 7 June 1938.

82. IAD, MSP, Minutes of PHC, 5 December 1937 (Location Superintendent to MOH, 4 December 1937).

83. IAD, MSP, Minutes of PHC, 15 August 1938, 12 September 1938.

84. IAD, MSP, Minutes of PHC, 10 May 1938, 9 August 1938.

85. IAD, MSP, Minutes of PHC, 10 May 1938, 7 June 1938.

86. IAD, MSP, Minutes of PHC, 6 September 1938, 5 October 1938, 10 January 1939; IAD, MSP, Minutes of PH and NEAC, April 1941, Report of the Acting MOH, 8 April 1941.

87. IAD, MSP, Minutes of PHC, 6 September 1938, 5 October 1938.

88. IAD, MSP, Minutes of PHC, 5 October 1938.

89. Ibid.

90. IAD, MSP, Minutes of PHC, 10 January 1939.

91. Ibid.

92. IAD, MSP, Minutes of PHC, 7 March 1939, 4 April 1939.

93. IAD, MSP, Minutes of PH and NEAC, 11 April 1939.

94. IAD, MSP, Minutes of PH and NEAC, 15 May 1939.

95. IAD, MSP, Minutes of PH and NEAC, 9 August 1939.

96. IAD, MSP, Minutes of PH and NEAC, 17 March 1941, Report of Acting MOH, 12 March 1941.

97. Ibid.

98. Ibid.

99. IAD, MSP, Minutes of PH and NEAC, 14 July 1941.

100. IAD, MSP, Minutes of PH and NEAC, 17 May 1945.

101. As, for example, when 100 gallons were destroyed in front of a house "occupied by a native female, Elizabeth"; IAD, MSP, Minutes of PH and NEAC, 5 September 1939.

102. IAD, MSP, Minutes of PH and NEAC, April 1941, Report of the Acting MOH, 8 April 1941.

103. Ibid.

104. Union of South Africa (U.G.56–'37), "Notes on Conference between

Municipalities and Native Affairs Department Held at Pretoria on 28th and 29th September, to Discuss The Provisions of the Native Laws Amendment Act (no. 46 of 1937)," p. 21; Benoni Municipal Archives, Minutes of NEAC, 11 January 1946, Report of Manager of Non-European Affairs, 9 January 1946; and Minutes of NEAC, 9 April 1946, Report of Manager of Non-European Affairs, 4 April 1946.

105. CAD, NTS, vol. 7725, file 166/333, Acting Director of Prisons to SNA, 16 April 1942; DNL to SNA, 30 April 1942; CNC Witwatersrand to SNA, 11 February 1954; Director of Prisons to SNA, 18 March 1954; SNA General Circular no. 34 of 1954, 18 August 1954.

106. U.G.56–'37, "Notes on Conference."

107. IAD, MSP, Minutes of PHC, 9 June 1937 (Encl. Advisory Board Minutes, 28 May 1937); and Minutes of PHC, 11 August 1937 (encl. Memo from Advisory Board, 27 July 1937).

108. IAD, MSP, Minutes of PHC, 13 October 1938, 8 November 1938.

109. IAD, MSP, Minutes of PH and NEAC, June 1940 (Report of Manager of Non-European Affairs, 6 June 1940).

110. Ibid.

111. CAD, NTS 7676, File 110/332, District Commissioner SAP to Deputy District Commissioner, 23 July 1945; Sapire, "African Urbanisation," pp. 169–200; Cohen, "Pledge for Better Times," pp. 41–51; *Guardian,* 18 May 1946, 25 May 1946. For more discussion of Benoni and Germiston, see P. Bonner, "The CPSA and the ANC on the Witwatersrand, 1940–1960" (University of Witwatersrand, forthcoming).

CHAPTER TWELVE

DRINKING, APARTHEID, AND THE REMOVAL OF BEERHALLS IN JOHANNESBURG, 1938–1962

Christian Rogerson

INTRODUCTION

JOHANNESBURG'S AFRICAN BEER drinkers may recall 16 June 1959 as a small landmark in the making of urban apartheid. On that particular Tuesday the city's Central beerhall failed to open after over twenty-one years of furnishing municipally brewed beer to Johannesburg's African male population. Despite the irony of misgivings expressed by Patrick Lewis, chairman of Johannesburg's Non-European Affairs Committee, that 16 June was "an unsuitable date" because "the 26th June was the big day for the African National Congress," the closure was effected without incident.[1] The truckload of armed police who guarded the closed premises for several hours in anticipation of trouble stood by idly, and in the immediate aftermath Lewis could remark that nobody "mourned" the death of Central beerhall.[2]

The closure of Central beerhall was, however, a significant event in the historical geography of Johannesburg. Since the adoption during 1937, and implementation in 1938, of a municipal monopoly in the city, the consumption of "kaffir beer" had been concentrated at a series of large centrally located beerhalls, the most important being Cen-

tral.[3] As a result of two decades of policies that fostered mass drinking, each weekend 100,000 Africans gathered at Johannesburg's three
central beerhalls to quaff 50,000 gallons of "pink gold." But with the
closure of Central beerhall and the restriction of beer sales at Mai Mai
and Wolhuter to bona fide hostel residents, alternative drinking places
had to be found and a new spatial articulation of African beer-drinking
places began to form. Henceforward the reconstituted map of African
beer drinking took on a more decentralized appearance, marked by a
progressive shift of municipal beer sales toward township sites.
Therefore, 16 June 1959 represents a key watershed in the creation of
"drinking apartheid" by which officially sanctioned African consumption of alcohol was gradually deflected away from central Johannesburg and confined to township locales.

This chapter charts the crystallization of drinking apartheid in Johannesburg, interrogating the causes, consequences, and struggles surrounding the changing location and removal of beerhalls in the city
from 1938 to 1962.[4] Issues of beerhall location and spatial policy constitute important themes that have not been directly addressed in historical writing on South African beerhalls.[5] Yet in Johannesburg, at
least, locational conflict surrounding beerhalls was at the core of what
was described in 1959 as "the year of the beerhall crisis."[6] First, the
growth and contouring of Johannesburg's network of municipal
beerhalls from 1938 to 1954 is investigated. The focus then turns to
the rethinking of beerhall location policy, which was occasioned jointly
from above by central government pressure for drinking apartheid
and from below by rising conflict and protest surrounding beerhalls
as "noxious" locational facilities. Finally, attention is directed to the
new official spatial dispensation of African beer drinking, chronicling
moves for decentralized drinking within "white" Johannesburg and
the emergence of municipal beer provision in township areas.

THE GROWTH AND LOCATION
OF BEERHALLS, 1938–1954

The basic geography of municipal beer drinking in Johannesburg
was etched between 1938 and 1941 (see fig. 12.1). The city's first mu-

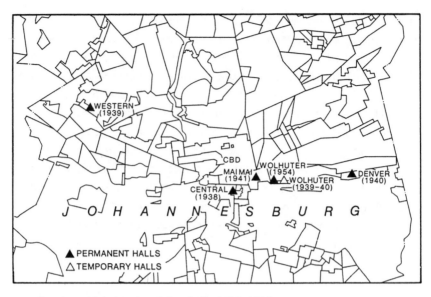

12.1 Location of Johannesburg's beerhalls, 1938–1954

nicipal beerhall commenced business on 1 January 1938 at the site of the Salisbury and Jubilee Compound, a notorious focus for the illicit liquor trade. The temporary wood-and-iron structure was divided into three areas: the brewery, the drinking area, and an eating house. Municipal officials expressed delight at the successful launch of the "canteen" and the sight of queues of patrons "long before the opening time of 8 A.M." At the 9 P.M. close the new beerhall had recorded 1,600 customers. Patronage expanded rapidly, escalating to daily attendance figures of 3,600 by 8 January and an estimated 5,000 one week later. In the initial financial statement concerning beerhalls, turnover for the Salisbury-Jubilee establishment during the first three weeks of January 1938 was £1,216, of which a staggering 45 percent was profit.[7] Beyond financial considerations and the growing popularity of the beerhall among African customers, municipal officials claimed added benefits in the suppression of the activities of "skokian queens" and the elimination of serious crimes of violence in the vicinity of the hall. The manager of Johannesburg's Non-European Affairs Department averred that the municipal canteen "is now the native's club, in which he can meet his kinsmen in a social capacity and enjoy a clean wholesome drink, under decent conditions and immune from the importunities of undesirables."[8]

In the wake of the success of Johannesburg's fledgling experiment with municipal monopoly, plans were announced during February 1938 for the building of four additional beerhalls. Six months later the Minister of Native Affairs sanctioned approval of a loan of £100,000 to finance a new municipal brewery and the establishment of five permanent beerhall structures. The proposed siting of these beerhalls was one in central Johannesburg "and the rest in the native townships."[9] However, in joint discussions held "just after the monopoly system was introduced" between the Non-European Affairs Committee and members of Native Advisory Boards, the suggestion for beerhalls within "location areas" was firmly rejected in favor of pleas for home brewing.[10] The city council agreed not to establish such beerhalls but failed to support proposals from members of the Native Advisory Board "to permit home brewing to operate *pari passu* with the monopoly system in the industrial parts of the urban area."[11]

The abandonment of schemes for beerhalls in township areas was hastened by the unpromising record of the Western beerhall, which was initiated on land adjoining the boundary of Western Native Township. Expectations of great success and considerable profit attached to the location of this second beerhall in Johannesburg. In October 1938 it was observed that the market potential of the Western areas "is likely to be the most lucrative in the city" and that completion of the beerhall should be speeded "so that potential revenue is not lost."[12] Nonetheless, the success of the Salisbury-Jubilee beerhall was not repeated after the initial opening of Western beerhall on 1 April 1939. The new beerhall became a focal point of organized opposition, a boycott by township residents, and even threats of being burned to the ground. Defense of shebeen livelihoods and pressures for home brewing combined to fuel continuing protests directed at the Western beerhall. Six months after inauguration, officials ruefully admitted that the project "is not proving a success" and "there seems little prospect of a substantial improvement in the near future."[13] By 1940 the position was little improved, with monthly sales at Western a meager £391 as compared to £5,160 for Salisbury-Jubilee.[14] Moreover, in evidence submitted to the 1941 Kaffir Beer Inquiry, officials again disclosed that the Western beerhall "is far from popular" and "is not supported to the same extent as any of the other beerhalls in Johannesburg."[15]

With plans aborted for additional beerhalls to be sited within townships, the axis of municipal policy shifted toward setting up a chain of beerhalls located in industrial areas and "at points outside native townships where large numbers of industrial natives congregate."[16] Underpinning this geographical shift in the location of beerhalls was a recognition that their principal patrons were "industrial natives not living under family conditions."[17] Alongside the city's daytime communities of workers in factories, the core market for beerhalls comprised the large number of African workers who continued to reside outside townships. This group included a mass of private-sector employees of industrial and commercial establishments who lived in hostels, compounds, or on the overcrowded rooftops of Johannesburg's newly christened "locations in the sky."[18] In addition, the African population of central Johannesburg was boosted by the groups of essential public-service employees resident in compounds and the army of nocturnal cleaners, laborers, security guards, and maintenance workers who sheltered "on site" throughout the inner suburbs of white Johannesburg.[19] Much of the potential alcohol market offered by these communities was served by the shebeens that proliferated throughout central Johannesburg during the 1940s and 1950s.[20]

The selection of appropriate beerhall sites to capture that market niche proved a difficult task. The Denver industrial area, situated in the eastern part of the city, was an obvious location for a new beerhall, which was established in November 1940. A captive market for this beerhall was furnished by the relative geographical isolation of Denver, three miles from the city center, and by the proliferation of industry in its environs. Much greater difficulty arose in finding inner-city sites for new beerhalls that would be both convenient as well as publicly acceptable. The dilemmas faced by the municipality in locating new beerhalls were sharply exposed in the founding during May 1939 of the Wolhuter beerhall. From the perspective of tapping potential

African consumers working in the eastern edge of the inner city the location of this new beerhall was admirable. But its situation as a noxious facility close to white residential areas was a recipe for conflict. During early 1940 an increasing chorus of complaints began to be sounded by white residents. Protests were lodged concerning "the intolerable state of affairs" caused for residents by the noise of "drunken natives" shouting and yelling and by the disruption of church services through their persistent singing.[21] In deference to the wishes of objecting taxpayers the Wolhuter beerhall was moved 500 yards to a site known as the Old Meyer and Charlton compound. Once again the market for the beerhall was not problematical, with reported monthly sales averaging £2,411 between March and July 1940.[22] The beerhall, however, was forced to close at this new location in late 1940 when the mining commissioner drew attention to the fact that its presence constituted a possible infringement of the regulations governing trading on mining ground.[23]

During 1939 and 1940 a series of events around the Salisbury-Jubilee hall culminated in the initiation at Mai Mai, City and Suburban, of a new inner-city beerhall, which opened on 15 February 1941. Attached to the Salisbury-Jubilee compound was a traditional trading bazaar that comprised a mass of boot repairers, bangle makers, leather workers, sjambok makers, herbalists, skin dressers, and tailors.[24] This successful bazaar attracted many customers who patronized the adjoining beerhall. But the symbiosis of beerhall and bazaar was broken when it was announced that the community of traders and craftsmen would be transferred to new premises at the Natalspruit Compound.[25] Between 10 and 15 June 1940 the bazaar was moved into the converted former mule stables of the city's sanitary department and the outspan yard for the carts formerly used for collecting night soil. Although the traders and craftsmen at Mai Mai pleaded for the establishment of a branch beerhall to improve business, the only assistance offered by municipal authorities was advertisements in the African press announcing the new location of the bazaar. In the vicinity of the new bazaar, however, there arose a mass of illicit shebeens seemingly "carrying on a lucrative trade."[26] Equally worrying to officialdom was a sharp downturn in sales at the Salisbury-Jubilee beerhall following the bazaar's relocation. To kill the illicit shebeens and recapture the lost trade in municipal brews, the Johannesburg authorities proposed that a beerhall be sited at Mai Mai, adjacent to the existing small hostel. The new Mai Mai beerhall was optimally situated with respect to the geography of demand in central Johannesburg and flourished accordingly. Indeed, the combination of beerhall and trading bazaar at Mai Mai drew attention from the Faure Committee, which undertook a national investigation during 1945 and 1946 of the manufacture and distribution of kaffir beer. Mai Mai was commended as a "fine example" of the development of beerhalls as joint social and shopping centers, a trend "strongly advocated by the Committee."[27]

The final step in the forging of the early geography of municipal beerhalls in Johannesburg was the reestablishment in 1954 of a beerhall in Wolhuter (fig. 12.1). After the temporary closure of Western and Denver beerhalls due to wartime shortages of sorghum, buoyancy was renewed in the municipal beer trade, and Johannesburg authorities announced plans to extend the beerhall grid "to serve adequately natives employed and housed in industrial areas."[28] The decision to expand at Wolhuter was motivated by the drive for expanded municipal beer profits and the authorities' desire to stamp out a thriving shebeen trade in the vicinity of Wolhuter Men's Hostel. By 1950 conditions at Mai Mai, Denver, and the renamed Central beerhall (the former Salisbury-Jubilee beerhall) were becoming "crowded beyond their capacity."[29] The rush of potential customers was such that demand could not be adequately catered for within these existing beerhalls, which, in the case of Mai Mai in particular, could not be enlarged. Moreover, in 1951 Johannesburg's town clerk was aware that the city's rising beer revenues not only substantially reduced the deficit transfer to the General Rate Fund but also could "be considerably increased by the provision of additional beerhalls."[30] Accordingly, he proposed that an additional beerhall be sited on land owned by the council adjacent to the Wolhuter Men's Hostel. The land was appropriate since it was (unproclaimed) and thus not subject to the trading restrictions on mining land, legislation that felled the earlier Wolhuter hall. Fears of renewed white opposition to a beerhall in the locality were reduced by the metamorphosis of Wolhuter into an industrial zone rather than a white residential area. In addition, the Secretary for Native Affairs pointed out that a railway line constituted an effective geographical buffer zone between Wolhuter and the closest areas of white residence. Nonetheless, with an eye to possible complaints from white residents in Jeppestown, the authorities decided to construct a twelve-foot-high brick wall in order "to isolate the hall area."[31] With such assurances, the Secretary for Native Affairs granted Johannesburg authorities the necessary approval for the siting of the new Wolhuter beerhall under section 34 (3) of the Natives (Urban Areas) Consolidation Act of 1945.

RETHINKING THE LOCATION
OF MUNICIPAL BEER HALLS

With the return of economic prosperity after World War II, an escalating number of new job opportunities opened for African workers amid the boom in Johannesburg's new factories, offices, and shops. From 1943 to 1953 African industrial employment more than doubled—from 48,000 to 108,000 workers.[32] Expanded market opportunities for the city's chain of beerhalls were offered by the thriving new metal and engineering complexes and light-consumer manufacturers that dotted new industrial townships growing in the eastern and southwestern zones of Johannesburg.

Capitalizing on these new market opportunities, the city's municipal beer trade attained new levels of prosperity (see fig. 12.2 and table 12.1). Johannesburg's municipal beer profits soared from £47,952 in 1946–1947 to £201,576 by 1951–1952, reaching the dizzy financial heights of £525,101 by 1956–1957.[33] Beerhall patronage grew steadily after 1950, climbing by 1958 to average attendances of 82,000 on weekdays, 71,000 on Sundays, and exceeding 100,000 customers on peak days.[34] The demands of drinkers were accommodated on weekdays by two sessions of selling, between 10:30 A.M. to 3:00 P.M. and 4:00 to 6:30 P.M.; on Saturdays and public holidays from 10:45 A.M. to 3:30 P.M.; and on Sundays from noon to 4 P.M. Accompanying the rapid growth of the municipal beerhall trade, however, was an array

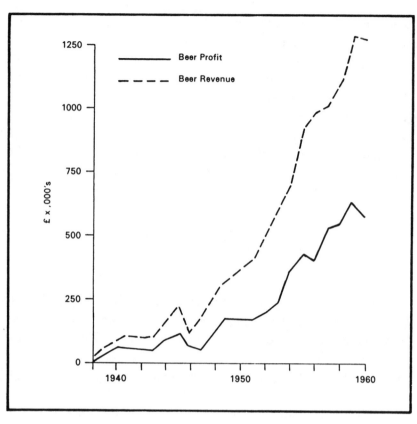

12.2 Growth of Johannesburg's municipal beer trade, 1938–1960

Table 12.1: Attendance at beerhalls in Johannesburg, 1958

	Average Daily Patronage		
	Weekdays	*Sundays*	*Peak*
Central	33,000	20,000	40,000 (Friday)
Mai Mai	18,000	14,000	22,000 (Friday)
Wolhuter	13,000	10,500	17,000 (Friday)
Denver	9,000	15,000	15,000 (Sunday)
Western	9,000	12,000	12,000 (Saturday and Sunday)

Source: Intermediate Archives Depot, Johannesburg, Files of West Rand Development Board, 401/8/15, vol. 1.

of problems that ultimately precipitated a rethinking of the policy surrounding the appropriate location for such facilities.

Notwithstanding surging beer revenues, the authorities accorded scant consideration to suggestions by African patrons for improving facilities at the beerhalls. Official promises that the makeshift wood-and-iron structures would be refurbished into permanent beerhall social structures largely went unfulfilled.[35] Patrons complained bitterly of the "most unfavourable conditions" associated with the temporary buildings. Because inadequate provision was made for storm drains, during summer rains drinkers were "like pigs in the mud," ankle-deep in water and mud. The slippery quagmire surface conditions in beerhall yards exacted a toll in the strained and fractured ankles of many patrons. In winter, drinkers suffered from inadequate heating facilities, leading to one petition complaining that "we are freezing." Beerhall patrons were also dissatisfied with the inadequate provision of lavatories, shortchanging by white cashiers, and, most important, the condition of the beer. On windy days, patrons at Central endured "beer full of dust" and those at Denver confronted "particles of hair mixed with the beer" as a result of street hairdressers in the adjoining grounds.[36] These minor inconveniences paled beside the reaction of patrons to the exhaustion of beer supplies or the serving of fresh beer. At Central, patrons stoned the cashiers' offices when they were informed that beer supplies were sold out, and at Wolhuter the serving of fresh beer precipitated a riot that led to one death, many injuries, and damage to nearly forty automobiles.[37]

The policy agenda of Johannesburg's municipal authorities was scarcely influenced by these complaints. The council's chief concern was with the overcrowding of the centrally sited beerhalls and with associated problems of control. In 1952 "disturbances" at Mai Mai linked to overcrowding concentrated official minds on the imperative for reopening a beerhall in Wolhuter.[38] Nonetheless, resuscitating a beerhall at Wolhuter afforded no relief to the worsening conditions at Central. In March 1954 the tinder box of abject facilities and mass drinking was seemingly lit by persons outside the beerhall throwing eaten mealie cobs into the hall. These hit patrons, who mistakenly blamed other drinkers in the hall for the unwanted missiles. Rising tempers and the throwing of heavy beer mugs resulted in Johannesburg's worst beerhall riot for three years—with sixty-eight injuries, twenty of them serious—as the enclosure outside the building was turned into a battlefield.[39] Further rioting occurred at Central on 4 July 1954, with seven persons killed and fifty injured. The Manager of Non-European Affairs blamed "the grossly overcrowded conditions that prevail there."[40] He attributed the overcrowding to increased patronage as a result of new commercial and industrial expansion in the southwest of the city, an area in which there were no beerhalls. The fighting at Central beerhall was mirrored by similar events at Mai Mai. By far the worst incident occurred in July 1956, when faction fighting broke out between different groups of Zulus. The resulting clashes involved an estimated 2,000 to 3,000 patrons outside Mai Mai hammering each other "with stones and drinking mugs."[41]

The riots and disturbances threw into sharp relief the issue of control over the mass-drinking institutions Johannesburg authorities had nurtured. In 1952 municipal officials were observing that "it is becoming more difficult to control the beerhalls."[42] The disregard of regulations designed to prevent overimbibing contributed to the progressive problems of control in beerhalls. The manager of Johannesburg's Non-European Affairs Department expressed concern that at Central "natives obviously under the influence of liquor are being served with additional beer."[43] Although the regulations provided that patrons were only to be served on one occasion, avoidance was simple. At Mai Mai, for example, "you can drink a big bucketful all by yourself and nobody will worry you. If you lie down a police boy may move you, but if you can get your back against a wall you can order a second bucketful."[44] Nonetheless, in at least one instance when patrons at Denver were refused more beer, they smashed forty windows and stabbed a policeman.[45]

Problems of overconsumption were worse on Sundays, the peak day for riots, because the beerhalls opened at midday only. This later opening prompted many patrons to first frequent the numerous shebeens still functioning in the environs of beerhalls.[46] In order to counter the growing problems of control, frequent requests were submitted for the appointment of additional "police boys" at the beerhalls. In

1953, for example, the continuing expansion of patronage at Central caused queues outside the beerhall to become "unmanageable owing to the shortage of police staff."[47] However, the request for an increased police complement was denied, ostensibly on the grounds of lack of funds. One improvement to the appearance of Central beerhall was secured at no cost to the council, which happily conceded rights to an advertising company to install four huge advertising panels to screen this "noxious" facility from public view.[48]

The difficulties of controlling beer drinkers inside the halls were matched by a litany of problems outside their walls. Traffic congestion, hazards, and conflicts arose when the beerhalls closed for business and patrons streamed onto the streets. Further worsening the congestion outside the inner-city beerhalls were the throngs of street traders, whose operations commonly overflowed into the roadway. Closing time at the beerhalls was especially hazardous for white motorists driving in the vicinity, with collisions and accidents engendering a climate of great tension. Around the Wolhuter hall, closing time was normally "a nightmare . . . a scene of chaos, with Natives in their hundreds pouring onto the street, heedless of passing traffic."[49] The most serious incident was recorded on 31 January 1959 at closing time near Mai Mai, when a heated argument flared between departing patrons and a white truck driver; the driver died as a result of injuries sustained in the melee.[50] Such racial incidents fueled the ire of white residents and Nationalist politicians. Petitions denounced the dangers associated with beerhalls, the aggressive tone of "natives" toward whites, the stoning of vehicles and damage to property, the activities of "loafers" and *tsotsis* attracted to the environs, the degeneration of the areas surrounding beerhalls into zones akin to "native locations," and the sight of beerhall patrons urinating in the streets.[51]

The manifold problems of Johannesburg's beerhalls did not pass unnoticed by the central government. A directive from the Department of Native Affairs to the Johannesburg city council during August 1956 advised that the presence of all five of the city's beerhalls "in the European area" was contrary to current policy and that eventually they would have to be relocated in township areas.[52] In addition, the department stressed that "the profit motive must play no part whatsoever" in the municipal supply of beer and that local authorities should not seek to extend their beer operations "merely" for considerations of profit. In November 1956 the secretary of the Department of Native Affairs issued an important call for Johannesburg authorities to move toward apartheid planning in drinking places. Having carefully considered the most appropriate location for facilities such as beerhalls, perceived as "sources of potential danger," departmental policy was that all institutions "catering for the needs of urban Natives should be situated in areas specially demarcated for Natives." Furthermore, in terms of its powers under the Natives (Urban Areas) Consolidation Act of 1945, the department refused to sanction the location of new beerhalls "save where these are erected in accordance with policy." The department felt that the "time is now opportune for the City Council to consider the desirability of removing all such institutions to the Native Townships." Nevertheless, it conceded that this goal of engineering a spatial rearrangement in African drinking patterns "can only be a long term policy." However, it urged the Johannesburg authorities to begin by considering "the early removal of the Central Beer Hall."

The department planned to link excision of other beerhalls, such as Mai Mai and Wolhuter, with programs for the removal from the white city of African men's hostels and the enactment of "locations in the sky" legislation. With the projected march of residential segregation in Johannesburg threatening to choke off part of the market for inner-city beerhalls, the eventual objective was to situate all beerhalls in the areas of nascent Soweto. The only exception was an envisioned beerhall at Eastern Native Township to cater for the needs of residents and the planned extension of the hostel. This official policy that all social facilities for African residents of Johannesburg, including beerhalls, be provided "in their right place" was continually reiterated at meetings between officials of the Department of Native Affairs and municipal representatives.[53]

The proposals of the department for drinking apartheid were applauded by local Nationalist politicians but received only lukewarm acceptance by the United Party-controlled Johannesburg city council. No doubt mindful of the potentially large revenue shortfall that might result from an immediate closure of the lucrative inner-city beerhalls, municipal officials bruited alternative plans for reconstituting the map of African beer drinking. The council's plans emphasized decentralization and smaller beerhalls or beer gardens over the existing mass-drinking institutions. The notion of small "beer gardens" in Johannesburg appears to have been drawn from experience in Southern Rhodesia.[54] After a visit there in 1955, W. J. P. Carr, manager of Johannesburg's Non-European Affairs Department, advocated that lessons might be learned from beerhall policy in urban Rhodesia.[55] Planned beer gardens would be an element in the council's scheme for decentralized drinking facilities in townships. Nevertheless, the initial steps toward township drinking facilities involved the projected building of beerhalls appended to the new men's hostels at Dube (opened in 1956) and under construction at Nancefield (opened in 1957). Significantly, these new hostels would accommodate an estimated 5,000 former residents relocated from Johannesburg's "sky locations," potential patrons lost to the inner-city beerhalls.[56]

The major thrust of decentralized planning and small beerhalls was toward strategic points servicing the demands of African drinkers working within the commercial and industrial areas of Johannesburg. The council suggested that the problems of Central beerhall, "the biggest thorn in the flesh" of the central government, might be resolved by establishing a number of smaller decentralized beerhalls within the space of industrial Johannesburg. In light of past problems in securing sites for city beerhalls, the council admitted that finding appropriate locations might be "difficult, if not impossible." The need for such sites derived from the danger that in the absence of beerhalls within their daytime working areas, African drinkers would drift back to shebeens. By day 100,000 Africans were working in the city's offices and factories; additionally, hostel and compound dwellers, domestic servants, and residents of the "locations in the sky" also required the provision of city drinking places. Support for the council's suggestions of smaller decentralized branch beerhalls came from the Transvaal Chamber of Industry, which stressed the role of beer as workers' midday meal, and the local chamber of commerce, concerned that the spare time of an African employee be "used in such a way that he is absorbed and does not become a nuisance."[57]

After these proposals were formulated in 1957 and submitted for ministerial approval, no further action was taken on the issue of possible beerhall removal from inner-city Johannesburg. Without the consent of the newly christened Department of Bantu Administration and Development, the council's plans for a spatial reorganization of sanctioned beer-drinking facilities were quietly shelved. The killing of a white man outside Mai Mai on 31 January 1959 appears to have been the catalyst for a new frenzy of activity. Only two days before the incident the Minister of Bantu Administration denied the municipality permission to proceed with the planned township beer gardens; immediately afterward, he reversed the decision and ordered the municipality to ready such facilities.[58] Moreover, a meeting on beerhalls was hastily arranged between municipal officials and the watchdog Mentz Committee, appointed to oversee "solutions" to Johannesburg's problems. After this encounter two different plans for the location of beerhalls were submitted for consideration to the minister.[59] The first plan represented guidelines for the immediate enactment of drinking apartheid, with the suggested closure of Central, Wolhuter, and Mai Mai and their replacement by beerhalls in township areas. In 1957 the council formulated an alternative proposal to close the inner-city beerhalls, establish new "secluded" decentralized beerhalls in industrial areas, and gradually construct beer gardens in townships.

On 24 February 1959 the government announced that drinking apartheid was to prevail and no other provision should be made in "white" Johannesburg when the three inner-city halls were shut.[60] The minister stated that "in the interests of declared policy of the country I was obviously unable to accept the recommendation of alternative beerhall facilities outside the Bantu residential areas."[61] There was further bad news for the municipal beer trade of Johannesburg. After 16 June the remaining two beerhalls in the white city (Denver and Western) were compelled to close on Sundays as well as public holidays. The only element of the council's policy endorsed by the central government was the proposal for small township beer gardens in preference to "the dangers inherent in mass drinking emporia." The council reiterated its fear that the police would be unable to cope with the anticipated boom in shebeens after the demise of the city beerhalls and urged a stay of their execution. Moreover, it requested that the issue of Johannesburg's beerhalls be passed on to the Malan Commission, which was then investigating the wider question of a possible lifting of prohibition on the sale of liquor to Africans.[62] The central government turned down the proposal and insisted that the inner-city beerhalls be closed on or before 16 June.

The uncompromising tone of the minister confirmed that the removal of beerhalls from central Johannesburg was viewed as a step toward urban apartheid and a means to defuse potential racial conflict: "If the Bantu, in their present state of development, cannot enjoy an amenity such as a beerhall without creating disturbances and resorting to acts of violence, they have only themselves to blame if the State deems it necessary to take steps to protect members of other racial groups from such behaviour."[63] During April and May of 1959 representations continued to officials of the Department of Bantu Administration and Development seeking reversal of the decision on beerhalls. The Transvaal Chamber of Industry communicated its misgivings that the removal of beerhalls might "lead to more resentment on the part of the Native population" and exert "a disrupting effect" on industry by increasing absenteeism as workers sought out illicit liquor sources.[64]

The apprehensive views of the municipal authority were further pressed on the minister when he visited Johannesburg to open Orlando Stadium. At a further meeting with representatives of the department, municipal officials warned of the dire financial and social consequences of closure.[65] They raised the specter that a "sudden closing of the beerhalls would be disastrous and lead to riots." In addition, they claimed the council would lose £325,000 as a result of the impending loss of sales at the three beerhalls. Reduced beer profits would compel the council to apply to the European revenue fund to subsidize the Native Revenue Account with an increase of a half-penny on the property taxes. Denver was a "slum area" populated only by "low class Europeans" engaged in illicit liquor dealing. Sunday closure of the Denver and Western halls would drive beer drinkers to shebeens, where the more potent liquor and concoctions would "make them arrogant and dangerous." Council officials therefore argued that those beerhalls should be permitted to open during specified hours on

Sundays. The idea that city residents might go to the townships for their weekend beer was discounted as unrealistic even with reduced weekend transport fares. Finally, Johannesburg's Manager of Non-European Affairs unveiled a proposal for four sites, described as "sufficiently isolated from the public and public roads," within industrial zones to the south of the city where branch beerhalls might be initiated.

Less than two weeks before the deadline for closure, the minister agreed to meet Johannesburg officials and debate once again the matter of beerhall siting in the city. As a result of that meeting a recasting of the spatial fabric of official African drinking places was set in motion. First, Johannesburg authorities were permitted to establish "on a purely temporary basis" three new branch beerhalls providing some beer-drinking facilities in the city after the closure of Central, Mai Mai, and Wolhuter. The sites selected for these noxious facilities had to be in the mining belt south of the city and "so remote that there can be no possibility of friction."[66] The new beerhalls would be open on weekdays from noon to 2 P.M. and from 6:30 to 8:00 P.M. Second, the opening hours and functioning of the Denver and Western beerhalls would permit business both on Sundays and public holidays. Third, the minister consented to the supply of beer in hostels and compounds in order "to encourage Natives to go home and drink."[67] This decision meant that beer would still be available at Mai Mai and Wolhuter to hostel residents only, supplied for the first time to residents at Wemmer Hostel, and potentially soon available at seventeen municipal and sixteen large private compounds. Fourth, the minister agreed in principle that beer might be made available to large employers of African labor in industrial areas to supply to their employees. Lastly, he approved the construction of an array of at least nineteen beer gardens in the southwestern townships.[68]

REDRAWING THE MAP OF BEERHALLS

A new chapter had begun to unfold in the historical geography of Johannesburg's beerhalls. The agreed closure of the three inner-city halls triggered furious activity designed to prepare facilities for officially sanctioned drinking places after 16 June. An analysis of the redrawn map of African beer drinking in the city highlights the struggles surrounding decentralized drinking within the bounds of the white city and the implantation and extension of beer-drinking facilities in township areas.

Key features of the reconstituted geography of drinking places in the white city were the absence of Central, the continued functioning of Denver and Western halls as before, beer provision to hostel residents at Mai Mai, Wolhuter, and, for the first time, at Wemmer; and most importantly, the opening of three new beerhalls (fig. 12.3). This remarkable shift in the sites of officially sanctioned beer drinking had been engineered in great haste over a span of only eleven days. On 8 June 1959 the council identified suitable sites for three new decentralized beerhalls—two on mining ground and the third on municipally owned land.[69] All three sites were located in industrial-commercial zones and favorably situated with regard to patterns of beer demand. Next day the necessary approval was secured for the sites from officials of the Department of Bantu Administration and Development.

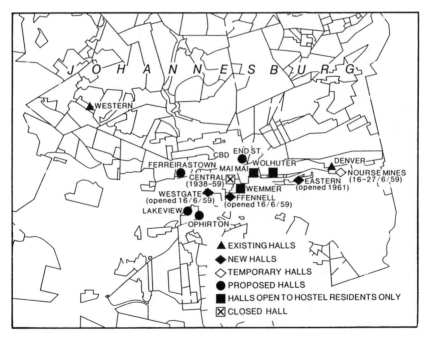

12.3 Changing spatial pattern of beerhalls in the "white" city, 1959–1961

A week later the prefabricated structures had been erected and prepared for business on 16 June. Inevitably, the new facilities were "rather rough and ready" and lacked any seating facilities for their patrons.[70] The council posted signs outside the three inner-city beerhalls and appointed attendants to advise and redirect beer drinkers to the new sites. Municipal officials enthused over the apparent smoothness of the transition proclaiming the three new halls furnished "excellent alternatives" and that "altogether the whole beerhall picture is peaceful and satisfactory":

> When the first thirsty Natives in dirty blue overalls at the heads of queues numbering several thousands started moving through openings in eight-foot-high fences past small wood and corrugated iron cashier's kiosks in three new beer halls at noon on Tuesday 16 June 1959 something not far short of a miracle had been achieved.[71]

To celebrate the perceived success of "Operation Beerhalls" fifty white workers who participated in building the new halls were guests of the mayor at a special cocktail party held in the now abandoned Central beerhall.[72]

Patrick Lewis, chairman of the Non-European Affairs Committee, was obviously delighted with the selection of sites for the new halls, which he anticipated would escape the opprobrium attached to the demised halls. Lewis commented that at the Nourse Mines, Ffennell Road, and Westgate sites, "it would indeed be impossible to find any sites where less Europeans of both sexes are working in close proximity anywhere within the municipal boundaries."[73] Situated close to the municipal dog pound the Westgate beerhall appeared admirably located, as did Ffennell Road, where "no accumulation or milling around of Natives or their vehicles need at any time occur in the street." To curb the possibility for "trouble and drunkenness" near the new halls the committee reduced the maximum quantity of beer an individual could purchase from half a gallon to one quart. Moreover, to ward off the overcrowding problems that afflicted the old inner-city halls, patrons of the new beer facilities were cautioned as to their fragile and uncertain status. A notice, issued at each of the three halls, drew the attention of drinkers to the new opening hours (noon to 2:00 P.M. and

6:30 to 8:00 P.M. on Mondays through Fridays; noon to 2:00 P.M. on Saturdays, and no opening on Sundays):

> Please do not come here earlier. It is in your interest that you do not congregate here in large numbers before the hall opens. This hall is a concession by the Minister of Bantu Administration and Development and can be closed at any time if it is found that large numbers of people congregate here long before the hall opens, or linger after it has closed. If you value your beer and the opportunity to drink it in this hall, please do not come here early or stay late.[74]

The new opening hours were evidently targeted at deterring mass after work drinking sessions by township residents, whose demand for beer henceforth would be satisfied by the new facilities in townships.

The planned market for the decentralized beerhalls in the city was spelled out clearly in the notice:

> This hall is intended for those people living in the city who find it difficult to go to the Townships for their beer. Residents of the Townships are requested to use the beer gardens in their own Townships as much as possible. . . . Please do not wait after work. Go straight home and have your beer in your own beer gardens which remain open until 9:00 at night.[75]

Official euphoria over the events of 16 June was soon shattered as white residents and other interest groups protested against the spatial contiguity of these noxious facilities. Nourse Mines beerhall in the Denver area almost immediately became a flashpoint of locational conflict. Within a day of the opening of Nourse Mines, petitions for its removal were being organized by the parent bodies of three schools, the employees of the adjacent mine, and the council of the local Dutch Reformed Church.[76] Familiar complaints, grounded deeply in class and race prejudices, began to echo from white residents in surrounding suburbs and received particularly sympathetic coverage in the Nationalist press. Beer drinking let loose "primitive passions," women working in the locality were anxious "about their safety," "Bantu again very reluctantly gave way" to passing motorists or "took up a threatening attitude" to pedestrians, and education "was thwarted by what the children saw in the vicinity of the beerhall." At rowdy protest meetings residents demanded the removal of the Nourse Mines beerhall to avert "the death of men, women and children."

The question of beerhall siting in Johannesburg became further inflamed by fears of a repeat of the rioting in Durban that followed the serious riots around the Cato Manor beerhall on 18 June 1959.[77] After the announcement of an impending visit to Johannesburg by the Minister of Bantu Administration and Development to inspect the functioning of the city's experimental beerhall system, the council conceded defeat. The Nourse Mines beerhall closed on 27 June 1959, eleven days after its inauguration.[78] The two remaining decentralized beerhalls at Westgate and Ffennell Road fared better, albeit without escaping controversy and becoming focal points for locational conflict.

Both halls were optimally sited to reap the financial rewards of beer demands furnished by employees in the burgeoning industrial and commercial zones to the south of the city center. Indeed, worries were sounded five weeks after their inception that they "were drawing too much custom."[79] Nonetheless, some relief was anticipated from plans that large employers of African labor might sell cartons of beer at lunchtime to their employees. Lewis envisioned that "big tankers" might ferry supplies of beer to industrialists around the city or that the council might set up "mobile canteens selling sealed containers of beer, with canteens to move on every 15 minutes."[80] Two major problems precluded the immediate implementation of such schemes. First, the proposals ran against existing liquor legislation, then under review, that employers might give but not sell supplies of beer to their workers. Second, and more important, the scheme was predicated on firms having "satisfactory canteens or rooms for use by Native employees."[81] Yet, with large numbers of African workers dependent on coffee carts for their sustenance during the work day, adequate canteen facilities were largely absent in Johannesburg at this time.[82]

The Westgate and Ffennell Road beerhalls survived a stream of protests directed at their ostensibly noxious character. Residents of the married quarters at Robinson Deep mine bemoaned "the endless trouble with drunken Natives streaming through the property," complained that "Natives shout, scream and accost our Native servants," and voiced the usual concern about workers' "aggressive attitudes towards any European in their path." Concerned about the control of workers due to "the increasing incidence of boys coming back to the compound under the influence of liquor," the mining company itself joined the chorus of complaints.[83] At Ffennell Road dissatisfaction centered on white women "in danger of interference by undesirable persons," on the rapid deterioration in "the character of the neighbourhood," and on the potentially "extremely dangerous" situation that "the intoxication of Natives" might create when machinery was used. The Mining Commision threatened that the operations of both Westgate and Ffennell Road beerhalls might contravene the regulations governing trading on mining ground.[84] That threat prompted a search for further potential sites for beerhalls in the event that Westgate and Ffennell Road were forced to close. Although the search uncovered four possible areas (see fig. 12.3), the municipal authorities acknowledged that the "absence of undeveloped land" close to the city center mitigated against "an easy solution."[85]

By the close of the 1950s the "anywhere but near us" syndrome, which constantly portrayed African beerhalls as noxious facilities, threatened to force the beleaguered municipal authorities to once again move on the beerhalls in Johannesburg (fig. 12.4). Fears of court injunctions against the continuing operations of these municipally run establishments on grounds of illegal trading on proclaimed mining land were well founded. Indeed, the continued operation of these two beerhalls seems to have been secured only by the clouded circumstances that surrounded future policy toward liquor supplies to Africans in South Africa. Due to the prevailing air of uncertainty during 1960 and early 1961, the Minister of Bantu Administration and Development considered "unwise" any proposals for the council to proceed with planning "any additional temporary beerhall sites."[86]

The geographical extension of municipal beer provision into township residential areas was a predictable outgrowth of the strengthening forces in the mid-1950s that sought to bring closer the ideal of a racially segregated city. A watershed event in the history of township beer provision was the passage in May 1955 of the "locations in the sky" act, designed to bleach the residential face of Johannesburg by ex-

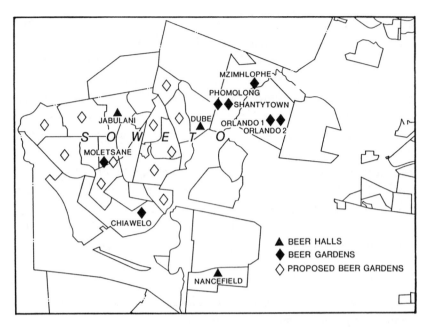

12.4 Location of beerhalls and beer gardens in Soweto, 1960

cising "surplus" Africans living on the city rooftops or illegally in backyard dwellings. During 1956 Dube Hostel, the unwilling reception point for those evicted from white space, was readied for occupancy.[87] The longstanding objections of most township residents to beerhalls were now overridden by the attractive financial logic attached to the proposal that "a Beerhall should be established at the Hostel, as has been done at all other Hostels."[88]

Ministerial approval for the erection of a beerhall at Dube hostel was given in November 1956 and a temporary hall commenced business in February 1957. The new beerhall was not merely restricted to hostel residents; officials hoped that "this beerhall will attract great numbers of patrons from all the neighbouring areas."[89] The experiment of municipal beer provision at the Dube hall (nicknamed "Ghana") was carefully observed by Johannesburg authorities with an eye to future planning. The scheme was viewed as a "spectacular success," leading to similar plans for beerhalls to be appended to the Jabulani and Nancefield hostels. Significantly, these three hostel-linked beerhalls, each planned to accommodate roughly 5,000 patrons, did not mark a major departure from policies favoring mass drinking institutions over small, decentralized drinking places.[90]

The decentralization of township drinking was linked to the fuzzy concept of introducing "beer gardens" as opposed to beerhalls. Although the appellation *beer gardens* was normally reserved for discussions of township drinking places, on several occasions that nomenclature slipped into resolutions relating to the planned, decentralization of beerhalls at Ffennell Road, Westgate, and Nourse Mines. Suspicions were aired that the term *beer garden* was merely a sanitizing mask designed to temper the opposition of township residents toward the municipal provision of beer. Nevertheless, officials stressed that the township beer gardens eventually would become "real gardens" and there appeared "no reason why the 'beerhall' of ominous memory in politics, should not become the 'beer garden' with music, if needed, and even such sophisticated additions as snacks."[91] One bemused researcher suggested that the only apparent distinction between township "halls" and "gardens" was that the former enjoyed facilities for the provision of meals.[92] This divide was not always clear, as many restaurants were attached to what were ostensibly planned as beer gardens.

Proposals for the implantation of beer gardens into townships were detailed first at council meetings in March 1957. The council envisioned that "a number of small beergardens should be established in the Native locations, attractively designed and suitably sited."[93] The chief function of such facilities would be "the selling of kaffir beer to local residents in sealed cartons for consumption at home."[94] Those ideas were not effected and lay dormant for almost two years when revived in the flurry of new proposals that followed the announcements that the inner-city beerhalls would be terminated. The notion of beer gardens as an integral part of Johannesburg's plans for redrawing the map of African drinking places was endorsed by the central government. But by 1959 the council recognized the need for decentralized, on-site consumption facilities and accordingly, while incorporating off-sales, it made provision for up to 750 customers to drink their beer within the gardens.[95] Construction of the new drinking points began apace, and Orlando East was selected for the dubious privilege of accommodating the first two township beer gardens. In May 1959, in the presence of officials from the Department of Bantu Administration and Development who traveled from Pretoria specially for the occasion, Patrick Lewis proudly declared that "it is of considerable moment to me that I am able to open the first two Beergardens."[96] Following the two Orlando East beer gardens five similar facilities were rapidly initiated, with at least a dozen more at various stages of planning by the fading of the decade.[97]

The setting up of beer gardens, both with and without offsale provisions, was a significant element in shaping drinking apartheid. By 1960 the contours of a new geography of township drinking had been sketched (see fig. 12.5). The relentless march of new beer gardens across the map of Soweto continued even in the wake of the bitter cry uttered by residents that the municipality should "give us schools— not beerhalls."[98] Moreover, no compromise was brooked in the location of new beer gardens, despite complaints that many were "wrongly

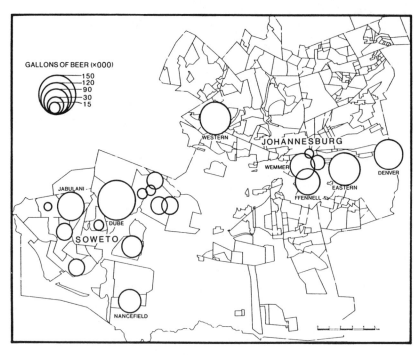

12.5 Geography of beer sales in greater Johannesburg, April 1962

sited near railway stations" or that women were afraid to visit their husbands "as they might be molested by gangsters or arrested by the Police."[99] Different rules clearly applied to dealing with locational conflict over beerhalls in white residential areas as opposed to townships.

The final act in remaking the geography of drinking, further extending municipal beer provision into townships, was the siting of a large new beerhall at Eastern Native township, a small township island that abutted commercial and industrial Johannesburg (see fig. 12.3). With special blessing from central government this anomalous "location in town," not under threat of removal, was the site of a new African worker hostel that opened officially in December 1961.[100] Planning for the beerhall had begun three years earlier. The closure of Central, the disastrous siting of a new hall at Nourse Mines, and worsening overcrowding at Denver all underscored the vital importance of constructing a beer facility at Eastern Native. Initially, temporary provision was made, the formal opening of the Eastern beerhall occurring at the same time as the hostel. Very soon after its inauguration, the Eastern beerhall became one of the busiest focal points of Johannesburg's municipal beer trade.[101]

CONCLUSION

The dramatic change in the geography of drinking in greater Johannesburg between 1957 and 1962 is evident from analyzing data concerning beer sales. In 1957, before the beginnings of drinking apartheid were first manifest in the opening of Dube beerhall, all Johannesburg's municipal beer sales were conducted through the five focal points at Denver, Western, Mai Mai, Wolhuter, and, most importantly, Central. The sixteenth of June 1959 was a landmark in the geography of beer sales, shifting the axis from a concentrated pattern to a spatially dispersed network with new selling points located both within the white city and increasingly in township areas.

By 1962 Johannesburg was a considerable way along the road to drinking apartheid (see fig. 12.5). In five years the geographical balance of sales tipped firmly from sites in the white city to township locales. Of total beer sales of 1.2 million gallons, 50 percent was accounted for by the three large beerhalls at Dube, Jabulani, and Nancefield and the scatter of eleven township beer gardens. If sales for Eastern are included with those of Soweto, township beer sales collectively accounted for almost 62 percent of the municipality's beer business. Although the Denver and Western halls remained individually significant drinking places (fig. 12.5), taken with the two other beerhalls in the white city, they represented only 25 percent of beer sales by 1962. The remaining 13 percent of sales was running through the three surviving inner-city hostels (Wemmer, Mai Mai, and Wolhuter) and over thirty small municipal and private compounds. The forging of this new drinking apartheid hinged around the manifold struggles, compromises, and conflicts that had surrounded the location and removal from Johannesburg of African beerhalls as "noxious" facilities.

ACKNOWLEDGEMENTS

Thanks are extended to Phil Stickler for the preparation of all the illustrations in this chapter.

NOTES

1. Central Archives Depot, Pretoria (CAD), Native Affairs Department (NTS), vol. 4857, file 51/313 (c) (3) (9), Statement by P. Lewis, Meeting in Pretoria with Department of Bantu Adminstration and Development, 6 May 1959, p. 2.

2. *Rand Daily Mail*, 15 June 1959; *Star*, 17 June 1959.

3. On the geographical spread of municipal monopoly in South Africa see C. M. Rogerson, "A Strange Case of Beer: The State and Sorghum Beer Manufacture in South Africa," *Area* 18 (1986): 15–24.

4. The year 1962 is an appropriate date to close this study, for on 15 August 1962 prohibition was finally lifted on the purchase of "white" liquor by Africans.

5. See P. la Hausse, "Drinking in a Cage: The Durban System and the

1929 Riots," *Africa Perspective* 20 (1982): 63–75; "The Struggle for the City: Alcohol, the Ematsheni and Popular Culture in Durban, 1902–1936" (M.A. diss., University of Cape Town, 1984); *Brewers, Beerhalls and Boycotts: A History of Liquor in South Africa* (Johannesburg: Ravan Press, 1988); "The Message of the Warriors: The ICU, the Labouring Poor and the Making of a Popular Political Culture in Durban, 1925–1930," in *Holding Their Ground: Class, Locality and Culture in 19th- and 20th-Century South Africa*, ed. P. Bonner et al. (Johannesburg: Ravan Press, 1989), pp. 19–57; and H. Bradford (in this collection).

6. University of Witwatersrand (UW), A 1132 C22, Report of Manager, Non-European Affairs Department, Johannesburg, 1 July 1958 to 30 June 1959, p. 1.

7. *Star*, 1 January 1938, 10 January 1938, 3 February 1938; *Rand Daily Mail*, 18 January 1938.

8. *Star*, 29 December 1938.

9. *Star*, 3 February 1938, 30 August 1938.

10. Intermediate Archives Depot, Johannesburg (IAD), files of the West Rand Development Board (WRDB), 385/17, Manager, Non-European Affairs Department to Native Commissioner, Johannesburg, 28 January 1941.

11. IAD, WRDB, 401/8/10, vol. 1, Minutes of Non-European Affairs Committee, 4 May 1950.

12. IAD, WRDB, 401/8/3, Draft Report Beer Hall Western Districts, 18 October 1938.

13. IAD, WRDB, 401/8/3, Report of Manager to Non-European and Native Affairs Committee, 3 August 1939; *Rand Daily Mail*, 13 and 14 April 1939; *Umteteli wa Bantu*, 8 April 1939.

14. Minutes, Johannesburg City Council (JCC), 6 September 1940, p. 1058.

15. CAD, NTS, vol. 7032, file 31/322/6, Kaffir Beer Inquiry (Native Affairs Commission) Annexures, p. 69.

16. *Star*, 15 June 1938 and 5 July 1938; Minutes, JCC, 26 March 1957, p. 558.

17. IAD, WRDB, 385/17, Manager, Non-European Affairs Department to Native Commissioner, Johannesburg, 29 January 1941.

18. See G. H. Pirie and M. da Silva, "Hostels for African Migrants in Greater Johannesburg," *GeoJournal* 12 (1986): 173–82; C. Mather, "Residential Segregation and Johannesburg's 'Locations in the Sky,' " *South African Geographical Journal* 69 (1987): 119–28.

19. G. H. Pirie, "Housing Essential Service Workers in Johannesburg: Locational Conflict and Constraint," *Urban Geography* 9 (1988): 568–83.

20. IAD, Public Health Department of Johannesburg (PHD), 11/1, vol. 3, "Special Report on Shebeens" by Can Themba, 20 November 1961. General accounts of shebeens in Johannesburg are provided by C. M. Rogerson and D. M. Hart, "The Survival of the 'Informal Sector': The Shebeens of Black Johannesburg," *GeoJournal* 12 (1986): 153–66; and C. M. Rogerson, "Consumerism, the State, and the Informal Sector: Shebeens in South Africa's Black Townships," in *Economic Growth and Urbanization in Developing Areas*, ed. D. Drakakis-Smith (London: Routledge, 1990), pp. 287–303.

21. For Wolhuter complaints see CAD, NTS, vol. 7032, file 31/322/6, Evidence of Rev. C. Moore to Kaffir Beer Inquiry, pp. 152–54; *Rand Daily Mail,* 17 February 1940, 25 March 1940; *Star,* 26 March 1940.

22. Minutes, JCC, 6 September 1940, p. 1058.

23. IAD, WRDB, 401/8/5, Acting Manager to Native Commissioner, 18 February 1953.

24. See *Rand Daily Mail,* 11 February 1936; IAD, WRDB, 122/54/1, Superintendent Wemmer, Native Men's Hostel to Manager Non-European Affairs Department, 9 March 1939.

25. *Star,* 27 April 1940.

26. IAD, WRDB, 122/54/1, Acting Manager Memo on Mai Mai, 26 July 1940; *Sunday Express,* 25 August 1940.

27. Union of South Africa, Department of Native Affairs, *Report of the Committee Appointed to Enquire into the Use of Profits Derived from the Manufacture, Sale and Supply of Kaffir Beer, 1945–46* (Chairman: J. C. Faure), p. 30.

28. Minutes, JCC, 27 November 1945, p. 1091.

29. IAD, WRDB, 90/17, Manager, Non-European Affairs Department to Non-European Affairs Committee, 4 July 1950.

30. IAD, WRDB, 401/8/5, Town Clerk to Non-European Affairs Committee, 7 December 1951.

31. Ibid., Secretary for Native Affairs to Manager, Non-European Affairs Department, 3 February 1954.

32. A brief account of the post–World War II industrial and commercial expansion of Johannesburg is given in C. M. Rogerson, "The Casual Poor of Johannesburg, South Africa: The Rise and Fall of Coffee-Cart Trading" (Ph.D. diss., Queen's University, Kingston, 1983), pp. 226–34.

33. Figures on Johannesburg's beer profits are provided by P. R. B. Lewis, Johannesburg's Native Revenue Account, *The South African Treasurer* 33 (December 1960): 28.

34. IAD, WRDB, 401/8/15, vol. 1, Non-European Affairs Department Memorandum on Hostels and Beer Halls, 22 August 1958.

35. See Minutes, JCC, 27 November 1945, p. 1091.

36. IAD, WRDB, 410/8/6/5, Petition of 247 patrons of Central Beer Hall to Manager Native Affairs, Johannesburg, 24 September 1944; Wemmer Residents to Superintendent, City Council, 5 November 1953; 401/8/6/2, Brewery Manager to Manager, Non-European Affairs Department, 28 September 1953; IAD, PHD, 2/6/1, Medical Officer of Health to Acting Manager, Non-European Affairs Department, 20 December 1951.

37. IAD, WRDB, 401/8/6/2, Acting Assistant-Manager to Manager, Central Brewery, 30 October 1952; *Star,* 9 March 1957.

38. IAD, WRDB, 352/4, Brewery Manager to Manager, Non-European Affairs Department, 15 September 1952.

39. For accounts of the riot see *Rand Daily Mail,* 22 March 1954; *Bantu World,* 27 March 1954.

40. IAD, WRDB, 90/17, Report of Manager, Non-European Affairs Department, 29 July 1954.

41. *Rand Daily Mail,* 24 and 25 July 1956.

42. IAD, WRDB, 401/8/6/2, Acting Assistant-Manager to Manager, Central Brewery, 30 October 1952.

43. IAD, WRDB, 401/8/1/1, Manager, Non-European Affairs Department to Acting Brewery Manager, Central Beer Hall, 5 November 1953.

44. *Rand Daily Mail,* 24 July 1956.

45. *Rand Daily Mail,* 30 March 1953.

46. IAD, WRDB, 352/4, Assistant Manager to Manager, Non-European Affairs Department, 5 July 1954.

47. IAD, WRDB, 401/8/6/5, Brewery Manager to Manager, Non-European Affairs Department, 24 November 1953.

48. *Star,* 2 September 1957.

49. *Star,* 5 October 1956.

50. For various accounts of the incident see *Star,* 11 and 12 June 1959 and *Drum,* April 1959.

51. IAD, WRDB, 401/8/5, Manager, Non-European Affairs Department to Chief Traffic Officer, 18 January 1957; *Star,* 6 August 1956, 3 May 1957, 4 February 1959; *Rand Daily Mail,* 24 July 1956, 9 March 1957.

52. IAD, WRDB, 352/4, Extract from Report of Non-European Affairs Department, 14 August 1956; *Star,* 10 August 1956.

53. IAD, WRDB, 401/8/15, vol. 1, Secretary, Department of Native Affairs to Chief Native Commissioner, Johannesburg, 8 November 1956; Notes of Meeting in Boardroom of Non-European Affairs Department, 12 August 1958.

54. The decentralization of beerhalls and the functioning of beer gardens

in Bulawayo is discussed in *Bulawayo Chronicle,* 7 July 1956; H. F. Wolcott, *The African Beer Gardens of Bulawayo* (New Brunswick, N.J.: Rutgers Center for Alcohol Studies, 1974).

55. *Star,* October 1955; IAD, WRDB, 401/8/15, vol. 1, Report by W. J. P. Carr, "The Manufacture and Sale of Kaffir Beer by the Non-European Affairs Department," 29 January 1957.

56. Mather, "Residential Segregation," pp. 120, 125.

57. IAD, WRDB, 401/8/15, vol. 1, Notes on Meeting in City Hall, 9 September 1958; Report by W. J. P. Carr, 29 January 1957.

58. *Rand Daily Mail,* 28 May 1959.

59. *Star,* 17 February 1959; *Rand Daily Mail,* 13 and 25 February 1959.

60. *Star,* 24 February 1959.

61. *Rand Daily Mail,* 24 February 1959.

62. *Star,* 17 February 1959, 13 March 1959; *Rand Daily Mail,* 25–27 February 1959; *Die Transvaler,* 17 March 1959.

63. IAD, WRDB, 401/8/15, vol. 1, Minister of Bantu Administration and Development to Town Clerk, 9 March 1959.

64. Ibid., Transvaal Chamber of Industry to Minister of Bantu Administration and Development, 2 April 1959.

65. CAD, NTS, vol. 4857, file 51/313 (c) (3) (9), Notes of a Meeting in Pretoria 6 May 1959 with Representatives of the Johannesburg Municipal Non-European Affairs Department.

66. IAD, WRDB, 401/8/15, vol. 1, Statement by Minister of Bantu Administration and Development, 5 June 1959.

67. *Star,* 8 June 1959.

68. UWL, A1132 A1/2, P. R. B. Lewis Press Statement re Bantu Beerhalls, 8 June 1959; *Rand Daily Mail,* 9 June 1959; *Star,* 9 June 1959.

69. *Star,* 12 June 1959.

70. IAD, WRDB, 401/8/15, vol. 2, P. Lewis to Minister of Bantu Administration and Development, 22 June 1959.

71. *Star,* 17 June 1959; IAD, WRDB, 401/8/15, vol. 2, Non-European Affairs Department Memo, "The Wonder of the Beerhalls," 18 June 1959.

72. *Rand Daily Mail,* 23 June 1959. Predictably, African workers were not invited to this celebration; a separate party was held for them three days later.

73. IAD, WRDB, 401/8/15, vol. 1, P. Lewis to Editor, *Die Vaderland,* 17 June 1959.

74. Ibid., vol. 2, Notice by W. J. P. Carr on Opening of Temporary Beerhalls, n.d.; see also *Rand Daily Mail,* 25 June 1959.

75. Ibid.

76. *Star,* 24 June 1959.

77. See *Vaderland,* 17 and 18 June 1959; *Transvaler,* 17, 24, and 25 June 1959; *Rand Daily Mail,* 24 June 1959. Accounts of the riots in Durban are provided in *Star,* 19 June 1959; and *Rand Daily Mail,* 19 and 20 June 1959; see also M. Blumberg, "Durban Explodes," *Africa South* 4(1) (1959): 9–17.

78. IAD, WRDB, 401/8/15, vol. 2, Minutes of Non-European Affairs Committee, 25 June 1959; *Rand Daily Mail,* 26 June 1959; *Star,* 26 June 1959.

79. IAD, WRDB, 401/8/15, vol. 2, Remarks by P. Lewis, 28 July 1959.

80. *Star,* 26 February 1959; *Sunday Times,* 7 June 1959; *Rand Daily Mail,* 4 July 1959; IAD, WRDB, 401/8/15, vol. 2, Remarks by P. Lewis, 28 July 1959.

81. CAD, NTS, vol. 4857, file 51/313 (c) (3) (9), Notes of a Meeting in Pretoria 6 May 1959, p. 4; IAD, WRDB, 401/8/15, vol. 2, Johannesburg Chamber of Commerce to Manager, Non-European Affairs Department, 26 June 1959.

82. See C. M. Rogerson, "Feeding the Common People of Johannesburg, 1930–1962," *Journal of Historical Geography* 12 (1986): 56–73; C. M. Rogerson, "Humanizing Industrial Geography: Factory Canteens and Worker Feeding on the Witwatersrand," *South African Geographical Journal* 70 (1988): 31–47; C. M. Rogerson, "From Coffee-Cart to Industrial Canteen: Feeding Johannesburg's Black Workers 1945–1965," in *Organisation and Economic Change: Southern African Studies Volume 5,* ed. A. Mabin (Johannesburg: Ravan Press, 1989), pp. 168–98.

83. IAD, WRDB, 401/8/15, vol. 2, details these complaints.

84. Ibid.

85. IAD, WRDB, 401/8/15, vol. 3, Resolution of Non-European Affairs Committee, 11 July 1961.

86. Ibid., Deputy Clerk of Council to Manager, Non-European Affairs Department, 6 November 1961; Chairman, Robinson Deep to Secretary, Bantu Administration and Development, 2 December 1960; Minister of Bantu Administration and Development to Manager, Non-European Affairs Department, 12 December 1960.

87. Mather, "Residential Segregation," p. 125.

88. See, IAD, WRDB, 401/8/13, Minutes of Eastern Dube Advisory Board, 1 November 1955 and undated notes; WRDB, 401/8/15, vol. 1, Minutes of Dube Advisory Board, 19 March 1957.

89. IAD, WRDB, 262/3/37, Non-European Affairs Department Memo,

19 November 1956; WRDB, 401/8/13, Assistant Manager, Native Areas to Manager, Non-European Affairs Department, 21 February 1957.

90. *Star,* 13 March 1959.

91. IAD, PHD, 2/6/2, vol. 1, Extracts from Minutes of Non-European Affairs Committee, 29 May 1959, 25 June 1959; IAD, WRDB, 401/8/13, Extract from Minutes of Dube Advisory Board Minutes, 1 November 1955; *World,* 18 March 1959; *Rand Daily Mail,* 27 and 28 March 1957.

92. H. Sachs, *The Role of the Beerhalls in the Municipal Townships of Johannesburg: A Social Psychological Study—Second and Final Report* (Johannesburg, 1962), p. 34; see also CAD, NTS, vol. 4857, file 51/313 (c) (3) (9), Non-European Affairs Department, Application for Specific Approval (a) Beergardens (incorporating off-sales); (b) Provision of Restaurants at Beergardens; (c) Off-sales Depots: South Western Townships, 1959.

93. Minutes, JCC, 26 March 1957, p. 560.

94. Ibid.

95. *Star,* 13 March 1959.

96. IAD, WRDB, 401/8/10, vol. 1, P. Lewis to City Engineer, 21 May 1959; *Star,* 25 May 1959.

97. *Star,* 2 and 22 April, 1959; *Rand Daily Mail,* 28 April 1959; and CAD, NTS, vol. 4857, file 51/313 (c) (3) (9).

98. *World,* 4 July 1959.

99. IAD, WRDB, 401/8/15, vol. 2, Non-European Department discussions with Joint Native Advisory Boards, 26 August 1959.

100. *Rand Daily Mail,* 4 June 1959.

101. IAD, WRDB, 262/5/46, Report of Manager, Non-European Affairs Department to Non-European Affairs Committee, 26 February 1960; WRDB, 401/8/4/1, Manager, Non-European Affairs Department to Chief Engineer, Housing, 31 October 1960. Monthly sales figures for each beerhall and beer garden operated by the Johannesburg municipality are in IAD, WRDB, 401/8/6/2.

CHAPTER THIRTEEN

ALCOHOL AND
THE CONTROL OF LABOR
ON THE COPPERBELT

Charles Ambler

INTRODUCTION

IN THE HISTORY of the Northern Rhodesia Copperbelt, conflict repeatedly developed over attempts to regulate the production, distribution, and use of alcoholic beverages intended for African consumers. Officials of the mining companies and of the central and local governments were determined that African drinking should not undermine public order and labor discipline in the mining district; and the Africans who migrated to the Copperbelt were equally determined to define their own lives outside work and hence their drinking practices. African workers and other town dwellers were, however, never united in their conceptions of appropriate patterns of drinking: some sought as much as possible to maintain rural patterns of drinking, while others embraced various new urban forms—whether legal or illegal. Colonial officials, employers, and white settlers were similarly divided in their views of what constituted the best means to regulate and control African production and consumption of alcohol.[1] Thus, if the struggle to define African drinking was protracted and often bitter, it was by no means a straightforward test of will and power be-

tween the African population on the one hand and an alliance of state
and capital on the other.

ALCOHOL USE AND THE
DEVELOPMENT OF THE COPPERBELT

The creation of a copper-mining industry in Northern Rhodesia in
the 1920s and 1930s brought large-scale employment and urban settlement to a sparsely populated country that had previously served as
a labor reservoir for the agricultural and industrial enterprises of
Southern Rhodesia and the Belgian Congo (fig. 13.1). The rapid
growth of towns and the establishment of labor compounds in the
mining area made alcohol regulation an issue of serious contention
for the first time in the territory.[2] International agreements dating
from the late nineteenth century obligated the European powers to
ban the production of spirits and their consumption by Africans; and
in east and central Africa the British broadened that ban to include all
European-type beer and wines as well. This prohibitory zeal did not
extend, however, to the various fermented grain drinks that were
consumed in rural communities across Northern Rhodesia. Through
the mid-1920s Northern Rhodesia officials remained convinced that
attempts to control consumption of these beers were bound to fail
and might well prove counterproductive.[3] The effort to impose prohibition on the Witwatersrand—widely regarded as a disastrous
failure—had persuaded many colonial officials that active regulation
would encourage criminality and accelerate the spread northward of
the various types of dangerous spiked drinks and bathtub gins that
they associated with the worst aspects of urban life in the South African mining regions.[4]

In the chaotic first years of the development of copper mining,
when labor was in short supply, neither company nor government officials made much effort to regulate life in urban African settlements;
and the Copperbelt migrants were thus left largely to their own de-
vices in shaping their lives outside work.[5] By 1930 the mines alone
were employing 30,000 African workers, and many thousands more

13.1 Copperbelt towns and mines, Northern Rhodesia

men, women, and children had flooded into the Copperbelt towns and settled in ramshackle municipal townships, the backyards of white employers, or in the shantytowns that ringed each Copperbelt town.[6] The mine companies constructed compounds to house their workers, but in contrast to South African practice the Copperbelt compounds were not closed, and the companies encouraged miners to bring their families to the mines with them.[7]

Migrants to the Copperbelt made drinking the center of African social life in town, just as it was in the rural areas.[8] Many tried as much as possible to reproduce rural patterns of beer production and consumption: they brewed beer in their households for family use, for ceremonial occasions, and for beer parties to which neighbors and friends were invited.[9] Others, however, already had considerable experience of town or mine life in Southern Rhodesia or South Africa and thus were accustomed to urban styles of drinking.[10] In any case, brewing rapidly became commercialized in the towns, even though private sales of grain beer were clearly illegal.[11] There was a ready market of single men on the mines with no way to obtain beer except by purchase, and urban women had the time to brew on a regular basis. In towns brewing was no longer tied to the agricultural cycle, since the ingredients to make beer were always available for purchase. Women migrants quickly recognized that brewing was one of the few ways they could support themselves or contribute to family income.[12] As beer became a commodity, the patterns of drinking changed also. The unfamiliar rhythms of industrial employment forced drinking into restricted periods—the hours after work and especially the weekend. And since beer had to be purchased, treating and buying rounds became customary.[13] To encourage compound residents to drink in small circles of family and friends, several mines issued brewing permits to households in rotation, but compound residents paid little attention to these regulations.

Some women only prepared and sold beer occasionally, but others made it a business.[14] The industry policy of encouraging the presence of women in the mine compounds probably prevented the growth of a shebeen subculture on the Copperbelt similar to that found in the African urban communities of the Rand. The steady growth in the number of women settling in the Copperbelt during the 1930s brought a corresponding growth in the number of women anxious to earn cash by brewing. The result was that no one had to go very far for a drink.[15] Regular payoffs to the compound police ensured that raids would be relatively infrequent; and officials and police suspected of turning in brewers often faced harassment.[16]

People living in rural areas surrounding the new mining towns also seized on the possibilities of the beer trade and began brewing for sale to town residents. In the late afternoons and especially on the weekends, miners and their fellow town dwellers streamed to nearby settlements looking for beer and entertainment.[17] Since beer regulations were rarely enforced beyond urban areas, women in neighboring villages could produce beer openly and thus did not need to resort to the shortcuts often employed by town brewers, who had to keep an eye out for the police. Visitors from town could drink in these villages relatively free of the threat of raids and in conditions of privacy that urban life did not provide. These jaunts provided an escape from the crowded and unpleasant conditions of the towns and mining compounds and evoked for urban migrants the ambiance of their rural home areas and of customary forms of leisure.[18]

ALCOHOL REGULATION

In towns and labor compounds the authorities saw danger and disorder in drinking practices that in a rural setting they might have considered harmless or even quaint. In 1942 a white official argued that Africans "brew too large a quantity. Perhaps it did not matter when they were living in their villages, but when there are hundreds of men working on dangerous work on the mines, it would be very bad for everyone if they went to work drunk."[19] Employers worried especially that drinking threatened industrial discipline by encouraging absenteeism and undermining job performance.[20] White settlers displayed even greater concern about the dangers they perceived in African drinking and inebriation. Drunken men returning home to the residential compounds or to servants' quarters often ignored the obsequious rituals of a colonial order steeped in white supremacy and presented a frightening prospect to the whites who observed them. In short, the freewheeling drunken comportment of African urban dwellers offended the sensibilities of white women and men, who believed that "gentlemen" should know how to hold their liquor.[21]

Responding to these concerns, the Northern Rhodesia government adopted a new Native Beer Ordinance in 1930. That law maintained most elements of the existing—weakly enforced—regulations: it prohibited beer sales in rural areas outright and permitted sales in urban areas only under municipal license and only for consumption on premises. The regulations also gave to local authorities the power to set prices and the responsibility to enforce bans on gambling, drunkenness, and other behavior that whites found objectionable. In contrast to the former regulations, however, the new ordinance firmly enshrined the notion of state monopoly that was central to the South African "Durban system" and committed the state to the creation of a system of public beerhalls. This change signaled an emerging official determination to gain greater control over the social lives of urban Africans.[22] According to the Secretary for Native Affairs:

> Experience of Europeans who are responsible for the good order of townships where Europeans and Natives live together has shown that it is as a rule the private native drinking party, and the week end at the village, which lead to excessive drinking, drunkenness and disorder. It has therefore seemed to them more desirable that reasonable opportunity should be given for Natives to obtain beer to a moderate amount regularly in public and to take away the opportunity of consuming an excessive amount privately at intervals.[23]

Although some colonial officials worried that the state lacked the manpower and police powers to enforce any comprehensive regulation of alcohol, the central administration nevertheless began providing loans to municipalities to build beerhalls and otherwise facilitated their construction.[24] By the end of the 1930s all the Copperbelt towns and most of the mine compounds had small breweries and beerhalls owned and operated either by municipal governments or by mining companies.[25] The growth in unemployment during the Depression years and the proliferation of makeshift "loafer compounds" convinced many whites that such action had to be taken to preserve public order and safety; in the view of many mine and municipal officials the construction of public beerhalls represented the best way to stamp out disorderly drinking.[26] The ordinance mandated that beer profits had to be used for "native welfare," defined in practice as the provision of minimal recreation and social services for the African population. Thus, the halls promised to generate revenue that the financially strapped municipalities could use to maintain segregated African residential areas.[27] By forcing drinking into public beerhalls, the state and the mines sought also to monitor and regulate leisure activities that had previously been hidden from scrutiny. At the same time, officials located the beerhalls to put African drinking out of the view of most whites and to reduce contact between the races. Indeed, the 1930 ordinance explicitly forbade whites to enter beerhalls except on official business. At the same time, as a defense against socializing across racial boundaries, mine management made certain that company-sponsored social and sports clubs were open to white employees of all ranks.[28] The imposition of limited hours—generally from 9:00 A.M. to noon and 3:00 to 6:00 P.M.—restricted legal drinking to daylight hours and made it difficult to use beerhalls for the extended drinking parties that were features of village life but which Europeans found unacceptable in the town setting. By opening beerhalls in the compounds, the mine companies also sought to keep their workers near home after their shifts and on the weekend and thus ready to return to work in the morning or on Monday.[29]

PATTERNS OF DRINKING
IN THE MINING AREAS

The attempt to control and regulate African drinking on the Copperbelt failed in two crucial respects. First, neither the municipalities nor the mining companies ever managed to suppress illicit competition to the beerhalls; indeed, during the 1940s illegal brewing and sales of beer increased rapidly. Second, the beerhalls themselves did not evolve into the instruments of control and improvement that the authorities had envisioned, and officials became increasingly concerned about the dangers that beerhalls represented to them. Those failures reflected both the determination of African urban residents to resist regulation and the lack of determination on the part of European officials to enforce it.

Despite the clear message of the 1930 ordinance, many in authority doubted that public beerhalls represented the most desirable approach to alcohol regulation. Whatever theoretical advantages they saw in the public control of drinking, many whites regarded the Copperbelt beerhalls as tawdry and disruptive. Since few municipalities were in fact willing to invest much in beerhall construction, they were often dismal and rundown; and because few towns had more than one beerhall, they were often overcrowded—especially on Sundays.[30] Europeans wanted control over African drinking, but at the same time they feared an institution that brought together such large numbers of Africans to drink. Expressing a point of view that would gain increasing support during the next two decades, the Secretary for Native Affairs declared in 1934 that "a large crowd of natives excited with beer is like a volcano liable to blaze up at any moment and the larger these crowds the more likelihood of trouble."[31]

The fiscal health and institutional success of the beerhalls required active steps to crush illicit competition through a program of police raiding, but the administration was unwilling to make such a commitment before the late 1940s. Not only would strong enforcement have been prohibitively expensive at a time when resources were limited, but also highly unpopular and disruptive. Local government would later apply pressure for enforcement of the monopoly, but during the 1930s the municipalities had not yet come to depend on the revenues produced by beer sales.[32] Industry support for beerhalls was in any case lukewarm; and well into the 1940s some of the mines preserved a permit system in preference to the establishment of beerhalls.[33] Mine managers saw access to alcohol as important in the recruitment and maintenance of a stable labor force and thus tended to be more concerned with complaints about the quality or availability of beer than with enforcing the state monopoly.[34]

Through the mid-1940s Copperbelt women defied the beerhall

monopolies and continued to produce illicit beer. Brewing had become an essential element of the economies of many households, and brewers refused to abandon that source of income. For drinkers, buying beer from illegal private brewers was often more convenient than patronizing beerhalls that had limited hours and which were few in number and thus often located several miles from residential areas. The private brewer—perhaps a person from the patron's home area—produced beverages that more nearly resembled the ones people were accustomed to drinking at home than the mass-produced and standardized beerhall brews.[35] By the mid-1940s brewers faced increased harassment; in 1945 in Mufulira, for example, the authorities prosecuted some twenty women each month for offenses related to illegal brewing.[36] However, the penalties imposed did little to discourage the brewers. They organized themselves into circles whose members contributed to pay the fine of any of their number unlucky enough to be arrested; and those arrested were soon back in business, the costs involved in brewing being relatively small.[37] They also produced various drinks, such as honey beer, that did not fall within legal definitions of "native beer," and which therefore could be "made and consumed quite openly."[38] Illegal brewing continued with the knowledge and connivance of African police and petty officials, whose reluctance to battle private brewers clearly reflected popular opinion.[39] Africans not only flagrantly ignored the alcohol monopoly, they apparently refused to recognize its legal legitimacy. Most had little patience with the official argument that beerhall profits were being returned to them in the form of community amenities.[40] Town residents simply saw beerhalls as one of a variety of sources of alcohol, and thus they generally saw police actions against brewers not as the suppression of illegal activities but as the harassment of competitors to the beerhalls.[41] Appointed tribal representatives in the mining compounds protested repeatedly that the fines imposed on brewers were too high, and on one occasion they asked that brewing paraphernalia that had been seized be returned after fines had been paid.

For some members of the colonial administration the creation of beerhalls represented an opportunity to reshape African drinking customs and behavior or, in the words of the Secretary for Native Affairs, "to educate them to 'take their liquor like gentlemen.'"[42] In fact, although the authorities might fence the beerhall grounds and impose drinking hours, they could not really control or even monitor the behavior of the hundreds of patrons crowded inside. To the dismay of white officials, the beerhalls gradually evolved into centers of a distinctive African working-class leisure culture. Although envisioned as instruments of control, the beerhalls in fact offered a freedom of behavior and association that other forms of drinking did not; indeed, many urban Africans found the beerhall scene very appealing.[43] Since beerhalls were already well-established fixtures of urban life in parts of Southern Rhodesia and South Africa, as well as in the towns of Livingstone, Lusaka, and Broken Hill in Northern Rhodesia, many migrants to the Copperbelt regarded them as essential amenities.[44]

In the 1930s and 1940s the typical beerhall or beer garden included a brewing house whose employees prepared large quantities of beer that was then sold from a simple hall. Drinking was permitted in the halls, but most patrons gathered under trees or kiosks in the enclosed grounds.[45] By the late 1930s beerhalls had become public meeting places where men could search out women and find friends, demonstrate their generosity, and assert their status by purchasing rounds for friends and showing off new and expensive clothes:

> The Beer Hall is one of the few social centres, crowds . . . foregather there every afternoon, but particularly on Sundays. They pass in their crowds down the paths leading to the beer palace, all well turned out. They come in felt hats with saucy feathers, dark glasses with pink rims, white collars and bright bows, coloured trousers neatly pressed, full at the bottom with pointed shoes and swagger canes or knob-kerries. The ladies are correspondingly flashy. There are many dazzling frocks . . . evening dresses bought from ladies in the European town, coloured handkerchiefs on heads, crocheted caps or stylish hats worn on one side.[46]

At the beerhalls people gathered in groups according to age, gender, or home area to drink, talk, or dance. For the more urbanized and affluent segments of the African population, the beerhalls also provided the opportunity to establish distinctions between themselves and their fellow town residents. These well-dressed men and their female guests

drank in a more decorous fashion, at separate tables that they sometimes decorated with cloths and flowers. These were the same people
who participated in the ballroom dancing clubs and competitions that
were a fixture of Copperbelt life, and they often looked with considerable disfavor on the behavior of the less sophisticated mass of
people who frequented the beerhalls.[47]

The atmosphere was indeed often raucous. After many hours on
the job or after a long work week, men saw drinking not only as a
traditional pleasure, but as an escape from the pressures and rigidity
of life in industrial communities. Inexpensive beer prices and limited
beerhall hours combined to encourage patrons to consume large quantities of beer in short periods. Whereas in the rural areas beer was
available only periodically and then in limited quantities, in the towns
those with money could buy beer every day in the week. The result
was considerable drunkenness, although it is difficult to determine
how much inebriation resulted from the amount of alcohol consumed
and how much from the drinkers' determination to get drunk.[48] Where
alcohol flowed, and where a thousand or more women and men
might crowd together on a weekend in the afternoon heat, trouble
was not uncommon. In the relatively anonymous atmosphere of the
beerhalls, small slights could rapidly escalate into fights. Above all,
men fought over women. Workers often worried that their wives frequented the halls during their shifts; and women worried that their
husbands were taking up with other women when they went to drink.
Very often, "broken heads or matrimonial troubles were brought
about."[49]

Through much of the 1930s mine and municipal officials preferred
to ignore the rakish and disorderly qualities of beerhall culture. But
with the revival of the copper industry toward the end of the decade
and the growth in the concern of white residents over African drunkenness, officials came to see cracked skulls and marital conflict as barriers to their larger program of creating and sustaining a stable and
disciplined work force. European observers frequently described the
beerhalls in sordid terms, as filthy and crowded institutions that lacked
the "village atmosphere" and promoted violence, criminality, and
immorality. A growing number of Africans supported that assess-
ment.[50]

In the years immediately following World War II colonial and mine officials became increasingly concerned about the apparent failure of alcohol regulation, and concerned also that widespread flouting of liquor laws encouraged general disrespect for the law.[51] The expansion of the mining industry during the 1940s drew large numbers of people into the Copperbelt towns, creating conditions of overcrowding and squalor in mine and municipal compounds and especially in the communities of squatters that surrounded them.[52] Industrial prosperity and population growth also fueled a rapid expansion in illegal brewing and drinking, which in the view of the authorities both fed off and contributed to urban poverty and disorder. By the mid-1940s illicit brewing had become pervasive in many areas. In the mining town of Kitwe, for example, more than half the women brewed on a regular basis, and a small but increasing number had become professional brewers.[53] Officials saw a clear link between this expansion of commercial brewing and the growth of squatter settlements.[54] At a 1944 meeting in Kitwe attended by the governor, the Secretary for Native Affairs, and provincial and district officials, "all agreed the loafer and beer situations [were] serious, requiring early and drastic action."[55]

In the aftermath of the war the administration intensified pressure on illegal beer production. Police increased their raids on private brewers and the municipalities eradicated most of the squatter compounds. But official fears of the supposedly dangerous impact of the beerhalls on urban society tempered official enthusiasm for a campaign to enforce the beer monopoly. In the face of a growing and seemingly intractable problem and a steady chorus of complaints from municipal, district, and corporate officials, the Northern Rhodesia Government commissioned a thorough investigation of the issue in 1948.[56] The resulting report downplayed the extent and danger of urban drunkenness, but made plain that illegal brewing was rampant and noted that many town residents resented the beerhall system.[57] The report recommended that private, licensed drinking establishments gradually replace the beerhalls.[58] Some mine officials had in fact already begun to think along similar lines. In 1942 a manager at the Mufulira mine had prepared a memorandum in which he criticized the establishment of beerhalls as a regrettable state intervention into the commercialization of alcohol production and distribution. He argued that because in Northern Rhodesia "control became difficult as the population increased, . . . instead of a gradual evolution through the medium of the inn or pub, the native was suddenly and rudely thrust into the beerhall system, which is a system entirely foreign to all his traditions."[59] By the end of the decade many officials of the mining companies and of the central government had likewise concluded that beerhalls should be eliminated.[60] Yet more than ten years would pass before that step was taken.

The beerhalls endured because there was no consensus as to what should replace them. In the postwar years the halls began to make substantial profits, and white settler-controlled town governments became correspondingly dependent on that income to maintain minimal services for Africans—services that would otherwise have had to have been paid for out of general revenues. Not surprisingly, the Copperbelt municipalities resisted any plan that threatened the income that beer sales produced.[61] At the same time, many colonial officials were simply uncomfortable with the idea of privatizing the beer trade. That discomfort betrayed both a paternalistic desire to protect African consumers from the exploitative tendencies of the free market and a general reluctance to cede direct supervision over African drinking to a new class of African license holders.[62] Thus, through the 1950s the mine companies, followed later by some of the municipalities, attempted to devise alternatives that would incorporate the supposedly desirable elements of the English pub, while retaining the fundamental control of whites over African drinking.

During the 1950s the character of the mine labor force changed dramatically, reflecting the industry program of stabilization and advancement for African labor.[63] Turnover among African workers, which had remained high through the 1940s, declined sharply; and between 1951 and 1960 the proportion of miners who lived with their wives at the mines rose from 60 to 87 percent.[64] By 1960 the typical African mine worker was the head of a relatively settled urban family.[65] As the companies pursued stabilization, they also sought a far greater degree of involvement in the lives of workers and their dependents. Before the Second World War, the industry provided only basic amenities in the residential compounds: a few clinics, small schools and simple recreation halls, occasional soccer fields, and of course the beerhalls.[66] The copper boom of the late 1940s and early 1950s, however, provided the resources for the mines to develop a much more ambitious and intrusive presence in worker compounds.

The industry set out first to define clearly the boundary between the compounds and the surrounding settlements. Companies began requiring all workers to live within the compound perimeter and introduced a program of police sweeps to evict all those who were not employees or their dependents.[67] To ensure the paramountcy of industry objectives, the companies also moved to end any division of responsibility for the management of the compounds. During the 1940s and 1950s the companies took over control of welfare programs that previously had been run by missions; they also assumed management of beerhalls—many of which had been operated by municipalities.[68] Company officials aimed most of their new programs of leisure and improvement at semiskilled and skilled African workers. In particular, the mines invested considerable effort and money during the 1950s in developing exclusive social clubs that would meet the putative recreational requirements of those workers and their families. Management hoped that the clubs would draw "respectable" men away from the beerhalls, where clearly they did not belong.[69] Such policies were part of a broader program of nurturing a new elite of privileged workers. The larger goal was that these men and their wives and children would assimilate middle-class family customs and, at a time when the power of the African miners union was growing, comprise a bastion of support for corporate values.[70]

The mining companies soon came to realize, however, that they would have to provide alternative sources of alcohol if they were to reshape the social lives of skilled and semiskilled miners. During the 1940s several of the mines had already introduced sales of beer for consumption off-premises so that such men and women could drink at home—in the "family circle."[71] At the end of that decade, after substantial protest from African political leaders, Northern Rhodesia had also begun permitting Africans to drink European-style bottled beer and wines—consumption of which became a mark of status.[72] But neither of those reforms provided for the establishment of premises where better-off Africans could drink in the company of their peers and separate from others.[73] The new clubs established in the mine compounds during the 1950s failed to attract much interest specifically because they could not serve any form of liquor. As a result, companies began experimenting—very cautiously—with the creation of licensed drinking clubs that would serve beers to dues-paying members.[74]

By the late 1950s African social clubs at several of the mines sold beer to members, and a number of the companies had also opened public "luxury saloon bars."[75] At the Roan mine a compound manager suggested developing "high quality beerhalls" that might include libraries, while his counterpart at Bancroft noted that "African opinion inclines toward provision of premises which would be in some way restricted to senior men, and with a 'collar and tie' rule and it has been suggested that a small additional charge should be made for drinks or membership fee levied to restrict entry."[76] According to a report from Roan, such clubs might become "the one place where the European could reach the better educated and more moderate African."[77] Those efforts received considerable support from Africans. In a 1954 letter to the *Central Africa Post,* for example, a Kitwe resident welcomed the establishment of "a bar where decent people can drink quietly, free from much noise and fighting, which are very common in an ordinary beer hall or bottle store. This is something decent Africans have been wanting for a long time."[78]

The introduction of clubs, however, had little effect on the lives of ordinary miners, who continued to patronize the beerhalls and illegal drinking places. In 1955 an official investigation of alcohol regulations concluded once again that beerhalls should be eliminated and replaced with a general licensing system. But the report acknowledged that the scale of beerhall profits made it unlikely that such a change could be accomplished.[79] Hence, as the complaints against the beerhalls mounted, companies and municipalities responded by making improvements in the beerhalls rather than closing them down. In the mid-1940s several of the mines began opening branch beerhalls, both to bring halls nearer to the main residential areas and to reduce the numbers patronizing the main beerhalls. Eventually, several of the companies also began to invest substantial sums in the construction of more spacious and better-appointed buildings.[80] The mine managers also tried to improve the quality of beer served, but complaints only subsided after the mid-1950s, when the Heinrichs Company established a modern brewery and began mass-producing Chibuku brand grain beer to supply the Copperbelt beerhalls.[81] In an attempt to project a new image for traditional-style beer, Heinrichs promoted Chibuku with advertisements picturing well-heeled Africans driving late-model convertibles, or African ballroom dance champions attired in evening dress.[82] But this sophisticated image collided with the persistent reality of Copperbelt beerhalls—institutions into which crowded hundreds, even thousands, of working-class drinkers. Wrote one African critic, "All these boxers and athletes pictured in beer advertisements are just illusions created by the advertisers."[83]

THE DEMISE OF THE BEERHALLS

African and European critics increasingly denounced the beerhalls in strongly moralistic terms. The halls, they argued, bred crime and juvenile delinquency and encouraged women and men to waste their time and money. Repeatedly, African correspondents used the local press to advance their view that beerhalls promoted immorality, adultery, and disorderly behavior.[84] Whereas the mine company newspapers of the 1930s and 1940s had generally ignored beer drinking or presented it in a positive light, by the late 1950s a stream of articles and letters appeared suggesting that drinking itself might be socially disruptive and dangerous. The writers, all Africans, placed particular emphasis on the ways that excessive alcohol use threatened family life.[85] Moreover, physicians and social welfare workers began expressing public concern for the first time about the growth of alcohol abuse in the African population.[86] Criticism also came from those who objected to the beerhall monopoly because it excluded Africans from a potentially lucrative area of commerce and gave control over beer profits to municipal governments dominated by white settlers.[87] But in the end, political fears rather than moralistic concerns killed the beerhalls. Beginning in 1957, African political leaders organized a series of boycotts of Copperbelt beerhalls that resulted in considerable destruction of property and some violence. After 1960 conflict intensified on the Copperbelt with the disintegration of the Central African Federation and the subsequent movement toward African majority rule. In an atmosphere of bitter competition the beerhalls emerged as centers of political mobilization and confrontation.[88] These developments made the authorities understand that the beerhalls had become genuine popular institutions. In response, the mine companies not only pushed ahead with the development of clubs but moved to eliminate beerhalls entirely and replace them with smaller taverns and facilities for the purchase of beer for consumption off premises.[89] Whereas in 1958 the Roan mine had only one beerhall for a compound population of about 50,000, by 1964 African workers could buy beer at thirteen different locations.[90] During the same period both the Nchanga and Mufulira mines also gradually expanded the number of clubs and off-license stores where beer could be purchased.[91] In 1964 the Nchanga mine management launched an ambitious and expensive Tavern Development Scheme that was intended "radically to change African drinking habits."[92] The mine planned to close the three existing beerhalls and replace them with six bottle stores and a number of taverns to be managed by Africans who would be trained to regard themselves as independent proprietors. Management blatantly advertised its intentions in the translations for the names chosen for the new taverns: Let Us Be Decent, Mutual Understanding, and Calmness.[93]

Although white settlers often linked the beerhalls to political agitation and to crime, local municipalities still remained reluctant to commit the capital and risk the loss of revenue that closing the beerhalls would entail.[94] Finally, in April 1964, with independence only six months away, the Northern Rhodesia administration forced local governments to act, ordering that "large beerhalls, which have for long been condemned as giving rise to much social unrest must be closed down."[95] Even then the towns resisted regulations that they claimed would provide insufficient "gallonage" to maintain adequate revenue. The central administration rejected this response, making it clear that "the prime intention is to achieve a complete departure from the system of large beerhalls and to erect bars which can serve . . . a strictly limited number of persons."[96] The demise of the beerhalls did not bring an end to state monopoly, however. The gradual dismantling of racially discriminatory legislation gave Africans the opportunity to patronize and operate bars and bottle stores that sold European-style beer and spirits; but the state kept close control over the sale of Chibuku and similar drinks aimed at a low-income clientele. The government would set hours and prices and impose design restrictions for the new, smaller drinking establishments. Most important, the regulations clearly encouraged local authorities and employers—and not private individuals—to build and operate those establishments. Notwithstanding official investigations in 1948 and 1955 that advocated private licensing, the Northern Rhodesia government (and its Zambian successor) continued to resist popular demands for the introduction of a system of private licenses for the sale of grain beer.[97] The argument that small, privately owned bars or pubs on the English model represented a highly efficient means of control and improvement collided with a deeply held paternalistic tradition of protecting ordinary Africans from the vagaries of the market. At a time when municipal finances were very much in doubt and urban areas seethed with unrest, officials apparently preferred not to experiment. Thus, while the relatively affluent could buy bottled beer in many bars and clubs, large numbers of poorer town dwellers continued to patronize private illegal brewers in preference to the new public taverns. The introduction of beerhalls more than thirty years earlier had nurtured the development of distinctive forms of urban leisure, but three decades of alcohol regulation had failed entirely to give the state and employers control over the leisure lives of Africans. These women and men continued to define to a very great extent their own drinking customs—whether within or beyond the law.

ACKNOWLEDGEMENT

This chapter is based on research funded by a grant from the University Research Institute, University of Texas at El Paso.

NOTES

1. For the relationships between the state, capital, and labor on the Copperbelt see J. Parpart, *Labor and Capital on the African Copperbelt* (Philadelphia: Temple University Press, 1983). While historians have focused considerable attention on the history of labor and labor organization, they have had little to say about the history of work, and even less about leisure. See M. Burawoy, *The Politics of Production: Factory Regimes under Capitalism and Socialism* (London: Verso, 1985), pp. 5–8; and F. Cooper, *On the African Waterfront: Urban Disorder and the Transformation of Work in Colonial Mombasa* (New Haven: Yale University Press, 1987), pp. 5–6.

2. In addition to Parpart, *Labor and Capital*, the large literature on the history of the copper industry includes, S. Cunningham, *The Copper Industry in Zambia* (New York: Praeger, 1981); E. Berger, *Labour, Race and Colonial Rule: The Copperbelt from 1924 to Independence* (Oxford: Oxford University Press, 1974); and C. Perrings, *Black Mineworkers in Central Africa* (New York: Holmes and Meier, 1979). During most of the colonial period, mining was concentrated in four mines—Nchanga and Nkana, controlled by the Rhokana Corporation (Anglo–American), and Roan Antelope and Mufulira, controlled by the Rhodesia Selection Trust (see fig. 13.1). The British South Africa Company administered Northern Rhodesia until 1924, when it came under the control of the Colonial Office.

3. From 1914 alcohol control regulations were on the books, but they were little enforced; National Archives of Zambia, Lusaka (NAZ), BS 3/168, no. 13, Legal Advisor, Northern Rhodesia Public Prosecutor to Chief Secretary, 20 December 1913. The unsuccessful attempt of Lewanika, paramount chief of the semiautonomous province of Baroteseland and a temperance advocate, to impose alcohol prohibition in his domain only reinforced official determination to avoid such policies; NAZ, BS 3/168, no. 33, High Commissioner, Cape Town to Acting Administrator, Northern Rhodesia, 25 February 1914; BS 3/168, no. 33, Acting High Commissioner, Cape Town to Administrator, Northern Rhodesia, 5 January 1912.

4. NAZ, BS 3/168, no. 33, High Commissioner, Cape Town to Acting Admininstrator, Northern Rhodesia, 25 February 1914. See also J. Baker and D. Moodie (in this collection).

5. F. Spearpoint, "The African Native and the Rhodesia Copper Mines," *Journal of the Royal African Society,* 36 supplement (July 1937). Spearpoint was for many years compound manager at the Roan Antelope mine in Luanshya.

6. Yale University Library, Manuscripts and Archives, J. L. Keith and A. Stephenson, "Administrative Control of Industrial Population," Report of the Sub-Committee of the Native Industrial Labour Advisory Board (Lusaka, Government Printer, 1936), esp. p. 4.

7. Parpart, *Labor and Capital,* pp. 30–44.

8. C. W. Coulter, "The Sociological Problem," in *Modern Industry and the African: An Enquiry into the Effect of the Copper Mines of Central Africa upon Native Society and the Work of Christian Missions,* ed. J. Merle Davis (London: Macmillan, 1933), pp. 72–73. This was the report of a commission that visited the Copperbelt in 1932.

9. For a description of drinking in rural areas in the 1930s see A. Richards, *Land, Labour and Diet in Northern Rhodesia: An Economic Study of the Bemba Tribe* (Oxford: Oxford University Press, 1961 [1939]), pp. 77–81.

10. Spearpoint, "Rhodesia Copper Mines," p. 26; and Parpart, *Labor and Capital,* p. 31.

11. During the 1930s cash sales of beer also became common in rural areas. Men returning home from wage employment often wanted regular access to beer, and women left behind when men migrated found brewing a convenient way to earn increasingly necessary cash; Richards, *Land, Labour and Diet,* p. 77.

12. See G. Chauncey, "The Locus of Reproduction: Women's Labour in the Zambian Copperbelt, 1927–1953," *Journal of Southern African Studies* 7 (1981): 135–64.

13. R. J. B. Moore, *These African Copper Miners: A Study of the Industrial Revolution in Northern Rhodesia,* rev., with appendices by A. Sandilands (London: Livingstone Press, 1948), p. 51. This account by a missionary is based on evidence collected during the late 1930s and early 1940s. Audrey Richards has pointed out that the notion of the weekend was beginning to spread in the Northern Rhodesia countryside by the 1930s; *Land, Labour and Diet,* p. 392. See also K. Atkins, " 'Kafir Time': Preindustrial Temporal Concepts and Labour Discipline in Nineteenth-Century Colonial Natal," *Journal of African History* 29 (1988): 229–44.

14. R. T. Chicken, *A Report on an Inquiry into the Prevalence of Illegal Brewing and Its Causes and Effects on Urban Areas near the Railway Line in Northern Rhodesia* (Lusaka: Government Printer, 1948), p. 7.

15. A. Lynn Saffery, *A Report on Some Aspects of African Living Conditions on the Copper Belt of Northern Rhodesia* (Lusaka: Government Printer, 1943), p. 15; Chauncey, "Locus of Reproduction," pp. 144–47; and K. Hansen, *Distant Companions: Servants and Employers in Zambia, 1900–1985* (Ithaca: Cornell University Press, 1989), pp. 161–62.

16. Spearpoint, "Rhodesia Copper Mines," pp. 29–30.

17. Ibid., p. 33.

18. G. Wilson, "An Essay on the Economics of Detribalisation," part 2, *The Rhodes–Livingstone Papers* no. 6 (Livingstone, Northern Rhodesia, 1942), p. 33; NAZ, SEC 2/421, vol. 1, no. 34, Provincial Commissioner, Northern Province to Chief Secretary, 28 November 1939; Great Britain, Colonial Office, *Report of the Commission, Appointed to Enquire into the Disturbances in the Copperbelt* [Russell Commission] (Lusaka: Government Printer, 1935), p. 34. This report emphasizes the desire on the part of compound residents for greater privacy. See also Chauncey, "Locus of Reproduction," p. 138.

19. NAZ, SEC 2/421, vol. 1, no. 250, Extract of Minutes, African Provincial Council, Central Province [1945].

20. L. H. Gann, *A History of Northern Rhodesia: Early Days to 1953* (London: Chatto and Windus, 1964), p. 209; Parpart, *Labor and Capital,* pp. 30–44; Keith and Stephenson, "Administrative Control of Industrial Population," p. 4; and NAZ, SEC 2/421, vol. 2, no. 314, Secretary for Native Affairs, Extract of Minutes, African Provincial Council, Western Province, Ndola, 8–9 October 1945.

21. NAZ, ZA, 1/9/83/1, no. 31, Secretary for Native Affairs to Commissioner for Lands, Mines and Local Government, "Native Beer Halls," 16 February 1934. White mine workers had a reputation for drunkenness as well; NAZ, SEC 1/1573, no. 60, minutes by H. C. S., 1 September 1936.

22. NAZ, ZA 1/9/83/1, no. 13, Notes on Complaints of Mine Managers [1930].

23. NAZ, ZA 1/9/83/9/1, no. 2, Secretary for Native Affairs to E. A. Muwamba, 25 September 1928.

24. NAZ, ZA 1/9/83/9/1, no. 13, Notes on Complaints of Mine Managers [1930]; and no. 3, Chief Secretary to District Commissioner, Ndola, 16 April 1931.

25. NAZ, ZA 1/9/83/1, no. 29, extract of minutes of interview between

the Governor and African residents of Lusaka, 8 November 1932; ZA 1/9/83/2, no. 19, Luanshya Native Beer Report, 1932–1933; ZA 1/9/83/4 no. 21; Manager, Mufulira Beer Hall, Half Yearly Report, 21 July 1931; ZA 1/9/93/9/1, no. 3. Chief Secretary to District Commissioner, Ndola, 16 April 1931.

26. Chicken, *Prevalence of Illegal Brewing*, pp. 4, 7. Concerns regarding African drunkenness reflected the preoccupation of white settlers with their fears of African sexual interest in white women; Moore, *African Copper Miners*, p. 42.

27. NAZ, ZA 1/9/83/2, no. 6, Acting Provincial Commissioner, Broken Hill to Secretary for Native Affairs, 2 September 1929; ZA 1/9/83/9/1, no. 2, Secretary for Native Affairs to E.A. Muwamba, 25 September 1928; ZA 1/9/83/1, no. 31, Secretary for Native Affairs to Commissioner for Lands, Mines and Local Government, "Native Beer Halls," 16 February 1934.

28. NAZ, ZA 1/9/83/1, no. 31, Secretary for Native Affairs to Commissioner for Lands, Mines and Local Government, "Native Beer Halls," 16 February 1934; RMC/RST (Roan Consolidated Mines, Ltd. [former Rhodesia Selection Trust], Archives, Zambia Consolidated Copper Mines, Ltd., Ndola, Zambia), 202.7, Letter to Chief Medical Officer, RACM, 11 February 1943; and NCCM/RC/HO (Nchanga Consolidated Mines, Ltd. [former Anglo American Corporation], Archives, Zambia Consolidated Copper Mines, Ltd., Ndola, Zambia), 159, Rhokana Corp., "Memorandum on Mine Recreation Clubs," 21 June 1932.

29. NAZ, ZA 1/9/83/9/1, no. 2, Secretary for Native Affairs to E. A. Muwamba, 25 September 1928.

30. NAZ, ZA 1/9/83/1, no. 35, extract from tour report of Acting Secretary for Native Affairs, Tour of Copperbelt, minute no. 606/99, 7 August 1934.

31. NAZ, ZA 1/9/83/1, no. 31, Secretary for Native Affairs to Commissioner for Land, Mines and Local Government, "Native Beer Halls," 16 February 1934.

32. *Report of Disturbances in the Copperbelt* [Russell Commission]; and Parpart, *Labor and Capital*, pp. 75–77; NAZ, ZA 1/9/83/1, no. 35, extract from tour report of Acting Secretary for Native Affairs, Tour of Copperbelt, minute no. 608/99, 7 August 1934.

33. RCM/RST 203.6, R. Moore, Mindolo Mission to F. Ayer, General Manager, RACM, "Comparison of Beer System and Permit System of Controlling Native Beer Drinking," January 1935.

34. See, for example, *Mufulira Compound Magazine*, 1939–1941; also,

RCM/RST 202.7, Memorandum from Compound Manager, Mufulira to General Manager, "Native Labour Policy: Beer Hall," 1 September 1942. For the continual complaints about beer quality, see notes on "Boss Boy" and "Tribal Representative" meetings.

35. Chicken, *Prevalence of Illegal Brewing*, pp. 5–7; and NAZ, SEC 2/420, vol. 1, Acting Provincial Commissioner, Western Province, Ndola to Chief Secretary, 27 March 1940.

36. Minutes of the African Provincial Council, Western Province, Ndola, 8–9 October 1945.

37. Interview, Mr. Jubani, Lusaka, 5 July 1988. Unless otherwise noted, interviews were conducted by the author and transcripts are in his possession.

38. NAZ, SEC 2/421, vol. 2, no. 447, extract of the May report of the Labour Officer, Luanshya, enclosed in Labour Commissioner to Secretary for Native Affairs, 29 June 1948.

39. NCCM/WMA 202.9, notes on meetings of Boss Boys and Tribal Representatives, RACM, 30 August 1944, 2 December 1944, and 28 December 1944.

40. Ibid.

41. NCCM/WMA 202.8, notes on meeting of African Tribal Representatives, Mufulira, December 1944.

42. NAZ, ZA 1/9/83/9/1, no. 2, Secretary for Native Affairs to E. A. Muwamba, 25 September 1928.

43. Burawoy, *Politics of Production*, p. 230.

44. NAZ, RC/29, no. 34, District Commissioner, Broken Hill to Chief Secretary, 11 October 1923; RCM/RST 202.7, letter to Chief Medical Officer, RACM, 11 February 1943.

45. NAZ, ZA 1/9/83/3, no. 1, Provincial Commissioner, Broken Hill to Secretary for Native Affairs, 31 December 1929; Coulter, "Sociological Problem," p. 84; Spearpoint, "Rhodesia Copper Mines," pp. 30–34.

46. Moore, *African Copper Miners*, pp. 51–52.

47. Ibid., p. 52; and interview, Mr. Jubani, Lusaka, 5 July 1988.

48. H. Powdermaker, *Copper Town: Changing Africa. The Human Situation on the Rhodesian Copperbelt* (New York: Harper and Row, 1962), pp. 296–97; Moore, *African Copper Miners*, p. 51; and Richards, *Land, Labour and Diet*, pp. 77–81. White observers very likely exaggerated the extent of drunkenness.

49. Spearpoint, "Rhodesia Copper Mines," p. 32; also NAZ, ZA 1/9/83/4, no. 21, Manager, Mufulira Beer Hall, Half Yearly Report, 21 July 1931; and Moore, *African Copper Miners*, p. 55.

50. Spearpoint, "Rhodesia Copper Mines," p. 31; RMC/RST 203.6, Compound Manager, Luanshya to Estate Agent, 15 December 1930; and RMC/RST 203.6, R. Moore, Mindolo Mission to F. Ayer, General Manager, RACM, "Comparison of Beer Hall System and Permit System of Controlling Native Beer Drinking," January 1935.

51. Saffery, *Living Conditions on the Copperbelt,* p. 57; NAZ, SEC 2/421, vol. 2, no. 343/1, District Commissioner, Broken Hill to Provincial Commissioner, 28 June 1946; and SEC 2/421, vol. 1, no. 56, Labour Commissioner, Lusaka to Chief Secretary, 29 October 1940.

52. Northern Rhodesia, *Report of the Commission to Inquire into the Administration and Finances of Native Locations in Urban Areas* (Lusaka: Government Printer, 1943), p. 11; and Saffery, *Living Conditions on the Copperbelt,* for example, p. 52.

53. Saffery, *Living Conditions on the Copperbelt,* p. 15; also, Wilson, "Economics of Destribalisation," p. 31.

54. Chicken, *Prevalence of Illegal Brewing,* p. 4.

55. NAZ, SEC 2/421, vol. 1, no. 235, notes on discussions on the loafer and illicit beer brewing problems held at Kitwe, 20 November 1944.

56. Chicken, *Prevalence of Illegal Brewing,* esp. p. 4; and extract of minutes of the meeting of the African Provincial Council, Western Province, Ndola, 8–9 October 1945.

57. Chicken, *Prevalence of Illegal Brewing,* p. 4.

58. Ibid., p. 9.

59. RCM/RST 202.7, Compound Manager, Mufulira to General Manager, "Native Labour Policy: Beer Halls," September 1942. For scholarly discussion of the commercialization of alcohol in England, see P. Clark, *The English Alehouse: A Social History 1200–1830* (London: Longman, 1983), pp. 1–63.

60. Northern Rhodesia, Legislative Council Debates, 10 December 1941; and Great Britain, Colonial Office, *Report of the Commission Appointed to Inquire into the Disturbances in the Copperbelt, Northern Rhodesia, July 1940* (Lusaka: Government Printer, 1940), p. 36. Concern was often expressed that it was inappropriate to use the income from alcohol consumption to fund social welfare.

61. *Northern News,* 8 August 1957; Northern Rhodesia, *Report of the Liquor Licensing (Application to Coloured Persons and Africans) Committee* [Ridley Committee] (Lusaka: Government Printer, 1955), p. 12; and A. H. Ashton, "Liquor Laws of Central Africa" (Paper delivered at the Confer-

ence of Non–European Administrators, Livingstone, Northern Rhodesia, 1960), p. 11.

62. African Provincial Council Debates, Western Province, Ndola, 8–9 October 1945. Some argued that a system of private bars would actually constitute a more sophisticated form of control. Proponents of a license system often pointed out that such a system seemed to work well in the neighboring Belgian Congo; *Report of the Liquor Licensing Committee* [Ridley Committee], pp. 12–14.

63. See Parpart, *Labor and Capital,* chaps. 6–8. It was not, of course, company policy alone that produced these changes.

64. Ibid., pp. 138, 165–166; and Powdermaker, *Copper Town,* pp. 89, 97.

65. Parpart, *Labor and Capital,* p. 168; and Yale University Library, Manuscripts and Archives, group 605, box 27, folder 498, "Africans at Roan Antelope," 3rd. ed. (May 1961).

66. Spearpoint, "Rhodesia Copper Mines," pp. 41–43.

67. RCM/RST 202.7, Northern Rhodesia Chamber of Mines, "Memorandum on African Labour Policy," 29 January 1945; and RCM/C 205.2, no. 3, Mine Compound Police, 1956–61.

68. NCCM/RC/HO 160, General Manager, Rhokana to Consulting Engineers, Johannesburg, 28 September 1954; NCCM/CSD/MO/220, Information on Beerhalls in the Copperbelt, 18 July 1962; RCM/RST 203.5.1, J. D. Rheinallt Jones, "Report on Health and Social Welfare," 1949, RCM/RST 202.7; Compound Manager, Rhokana to General Manager, Memorandum on Native Labour Policy, 31 January 1944; RCM/RST 203.5.1, Compound Manager, Roan to General Manager, Memorandum on Missionary and Welfare Societies, 3 September 1944; and RCM/RST 203.5.1, Compound Manager, Roan To General Manager, notes on a visit to Nkana and Mufulira mine compounds, 13 October 1947; see also Parpart, *Labor and Capital,* pp. 101–3.

69. RCM/RST 203.8.1, notes for a speech on the occasion of the opening of the first "neighbourhood" welfare subcenter, 14 October 1955 [Roan]; and RCM/RST 203.8.1.69, Men's Social Club, Nchanga Mine Township to Welfare Officer, Nchanga, 23 October 1959.

70. Parpart, *Labor and Capital,* pp. 140–43; and "Drunkenness Destroys a Family's Unity and Happiness," *Mufulira African Star,* May 1960.

71. Secretary for Native Affairs, Northern Rhodesia Legislative Council Debates, 15 March 1948; RCM/RST 202.7, Northern Rhodesia Chamber of Mines, Memorandum, "African Labour: Subsidiary Canteens in Compounds—Off Sales," 10 February 1945.

72. See C. Ambler, "Alcohol, Racial Segregation and Popular Politics in Northern Rhodesia," *Journal of African History* 31 (1990): 298–302, for discussion of legalization of beer and wine.

73. Some beerhalls did provide separate areas for the consumption of bottled beer and wine, but the atmosphere was not noticeably different from the rest of the beerhall.

74. RCM/RST 203.8.1, Roan Antelope Mine, Memorandum, "Clubs in African Townships," 2 July 1958; and RCM/RST 203.8.1, Acting Manager, Bancroft Mine to Secretary, Chamber of Mines, 3 August 1957.

75. RCM/RST 203.8.1, Assistant African Personnel Manager, Roan, memorandum (on clubs), 3 July 1958; RCM/RST 203.8.1, Secretary, Men's Social Club, Nchanga Mine Township to Welfare Officer, Nchanga, 23 July 1959; and *Nchanga Drum,* 5 September 1958. Also, *Northern News,* 17 July 1957. The object of these new institutions was rapidly undermined by the fact that too many people wanted to patronize them; NCCM/CISB/HO 111/1, Nchanga Mine, Progress Report no. 10, Nchanga Mine Township Public House Development Scheme, 5 August 1954.

76. RCM/RST 203.8.1, Assistant African Personnel Manager, Roan, Memorandum (on Clubs), 3 July 1958.

77. RCM/RST 203.8.1, Chief of Study to Personnel Manager, Roan, 23 July 1958.

78. Godwin Lewanika to the editor, 17 May 1954.

79. *Report of the Liquor Licensing Committee* [Ridley Committee], p. 12.

80. *Nchanga Drum,* 12 May 1959, notes the opening of a "smart new beer hall," in the Nchanga African Township.

81. Complaints about beer appear repeatedly in the notes and minutes of meetings of Tribal Representatives and Boss Boys at the various mines. See also the comments by N. Nalumango, Northern Rhodesia Legislative Council Debates, 6 December 1950. For the establishment of the corporate breweries see C. M. Rogerson and B. A. Tucker, "Commercialization and Corporate Capital in the Sorghum Beer Industry of Central Africa," *Geoforum* 16 (1985): 360–61.

82. See, for example, *Nchanga Drum,* issues for 1959.

83. "Drunkenness," *Mufulira African Star,* April 1960. This article was the first in a series of what were described as "outspoken articles on drunkenness written by African Welfare Workers."

84. See *Northern News,* 15 May 1957; and *Mufulira African Star,* July 1956 and June 1960.

85. "Drink, the Destroyer," *Mufulira African Star,* June 1960, also April and May 1960; *Luntandanya* (Nkana Mine newspaper), March 1956 and December 1957; and *Northern News,* 24 July 1957.

86. NAZ, HM 48/1(c)iii, Northern Rhodesia Society on Alcoholism, Minutes, 1961–1964.

87. *Nchanga Drum,* 7 March 1958; and *Northern News,* 9 August 1957 and 22 July 1957.

88. See NAZ, ZP 30/1, Northern Rhodesia, "Report and Minutes of Evidence of the Commission of Inquiry into the Unrest on the Copperbelt, July-August 1963," mimeographed (Lusaka, 1963), esp. p. 100. These protests are described in Ambler, "Alcohol and Politics."

89. RCM/RST 203.8.1, "Scheme for the Further Development of African Welfare Services," Roan, March 1960; "Short History of the Fisansa Recreation Club," Roan [ca. 1961]; African Personnel Manager, Roan, memorandum, "African Beer," 11 May 1961.

90. NCCM/CISB/HO 111/1, no. 18, "Liquor Undertaking in Roan and Impact on Mine Township," Roan, 16 April 1964.

91. "Africans at Roan Antelope," p. 43; *Mufulira African Star,* March 1961; NCCM/CISB/HO 111/1, no. 7, Anglo-American Corp. Group of Mines, "Report of the Sub-Committee Appointed by the Community Services Managers to Investigate the Establishment of Neighbourhood Community Centres (Clubs)," 7 March 1964; and NCCM/CISB/HO 111/1, no. 50, Nchanga Mine, "Preliminary Report on Liquor Undertakings," 24 June 1964.

92. NCCM/NCCM/HO 551/1, Nchanga Mine, "Report on Liquor Undertakings," 16 July 1964; and NCCM/CISB/HO 111/1, no. 21; Anglo-American Corporation (C.A.), notes of a meeting held to discuss the implications of replacement of beerhalls by bars, Kitwe, 23 April 1964.

93. NCCM/RAA/KO 187/1, Nchanga North Township Public House Development Scheme, Progress Report no. 8, 9 July 1964.

94. NCCM/CISB/HO 111/1, Nchanga Mine, Progress Report no. 10, Nchanga Mine Township Public House Development Scheme, 5 August 1954.

95. Northern Rhodesia, Ministry of Local Government, Circular 5/64, 11 April 1964, "Local Authority Liquor Undertakings."

96. Northern Rhodesia, Ministry of Local Government, Circular 23/64, 8 July 1964.

97. RCM/RST 202.7, Compound Manager, Mufulira to General Man-

ager, Memorandum, "Native Labour Policy:—Beer Halls," 1 September 1942; NCCM/ZAM/HO 254/1, Northern Breweries, Ltd., "The Implications of Changing from Beerhalls to a Better Type of Amenity in the Municipal Townships," 10 February 1964 (Northern Breweries was by this time a subsidiary of Rhokana); and *Report of the Liquor Licensing Committee* [Ridley Committee], pp. 12–14.

CHAPTER FOURTEEN

THE CONSTRUCTION OF COMPOUND AUTHORITY: DRINKING AT HAVELOCK, 1938-1944

Jonathan Crush

INTRODUCTION[1]

FROM THE LATE 1930s, the economic and political landscape of colonial Swaziland was transformed by South African and British mining and agribusiness capital. The growth of a new internal working class, and its concentration in much larger production units, greatly enhanced the opportunities for coordinated labor action within the country.[2] Yet between 1940 and 1962, the country experienced only one major confrontation between labor and capital: the strike at the Havelock asbestos mine near Piggs Peak in February 1944. There were few injuries and no loss of life though the protesters did considerable damage to carefully selected buildings on the mine property, including the mine beerhall. Unable to reconcile the riot with the pervasive colonial myth of a docile and contrite Swazi worker, officials initially reacted by blaming the violence on foreign agitators.[3] Subsequently, they confirmed that the strike was simply another, albeit more serious, incident in an escalating domestic conflict over the control of alcohol production and consumption at the mine and in colonial Swaziland more generally.

The Havelock mine had been in production for five years when the strike occurred. During that time, Havelock's owners had negotiated workable structures of labor control at the mine. By incorporating figures of rural authority into these structures, Havelock management drew close to the Swazi aristocracy under Sobhuza in the years leading up to the strike. There is a tendency in the recent literature on Swaziland to see the growing rapprochement between Sobhuza and foreign capital after 1940 as advantageous to both parties and therefore unproblematic. The events surrounding the strike revealed that the relationship could be contradictory, particularly where the needs of capital conflicted directly with the defense of customary rights by the aristocracy. The strike also forced the colonial state into a much closer public and private identification with the interests of foreign capital in Swaziland. The key to the events at Havelock in February 1944 lies in an understanding of the implicit moral contract between employers and employed that governed alcohol transactions in the compound.

REPRESENTATIONS OF SWAZI DRINKING

Reporting to the Transvaal Liquor Commission in September 1909, Swaziland Resident Commissioner Robert Coryndon typecast the Swazi as "the greatest beer drinkers south of the Zambesi."[4] He went on to observe that almost every homestead had several recognized beer drinks every season, and that beer making at homesteads in the vicinity of the country's smaller gold and tin mines went on "almost continually." The beer drinks, he claimed, frequently developed into "drunken orgies" that led to violent stick fights and ended up in colonial courts. In the 1930s sporadic colonial criticism of the "orgiastic" character of Swazi drinking practices reached a crescendo. In one fairly typical outburst, Sidney Williams complained that beer was now being sold in vast quantities, as a result of which "drunken orgies occur at weekends all over the country to the detriment of a nation's pockets, health or morals."[5]

Although it is impossible to quantify, it seems likely that by the 1930s many Swazis were in fact drinking a great deal more than they had earlier in the century. "Beer is drunk whenever we can get it," went one Swazi saying, "[and] when I have had enough beer I feel the day is ended."[6] The reasons for this are not hard to see. First, a great deal more beer was available for drinking than in the distant past. Some years earlier, when colonial taxation was first imposed, homesteads began to sell beer to raise taxes and avoid wage work. As well, women began to brew and sell beer as a way of asserting their own economic and social independence within the homestead. If they could obtain access to cash (through migrant remittances, for example) they bought grain and brewed.[7] In the 1930s four shillings worth of purchased grain, when converted into beer, would sell for eight shillings or more.[8] Missionary societies were continually disciplining their female members, who were prepared to renounce virtually everything, except their right to brew and sell beer. The availability of grain for purchase also meant that brewing and drinking were no longer as tightly tied to the rhythms of the agricultural calendar. At earlier times, periods of abundance and indulgence after the harvest alternated with periods of dearth and enforced abstinence. Now beer was available at any season for those with the means to buy it.

Accounts of Swazi brewing in the 1930s indicate that beer (or *tshwala*) was made from both of the two major subsistence crops, maize and sorghum, either together (usually in equal quantities) or separately. Like drinkers everywhere, Swazi consumers were closely attuned to variations in taste, consistency, and strength. Brewers who made good beer had a "light hand," while others made beer "which is only water."[9] Most drinkers preferred the taste of pure sorghum beer but were prepared to stomach maize beer as long as it was made from white maize. In northern Swaziland, *mpekwa* beer, which underwent a double boiling, was popular since it was much stronger than ordinary *tshwala*. In the lowveld, where grain harvests were smaller and more unreliable, the residents tended to drink more palm wine and marula beer (*emagunu*). *Emagunu* drinking was more widespread in the hot summer months, when *tshwala* was less freely available.[10]

Women produced beer as often as they reasonably could, though the task was lengthy and arduous and had to be performed with great care and precision. Mbonwa Hlope recalled beer-making in the 1920s:

> We used to use *umtfombo* [malt] and *emabele* [sorghum] which we planted ourselves. We'd take the sorghum and soak it in water, then leave it to dry before putting it into the clay pot. We'd first put water into the clay pots, and make a fire. The clay pots were put near the fire, not over the fire, so that the flames just lick the sides of the pots. When the water has boiled, you would pour some of the water into the other pot and then you had to keep on doing that from time to time. Then we covered the pot with special leaves called *imihlapho*. The malt would ferment—meanwhile we would stir the malt from time to time, and then leave it to ferment. Then after that we would dry it outside in the sun. Once it had dried, the malt would be ground using a grinding stone.[11]

How often women actually brewed depended on the state of home-stead grain stocks, the price of purchased grain, and the social and economic pressures to brew. In the patriarchal Swazi homestead, a "good" wife was one who made sure that her husband always had a pot of beer or *mahewu* (a soft fermented porridge) ready on demand.[12] Women who did not brew at least once a month were seriously criticized by husbands and their acquaintances. Criticism was more muted when grain stores were low. In practice, most rural women brewed no more than four times a year, although they brewed in quantity when they did so.

Brewing for domestic use was a long-standing practice, but no homestead existed in isolation from the broader community. Beer played a central role in local ceremonies such as moving a homestead, attesting an agreement or marriage contract, weddings and funerals, and sacrificial libations to the ancestors, as well as national rituals such as the annual *Incwala* festival.[13] Good neighbors always had beer available for each other and for casual visitors, and beer was the most common form of reward for agricultural services rendered. Voluntary workers at communal work parties expected to be rewarded with a feast and beer party. People called by the local chief to work on his fields expected no less.[14] With the entrenchment of mass labor mi-grancy in the first two decades of the century, the agricultural re-sources available to the homestead were reduced, since many men were away for long periods. As homesteads declined in size, young men used the proceeds of migrancy to establish themselves independently. One result was that communal work parties (with their accompanying beer drinks) increased in frequency as homesteads began to rely on other homesteads for help during the agricultural cycle.[15]

Beer-giving also played a central role in the symbolic and ideological reproduction of relations of domination and dependence within Swazi society. Chiefs and wealthier commoners were in a position to organize larger work parties and offer greater rewards:

Dancing, singing, boasting, and display are as essential as the feast. . . . When the work is over, the feast is enjoyed at leisure; if the work ends late, the feast is postponed to the following day. Then the entertainment begins: men and women sit in their separate groups chanting old national songs, and every now and then an individual rises and flaunts his or her dancing skill to honour the host and rejoice the spectators. The host sits on his mat or sheepskin rug apart from the rest of the people. He keeps the workers under control, distributes the food, and calls any man whom he wishes specially to honour to drink from his own pot of beer.[16]

Beer flowed in abundance on such occasions. In contrast, a poor commoner might be able to afford no more than a couple of gallons of beer to be divided up among those present.[17] Even if he was not organizing the party, the district chief expected either to be invited or to receive a portion as tribute.

Commoners regularly paid tribute to local notables, chiefs, and royalty with gifts of agricultural produce and beer. At one dance attended by Sobhuza in the Peak district, fifty-four large pots of beer were brought on one afternoon from eight different centers. Each group of carriers received a pot for their efforts, three bowls went to Sobhuza's entourage, and he distributed the remainder among the dancers and onlookers according to rank, sex, and locality. Incidents like this, reproduced at various scales up and down the country, were critical to the cultural and social reproduction of the hierarchy of power and privilege within Swazi society.[18] The receiver of gifts—in this case Sobhuza, but more often a local chief—used those same gifts, at no personal cost to himself, in a widely-acknowledged act of generosity to reinforce his own status and reputation. The order of gift giving was no less important since it allowed the chief to make a series of highly visible statements about the rank and place of various people, clans, and localities. It was precisely this set of social transactions and cultural meanings that Sobhuza sought to reproduce in the mine compounds.

Growing colonial hysteria in the 1930s and 1940s about the extent and effects of Swazi drinking was certainly related to the increasingly visible character of alcohol consumption. With the growth of mine camps and urban centers such as Manzini and Mbabane, weekend Swazi drinking became far more visible, and threatening, to whites. As new industrial concerns such as the Havelock Mine began to open up within the country, employing large workforces in concentrated areas, so the domestic market for beer also began to increase. Various new alcoholic concoctions made their appearance in the country as well.[19] At Havelock, the workforce consisted of migrants from Nyasaland and Mozambique, as well as Swazis with previous experience on the Witwatersrand mines. All had acquired a taste for some of the stronger beverages available in places like Johannesburg.

The evangelistic fervor of colonial denunciations of Swazi drinking was primarily an expression of the administration's deep uncertainty over its ability to secure a disciplined and reliable workforce for the new wave of foreign capital reaching the country. The dismal history of capitalist production in Swaziland gave them little encouragement.[20] As one white settler observed, the country's existing mines "have to keep on their roll say 300 Natives because they cannot at any one time get more than perhaps 150 actually working, because when the Swazi is near his home, like this, he just goes off at any time he feels like it."[21] He pointed out that labor inefficiency had plagued the industry for "something like 30 or 40 years" but that employers had "become accustomed to it."

Neither employers nor the state could afford to be as sanguine about the labor force at a massive new project such as the Havelock Mine. At the very least, the imposition of industrial work discipline demanded controls over the drinking habits of black miners. The country's smaller tin and gold mines had long been plagued by labor inefficiency due to unregulated alcohol consumption at nearby homesteads.[22] Swazi miners were also called upon by neighboring chiefs to participate in communal agricultural activities. At the end of the day there was invariably a beer party. The chiefs adapted the timing of their demands to coincide with the work week. But the effects of a beer party on Saturday or Sunday often extended into "Saint Monday":

> Every week, especially on Monday mornings, a number of workers are absent as a result of excessive drinking; fights, usually over women, are frequent. Women from the neighbourhood do a profitable business in the sale of beer to workers, and the compounds are recognized as centres of drunkenness and immorality.[23]

The drinking practices and preferences of the mine workforce threatened to pose a similar challenge to efficiency and productivity at the new Havelock Mine. Havelock management became determined to stamp out off-mine drinking at nearby homesteads, and over the border in the Transvaal.

THE MINE

In 1929 the British corporation Turner and Newall acquired a block of 1,000 prospecting claims over asbestos-bearing land on the slopes of the Emlembe Mountain of the Makonjwa range in northwest Swaziland.[24] The terrain was rugged and the area remote. Although the grazing was good, the soils were poor and few Swazis lived there; it was, to quote one colonial official, "the most valueless of all the Native Areas in Swaziland."[25] But for the existence of a royal cattle post and forest stand, the area would probably have been swallowed up into a winter grazing farm for Boer farmers from the eastern Transvaal at the time of the land partition in 1907.[26]

With unfavorable market conditions in the early 1930s, the veins of chrysotile asbestos remained in the ground. In 1936, however, the market improved and Turner and Newall's New Amianthus Company began development work.[27] The company spent £250,000 equipping the mine and trekking in 12,000 tons of heavy machinery.[28] It constructed roads and bridges and an overhead cableway to connect the mine with Barberton (fig. 14.1). The mine went into production for the first time in 1938 on a scale that dwarfed the small, undercapitalized tin and gold mines operating elsewhere in the country. By the

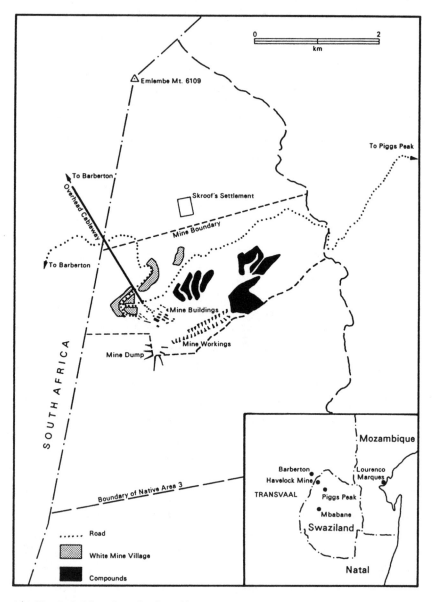

14.1 Havelock Mine, Swaziland, 1944

early 1940s the mine was hoisting 2,000 tons of ore per day and shipping 600 tons on the cableway to the railhead at Barberton. The employment roll rose continuously, so that by February 1944, the mine employed 2,373 black workers (1,915 on the surface and 458 underground) and 108 white.[29] The mine property was home to a further 1,500 people—the relatives of both white and black employees.

In establishing its company town, New Amianthus Mines introduced an approach to labor management and control quite foreign to Swaziland and to mining south of the Limpopo. Turner and Newall's Shabani asbestos mine in Southern Rhodesia was one model for Havelock, though broader trends in managerial ideology also made their mark.[30] From the outset, the mine made plans to stabilize skilled and supervisory black workers in settled accommodation. In practice, it found that family housing was a powerful complement to its local recruiting efforts.[31] Married Swazi migrants, many with long experience on the Witwatersrand, found conditions at Havelock more to their liking. By the mid-1940s the mine village contained 260 semi-detached housing units for married workers and their families. Unmarried migrants were housed in an adjoining open compound in single-sex, ethnically segregated dormitories. The mine deliberately employed an ethnically diverse workforce "so that they wouldn't give management any trouble."[32] Workers from outside the country were also reckoned to be less vulnerable to the lure of ceremony, communal activity, and beer parties in the surrounding countryside. By the mid-1940s Swazis, Mozambicans, and long-distance migrants from Nyasaland were employed in roughly equal proportions.

Living conditions at Havelock contrasted sharply with the squalor in Swaziland's tin- and gold-mining camps near Mbabane. Management at Havelock adopted a "welfarist" approach to the organization of life and leisure on the mine. Through detailed attention to the social environment of the mine, the owners hoped to encourage long service and workforce stability and to raise worker productivity. In addition to providing such amenities as a mine hospital, adequate storm drainage, latrines with waterborne sewerage, and generous food rations, the company required that all black employees belong to the mine's Native Welfare Society. The society organized wide-ranging "entertainment of a mental nature" with the profits from membership dues and the mine beerhall. Every Sunday, there were dance competitions and the compound manager organized a brass band, which regularly performed "military airs."[33]

The company built a soccer stadium and gave the mine team a bus for away matches. It provided a large recreation hall near the compound and showed free films every weekend to workers and their families. One visitor to the mine in 1945 noted that the workforce seemed relatively contented, though he admitted that the calm may have been illusory.[34] Only a year earlier, he recalled, there had been an unexpected "riot." In accounting for their actions, however, workers had made little reference to wages or working or living conditions at the mine (in marked contrast to the later 1963 strike at the same mine). The 1944 strike was directed more at the web of social relationships that governed life on and around the mine.

Somewhat problematically for the company, its mineral rights lay squarely within a block of land known as Native Area No. 3 (NA3). At various points in the 1930s, the colonial administration saw evidence of a looming conflict between the company and the Swazi owners of the land rights. Resident Commissioners Dickson and Marwick negotiated with Sobhuza on several occasions to persuade him to exchange NA3 for better land elsewhere in the country.[35] For various reasons Sobhuza refused, and the company had to be content with a ninety-year lease of a 4,000-acre tract of land in the middle of NA3 (see fig. 14.1). In that area the landscape was quickly transformed according to company designs. But the company had no control over events outside the boundaries of its leasehold.

As the Havelock mine developed, a shack settlement began to grow just north of the mine property on reserve land. Residents of the area were allocated land by the local chief—Sikuluvu "Skroof" Dlamini—once they had *khonta'd* (pledged allegiance) in customary fashion. Sikuluvu himself moved to the settlement in 1938 and set up business as a general dealer and trader with a partner, Moses Shiba. By the early 1940s "Skroof's" was inhabited by a diverse group of close to 200 people. In addition to current and ex-mine employees with their families, there were recent immigrants from the Transvaal, several people from other parts of Swaziland (including tradesmen, a Zionist pastor, and a Swazi woman abandoned by her Nyasa husband) and homesteads recently evicted from white farms bordering NA3.[36] Most of the business at Skroof's was perfectly legal and mine management had little objection to workers obtaining various services there at low cost. Management could not afford to be as sanguine about other activities at Skroof's—particularly large-scale illicit liquor production.

Throughout 1938 and early 1939, management had continual run-ins with Chief Sikuluvu and the other residents of Skroof's. In June 1938, for example, the compound manager visited the settlement after a number of miners turned up for work completely intoxicated. He found eighty gallons of doctored beer still unconsumed.[37] As a grain trader, Skroof was able to supply the brewers with maize and sorghum at low cost. He also sold many additives. The settlement consequently supplied the market for *sigomfane, makajano, skokian,* "barberton," and "kill-me-quick"—stronger brews with additional ingredients such as carbide, yeast, brown sugar, and potatoes.[38] The local colonial administration often assisted mine police in raids on Skroof's and prosecuted the brewers under the regulations of the 1936 Liquor Licensing Act. But the ingenuity of the brewers and the volume of demand nullified the power of the law. In April 1940 Sikuluvu himself was prosecuted in the Piggs Peak court for illicitly brewing and selling beer. On this occasion he was acquitted on a technicality when the District Commissioner's own clerk pointed out that the beer was unfermented.[39]

By the mid-1930s the colonial state had begun to acknowledge the futility of prohibition. If workers and urban residents could not be stopped from drinking, then the quantity and quality of alcohol consumed had to be regulated. By selling and issuing free rations of beer with high nutritional value and low alcohol content, employers sought to improve productivity and dissuade workers from drinking the more potent home brews available nearby. In the late 1930s the company applied to the Swaziland Administration for permission to build its own beerhall and brewery:

The applicant company is experiencing difficulty in keeping control over the Native Labourers employed, who wander away from the mine at week-ends in search of beer, and many of whom fail to return to work on Mondays. It is thought that the establishment of a beer-hall in the compound will stop, to a certain extent, this serious loss of labour at the beginning of each week.[40]

By making alcohol available on the mine property, management hoped to persuade workers to abandon the Skroof brewers. Through brewing and rationing its own beer, it aimed to control the amount, type, and alcoholic content of liquor available to the workforce.

Despite vigorous protests from missionaries and many white settlers, the administration amended the Liquor Act in early 1939 to allow employers to sell beer to their employees. New Amianthus Mines built its beerhall at Havelock and began handing out rations and selling diluted *tshwala*. The livelihood of the inhabitants of Skroof's was immediately threatened. In February and March 1939 there were work stoppages in protest at the company's demands that all drinking take place at the beerhall. On 13 March a crowd of 1,000 workers gathered at Skroof's and then marched to the beerhall, where they staged a peaceful demonstration.[41] To cope with the situation, the company adopted a strategy of coercion and concession. Management reasoned that freer on-mine regulations might tempt workers to patronize the beerhall rather than Skroof's. They therefore lifted the limit on the amount of beer which could be purchased, and agreed to the workers' request that they be allowed to consume the beer in the compound rather than just at the beerhall. Management sincerely hoped that this concession might dampen opposition to their plan to have Chief Sikuluvu and his followers evicted.

The company's desire to eradicate Sikuluvu's settlement became an obsession as time passed. In management thinking, all problems of labor indiscipline and productivity originated at Skroof's. John Starkey, the mine manager, castigated the administration for its "failure to control and liquidate settlements of undesirable natives surrounding the Mine, which . . . are responsible for the brewing of illicit Beer, establishment of Brothels and provision of sanctuary of undesirable agitator elements, which have been and still are a source of trouble to the Mine Management."[42] To management, the remedy was clear. For their part, colonial officials would have liked nothing better than to flatten Skroof's. They ordered repeated raids on the settlement and prosecuted vigorously, but there were self-imposed constraints on how far they could go.

Colonial land legislation in the reserves was designed to bolster the power and prestige of traditional leaders. It therefore gave the Swazi chiefs proprietary rights over all reserve areas and allowed them to allocate land to whom they wished.[43] Sikuluvu himself refused to move away from the mine on the grounds that he had every right to live there with his followers. Asked to order Sikuluvu to disband the settlement, Sobhuza backed the chief. Though sympathetic to the company's viewpoint, Sobhuza was adamant that the forced removal of Skroof's violated a basic constitutional principle which the colonial administration itself held dear.[44] Asked to allow the District Commissioner to vet the residents of Skroof's, Sobhuza responded that the movement and settlement of Swazis in and over the reserves had "never been referred to District Commissioners for sanction."[45] The contradictions between colonial land policy and labor policy were never clearer.

The beer protests in 1939 also proved critical in the construction of the "moral economy" of the Havelock mine. Dunbar Moodie has recently argued that everyday relations in the mine compounds of the Witwatersrand were tempered by an implicit moral contract between workers and low-level mine management.[46] The "moral economy" of the mine implied certain obligations on the part of mine officials and set informal limits on the coercive treatment of the workforce. It also allowed a considerable measure of latitude for workers to regulate their private lives with regard to various technically forbidden practices, including compound brewing and drinking. In this autonomous social space, workers could construct a life and culture in which "the definitions and performances imposed by domination [did] not prevail."[47] The boundaries of the contract were fluid and negotiable, consisting not of a consensus of agreed-upon rules but a fluid set of practices and norms that could be interpreted in very different ways by management and workers. The workers' version of the contract was in large measure created and recognized only in the context of its violation.[48] Deliberate or inadvertent violation of its bounds could precipitate moral outrage, mass organization, and collective action.

Such protest was often, in Thompson's words, "a complex form of direct popular action, disciplined and with clear objectives," informed by the belief that certain rights or customs were under attack and had to be defended.[49] The protests were often completely unanticipated and incomprehensible to mine management, who might put an entirely different construction on the terms of the moral contract. Part of the reason for this was management's failure to recognize that migrant workers brought to compound life a set of resources, practices, and social meanings that were rooted in the countryside.

In negotiating the moral economy of the mine, control over the supply and consumption of alcohol was always contested terrain. That was largely because the productivity of the workforce was powerfully shaped, in the eyes of management, by the drinking habits and practices of the mine workforce. For their part, workers jealously guarded what they saw as their right to drink what they chose whenever it was available. When management attempted to control the quantity, quality, and place of drinking, few workers uncritically acquiesced.

At the Havelock Mine, the beer protests of the late 1930s ushered in a set of informal rules governing drinking practices on mine property and a new chain of command within the compound. As elsewhere, compound life was governed by an enormously powerful white compound manager. Under his control was a fleet of mine policemen ("boss-boys"). Between workers and the compound manager sat the *indunas* (headmen). Their task was to communicate the manager's orders to workers and to keep him informed of events in the compound.

The *induna* system had its roots in the mine compounds of the Witwatersrand. It was introduced at Havelock in modified form in response to the beer protests of the 1930s, when the mine management decided to strengthen its lines of communication with the workforce. The company appointed its own Mozambican and Nyasa *indunas*, but asked Sobhuza and his advisors to appoint the Swazi *indunas* and to designate a personal representative to live on the mine. Sobhuza jumped at the chance to enhance the status and image of the aristocracy in a new setting.[50] His representative was usually a hereditary clan chief, "a senior person of stature and wide authority," often a member of the Dlamini aristocracy.[51] Though he rarely visited the mine itself, Sobhuza also constituted a second line of authority upon whom employers and the state could call for more direct intervention in the event of industrial disputes.

In mid-1939 Sobhuza appointed Chief Mhau Dlamini as his representative at Havelock. Mhau already had some experience performing a similar role among Swazi workers in Johannesburg, first on an individual mine and then at Sobhuza's house in Sophiatown.[52] Mhau and his successor Zece were inserted into the compound hierarchy between the compound manager and the *indunas*. Their position was thoroughly ambiguous. They were on the company payroll and the mine clearly saw them as an arm of management, there to keep the peace and to communicate the orders of the compound manager. But to secure their own legitimacy among the workers (and ultimately Sobhuza's as well) they played a more delicate game in the moral economy of the mine. The ambiguities were resolved, with regard to the alcohol question, by an implicit contract between the various parties. The government inquiry into the 1944 strike spent an inordinate amount of time trying to reconstruct the events of the strike and to ascertain what those procedures were and why they had been violated.

THE STRIKE

On the evening of 1 February 1944 a group of Havelock mine *indunas* met to discuss what action to take to protest against the dismissal of two of their number. One of those present, Manuel Sibuyi, argued that they should "tell the Shangaans and then go down and wreck the beerhall and break it." Fenisi Mtombela, another *induna*, described what happened after the meeting:

> There were many people led by Sibuyi and Mhlanga armed with sticks. Sibuyi had a whistle. From the beerhall the crowd went to the Compound Manager's hut and broke all the windows. Mhlanga and Sibuyi were leading the mob. They marched to the football ground. Mhlanga said "We must go to the aerial station." The mob refused saying "We have no griev-

ance with those Whitemen, but only with the one in charge of the beer-hall." They all agreed, and the majority went past the Blantyre compound to the top Compound. Mhlanga and Sibuyi said to the Swazis "Why are you idling? Hasn't your Nduna been dismissed?" That was when the Shangaans and the Swazis went to Bhayi's hut, broke into it and scattered all his belongings.[53]

Mineworkers from Nyasaland were neither asked nor expected to participate. As one Nyasa worker recalled, "Strikes of that nature did not involve everybody, they were like family issues, they involved only those directly affected by the incident."[54]

The crowd of Swazi and Mozambican workers moved off to the beerhall and set about the premises with axes. They hacked the beer vats and steam pipes to pieces, broke into an adjoining storeroom, and removed 141 pairs of boots, as well as bags of sugar, malt, and beans.[55] When they gathered again on the football field early next morning, the compound manager, Herbert Johnson, tried to address them. He was unable to make himself heard above the jeering and quickly turned and ran when sticks and rocks began to rain down on his head. The crowd chased after him but turned back when armed white employees fired several warning shots from the top of the mine dump next to the field.[56]

The workers then returned en masse to their compound and refused to negotiate with management or the local Assistant District Commissioner. Government Secretary Armstrong arrived from Mbabane that evening as did a large contingent of South African Police from Barberton and Ermelo who were immediately sworn in as Special Constables in Swaziland and stationed around the mine. South African intervention had been requested by the Resident Commissioner and authorized by Prime Minister Jan Smuts himself. A relieved High Commissioner noted to his superiors that "the timely arrival of the Union police . . . was of the greatest utility in preventing any further outbreak."[57]

Throughout the morning of 3 February the workers demanded that Sobhuza be present before they would begin negotiations. Sobhuza refused to go to the mine on the grounds that "it was not in accordance with native law and custom [for him to] deal personally with such a disturbance."[58] He did appoint three high-ranking members of the Swazi *liqoqo* (Council) to mediate on his behalf. They were rushed from Mbabane to the mine in a car hired by the administration. Protracted negotiations between mine management, workers, and Sobhuza's envoys ensued. The envoys were unable to persuade the strikers to return to work before their grievances were addressed. These were presented on 4 February, whereupon the Government Secretary initiated a full-scale enquiry that lasted almost a week.[59]

The strike came as an enormous shock to colonial officials and local whites. The *Times of Swaziland,* for example, remarked that "nothing occurring in Swaziland for 47 years has surprised and distressed [us] more than the riot which took place recently."[60] In his annual address to the Swazi, the Resident Commissioner went further: "Everyone [is] ashamed of this action by the Swazis at Havelock because previously no such violence has been committed by Swazis during their history."[61] The workers' grievances were very specific, surprising the Government Secretary, who was anticipating a broad-ranging attack on wages and general conditions at the mine. Instead the workers demanded the reinstatement of the two *indunas* and filed a list of petty complaints against the compound manager, Herbert Johnson. Colonial officials found it hard to believe that these complaints could have been responsible for the level and intensity of emotion demonstrated during the strike. They were also intrigued by the behavior of "the mob" on the first night:

> There was a great deal of other property close to the compound (for example hospital, kitchens and store) which they might have attacked. . . . this is significant when considered with the complaints of the labourers who took part in the riot and strike. There were no complaints as to the general conditions of work at the mine, nor against the higher authorities of the mine or the European employees in general.[62]

To explain the obvious logic of the workers' actions it is necessary to return to the moral economy of the compound and the informal set of procedures governing alcohol transactions on the mine property.

The company's earlier willingness to allow workers to consume mine beer in the compound may have reduced the attraction of Skroof's but it also provided new opportunities for illicit activity. Brewing using traditional methods would have been virtually impossible to conceal in the compounds. Now the brewers could take the weak compound issue and quickly doctor it with sugar and other ingredients to enhance its potency and desirability. Competition was probably brisk in the early stages, but the compound *indunas* and their wives quickly used their privileged position to corner the market.[63]

The compound manager regularly raided the compound for illicit beer, but never before certain mutually understood procedures were followed. The system worked this way. When management periodically cracked down on compound brewers, the mine police were detailed by the compound manager to raid the rooms for beer. Before doing so they were to notify the chief and the *indunas* of their intentions. Rather than taking confiscated liquor directly to the compound manager they reported to the *induna* of the compound. The *induna* took the beer to Sobhuza's representative, Mhau or Zece. The chief then reported the details to the compound manager, who destroyed the alcohol and fined (or discharged) the offender.

There was thus a clear chain of command within the compound, recognized by both workers and management, that gave Sobhuza's representative a great deal of discretionary power over who would and would not be prosecuted. The evidence is clear that he exercised those discretionary powers and that not all cases were reported. The testimony of Dick Bhayi, a mine policeman, is particularly instructive here:

> I took the [confiscated] beer to the chief because I understood that anything illegal which was found should be taken to the chief. I thought the chief would send for me. When I came through the chief I did it according to native custom. When I realized that native custom was getting me no further I had to take other action. The Compound Manager might have got to hear on his own and he would have blamed me.[64]

Bhayi's reference to "native custom" is suggestive. It indicates, first, that the chief had successfully reproduced his rural authority in the mine compound. Although the circumstances were different, the bringing of confiscated beer to the chief would have been perfectly acceptable, since it probably resonated with the rural practices of tribute and gift giving outlined above. The redistribution of such "tribute" to clients, followers, and visitors was a persistent feature of rural society. In the compounds, by redistributing confiscated alcohol, rather than passing it on to mine management, the chief could draw on existing rural practices to enhance his prestige, confirm his generosity, and secure his reputation. By going first to Zece, Bhayi indicated that he was perfectly aware of the procedures of the moral economy. In defense of his subsequent decision to violate those procedures, he claimed that he had been scared of the compound manager, Herbert Johnson.

Johnson had been on the mine since 1939 and was never particularly popular with the workers. However, he appears to have observed the informal rules of the moral economy for much of the time. In 1943 the company began a major production drive to increase the output of an important war material. Production at Havelock doubled in a year (table 14.1). As part of that process, the company decided to tighten up on discipline in the compound. In late 1943 Johnson began to systematically break the bounds of the moral economy. He began by introducing a system of fines for "loafing" and warned that any worker caught shirking would be "given a hiding." He began administering corporal punishment—"I give them two strokes on the buttocks"—for such offenses as trying to obtain more than one meat ration, changing a work ticket, and "cheek." Beerhall profits had been

Table 14.1: Wartime asbestos production in Swaziland, 1939–1946

Year	Quantity (Tons)	Value (£)
1939	4,591	95,903
1940	20,804	436,756
1941	21,127	507,364
1942	25,595	647,200
1943	16,907	444,413
1944	32,659	886,090
1945	23,416	665,362
1946	32,138	844,631

Source: *South African Mining and Engineering Journal,* 8 March 1947.

falling, so in January 1944 he launched a systematic attack on illegal brewing in the compound. He started raiding the compound himself and made the mine police personally responsible for beer found in their sections. If the police failed to notify the manager about brewing activity, both they and the brewer were fined or discharged.[65] This policy placed the police in an invidious position.

At the end of January 1944, Dick Bhayi became aware of brewing activity in a house in the married quarters. He raided the house without telling Chief Zece and confiscated six drums of fermenting beer. He took the beer to Zece's. It became apparent to him that Zece had no intention of telling the compound manager when the chief later began handing out the beer to people in the compound. To save his own skin, Bhayi then took the unprecedented step of reporting the incident to Herbert Johnson.[66] Johnson was furious. He rebuked Zece in public, launched a series of personal raids on the compound, and fired two *indunas* for failing to control brewing. That night the *indunas* met to plan their protest against Johnson's violations of the moral economy of the mine.

Mobilizing the workers proved extremely easy. In the ensuing riot, the logic of the mob was transparent. The protesters attacked Johnson's offices (and Johnson himself the next day on the soccer field), ransacked Dick Bhayi's quarters, and destroyed the beerhall and brewery. Nothing and no one else on mine property was touched. After completing their job the workers returned to their compound and refused to move until their grievances against Johnson were addressed.

THE AFTERMATH

The strike had demonstrated that what Michael Burawoy calls the "apparatuses of the company state" could not effectively function without more direct colonial involvement.[67] To that point, the colonial state had played a largely passive role, collecting its share of mine profits and intervening in "production politics" only when requested.

After the strike, the colonial state became more interventionist and therefore assumed a much closer and public identification with the interests of big capital in the country. In dealing with the strikers, colonial officials were determined to demonstrate that violence was an unacceptable response to worker dissatisfaction. Sobhuza's representatives concurred in speeches to the workforce at the end of the inquiry. Twenty-three workers were tried away from the mine property and convicted of public mischief, with sentences ranging from six months' to three years' imprisonment.[68]

The Assistant District Commissioner at Piggs Peak was officially reprimanded for failing to visit the mine regularly before the strike. Thereafter, he was ordered to keep in weekly contact with the mine manager, compound manager, and Sobhuza's representative. Funds were also appropriated from the public purse to pay for him to place "trusties" (spies) in the compound.[69] The District Commissioner was instructed to hold a weekly court at the mine and the administration built, equipped, and staffed a police station on the mine property. The station was paid for out of a disguised grant from Colonial Development and Welfare Act funds.[70] The administration also decided to swear in the mine's 120 white male employees as special police. The state later equipped the force with a Bren gun, seventy rifles, training, and a rifle range.[71]

In the aftermath of the strike, mine management intensified its rhetorical onslaught against the brewers and residents of Skroof's, virtually blaming Sikuluvu and his followers for the whole affair. The investigation uncovered no direct evidence of any collusion, and colonial officials repeatedly exonerated Sikuluvu in private conversation and correspondence.[72] But they were alive to the possibilities of the moment. In public meetings with Sobhuza they adopted the company's position:

> You will all know how the Swazis working at Havelock Mine were foolish enough to join in a riot and do a lot of damage to the mine. . . . Many people also lived on the Native Area next to the mine, where the Chief had allowed them to come and live, although they had no claim to land there. Many of these people were brewing beer and putting medicine into

it, and selling it in the mine compound, which is forbidden by law. I cannot allow a lot of undesirable good-for-nothing lawbreakers to hang about the neighbourhood of the mine.[73]

Police raids on Skroof's intensified dramatically in the weeks after the strike.[74] Large quantities of *sigomfane* and *makajano* were destroyed. South African police joined in the effort by cracking down on brewers over the Transvaal border.

The state ordered a census of Skroof's and began evicting "undesirables" (including the Zionist pastor). To get round the constitutional issue, the Resident Commissioner used the Swaziland Defence Regulations of 1939, which gave him the power to protect the interests of a vital wartime industry.[75] The use of emergency regulations in this context was a patent abuse of the Regulations, as the Resident Commissioner privately admitted. Sobhuza protested vigorously. The administration backed down on its plans to completely eradicate Skroof's, adopting instead a policy of intensive policing of the settlement.[76] The "constant irritant" of police harassment produced numerous convictions in the years following the strike. By the late 1940s the number of prosecutions had fallen markedly.[77] In 1947 the state reopened negotiations with Sobhuza for the exchange of NA3.[78]

The inquiry into the strike placed much of the blame on the compound manager, though it failed to place his behavior in the context of the production imperatives of the mine. Despite a long history with the company, Johnson was viewed as "temperamentally unsuited" for the post by the government secretary. The administration recommended his transfer from Havelock. The company initially agreed to remove Johnson and then refused.[79] Starkey, the mine manager, argued that to transfer Johnson right after the strike would be seen as a victory for the workers and a vindication of their protests. The local administration referred the issue to London. In November 1944 the Undersecretary of State met with the chairman of Turner and Newall and urged that Johnson be removed.[80] Johnson was reigned in by management and finally transferred to Shabani in September 1945. As Dunbar Moodie suggests, the security of tenure of the compound manager and the bounds of the moral economy were inseparable.[81]

Burawoy has argued that strikes on the Zambian Copperbelt in the early 1940s dramatically demonstrated that tribal elders were becoming ineffective for industrial conciliation and therefore unreliable for social control.[82] In Swaziland the outcome of the 1944 Havelock strike was exactly the opposite. The strike reinforced rather than undermined the chain of command within the compound. Dick Bhayi, for example, was easily sacrificed and the mine dismissed him immediately; ironically, for following orders that transgressed the moral economy of the compound. Chief Zece played no role in the strike and, indeed, was unable to exercise any control over the rioters. Yet at no point in the enquiry did any of the numerous witnesses question his authority and actions. On the contrary, the witnesses worked hard to keep Zece on side by protesting his treatment by the compound manager. Prominent among the list of grievances was an extraordinary complaint that Johnson had called Zece a "bloody swine" in an exchange fully four months before the strike.[83]

The authority of Sobhuza's representative was enhanced by the king's speedy reaction to the workers' call for outside mediation in the strike. In the aftermath of the strike, the company restructured its lines of communication with the compound. The chief was now given immediate and regular access to both the mine manager and the district commissioner. This simultaneously reduced the autocratic power of the compound manager and enhanced the prestige of Sobhuza's representative on the mine. This system was to prove a workable option on the mine for at least another decade. By the mid-1950s all the major industrial concerns in Swaziland employed Swazi *indunas* and a chief appointed by Sobhuza to keep the peace.[84] Ten years later, however, the limitations of the system were beginning to show. When the entire workforce went on strike again at Havelock in 1963, one of their major grievances was against the mine *indunas* and Sobhuza's representative on the mine.[85]

ACKNOWLEDGEMENTS

I am grateful to the Social Sciences and Humanities Research Council of Canada for funding the research on which this paper is based. I wish to thank Miranda Miles and Wiseman Chirwa for their assistance with oral interviews, and Hilda Kuper for her insights into the situation in Swaziland in the 1930s.

NOTES

1. An earlier version of this paper was published as "Customary Rights and Compound Control in Late Colonial Swaziland," *South African Sociological Review* 2 (1989).

2. A. Booth, "The Development of the Swazi Labour Market, 1900–1968," *South African Labour Bulletin* 7 (1982): 34–57; and A. Booth, "Capitalism and the Competition for Swazi Labour, 1945–60," *Journal of Southern African Studies* 13 (1986): 125–50.

3. Swaziland National Archives (SNA), file 15A, Resident Commissioner's Speech to Swazi National Council, 22 May 1944; also reported in the *Times of Swaziland,* 1 June 1944.

4. SNA, RCS 647/09, Coryndon to Secretary, Transvaal Liquor Commission, 30 September 1909.

5. SNA, RCS 171/39, Letter of S. B. Williams, 5 May 1930; see also "Editorial: Beer and Business," *Times of Swaziland,* 14 December 1939.

6. H. Beemer, "Notes on the Diet of the Swazi in the Protectorate," *Bantu Studies* 13 (1939), p. 200.

7. See J. Crush, *The Struggle for Swazi Labour, 1890–1920* (Montreal and Kingston: McGill–Queen's Press, 1987), pp. 56, 73–75.

8. Beemer, "Diet of the Swazi," p. 217.

9. Ibid., p. 218.

10. Ibid., p. 221; SNA, RCS 647/09, Coryndon to Secretary, Transvaal Liquor Commission, 30 September 1909, pp. 3–4.

11. Interview with Mbonwa Hlope, Enkamazi, August 1990 (conducted by Miranda Miles).

12. Beemer, "Diet of the Swazi," p. 217.

13. H. Kuper, *An African Aristocracy* (London: Oxford University Press, 1947), pp. 186, 197–225; B. Marwick, *The Swazi* (Cambridge: Cambridge University Press, 1940), pp. 13, 33–36, 102–3, 131–32.

14. Kuper, *African Aristocracy,* pp. 144–48.

15. Crush, *Struggle for Swazi Labour,* p. 205.

16. Kuper, *African Aristocracy,* p. 147.

17. Kuper contrasts three weeding parties that she observed. One, called by a chief, lasted two days, involved about 30 workers, who were rewarded with approximately 20 gallons of beer. The other two lasted a day. At the first, given by a "rich" homestead, there were 36 workers, who shared 8 gallons of beer (with pumpkins for the Christian converts). At the other, given by a "poor" homestead, 18 workers had to share 1 gallon of beer; see Kuper, *African Aristocracy*, p. 146.

18. Ibid., p. 154. Interview with Hilda Kuper, Los Angeles, November 1990.

19. SNA, Minutes of the 4th Session of the 6th European Advisory Council, 22 December 1937; and Beemer, "Diet of the Swazi," p. 227.

20. Crush, *Struggle for Swazi Labour,* pp. 167–89; and J. Crush, "Tin, Time and Space in the Valley of Heaven," *Transactions of Institute of British Geographers* 13 (1988): 211–21.

21. SNA, Minutes of the 3rd Session of the 7th European Advisory Council, 1941.

22. Crush, "Tin, Time and Space"; and Crush, *Struggle for Swazi Labour,* pp. 126–27.

23. H. Kuper, *The Uniform of Colour* (Johannesburg: University of Witwatersrand Press, 1947), pp. 12–13.

24. A. Pim, *Financial and Economic Situation of Swaziland: Report of the Commission Appointed by the Secretary of State for Dominion Affairs* (London: Dominions Office, 1932), pp. 16–17.

25. SNA, file 1246I, Suggested Exchange for Adjoining Land, New Amianthus Mines.

26. SNA, DO9/2, Partition notes of George Grey, 1909.

27. P. Scott, "Mineral Development in Swaziland," *Economic Geography* 26 (1950): 196–213.

28. "Swaziland's Great Mine," *Times of Swaziland,* 6 March 1941.

29. SNA, Piggs Peak District Commissioner, file 44c, Mining Returns, 1944.

30. I. Phimister, "African Labour Conditions and Health in the Southern Rhodesian Mining Industry, 1898–1953," in *Studies in the History of African Mine Labour in Colonial Zimbabwe,* ed. I. Phimister and C. van Onselen, (Gwelo: Mambo Press, 1978), pp. 102–50.

31. SNA, C191, vol. 1, Annual Report by Chief of Police, 1936.

32. Interview with D. Fitzpatrick, Mbabane, 17 March 1982.

33. For descriptions of conditions at Havelock see "Native Welfare at the Havelock Mine," *Times of Swaziland,* 15 May 1941; "Swaziland's Great

Mine," *Times of Swaziland,* 6 March 1941; "A Swazi Visits the Havelock," *Times of Swaziland,* 22 November 1945, 29 November 1945; Kuper, *Uniform of Colour,* p. 13.

34. "A Swazi Visits the Havelock," *Times of Swaziland,* 22 November 1945, 29 November 1945.

35. SNA, file 1246I, Suggested Exchange for Adjoining Land, New Amianthus Mines.

36. SNA, RCS 659, List of Habitations and Population on Reserved Portion NA3.

37. SNA, RCS 659, Memorandum on Sikuluvu Dlamini, 21 August 1944.

38. "Native Beer Hall," *Times of Swaziland,* 18 January 1940.

39. SNA, RCS 659, Memorandum on Sikuluvu Dlamini, 21 August 1944.

40. SNA, Minutes of the 4th Session of the 6th European Advisory Council, 22 December 1937, statement by Resident Commissioner; SNA, RCS 726/37, Application to Establish Brewery at Havelock Mine.

41. Ibid., and SNA, RCS 630/39–55/40, Annual Reports from District Commissioners, Peak District, 1939.

42. SNA, C191, vol.1, Starkey to Armstrong, 22 February 1944.

43. Crush, *Struggle for Swazi Labour,* pp. 131–66.

44. SNA, RCS 726/37, Notes of Meeting of Resident Commissioner with Paramount Chief, 15 March 1939; RCS 37A, Minute by E. Featherstone, 11 May 1944.

45. SNA, RCS 659, Sobhuza II to Armstrong, 5 May 1944. Sobhuza's view that this was an important question of principle was clearly influenced by his involvement at the time in renewed attempts to regain land lost earlier in the century; see H. Kuper, *Sobhuza II: Ngwenyama and King of Swaziland* (London: Duckworth, 1978), pp. 75–96.

46. D. Moodie, "The Moral Economy of the Black Miners' Strike of 1946," *Journal of Southern African Studies* 13 (1986): 1–35; and D. Moodie, "The 1946 Black Miners' Strike" (Paper presented at African Studies Seminar, Queen's University, 1988); see also E. P. Thompson, "The Moral Economy of the English Crowd in the Eighteenth Century," *Past and Present* 50 (1971): 76–136.

47. J. Scott, *Weapons of the Weak* (New Haven: Yale University Press, 1985), p. 328.

48. Ibid., p. 345.

49. Thompson, "Moral Economy of the English Crowd," pp. 78–79; see also A. Charlesworth and A. Randall, "Morals, Markets and the English Crowd in 1766," *Past and Present* 114 (1987): 200–13.

50. This was one element in Sobhuza's broader strategy to shore up the monarchy and consolidate Dlamini power; see H. Macmillan, "A Nation Divided? The Swazi in Swaziland and the Transvaal, 1865–1986," in *The Creation of Tribalism in Southern Africa*, ed. L. Vail (London: James Currey, 1989), pp. 299–310; H. Macmillan, "Administrators, Anthropologists and 'Traditionalists' in Swaziland: The Case of the amaBhaca Fines" (unpublished paper, Department of History, University of Zambia, nd); and L. Vail and L. White, *Power and the Praise Poem* (London: James Currey, 1991), pp. 155–97.

51. Interview with Hilda Kuper.

52. Kuper, *Sobhuza II,* p. 100.

53. SNA, C191, vol. 1, Report on Havelock Mine Disturbance, 15 February 1944, statement by Fenisi Mtombela.

54. Interview with B. C. Chirwa, Malawi, March 1990 (conducted by Wiseman Chirwa).

55. SNA, C191, vol. 1, Statement by Herbert Johnson.

56. Ibid., Featherstone to Harlech, 17 February 1944.

57. Public Records Office (PRO), DO 35/1179, Harlech to Machtig, 10 February 1944.

58. PRO, DO 35/1179, Featherstone to Harlech, 3 February 1944.

59. See SNA, C191, vol. 1, Inquiry into Complaints of Native Strikers on the Havelock Mine; and PRO, DO 35/1179, Swaziland Mining: Disturbance at Havelock.

60. "The Havelock Riot," *Times of Swaziland,* 17 February 1944.

61. SNA, file 15A, Resident Commissioner's Speech to Swazi National Council, 22 May 1944.

62. SNA, C191, vol. 1, Featherstone to Harlech, 17 February 1944.

63. Interview with B. C. Chirwa.

64. SNA, C191, vol. 1, Statement by Dick Bhayi.

65. Ibid., Statement by Herbert Johnson.

66. One informant suggests that Bhayi was "loyal" to Johnson and was receiving special privileges from him. The potential loss of these privileges may have been another reason for Bhayi's actions; see interview with B. C. Chirwa.

67. M. Burawoy, *The Politics of Production* (London: Verso, 1985), p. 220.

68. "Havelock Riot," *Times of Swaziland,* 13 April 1944.

69. SNA, RCS 657, Police: Havelock Special Constables.

70. SNA, RCS 658, Police Post at Havelock Mine

71. SNA, C191, vol. 2, Brigadier to Resident Commissioner, 23 May 1946.

72. PRO, DO 35/1179, Tait to Shepherd, 12 May 1944; SNA, RCS 37A, Government Secretary to New Amianthus Mines, July 1944; RCS 659, Assistant District Commissioner (Peak) to Acting District Commissioner (Mbabane), 13 July 1944.

73. Speech by Resident Commissioner, reported in *Times of Swaziland,* 1 June 1944.

74. SNA, RCS 659, Starkey to Armstrong, 21 August 1944.

75. High Commissioners Notice no. 123 of 1939.

76. SNA, RCS 659, Minutes of Annual Meeting of General Council of Chiefs, 22–31 May 1944.

77. SNA, DC Peak District, file 37A, Minute by E. Featherstone, 11 May 1944; Assistant District Commissioner to Government Secretary, 6 December 1946.

78. SNA, file 1246II, Minutes of Meeting of Resident Commissioner and Native Authority, 1 August 1947.

79. PRO, DO 35/1179, Huggard to Machtig, 14 September 1944.

80. PRO, DO 35/1179, Machtig to Baring, 27 December 1944.

81. Moodie, "Moral Economy."

82. Burawoy, *Politics of Production,* p. 229.

83. SNA, C191, vol. 1, Inquiry into Complaints of Native Strikers on the Havelock Mine, Complaint no. 3.

84. D. McCullough, "Labour in the Swaziland Sugar Industry, 1945–1965," (M.A. thesis, Ohio University, 1989).

85. SNA, DC 262A, "A Board of Enquiry into the Trade Dispute at the Havelock Mine. Report of the Board of Enquiry," pp. 15–22.

CHAPTER FIFTEEN

THE SHEBEEN QUEEN AND THE EVOLUTION OF BOTSWANA'S SORGHUM BEER INDUSTRY

Steven Haggblade

INTRODUCTION

IN BOTSWANA, AS in much of Africa, sorghum beer is big business. Households consume 15 to 20 percent of all grain in the form of sorghum beer, making it by far the most popular prepared beverage in the country (table 15.1).[1] Its prominence arises from historic importance in the social and religious spheres, which has translated, in modern times, into strong preference for its characteristic murky consistency, effervescence, and refreshing sour taste. Sorghum beer retails for only 10 to 15 percent of the cost of western "clear" beer. This modest price combined with low alcohol content and acknowledged nutritional reputation ensures continued widespread popularity.[2] For many years, home brewers met Botswana's entire demand for sorghum beer. They produced small batches, 50 to 200 liters at a time, with simple metal drums, woven strainers, and wooden paddles. Catering to steadily growing demand, the women home brewers gradually developed a vast cottage industry. In the early 1980s, roughly 30 percent of all households earned regular income from sorghum beer production, making it the largest nonfarm employer in the country.[3]

Table 15.1: Botswana liquor market, 1981

Beverage	Sales			
	Volume		*Value*	
			*Pula**	
	('000 liters)	*percent*	*million*	*percent*
Sorghum beer (home-brewed)	74,000	55.3	7.2	17.8
Sorghum beer (factory)	28,725	21.5	6.7	16.5
Other homemade brews	16,300	12.2	2.1	5.2
Clear beer	13,441	10.0	18.1	44.7
Wine	760	0.6	2.1	5.2
Hard liquor	552	0.4	4.3	10.6
Total	133,778	100.0	40.5	100.0

* Pula = $0.83 (mid-1990)

Source: Haggblade, "Shebeen Queen."

The huge domestic market for sorghum beer attracted Botswana's first modern manufacturing industry in 1965, when factory brewers expanded into Botswana from their base in Rhodesia and Zambia. Since the mid-1960s, factory-brewed sorghum beer has spurted to prominence, increasing its market share while eroding the position of the home brewers. The economic implications of that transition are considerable. This chapter aims to describe the changes which have taken place in Botswana's sorghum beer industry as well as the forces shaping that evolution. After tracing the emergence of commercial brewing, discussion focuses on the interactions among four key actors in the industry: home brewers, factory brewers, district governments, and licensed retailers.[4]

THE RISE OF CASH HOME BREWING

Women have been brewing sorghum beer in Botswana since at least the eighteenth-century immigration of Tswana peoples to the perimeter of the Kalahari.[5] Until the late nineteenth century women produced not for sale but primarily for social functions—weddings, funerals, celebrations of the harvest, for visitors and ceremonies of all kinds. Beer served as a medium of exchange in a network of reciprocal village relationships, the most important of which involved brewing to mobilize village labor for collective work on individual fields. During that era, brewers allocated their beer according to social protocol. They presented the communal gourd first to those of high social rank—the elders and the men. Women followed or drank separately, while youths and children primarily received the recycled dregs.[6]

Several forces combined to transform socially allocated home brewing into a huge, cash-based cottage industry. First was the gradual emergence of a cash economy, promoted initially by traders who opened up shops in Bechuanaland in the mid-nineteenth century.[7] Later, the protectorate government accelerated that monetization by demanding cash payment of a hut tax beginning in 1899 and a supplementary native tax in 1919.[8] Second, mine labor migration to South Africa directly propelled cash brewing to prominence by boosting both supply and demand. On the supply side, many observers have highlighted the causal link between the rise of mine labor migration, the emergence of female-headed households in rural areas, and the beginning of cash home brewing as these households attempted to support themselves with one of the few marketable skills they all possessed, the ability to brew beer. On the demand side, because young mine workers returned to the villages with cash in hand, they were able to command through purchase the quantities of sorghum beer that social allocation procedures had previously limited.[9] As Cooper has observed, "female beer selling is simply the reverse side of the male migrant labor coin."[10] Consequently, the beginning of mine labor migration to South Africa in the 1870s provides probably the best guide for dating the emergence of cash brewing in Bechuanaland.[11]

From its modest beginnings in the late nineteenth century, cash home brewing rode successive waves of increased demand. As the only alcoholic beverage legally available to blacks under protectorate rule, sorghum beer captured the full benefit of growing cash income and migrant remittances. After 1934, when the protectorate government lifted restrictions on mine labor recruitment north of twenty-two degrees south latitude, spending surged rapidly as the growing number of returning young mine laborers substantially enlarged the demand for sorghum beer.[12] In the 1960s rapid erosion of tribal restrictions on drinking, which village leaders had previously imposed in many parts of Botswana, unleashed a second wave of increased beer consumption.[13] As a result, Botswana's sorghum beer industry was growing rapidly when factory brewers emerged to contest the market in the mid-1960s.

THE INTRODUCTION OF FACTORY BREWING

Factory brewing of sorghum beer began in South Africa and Southern Rhodesia around 1910 to supply growing concentrations of black male workers in mines and emerging urban centers.[14] While some centers attempted to supply sorghum beer by supervising batteries of licensed women brewers, the frequent limits on female residence in urban areas and the possibility of generating township revenue motivated most municipalities to experiment with large-scale brewing, either on their own or under contract to private brewing firms.[15]

These emerging factory brewers encountered severe technical problems as they attempted to scale up production several orders of magnitude from the 50- to 200-liter batches common among cash home brewers. They experienced problems with malt quality, temperature during brewing, rapid spoilage, and uneven quality of their final product.[16] Consequently, factory brewing of sorghum beer languished until the late 1950s and early 1960s, when, with the aid of important applied scientific research, the brewers resolved the major technical problems involved in scaling up production.[17] During the intervening fifty years (between 1910 and 1960), private firms and municipal governments in Northern and Southern Rhodesia and South Africa experimented with factory brewing, enjoying varying degrees of success.

By the mid-1960s, two major forces had emerged among southern Africa's factory producers of sorghum beer. The first was a private company, Heinrich's Syndicate, which controlled the bulk of factory sorghum beer production in Zambia and was making considerable inroads in Rhodesia's municipal markets. Second, in contrast, were the publicly owned municipal breweries that supplied the entire urban sorghum beer market in South Africa, a hegemony legally enforced from 1962 onward by government-legislated monopoly.[18]

The expansion of factory brewing outside its initial spawning grounds in the mines and urban townships of Zambia, Rhodesia, and South Africa was largely the work of Heinrich's Syndicate. Municipal governments in the three countries had no mandate or incentive to expand beyond their own boundaries. But as a private, profit-making concern, Heinrich's did. Originally one of many small companies struggling to master the technology of large-scale sorghum beer production, Heinrich's Syndicate outlasted its rivals, buying some out and outcompeting others. Lonrho, the large Rhodesian-British multinational, bought out Heinrich's Syndicate in 1963, splitting the group into two separate companies: National Breweries, with headquarters in Zambia, and Heinrich's Chibuku, based in Rhodesia. Under Lonrho, Heinrich's Chibuku spearheaded much of the expansion of factory brewing outside its original three-country cradle to the surrounding countries of Malawi, Swaziland, and Botswana.[19]

In 1964, in the North East District of what was still the Bechuanaland Protectorate, the Tati Company established the first brewery in the territory to supply their new beerhall in Francistown. But Heinrich's Chibuku moved in quickly. In 1965 it entered into a partnership with the Tati Company to produce Chibuku brand sorghum beer for the Francistown beerhall. Incorporated as Bechuanaland Breweries, the local subsidiary opened a second brewery in Gaborone shortly after independence in 1966. Rechristened Botswana Breweries, Heinrich's Botswana subsidiary thus positioned its breweries in the country's two major towns, one at each end of the populous eastern strip that housed 80 percent of the country's population (see fig. 15.1).

The initial injection of factory-brewed sorghum beer generated tension, especially in rural areas of Botswana, where many observers feared it could displace home brewing. Speaking in the early years of Chibuku expansion into the rural communities around Francistown, a prominent local politician voiced this common concern. He empha-

ANGOLA

ZAMBIA

ZIMBABWE
Southern Rhodesia

NAMIBIA

Chobe

Ngamiland

North East
District

Central

△ FRANCISTOWN

△
Mmandinare

Ghanzi

Palapye △

Kweneng

Kgatleng

GABORONE

Southern

Kgalagadi

South East
District

SOUTH AFRICA

—·— International Boundary

——— District Boundary

——— Railway

▲ Breweries

△ Failed Breweries

0   200

km

15.1 Breweries in Botswana

sized that "the failure of parents to pay school fees for children was
created by the sale of Chibuku which has now made traditional beer a
thing of the past from which parents used to get money to educate
their children."[20] Home brewers likewise feared the repercussions of
a declining market share in the face of competition from factory-
brewed Chibuku.[21] They resisted when Chibuku was first introduced

into the villages surrounding Francistown in late 1968 and early 1969. In the villages of Mapoka and Moroka in North East District, home brewers destroyed crates of Chibuku as the first distributors attempted to unload it. Strong-arm escorts reportedly accompanied subsequent deliveries, assuring the unloading of Chibuku and upending drums of home-brewed sorghum beer in retaliation.[22]

GOVERNMENT RETAILING LEGISLATION

The dramatic expansion of Chibuku sales in the late 1960s and the protest it generated attracted government attention. The authorities responded in short order, promulgating the Traditional Beer Retailing Bye-Laws in 1970. Formulated during the initial conflagrations and undoubtedly influenced by them, these retailing regulations embodied four principles that continued to govern sorghum beer retailing in Botswana into the 1980s.

First, local government authorities—the town councils in urban communities and district councils in rural areas—were charged with regulating the retailing of sorghum beer. That stance emulated precedents recently established in Zambia and Rhodesia. It was likewise consistent with local government regulation of all other retailing in Botswana. Second, the legislation specified that retailing of home-brewed sorghum beer was to remain, as in the past, unregulated by government authorities. Third, the law required that retailers setting up businesses to retail factory-brewed sorghum beer obtain a license from the district or town council in whose jurisdiction they wished to operate. Fourth, the new regulations exempted home retailers of factory-brewed sorghum beer from licensing requirements. The legislation provided special dispensation for shebeen owners (the "shebeen queens"), stating that "within the boundaries of a *lolwapa* [the traditional family compound] traditional beer may be sold and bought from persons engaging, for the purposes of subsistence or the maintenance and education of children, in the sale of traditional beer."[23] Since all households have subsistence needs or children to educate, the law effectively exempted home retailers of factory-brewed sorghum beer from the licensing requirement.[24] By extending to home brewers the privilege of retailing factory-brewed sorghum beer without a license, the retailing statute enabled home brewers to supplement sagging home-brewing revenue by selling Chibuku.

FACTORY EXPANSION STRATEGIES

Heinrich's Syndicate, formed in 1955, quickly established itself as the only major private company to have mastered the technical difficulties involved in factory brewing of sorghum beer. They combined that technical expertise with attractive packaging and clever marketing to expand sales in Zambia, Rhodesia, and subsequently Botswana. That strategy, coupled with consistent product quality, helped them supplant municipal brewers in Zambia. In Rhodesia, too, it helped as they encircled often defiant municipalities, ultimately outcompeting all but Bulawayo.[25] The trademark red-white-and-blue one-liter carton contributed to their success in Botswana as did their "shake shake" slogan with its admonition to "shake before you drink." The modern image conferred by the brightly colored Chibuku cartons also enhanced its popularity, especially among the young.

But solid technical and marketing fundamentals were not enough to guarantee expansion, as Heinrich's knew from previous uncomfortable experience in the spotlight. Heinrich's forced retreat from Malawi in 1964, Rhodesia's moratorium on Chibuku brewing licenses in the early 1960s after complaints by municipal brewers, the acknowledged resentment of home brewers in Rhodesia, the common venting of black outrage on beerhalls established to sell factory-brewed sorghum beer, and the outbursts against Chibuku by Botswana politicians and home brewers surely impressed management at Lonrho and Botswana Breweries.[26] These episodes convinced them that the key to survival and growth lay in widespread distribution of profits to influential individuals and institutions. The company preferred to retain a modest share of steadily growing Chibuku profits over no revenue at all.

The fundamental instinct for self-preservation led Botswana Breweries to adopt several practices that enlarged their market share by aligning the financial interest of powerful domestic institutions with the expansion of Chibuku sales. First, the company deliberately refrained from retailing its own product. Since retailing generated approximately two-thirds of all domestic Chibuku profits, that policy produced a network of Chibuku boosters among the country's 150 licensed sorghum beer retailers, many of whom were district councillors and influential political or business leaders. Not only did Botswana Breweries refrain from retailing, they actively promoted selling by others, offering informal supplier credits to both shebeens and licensed retailers. The brewery also regularly offered assistance in both design and construction finance to councils who wished to retail Chibuku.[27] As a further inducement, they actually helped some councils operate their municipal beerhalls.[28] To deflect criticism, the brewery periodically brandished this citizen-owned retailing network. In 1969, for example, in an article entitled "Chibuku Manufacturers Deny That Traditional Beer Is a 'Thing of the Past,'" the company argued that concerns about home brewer displacement were unfounded because "the retailing of Chibuku beer has been left in the hands of the local population."[29]

In another effort to entrench itself, Botswana Breweries followed standard practices developed in Zambia and Rhodesia by paying an excise tax to local government councils on every liter of Chibuku retailed in their jurisdiction. This Traditional Beer Levy provided a convenient source of revenue to cash-strapped local governments, since the brewery remitted payment directly to the councils each month. The beer levy effectively rendered the financial interest of the councils coincident with the commercial fortunes of Chibuku. Indeed, in 1981 a member of parliament publicly asked why government allowed the import of Tlokwe, a competing factory-brewed sorghum beer from South Africa, given that it did not pay the same excise levy as domestically manufactured Chibuku.[30]

The third pillar of Botswana Breweries' strategy was to attain a domestic monopoly on the production of factory-brewed sorghum beer. To that end, in the late 1960s the brewery offered to loan funds to each district and town council to construct a council beerhall if they, in return, would explicitly grant Chibuku a monopoly within the council's jurisdiction.[31] The Minister of Local Government and Lands short-circuited that attempt by forbidding the councils to enter into such agreements. As a result, during the 1970s at least two other companies attempted to compete with Botswana Breweries. One brewed sorghum beer in Mmadinare in the early 1970s, while another operated in Palapye for eighteen months in 1975 and 1976. Technical and quality control difficulties apparently forced the pretenders out of business.

In later years, Botswana Breweries made another important move in their effort to retain a production monopoly. In 1972 South African Breweries, the largest brewer of clear beer in South Africa, purchased Heinrich's Chibuku from Lonrho. Chibuku sales slumped after the transition, prompting South African Breweries to bring in an aggressive new management team in 1979. In addition to launching a surge in Chibuku sales (fig 15.2), the new managers successfully negotiated a partnership agreement with the Botswana Development Corporation (BDC), Botswana's government-owned investment company and

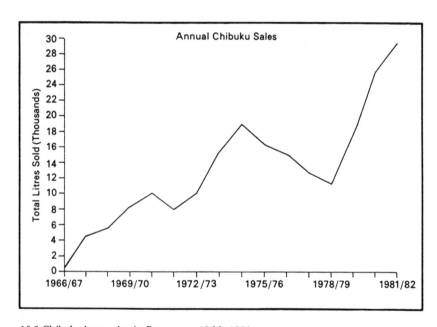

15.2 Chibuku beer sales in Botswana, 1966–1982

the last business group with the potential to mount a serious competitive threat to Chibuku's factory brewing supremacy.

Taken as a whole, this three-pronged spread-the-wealth strategy effectively harmonized the financial interests of Botswana Breweries with important political and business groups in the country.[32] Annual returns to capital in excess of 50 percent satisfied the Botswana Development Corporation and discouraged it from entering the arena to compete directly. By preempting competition from likely rivals and buying or outcompeting the others, Botswana Breweries retained its supremacy as the sole domestic producer of factory-brewed sorghum beer.

THE ROLE OF LICENSED RETAILERS

The decision of Botswana Breweries to stay out of sorghum beer retailing resulted in the development of an active network of licensed and unlicensed retailers. By the early 1980s over 58,000 home retailing establishments, or shebeens, operated in Botswana. Of those, 56,000 brewed and sold their own beer, while roughly 2,400 retailed factory-brewed sorghum beer. Chibuku was also sold through a network of 150 licensed retailers—beerhalls, beer gardens, and offsale outlets. Local councils owned a handful of those outlets, but the great majority were privately held. About 60 percent were owned by traders who expanded from other retailing lines into sorghum beer, while councillors or wives of civil servants owned most of the rest.

Licensed retailers, in particular, found sorghum beer retailing extremely attractive. One of the easiest imaginable businesses to operate, sorghum beer retailing meant dealing with a single supplier, stocking a single item in inventory, and charging a single price. It could therefore be run by unskilled staff. Moreover, because the short shelf life of sorghum beer guaranteed a complete stock turnover within three days, cash flow problems rarely arose. Large volumes combined with high margins and rapid turnover to make licensed retailing outlets immensely profitable cash machines. In 1982 the average licensed sorghum beer outlet earned annual returns of over 100 percent on investment, thereby generating profits of £2,800 in a country where per capita income stood at £600.[33]

The conduct of retail license holders was a central force shaping retail patterns. Because sorghum beer retailing was so lucrative, licensed retailers had incentives to control as large a volume of factory brew as possible. For that reason, many acted vigorously to prevent home retailers from obtaining Chibuku directly from delivery trucks at wholesale prices. They impressed on brewery drivers the necessity of delivering the factory brew to licensed depots and not stopping to unload at unlicensed shebeens along the way. The licensed retailers, some of them councillors, also lobbied district councils urging them to require shebeen procurement from licensed outlets. The shebeen queens, of course, strongly objected. Purchasing at retail prices eroded their profit margin considerably and relegated them to serving the riskier, high-price, credit sales end of the market.

The success of license holders in controlling the retailing of factory-brewed sorghum beer varied throughout the country. At one extreme was the South East District, where, for a time, the licensed outlets effectively prevented shebeens from selling any factory-brewed sorghum beer. In 1982 councillors held four of the eight sorghum beer retail licenses awarded by the council. At the same time, the council flagrantly misinterpreted the Traditional Beer Retailing Law by forbidding home selling of Chibuku. A complete enumeration of Tlokweng, the largest village in South East District, confirmed that no households were retailing factory-brewed sorghum beer.[34] While this case represented an extreme, licensed retailers in other regions also attempted to prevent the shebeens from obtaining factory-brewed sorghum beer except at retail prices. Distribution figures attest to their general success. Nearly 80 percent of all factory-brewed sorghum beer passed through licensed outlets. They retailed 70 percent directly and sold about 10 percent to the shebeens, who added further markups before redistributing to final consumers.

Easy to operate and extremely profitable, licensed sorghum beer outlets became an increasingly popular investment. Between 1980 and 1982 the number of outlets increased from zero to five in Serowe, Botswana's largest village. And in Kweneng District they nearly doubled, from thirteen to twenty-five. The expansion of production at Botswana Breweries, after 1979, coincided with the growing prominence of licensed retailers who, in turn, had every incentive to limit direct shebeen access to factory-brewed sorghum beer. Exclusionary practices by the licensed retailers diminished home brewers' prospects for a shift to Chibuku retailing in response to a declining market share for home-brewed beer.

HOME BREWER ACCOMMODATION

Initially, fearing they would be displaced, many home brewers opposed the introduction of "shake shake" in their villages. But since the late 1960s, Chibuku sales increased gradually across most of Botswana, so individual brewers did not feel the immediate impact of a competitive squeeze. Moreover, individual shebeen queens discovered that retailing Chibuku allowed them to earn satisfactory income without the physical effort required in home brewing. So in the 1970s and 1980s accommodation, rather than opposition, was the predominant response of home brewers to the expansion of Chibuku.

In the face of the increasing availability of factory-brewed competitors, some home brewers simply continued to brew their own beer for sale. Others retailed factory-brewed sorghum beer alongside their own. Still others specialized in Chibuku retailing. Where councils were hostile and shebeens had difficulty obtaining Chibuku, home brewers were left to contend with a shrinking market share for home brew. The choice of product mix was not simply a question of availability, however. It also depended on the resources available to the household, especially labor and working capital, and their opportunity cost. Equally important was the composition of consumer demand, which in turn depended on income levels, the prevalence of wage employment, and the proportion of young workers in the market.

Home brewers responded differently in urban areas than in villages. When Chibuku became available to village shebeen queens, most offered it for sale alongside their own home brew, allowing them to appeal to a range of consumers. In the small village of Serule in 1982, for example, 70 percent of the shebeens sold Chibuku along with their home brew. A few specialized Chibuku shebeens also emerged. Yet they retailed only a small fraction of total sorghum beer because of the large volume sold by licensed outlets and because the aggregate demand for home brew remained strong in village markets. In Serule, typical of many small villages, only 4 percent specialized in Chibuku sales. But in urban areas, substantially higher incomes, a high proportion of young consumers, and the prevalence of wage employment fueled demand for Chibuku. At the same time, scarcity of firewood, space constraints, and alternative employment opportunities for women diminished the profitability of home brewing. These twin forces—lower demand and increased costs—limited the home brewer market share in urban areas. Thus in the capital city of Gaborone, in 1982, over 50 percent of the shebeens selling sorghum beer sold only Chibuku; they offered no home brew. Of those shebeens, half also retailed clear beer to cater to the upscale urban income and tastes. Thus, the urban shebeens increasingly specialized in Chibuku because of its larger market share in the towns.

THE CONSEQUENCES

After nearly a century of steady growth, Botswana's cash home brewers have, since the mid-1960s, faced ferocious head-to-head competition from factory-brewed sorghum beer. Since 1965, when the technology necessary for domestic production of Chibuku poured in from surrounding countries, factory-brewed sorghum beer has captured 30 percent of the volume and 50 percent of the value of Botswana's sorghum beer sales. Because a cohort of specialized licensed outlets emerged to control 70 to 80 percent of Chibuku retailing, home brewers displaced by the growth of factory brewing were unable to fully substitute home retailing of Chibuku for lost brewing income.

The consequences of this transformation ran largely counter to the government's stated development objectives of income growth, employment creation, rural development, and improved income distribution. Instead, the introduction of factory-brewed sorghum beer led to the transfer of income from home brewers to wealthy traders and corporate balance sheets. Due to the introduction of Chibuku, full-time brewing employment—including home and factory brewing plus all retailing—dropped roughly 30 percent. At the same time, because of partial foreign ownership and the higher import content of Chibuku, national brewing and retailing income declined by about 6 percent.[35] And income distribution worsened considerably. The rise of factory brewing has consequently transferred earnings from poor and middle-income groups to the very wealthy, from women to men, and from rural to urban areas.

NOTES

1. For further details see S. Haggblade, "The Shebeen Queen" (Ph.D. diss., Michigan State University, 1984); and S. Haggblade, "Vertical Considerations in Choice-of-Technique Studies: Evidence from Africa's Indigenous Beer Industry," *Economic Development and Cultural Change* 35 (1987): 723–42.

2. L. Novellie, "Bantu Beer—Food or Beverage?" *Food Industries of South Africa* 16 (1963): 28; S. Haggblade and W. Holzapfel, "Industrialization of Africa's Indigenous Beer Brewing," in *Industrialization of Indigenous Fermented Foods*, ed. K. Steinkraus (New York: Dekker, 1989).

3. Haggblade, "Shebeen Queen."

4. The data reported in this chapter come from a five-month field study undertaken in 1982. The fieldwork included interviews with the only two sorghum maltsters operating in Botswana, the managers of the two sorghum beer breweries, and a stratified, nationally representative sample of 119 home brewers, 47 home retailers of factory-brewed sorghum beer, 9 licensed retailers and a control group of 138 households that did not brew or retail sorghum beer.

5. E. Rosenthal, *Tankards and Tradition* (Cape Town: Howard Timmins, 1961); C. Colclough and S. McCarthy, *The Political Economy of Botswana: A Study of Growth and Distribution* (New York: Oxford University Press, 1980).

6. D. Curtis, "Cash Brewing in a Rural Economy," *Botswana Notes and Records* 5 (1973): 17–25; J. Solway, "Socio-Economic Effects of Labour Migration in Western Kweneng," in *Papers Presented at National Migration*

Study Workshop, ed. C. Kerven (Gaborone: Government Printer, 1979); H. Wolcott, *The African Beer Gardens of Bulawayo* (New Brunswick, N.J.: Rutgers Center for Alcohol Studies, 1974); Rosenthal, *Tankards;* A. Richards, *Land, Labour and Diet in Northern Rhodesia: An Economic Study of the Bemba Tribe* (London: Oxford University Press, 1939).

7. I. Schapera, *Migrant Labour and Tribal Life: A Study of Conditions in the Bechuanaland Protectorate* (London: Oxford University Press, 1947).

8. D. Massey, "A Case of Colonial Collaboration: The Hut Tax and Migrant Labour," *Botswana Notes and Records* 10 (1977); Colclough and McCarthy, *Political Economy of Botswana.*

9. A. Sutherland, "Report on Research among the Bayei Peoples of the Okavango Delta" (Gaborone: Rural Sociology Unit, Ministry of Agriculture, 1976); O. Gulbrandson, *Agro-Pastoral Production and Communal Land Use* (Gaborone: Ministry of Agriculture, 1980); K. Kooijman, "Social and Economic Change in a Tswana Village," mimeographed (Leiden, 1978).

10. D. Cooper, "Rural-Urban Migration and Female-Headed Households in Botswana Towns," National Migration Study Working Paper no. 1 (Gaborone: Central Statistics Office, Ministry of Finance and Development Planning, 1979).

11. Schapera, *Migrant Labour and Tribal Life.*

12. On the importance of increased drinking by mine workers and young adults in expanding demand for home-brewed beverages see Curtis, "Cash Brewing in a Rural Economy"; Sutherland, "Bayei Peoples"; Solway, "Labour Migration in Western Kweneng"; Gulbrandson *Agro-Pastoral Production*; Kooijman, "Social and Economic Change"; S. Modimakwane, "The Beer Brewing Activity in Shakawe: The Party of Big Beer Brewers," in *UBS Student Surveys of Okavango Villages* (Gaborone: Ministry of Agriculture, 1978).

13. I. Schapera, *A Handbook of Tswana Law and Custom,* 2d ed. (London: International African Institute, 1959); Gulbrandson, *Agro-Pastoral Production;* A. Aguda, "Legal Development in Botswana from 1885 to 1966," *Botswana Notes and Records* 5 (1979).

14. Wolcott, *African Beer Gardens;* L. Novellie, "Kaffir Beer Brewing: Ancient Art and Modern Industry," *Wallerstein Laboratories Communications* 31 (April 1968); C. Rogerson and B. Tucker, "Commercialization and Corporate Capital in the Sorghum Beer Industry of Central Africa," *Geoforum* 16 (1986): 357–68; and R. Parry (in this collection).

15. L. Pan, *Alcohol in Colonial Africa* (Helsinki: Finnish Foundation for Alcohol Studies, 1975); Wolcott, *African Beer Gardens;* T. Oxford, *Journal of*

the Institute of Brewing 32 (1926): 314–16; C. Rogerson, "A Strange Case of Beer: The State and Sorghum Beer Manufacture in South Africa," *Area* 18 (1986): 15–24; Rogerson and Tucker, "Commercialization and Corporate Capital"; C. van Onselen, *Chibaro: African Mine Labour in Southern Rhodesia, 1900–1933* (London: Pluto, 1976).

16. Novellie, "Kaffir Beer"; and Haggblade and Holzapfel, "Africa's Indigenous Beer Brewing."

17. Novellie, "Kaffir Beer."

18. C. Rogerson (in this collection).

19. Rogerson and Tucker, "Commercialization and Corporate Capital"; and Haggblade, "Shebeen Queen."

20. *Botswana Daily News,* 14 January 1969.

21. Similar concern prevailed among home brewers in Rhodesia after the introduction of factory-brewed sorghum beer into rural areas; see J. May, "Drinking in a Rhodesian African Township," Occasional Paper no. 8, Department of Sociology, University of Rhodesia, 1973.

22. B. Egner (personal communication).

23. "Traditional Beer Model Retailing Bye-Laws," in *Laws of Botswana* (Gaborone: Government Printer, 1970), para. 3.1. In the language of the law, the term *traditional beer* refers to factory-brewed sorghum beer. A *lolwapa* is a traditional family compound.

24. This is not true for home retailing of clear beer and spirits. All retailing of those beverages does require a license. Shebeen queens who violate the requirement attract periodic confrontations with the law. See, for example, *Botswana Daily News,* 29 December 1979, 12 October 1982.

25. Rogerson and Tucker, "Commercialization and Corporate Capital."

26. Ibid.; Rogerson, "Strange Case of Beer"; I. Deacon, "The South African Liquor Industry" (Ph.D. diss., University of Stellenbosch, 1980); May, "Drinking in a Rhodesian African Township."

27. *Botswana Daily News,* 9 November 1969, 30 December 1981.

28. In 1982 Botswana Breweries operated council-owned beerhalls in Gaborone and Lobatse under a management contract with the town councils; see Haggblade, "Shebeen Queen."

29. *Botswana Daily News,* 14 January 1969.

30. *Botswana Daily News,* 4 December 1981. The Minister of Commerce and Industry responded that Tlokwe imports were consistent with Botswana's free-trade principles under the Southern African Customs Union Agreement. In 1982 Tlokwe accounted for 4 percent of factory-brewed sorghum beer sales in Botswana. Chibuku accounted for the remainder.

31. *Botswana Daily News,* 9 November 1969.

32. In 1981 Botswana Breweries earned about P32,000 (£19,000) in after-tax profit on every million liters of Chibuku they produced. They paid a roughly equal amount in taxes to both the central government and local government councils. Of the brewing income, 60 percent accrued to the Botswana Development Corporation. Meanwhile, retailers of Chibuku earned approximately triple the amount retained by the brewery. See "Botswana Breweries (Proprietary) Limited, Accounts 30th June 1981" (Gaborone: Registrar of Companies); and Haggblade, "Shebeen Queen," p. 213.

33. Haggblade, "Shebeen Queen," p. 190.

34. Ibid., p. 187.

35. Ibid., pp. 208, 233.

INDEX

European beer; Fruit beers; Grain beer; Honey beer; Hop beer; "Kaffir" beer; "Native" beer; Palm wine; Rum; Sorghum beer; Spirits; Sugar beer; traditional beer; *Utshwala;* Wine; and individual drinks: "Cape Smoke"; "Barberton"; Chibuku; *Doro; Gwebu; Isishimeyana; Khali;* "Kill-me-quick"; *Makajano; Mahewu/Marewu; Marula; Motopa; Mpekwa;* Palestine Bee Wine; *Oedeviki; Oilika; Rapoko; Sigomfane; Skokian;* Tlokwe

Alexandra, township of, 34

Amabutho system, 87

Amakholwa, 90

Amabele. See Sorghum

Amalaita. See Gangs

ANC. *See* African National Congress

Androcentrism, 209

Apartheid: controls over movement, 27; drinking under, 25, 307, 318–19, 320, 321, 330–32, 345; forced removals, 25, 178; protests against, 1; urban, 26, 306–7. *See also* Racism; Segregation

Asbestos production, Swaziland, 385

Assisted Voluntary Scheme (AVS), 282–83

Atkins, Keletso, 21

Ballenden, Graham, 175, 177

Balobedu, 8

Bambatha Rebellion (1906), 93, 96

Barberton (town), 374, 382

"Barberton" (drink), 290, 377

Barotseland, 14

Barracks. *See* Housing

Barrett-Young Committee, 21

Bars. *See* Beerhalls; Canteens; Shebeens; Taverns

Basutoland, 175, 280–83

Basutoland National Council, 281

Basotho, 201, 276; conflict with, 287–289; detribalization of, 283–84; employment of, 285; monopoly by, 283–84; pay for, 287

Basotho women, 270, 273, 280–82; abandonment of, 284–86; blame for, 277–78, 279, 291, 294; brewing by, 24, 286; immigration of, 279–80; liaisons with, 277; moral panic and, 274. *See also* Women

Baxter Committee of 1918, 44n64

Bazaars, 311–12

BDC. *See* Botswana Development Corporation

Bechuanaland. *See* Botswana

Bechuanaland Breweries. *See* Botswana Breweries

Beer: ceremonial, 255, 370–71, 397; on credit, 187, 193–96; fortifying, 143, 170, 176, 178, 194, 210, 384; health benefits of, 18, 121, 141, 142, 154; native, 18, 94–95, 347; quality of, 104, 125–26. *See also* Alcoholic beverages

Beer brewing. *See* Brewers; Brewing; Women brewers

Beer drinks, 30, 33, 200, 210, 240, 248, 252, 342, 344, 368, 370, 371, 373, 375, 397; attending, 167–68; communal, 34; crime and, 241; organizing, 262; regulating, 88; ritual killing and, 254–56, 257, 259–60, 264. See also *Umsindleko*

Beer gardens, 25, 32, 164; beerhalls and, 329; building, 319, 320, 322, 328, 330; description of, 32, 348; hours for, 325; locating, 329; map of, 328; sales at, 405

Beer-giving, significance of, 371–72

Beerhalls: attacks on, 1, 28, 34, 307, 315, 316, 347, 378, 382, 386, 402; attractiveness of, 31, 102, 194, 313, 314, 354; boycotting, 30, 104, 113n105, 130, 222, 226, 227, 288–89,

355; building, 99, 101, 210, 229n9, 295, 309, 312, 318, 322, 344–45, 346, 377, 403; closing, 20, 224, 228, 306, 321, 351, 353, 355–56; control of, 23, 25, 346, 352; criticism of, 26–28, 195, 212, 315–18, 331, 346, 349, 350, 351, 353, 354–55; decentralization of, 309, 319, 320, 323–26, 329; demise of, 354–55, 356; description of, 25, 99–100, 292–93, 307–8, 315, 346, 348, 354; establishment in Johannesburg, 307–9; exploitation by, 23, 103–4, 208; high quality, 353, 355, 364n75; hours for, 113n98, 324–25, 345; income from, 308, 310, 312–13, 315, 318, 332; inner-city, 310–11, 317–22, 324, 329; location, 20, 24–25, 307–9, 313–14, 320, 326–27, 331; map of, 308, 328; municipal, 20, 163, 173, 210, 218, 288–89, 313–14, 403; patronage of, 308, 313; political mobilization at, 355; profits from, 26, 27, 79, 98, 100, 126, 129–30, 131, 247, 295, 332, 347, 385–86, 405; raids on, 208, 216, 218, 219, 221–24, 350; relocating, 307, 310–11, 320–26; spatial pattern of (map), 323; support for, 310, 346; surveillance at, 19, 23, 31, 100–101, 348; white attitudes towards, 25, 311, 313, 317, 325, 327, 346; white exclusion from, 25; women and, 30, 133, 199, 212, 218. See also Canteens; Beer gardens; Mine beerhalls; various beerhalls

Beer monopoly, 1, 18, 21, 22, 26, 97, 123–31, 190, 196, 297, 306, 318, 344, 347, 356; beerhalls and, 309; benefits of, 100, 101, 113–14n108; development of, 18, 79, 95–96, 100, 102, 105, 105n3, 112n78; enforcing, 99, 127, 128, 135, 346, 350; morality

of, 102–3; opposition to, 27, 78, 112n90, 347, 355; problems for, 127, 128; profits from, 11, 79, 101, 125–26, 130, 351; segregation and, 22; spread of, 105, 105n3; support for, 26, 112n78

Beer parties. See Beer drinks
Beer protests, 24, 379, 380; male support for, 225–27; origins of, 209–16; women and, 209, 212, 214–17, 220, 222–25, 227–28. See also Boycotts; Resistance

Beer rations, 165, 200, 322, 326, 377, 378; drawing, 150–51; opposition to, 195; productivity and, 154; size of, 143

Beer sales, 229n11, 332, 358n11; attacking, 244–45; in Botswana, 346, 401–2, 404; control of, 116, 121, 135, 164, 190, 245–46, 251n34, 307, 401–2; decline in, 226, 293, 321; families and, 92; geography of (map), 330; increase in, 313, 315; labor migration and, 242–46; municipal, 293, 294, 311–12, 314; police and, 242; privatization of, 350–51; prohibiting, 241, 243, 344; revenues from, 26, 78, 96, 99–101, 124, 345, 346, 355; women and, 240, 247

Benoni, 176, 177, 273, 279, 289
Bhaca, 253
Binns, Percy, 97
"Black Christmas" campaigns, 34
Bloemfontein, 164
Boksburg, 176–77, 293
Botswana: beer selling in, 26–27; 396, 401–2, 404; breweries in (map), 400
Botswana Breweries, 399; beerhalls by, 403, 411n28; expanded production at, 407; income for, 412n32; market share of 402–3; monopoly for, 404; sorghum beer by, 402, 405; strategy of, 403–4

Botswana Development Corporation (BDC), 404–5, 412n32
Bottle stores, 1, 30. *See also* Offsale Outlets.
Boycotts, 30, 104, 126, 130, 133, 162, 170, 212, 214, 219, 221, 226, 288–89, 355; opposition to, 227; organizing, 34, 208; success of, 180, 213; women and, 209. *See also* Beer protests
Brailsford, E. A., 126, 127
Brakpan, 176, 273, 279, 290, 293
Brandy, 12, 14, 17, 68, 119, 144, 252
Brazil, 12
Breweries, 12, 25, 26, 124, 130; map of, 400
Brewers: canteens and, 131; confrontation with, 3, 241, 248, 293, 343, 384, 388; cunning of, 129; mine police and, 172, 342. *See also* Women brewers
Brewing: commercial, 26, 342, 343; community and, 163, 176, 264, 370; control of, 119, 123–26, 152, 176–77, 235, 241–43, 246, 289, 290, 291, 368; cottage industry, 26, 341, 343, 397; gender and, 131–32, 226, 370; illicit, 22, 23, 26, 27, 104, 123, 166, 199, 224, 245, 274, 275, 345, 377; income from, 33, 347; increase in, 238, 343; legalization of, 228, 243, 246; as political act, 247; prosecution for, 284, 294; rackets, 170–78; right to, 103, 170, 173, 215; ritual, 252, 370; rural, 27n11, 113n108, 239, 342, 371; syndicates and rings, 29; women and, 26–27, 132–33, 162, 218, 228, 235, 238–42, 244, 270, 281, 358n11. *See also* Factory brewing; Home brewing
Bridewealth, 282
British South Africa Company, 116, 357n2
Brothels. *See* Prostitution

Brussels Convention, 15
Buckle Commission, 165, 172
Bulawayo, 105, 402
Burawoy, Michael, 386, 388–89

Campbell, Robert, 189, 193, 195, 196, 199
Canteens, 62–63, 68, 124, 308–9; boycotting, 126, 133; brewers and, 131; closing, 68, 125; rural, 108n28; social interaction at, 62–63; women and, 133, 194–95. *See also* Beerhalls
Cape Colony: migration to, 237; slavery in, 13; taverns in, 12; temperance in, 20
Cape Colony Liquor Laws Commission, 7
Cape Coloured Commission, 44n64
Cape of Good Hope, 11
Cape Liquor Amendment Act, 23
Cape Province: prohibition in, 15.
"Cape Smoke," 16–17
Cape Town: labor market in, 63; taverns in, 12
Carr, W. J. P., 319
Cato Manor, 104; riots at, 30, 326; effects elsewhere, 326
Cattle: decline of, 268n25; marriage arrangements and, 268n27, 282, 283; theft of, 38n19
Central beerhall, Johannesburg, 312, 323, 331; closing of, 306, 307, 318, 320, 322, 324; improvements for, 317; problems for, 315, 316, 319; relocation of, 318
Ceremonies. *See* Customs; Rituals
Cetshwayo, on grain beer, 5
Chamber of Mines, 143, 149, 166, 178; recruiting policy, 178
Champion, A. W. G., 172, 212, 213–14, 221
Chibuku, 411n30; control of, 356; excise

tax on, 403; factory-brewed, 400–401; home brewers and, 401, 406; marketing, 354, 402, 409; selling, 399–404, 406–8, 412n32; shebeen queens and, 407–8; threat to, 402, 405

Chiefs: declining power of, 87; loss of control by, 91; power of, 379; proliferation of, 280–81

Chinese laborers, 237

Christians, boycotters and, 220–21

Churches, 88, 219–20

Ciskei, 253

Coal, 80, 187–88, 201. See also Natal coal mines

Coka, Gilbert, on liquor question, 78

Collieries. See Natal coal mines

Collisons of Cape Town, 61

Colonial Development and Welfare Act, 387

Colonial power, limits of, 21, 115, 123–31, 132, 134

Colonial space, creating, 116, 123

Colquhoun, Archibald, 116

Colson, Elizabeth: on drinking in Zambia, 8

Communist Party of South Africa (CPSA), 214, 298; African Protection League and, 297; effectiveness of, 297; resistance by, 270

Community: alcohol and, 4, 9; brewing and, 163, 176, 264; recognition of, 262, 264

Compound managers: bribes for, 172; dilemma for, 151, 167; illicit alcohol and, 150–53, 184n42; indunas and, 381, 384. See also Mine managers

Compounds: amenities of, 310, 352; bars, 163, 178; beer in, 29, 165, 322; brewing policies of, 164; brewing rackets, 163, 170–78, 184n42; building, 340, 342; closed, 17, 47n91, 82; drinking in, 33, 143, 146, 422–23;

enclosing, 152; golden syrup in, 166; incarceration in, 17, 19; intrusion in, 352, 389; loafer, 344–45, 350; map of, 147; open, 342–43, 352; popularity of, 149–50, 172; raiding, 152, 153, 170; social clubs and, 353; women and, 28–29.

Conference on Reef Municipalities, 271

Consumption. See Alcohol consumption

Control. See Labor control; Regulation; Social control

Copperbelt, 29, 340–41; alcohol in, 339, 340–41, 342–43; beerhalls on, 348–55; expansion of, 350; map of, 341; migrants to, 16, 340, 342

Coryndon, Robert: on Swazi drinking, 368

CPSA. See Communist Party of South Africa

Credit, extending, 18, 187, 193–96

Crime, 244, 270, 277, 349; beerhalls and, 354; decrease in, 294; drinking and, 155, 241, 273, 274, 308; illicit liquor trade and, 275, 291; increase in, 243, 275, 276, 278, 294; tolerating, 148

Crown Mines, 175, 185n57

Culture: alcohol and, 4–5, 79, 119, 287; alternative, 95; consumption and, 34, 62–63, 119, 132; drinking, 4, 145–46, 167–69, 347–48; leisure, 348, 349; plebian, 84. See also Shebeens

Customs: debate over, 87–88; invention of, 253; threats to, 380; upholding, 89, 247. See also Rituals

Dagga (marijuana), 132, 173, 231n41

Debt. See Tied-rent system; Token system

Deferred wages, 248, 283

de Jager, Ignatius W., 192, 195, 197

Delagoa Bay, 61

Demonstrations. *See* Boycotts; Protests

Denver beerhall, Johannesburg, 312, 323, 331, 332; closing of, 320; complaints about, 315; hours for, 321, 322; locating, 310

Denver (Johannesburg), 310, 321, 331

Department of Bantu Administration and Development, 320, 321, 323, 330

Department of Native Affairs, 241, 246

Dependence. *See* Alcoholism

Desertion, 198

"Detribalization," 283–84, 285

Diamonds: discovery of, 65; exploitation of, 16–17, 63

Diet, 5, 18

Dikobe, Modikwe, 2, 3

Discipline: and alcohol consumption, 16, 17, 22; industrial, 7, 343; and urban space, 22

Discourse, 9, 10, 38n19, 83, 155, 235, 274

Disease, 250n24; increase in, 278

Disorder, 2, 13, 15, 17, 84; causes of, 19, 272–73, 277–78, 289; control of, 264; ritual and, 265; roots of, 279–83; spread of, 278, 350, 354. *See also* Social order

Distilleries. *See* Liquor production

Division of labor, sexual, 237, 240

Dockworkers, 80, 92

Domestic service, 90, 92, 240, 241

Domestic workers, 84–85, 221, 239–40

Domination, 59, 70, 72, 83; affirming, 371; challenging, 95; tot and, 60. *See also* Subordination

Doro, 120; control of, 123; selling, 123, 124

Douglas, Mary, 265

Down Second Avenue (Mphahlele), 3, 34

Drinking: control of, 5–8, 17–19, 23, 95–96, 151, 176, 200, 345, 346, 372; dangers of, 5, 9; denunciation of, 241, 372; efficiency and, 22; employ-

ment and, 16, 22; escapist, 6, 111n65, 145, 179–80, 307, 349; geography of, 37n11, 330–31; rural, 33, 238, 241, 341, 343, 369, 380; scale of, 86, 94; tribal restrictions on, 398; urban, 8–9, 176, 342; women and, 211. *See also* Alcohol consumption; Beerhalls; Drunkenness

Drinking apartheid, 25, 318–19, 320, 321, 345; beginnings of, 307, 330–32

Drinking culture, 31, 167–69, 256; aspects of, 4; formation of, 145–46; reshaping, 347–48; in vineyards, 59

Drinking gardens. *See* Beer gardens

Drinking hours, 22, 99–100, 113n97, 313, 345; limiting, 22, 345, 349. *See also* Beerhalls

Drinking networks, 28, 167–69

Drinking parties. *See* Beer drinks

Drinking patterns, 37n11, 339, 345–46; authorities and, 343; changes in, 181, 341, 342, 345, 349, 355, 369; productivity and, 380; spatial arrangement of, 22–27, 318, 322, 329, 331

Drinking sets. *See* Drinking networks

Drinking space, 23–24

Drink-on-credit, 18, 187, 193–96. *See also* Token system

Drought, 214–15, 237, 280

Drunkenness, 5–6, 70, 85, 86, 125, 139, 244, 275, 316, 373, 377; accidents and, 199; arrests for, 93, 97, 127; concerns about, 13, 17, 19, 44n64, 59, 162, 242, 326–27, 343–44, 349, 350, 360n26, 364n83, 368, 372; crime and, 273; decrease in, 103, 113n96, 166, 324; increase in, 94, 124, 199, 243; productivity and, 140, 144; racism and, 360n26. *See also* Absenteeism; Drinking; Alcoholism

Dube beerhall, Johannesburg, 331, 332

Dube hostel, Johannesburg, 319, 328
Durban, 16, 18, 29, 79–105, 164;
  economic activity in, 80; map of, 81;
  monopoly system in, 79; prohibition
  in, 97–98; regulation in, 18, 21;
  shebeens in, 89, 91, 92; spatial
  control in, 24, 81; unrest in, 208, 212,
  213, 226–27, 326
Durban Corporation, 94
Durban Hop Beer Bill (No. 17) of
  1907, 97
Durban Navigation No. 2 Colliery, 191
Durban System, 19, 246, 344; implementation of, 123–24, 130, 134–35,
  248; interest in, 79; origins of,
  78–105; significance of, 101–2, 105
Durban Town Council, 78
Dutch East India Company, 12, 13–14, 56
Dutch Reformed Church, beerhalls
  and, 325
du Toit, J. P., 67

Eastern beerhall, Johannesburg, 331
East London, 169
East Rand, 21, 273; map of, 272; spatial
  control on, 24
East Rand Proprietary Mines (ERPM)
  beerhall, 168
Eating houses, 130, 308; beer at, 88, 94,
  97; licenses for, 96; municipal,
  99–100; raids on, 97; revenue from,
  96, 100
Economic and Wage Commission, 172
Ematsheni, 90, 99. *See also* Beerhalls;
  Durban; Durban System
Enyati Colliery, token system at, 198
Epworth Mission, brewing at, 126
Erika Theron Commission, 44n64
ERPM. *See* East Rand Proprietary Mines
European beer, 94, 340, 353;
  consumption of, 120; legalization of,

26, 200; preference for, 179; selling,
  119, 409

Faction fighting, 139, 164, 222, 275–76,
  278–79, 291–92, 316; increase in,
  286–88, 294–95; liquor control and,
  173. *See also* Fighting
Factory brewing: growth of, 26–27, 395,
  399, 402–5, 409; impact of, 409;
  income from, 412n32; introduction
  of, 396, 398–401. *See also* Brewing;
  Home brewing
Families, breakdown of, 215–17, 238,
  270–71, 277
Fanagalo, 183n31
Farmers, 98; bankruptcy for, 64;
  domination by, 57–60, 63, 65; labor
  shortage and, 64; liquor manufacture
  by, 147; opposition to token system
  by, 196. *See also* Agriculture
Farm shebeens. *See* Shebeens
Feminism, 209. *See also* Gender
Fences: control by, 290–92, 294, 348;
  effectiveness of, 293, 295, 297
Ffennell Road beerhall, Johannesburg,
  329; hours for, 324; protests at,
  326–27
Fighting, 224, 276, 294–96, 349, 368,
  373. *See also* Faction fighting;
  Violence
Fines, 94
Forced removals. *See* Apartheid
France, 44n62, 74n19
Francistown beerhall, 399
Free State, war of 1867–1868, 280
Fruit beers, 5–6

Gangs, 84, 92, 277; attacks by, 275. *See
  also* Fighting
Gender, alcohol and, 162, 225–28
Genetics, alcoholism and, 10, 41n39
Germiston, 273

383–84; Basotho women and, 273; compound managers and, 29, 152–53; control of, 23, 29–30, 146, 148, 149, 152, 195, 288, 294–95, 345–47; crime and, 291; harassment of, 293, 386; increase in, 14–15, 162, 288, 350; labor market and, 155; police and, 347; poor whites and, 146; women and, 148, 277, 278

Incwala festival, beer at, 370

Indians: alcohol and, 111n63; indentured, 189–90; recruitment of, 190

Indunas, 173, 380–81, 383, 389; complaints against, 184–85n47; compound managers and, 381, 384; protest by, 386; rights of, 173

Industrialization, 16, 269.

Industrial and Commercial Workers Union. *See* ICU

Industrial unrest. *See* Strikes

Inebriation. *See* Drunkenness

Infant mortality, 278

Informal economy, 118

Informers, 120, 242, 387; revenge on, 128

Innes Liquor Law (Act 28 of 1898), 69

Inns. *See* Taverns

Isiqataviki. See Kill-me-quick

Isishimeyana, 114n108, 210; names for, 108n29; prohibition against, 108n29; selling, 91, 95; taxation of, 87

Itimiti, 88

Jameson, Robert: Durban System and, 101; hop beer trade and, 96; on togt system, 82

Johannesburg, 29; beerhalls in, 27, 148–49, 307, 309; beerhalls (map), 308; beer sales in (map), 330; failure of prohibition, 139–40, 141–49, 155–56; industrial growth of, 313; municipal beer trade in, 314; regulation in, 18, 20; slumyards and

compounds (map), 147. *See also* Compounds; Illicit liquor trade; Mines; Witwatersrand

Johannesburg Consolidated Investment Group, 151

Johannesburg Town Council, 105

Johnson, Herbert, 383, 385–86, 388–89

Joint Councils, 196

Jones, Gareth Stedman: on leisure, 11

Jubilee Compound (Johannesburg), 308

Junod, Henri: on alcohol abuse, 7

Juvenile delinquency, 277, 354; increase in, 278

"Kaffir" beer, 85, 112n90, 210, 312; brewing, 129, 163–64, 165, 172, 240, 244, 249, 312; consumption of, 306–7; control of, 7, 101, 200; definition of, 94–95; nourishment from, 142; prohibiting, 121; restrictions on, 240–41; selling, 329. *See also* Beer; Grain beer

Kaffir Beer Act of 1912, 123

Kaffir Beer Act of 1920, 129

Kaffir Beer Committee, 194, 195

Kaffir Beer Inquiry, 310

Kaffir Beer Ordinance of 1920, 124, 128

Katzen, M. S., 147

Kenya, 38n18, 105

Khali: attraction of, 165; brewing, 143, 163–67, 171, 172. *See also Skokian*

Khama, temperance and, 14, 46n79

Khoikhoi, 56, 73n1

Kidd, Dudley, 6

"Kill-me-quick," 143, 210, 377

Kimberley, 16–17, 23, 82, 176

Kinship bonds, 87; decline of, 262; reinforcing, 146

Krige, Eileen, 8

Kruger government, prohibition and, 139–41

Kruger Republic, 17

transport of beer on, 85–86; working on, 74n14, 80

Randlords, prohibition and, 19–20, 139–40

Rapoko, 120, 123, 124, 129, 130. *See also* Grain beer

Rations, of wine, 9. *See also* Beer rations.

Recruitment. *See* Labor recruitment

Regulation, 18–19, 25, 99, 156, 198, 340, 356, 357n3, 368, 401–2; central government, 307, 327, 328; employers and, 20, 21–22; enforcing, 11–16, 17, 343–45, 357n3; failure of, 65, 69–71, 215, 350, 356; in England, 22; mining and, 21–22; reform of, 27; resisting, 19, 21, 26, 156, 346–47. *See also* Liquor laws

Rents, 127–28; control of, 116; tied system of, 66–69

Reserves. *See* Rural reserves

Resistance, to state control, 23, 28–29

Revenue. *See* Beer monopoly; Beer sales

Rhodes, Cecil B., 64, 116

Rhodes-Livingstone Institute, 8, 31

Ricksha pullers, 80, 85, 92, 111n68

Rinderpest, 88, 237

Riots, 316–17, 321, 326, 386. *See also* Violence

Ritual killing, 265; beer drink and, 259–60, 264; description of, 253–54. *See also* Umhlinzeko

Rituals, 33, 252; beer and, 370–71; changes in, 261. *See also* Customs

Roan Antelope Mine, 357n2, 358n5; beerhall at, 355

Robinson Clause, 23

Rum, 12, 16, 87

Rural poverty, 19, 214–15, 237, 280–81

Rural reserves, 19, 197–98; prohibition in, 211

Rural shebeens. *See* Shebeens

Rural society, alcohol and, 5–6, 8–9, 14–15, 21, 33, 36n11; cash in, 15; conceptions of time in, 21, 358n13; household production and consumption, 15, 260–62; migrancy, 33–34, 237–38, 244–48; sociability in, 167, 343

Rural values: consumption and, 62–63; disintegration of, 8

SAIRR. *See* South African Institute of Race Relations

St. Monday, 22, 62, 373

Sale of Native Beer Regulation Bill, 89

Salisbury, 29; Durban System in, 130; map of, 118; failure of prohibition in, 21; population of, 117; problems for, 116; tot system in, 119

Salisbury and Jubilee compound, 308

Salisbury Brewery, 124

Salisbury-Jubilee beerhall, 311, 312; sales at, 310; success of, 309

Schreiner, T. L., 102

Scott, James, 4

Scudder, Thayer, on drinking in Zambia, 8

Segregation, 83, 116, 246, 273; alcohol and, 2, 11, 25, 135; beerhalls and, 22, 24, 25, 234n83; maintaining, 345; monopolies and, 22; sexual, 134. *See also* Apartheid; Housing

Select Committee on the Working of the Native Liquor Laws, 145, 149

Sexuality, emphasis on, 215, 217–18

Shangaans, 164, 168, 169, 171, 381, 382

Shebeen queens, 226, 290, 293, 308, 401; home brewing and, 407, 408; raids on, 26; violations by, 411n24

Shebeens, 2, 4, 17, 31, 84, 89, 93–94, 98, 104, 132, 162, 163, 218, 311, 320, 403; beerhalls and, 312, 316; boycott of, 34; Chibuku and, 406, 407–8; Copperbelt and, 342–43; defense of,

309; description of, 92–93, 178–79, 227; farm, 173–74; high-class or elite, 32; meeting at, 30, 92; partial legalization of, 30; raids on, 23, 312; rise of, 85–95; rural, 173–75, 175; sorghum beer and, 46, 407; Sunday business for, 321; township, 175

Sigomfane: brewing, 377; destruction of, 388

Sikuluvu "Skroof" Dlamini, 393n50; allegiance to, 376; eviction of, 378–79; exoneration of, 387; prosecution of, 377; support for, 379. *See also* Skroof's

"Single" women. *See* "Unattached" women

Skillivaans, 190

Skokian, 114n108, 153; addiction to, 173; attraction of, 165; brewing, 143, 165, 167, 171, 290, 377. *See also* *Khali;* Alcoholic beverages

Skomplas. See Mine married quarters

Skroof's: brewing at, 378; elimination of, 378–79; establishment of, 376–77; illicit liquor trade at, 277, 383–84; raids on, 388. *See also* Sikuluvu "Skroof" Dlamini

Slavery: abolition of, 13; postemancipation, 59–60, 64; tot system and, 12

Slumyards, 148, 151, 177; Johannesburg, map of, 147

Smuts, Jan, 382

Sobhuza, 384, 389, 392n45; beer-giving by, 371–72; foreign capital and, 368; induna system and, 380–81; NA3 and, 376, 388; protest by, 388; Sikuluvu and, 379; strategy of, 393n50; strike and, 382–83, 387

Sobriety, 20, 97, 238

Sociability, drinking and, 62–63, 162–63, 167–70, 175, 178, 181, 238, 239, 342, 348–49, 397

Social clubs, 356; development of, 352–53, 355

Social control, 2, 22–23, 122, 135, 210, 235, 274, 293, 389; extending, 256–57, 298; search for, 270, 283–89; tot and, 60, 62–63, 71–72; "unattached" women and, 277. *See also* Labor control

Social disorder. *See* Disorder

Social networks, reinforcing, 57, 146, 175

Social order, 132, 274; drinking and, 9, 339; maintaining, 121, 238, 289, 298, 345; threats to, 2, 13–14, 88, 242, 288. *See also* Disorder

Somerset West, 63, 69

Songs of the Adventurers (film), 33

Sorghum, 107–108n27, 239

Sorghum beer: alcohol content of, 141; brewing, 292, 369; distribution of, 155, 397; factory-brewed, 396, 398–409, 411n21, 411n23; health benefits of, 141–42, 154; home-brewed, 401; illicit brewing of, 154, 293; income from, 395–96; marketing, 402; monopoly on, 288, 403; popularity of, 395–96, 398; selling, 401, 405–6, 408, 411n30; testing of, 142. *See also* Grain beer; Alcoholic beverages

South African Breweries, 404; beer from, 125, 135

South African Institute of Race Relations (SAIRR): on illegal liquor, 8; survey by, 36n6; token system and, 196

South African Police, intervention by, 290, 291, 382, 388. *See also* Police

South African Railways, 201

South African War (1899–1902), 17, 146; impact of, 84, 140

Southern Africa, map of, xvi

Southern African Customs Union Agreement, 411n30

Southern Rhodesia: colonial policy in, 20; beerhalls in 19, 32

Southern Rhodesian Missionary Conference, 133–34

Soweto, 177; beerhalls in, 332; beerhalls in (map), 328; 1976 uprising, 1, 34, 179–80

Spatial control. *See* Prohibition zones; Social control; Urban space

Spatial organization, 21, 23–24, 123; drinking and, 22–27, 307; protesting, 325; purpose of, 116–18; of wine farms, 60

Spatial strategy, 22–24

Spes Bona Mine, 152, 172

Spirits, 5, 12, 14, 15, 17, 18, 194

Springs, 271–72; map of, 272; serious crime in, 276

Squatters: brewing by, 350; prohibition on, 125–27

Stabilization. *See* Labor stabilization

Stallard, Colonel: Urban Areas Acts and, 271

Stellenbosch, 63

Stellenbosch district: canteens in, 63; map of, 58; tot system in, 57–60, 71–72

Stevedoring companies, 80, 83, 113n97

Storekeepers: profits for, 192–93; token system and, 194, 196–97

Strikes, 149, 166, 367, 368, 376, 378, 381–86; aftermath of, 386–89; behavior during, 383; mediation of, 389; token system and, 198; Van Ryn Deep, 170

Stuart, James S., 93, 106n14; on beer monopoly, 112n78

Sub-Nigel Mine, 174, 176

Substance addiction. *See* Alcoholism

Sudan, 105

Sugar beer, 12

Sugar industry. *See* Agriculture

Surveillance, state, 19, 23, 28, 31, 100–101, 345, 348

Swaziland, 29, 184, 377, 388; capital and mining development in, 368; drinking in, 24, 367–89; royal villages, 15

Swazis, 367, 385; aristocracy, 15; beer-giving by, 371; brewing by, 369; drinking habits of, 368–73; mining by, 375, 387–88; spatial control and, 24; strike by, 382, 383

Syrup. *See* Golden syrup

Tati Company, 399

Taylor, William: on drinking patterns in Mexico, 6

Taxation, 87, 91, 237, 397, 403; revolt over, 91

Teetotalism. *See* Temperance movement

Temperance movement, 8, 9, 102–3, 139, 164, 221; international, 4–5, 45n73; support for, 14–15, 19–20; tot system and, 71

Thabong township, Welkom, 178, 179

Themba, Can, 2

Thompson, E. P.: on moral economy and protest, 380

Tied-rent system, 66–69

Time. *See* Drinking hours; Rural society

Time-discipline, 59

Times of Swaziland, 383

Tlokwe, 411n30; import of, 403

Tobacco industry. *See* Agriculture

Togt Fund: fines by, 83; liquor profits for, 97; revenues from, 82

Togt Labour Amendment Act of 1902, 82

Togt workers, 80; accommodations for, 106n9; registering, 84, 101; strikes by, 84; unemployment for, 111n68

Token system, 11, 18, 187; description of, 190–91; end of, 196–201;

exploitation with, 193, 200, 201; investigation of, 197; use of, 190–96

Tot system, 10, 17, 18, 44n64, 119; accidents and, 142; contemporary, 44n64, 72–73; dispensing, 11–12, 57–60, 62; drawbacks of, 44n64, 69, 70–73; entrenchment of, 56–57, 61; farmers and, 59–60; in France, 44n62; on Kimberley mines, 17; labor control with, 66–68, 72; opposition to, 63; railways and, 71; size of tots, 57–58, 68; social interaction and, 62–63. *See also* Wine

Townships, 2, 19, 24, 34, 83, 126, 148; alcohol policy toward, 309-10, 321, 325, 327; carceral institutions, 19; fencing of, 24, 290–95; mineworkers in, 176, 177, 271–79, 286–89. *See also* Various townships

"Town women," 162, 183n21

Trading on Mining Grounds Commission, 177

Tradition. See *Customs*

Traditional beer: brewing, 179; control of, 119; definition of, 94, 411n23. *See also* Grain beer, Alcoholic beverages

Traditional Beer Levy, 403

Traditional Beer Retailing Law, 401, 406

Transkei, 33, 68, 235–37, 252–65; map of, 254

Transvaal: alcohol in, 17; prohibition in, 18; regulation in, 18

Transvaal Chamber of Commerce, 149

Transvaal Chamber of Industry, 319, 321

Transvaal Compound Managers' Association, 273

Transvaal Liquor Commission, 144, 368

Transvaal Medical Council, 147

Transvaal Mine Medical Officers' Association, 144

Transvaal Mines Traders' Association, 166

Transvaal Traders Association, 149

Trappers. *See* Informers

Trash money, 190, 218

Treaty of St. Germain-en-Laye, 15

Trusties. *See* Informers

Tshwala. *See Utshwala*

Turner, Victor, 265

Turner and Newall, 373–74, 375, 388

Turrell, Robert, 17

Uganda, 105

Ukubusa (labor service), 263

Umamlambo, 263, 265; acquisition of, 266–67n14; belief in, 258, 259

Umhlinzeko, 253, 254–56, 258, 267n24; end of, 255, 261, 262, 263–64; symbolism of, 265; *umsindleko* and, 254–56, 257, 259–60, 264–65. *See also* Ritual killing

Umsindleko, 253; change to, 261, 262, 265; description of, 255–58; *umhlinzeko* and, 254–56, 257, 259–60, 264–65. *See also* Beer drinks

Umsindleko beer, brewing, 263–64

Umtata: brewing in, 235–36, 243; labor migration in, 237; map of, 236; women in, 245–47

"Unattached" women, 287; brewing and, 270; concerns about, 273, 274, 277, 278; control of, 278, 288, 289; immigration of, 279–80; relationships with, 162, 271, 277. *See also* Women

Union Party, 214

Urban Areas Acts of 1923 and 1937, 270, 271

Urbanization, 145, 235, 284; alcohol abuse and 8; control of, 79, 100–101, 105, 269; disorderly, 270, 271; impact of, 19, 269; mining and, 270, 340

Urban Locations Ordinance of 1905, 122

Urban segregation. *See* Segregation

Urban space, 81, 82, 116–18

Utshwala, 94, 141, 216, 226, 240–41,

244; brewing, 86, 102, 214, 369; consumption of, 78–79, 86–87, 112n90, 218; control of, 246; cost of, 239; monopoly on, 210; prohibition on, 97, 98, 211; selling, 85, 88, 89, 91, 99–100, 108n28, 210, 229n11, 378

26–27, 209, 215, 280–81; exclusion
from compounds, 24; independence
for, 91; migration by, 30, 239–40,
342; beerhalls and, 194–95, 216;
oppression of, 215–17; population of,
90–91, 217, 231n34, 274, 299n11;
prejudice and, 227; presence in town
of, 7; protests by, 24, 211–12;
sentences for, 225, 296; wage labor
and, 237–40, 245, 246, 248; struggles
against male control, 30, 215–17,
221–25; white attitudes toward black,
90, 108n28, 210, 238, 243–44;
widows, 280. *See also* Basotho
women; Brewers; "Unattached"
women; Women brewers; Zulu women
Women brewers, 26–27, 85–95, 217,
271, 276, 281, 287, 297, 308, 342–43,
346–47, 350, 370, 397, 408; activism
of, 31; boycott by, 28, 30; control of,
24; income for, 211–12; licensed, 398;
migrant labor and, 33; relationships
with, 284; techniques of, 26–27, 28,
30, 239. *See also* Brewers; Home
brewers
Women's Auxiliary (ICU), 212, 214,
229n17

Women's Christian Temperance
Union, 102
Worger, William, 17
Work force. *See* Labor force
Work parties, beer for, 168, 371
Work stoppages. *See* Strikes

Xhosa, 170, 201, 252; brewing and, 170;
drinking groups of, 169; drinking
oratory, 33–34; homesteads and, 260;
labor migration and, 263; liquor and,
171; ritual killing and, 253

Yeo, Eileen and Stephan: on leisure, 11

Zambia, 8, 30. *See also* Northern
Rhodesia
Zuid Afrikaan, on labor shortage, 64
Zululand, 190, 198
Zulus: beer and, 5, 88, 100, 221–22;
clean-up campaign by, 292, 293, 294;
conflict with, 289; fighting among,
316; social sanctions of, 90; Togt
Fund and, 82; wage work by, 84
Zulu women, 85–90, 209, 220, 222. *See
also* Women